Value Wars

Also by John McMurtry

The Cancer Stage of Capitalism

'Deeply learned, relentlessly logical and corrosively liberating, McMurtry is an unconventional, idol-smashing philosopher imbued with passion and urgency; a dangerous man. Every word resonates.' Susan George

'Sometimes a great thinker or prophet comes along just when the world needs him.' William Krehm

'To compare capitalism with a disease such as cancer is a difficult task, but McMurtry does just this with a thought provoking analysis that should be embraced.' *Spectre*

'McMurtry analyses contemporary capitalist crises in terms borrowed from medical analyses of cancer ... It is an analogy which McMurtry sustains in an engaging and passionate manner.' *International Affairs*

John McMurtry

Value Wars
The Global Market Versus the Life Economy

Pluto Press
LONDON • STERLING, VIRGINIA

First published by Pluto Press
345 Archway Road, London N6 5AA
and 22883 Quicksilver Drive,
Sterling, VA 20166–2012, USA

British Library Cataloguing in Publication Data
A catalogue record for this book is available from
the British Library

ISBN 0 7453 1890 8 hardback
ISBN 0 7453 1889 4 paperback

Library of Congress Cataloging in Publication Data
McMurtry, John, 1939–
    Value wars : the global market versus the life economy /
John McMurtry.
        p. cm.
    ISBN 0–7453–1890–8 (hardback) — ISBN 0–7453–1889–4 (pbk.)
    1. Globalization—Economic aspects. 2. Globalization—Moral and
ethical aspects. 3. Globalization—Social aspects. 4. International
trade—Moral and ethical aspects. 5. Capitalism—Moral and ethical
aspects. 6. Values. 7. International economic relations. I. Title.
    HF1359 .M39 2002
    330.9'049—dc21
                                                      2002002246

10   9   8   7   6   5   4   3   2   1

Designed and produced for Pluto Press by
Chase Publishing Services, Fortescue, Sidmouth EX10 9QG
Typeset from disk by Stanford DTP Services, Towcester
Printed in the European Union by Antony Rowe, Chippenham, England

Contents

vi   VALUE WARS

Acknowledgements

I would like to thank the public institutions which have sustained this book's research and writing, in particular the University of Guelph, the numerous book, journal and policy research publishers who have disseminated shorter analyses as this work evolved, and the Royal Society of Canada which elected me to its membership while I was writing the manuscript.

I am above all indebted to my partner, Jennifer Sumner, who has been unfailingly supportive in every function from e-mail management to reading drafts of the typescript, and to Pluto's publisher, Roger van Zwanenberg who prompted the book, made excellent suggestions, and has always sustained a special integrity as publisher of controversial analysis. My colleague, Terisa Turner, has been a rich source of feminist and oil research as well as constant support. Jerry (G.A.) Cohen has, as always, provided acute inputs of counter-argument, sustaining words and targeted references. Alex Michalos has unstintingly assisted as a colleague, fellow researcher in the area and responsive reader. Other valued cross-disciplinary colleagues Howard Woodhouse, Bernard Hodgson, Allan Connolly, Bill Krehm, Peter McLaren, John Valleau and J.J. McMurtry stand out as penetrating co-investigators at many turns of the inquiry, with J.J. McMurtry performing the difficult and important task of constructing the book's Index. David Walmark, Matthew Stanton, Raymond Izareli, Mark Anielski, Dave Sherwood, George Freund, John Buchanan and Bob Olsen have continuously sent valuable source materials, while Griff Morgan, Michael Keefer, Jim Christoff, Jean Smith, Herb Wiseman and Tony Clark have also assisted in keeping me informed of movements on the front lines of our era. My doctoral students and now colleagues Jeff Noonan and Giorgio Baruchello have shared their research and disseminated their own creative understanding of life-ground analysis. John Bunzl, John Cobb Jr. and William Rees, along with some of those already mentioned, have independently and kindly read final drafts of the typescript for publisher comments.

It has been the nature of my recent research and writing that I have not been able to communicate its deepest connective patterns until the work has been completed. The layers of social conditioning, the normalised aversion of the eyes, the instituted rationalisations presupposed across subject disciplines and, overall, the pervasive culture of corporate globalisation all demand a reflective penetration beneath existing intersubjective resources and assumptions. The principles and connected meaning that finally crystallise have had to await the last rewrite to be disclosed, and so the readers of this book participate with me in what follows as a shared consciousness of a turning point of planetary life-organisation.

Preface

The typescript of this book was written through dramatic global change. As the work was nearing its completion, the attack on the World Trade Center and the Pentagon occurred on September 11, 2001. Universal norms in deadly planetary struggle underlie this event and its aftermath of 'America's New War', but a far wider field of life-and-death invasion, occupation and resistance is at work than the mass-homocidal collision that shook the world on 9–11. This deeper meta-war reaches back through an era of financial-military empire which now seeks global totalisation. Its unseen moral syntax and life-economy alternative are what this book investigates.

Propaganda looks only to the act and what it can justify in retaliation. Explanation seeks the meaning of the present in the structuring of its past. Working back through the chain of decisions and consequences to the 9–11 turn, we are first struck by the curiously unimpeded attack on the US's most populous city through so many unaccounted-for breaches of the US's $1 billion-a-day national security system. On September 12, I wrote a paragraph for publication that began with this connection back to 9–11's wider nexus of meaning.

The pervasive Echelon surveillance apparatus and the most sophisticated intelligence machinery ever built is unlikely not to have eavesdropped on some of the very complicated organisation and plans across states and boundaries for the multi-site hijacking of planes from major security structures across the US – especially since the World Trade Center had already been bombed in 1993 by the same known network of ex-allies of the CIA. Since the prime suspect, Osama bin Laden, is himself an ex-CIA-supported operative in Afghanistan, and his moves presumably under the most intense scrutiny for past successful terrorist attacks on two US embassies in 1998, one has to reflect on the connections.

The Lost Pattern of Facts

In subsequent months, documented evidence emerged that recurrently confirmed a behind-the-scenes structure of historical decision that has been abolished from view, like a stage being reset for another play. As Samuel Coleridge long ago advised, suspension of disbelief is a necessary state of mind for a drama to capture an audience's attention. As entertainment pervasively supplants understanding in global mass culture, suspension of disbelief regarding 9–11 seamlessly operates by liquidation of the facts that ground truth. The long line of repressed facts begins years before 9–11, most prominently with top-down blockings of FBI agents' investigations of mounting evidence of a plan for civilian aircraft hijacking and dive-bombing of major US buildings – a plan called 'Project Bolinka' and known about since before 1996. These blocks on FBI investigations were so obstructive that the Deputy-Director of the FBI and its Director of Anti-Terrorism, John O'Neill, resigned in a career-sacrificing protest at the top-down interference – before he too died on 9–11 as the World Trade Center's new Director of Security.[1]

There were also explicit warnings from the intelligence agencies of Sudan, France, Russia and a chorus of other international sources about the coming 9–11 attack. There were even statements by 'Israeli members of the intelligence community in the US' that they knew of the attack beforehand – reports which were not denied by US Secretary of State Powell when the question arose in a press conference which I observed on December 18. Perhaps most remarkably, there had been direct warnings from the Republican Party's own past Chief Investigative Council for the House Judiciary Committee to the Bush administration. Later representing FBI special agents suing the US Justice Department along with Washington DC Judicial Watch, David Philip Schippers reported in Houston on October 10 on the 'Alex Jones Talk Show' that these agents knew of a plan of bin Laden's network to attack Lower Manhattan with 'commercial airlines as bombs' long before 9–11, but were blocked from investigative and preventative action by FBI and US Justice Department command, and threatened with prosecution under the National Security Act if they published this information, with Attorney-General Ashcroft himself refusing to return calls to his fellow senior Republican for four weeks before 9–11.

The mass media, dominantly owned by military-industrial and infotainment corporations, declined to report any of these facts. This is because the regulating mind-set of official society blinkers out whatever exposes a disorder in the existing system of rule. The value system disorder behind 'America's War against Terrorism' is, accordingly, systematically obscured by a saturating media discourse of war and the threats of an omnipresent enemy. Yet, in the world of forgotten fact, US logistical and financial support of death-squads, terrorist networks and narcotic-financed 'wars of liberation' had been systematically fomenting chaos around the world for decades before 9–11. Sowing chaos is, in truth, the distinguishing strategy of this empire's movement of military-political perimeters across borders. In the case of al-Qaida and the Taliban, the CIA's partnership with Pakistan's Intelligence Services (ISI) had financed and trained both as well as the Afghanistan-based terrorist camps. The ISI's commander-in-chief, Lieutenant-General Mahmoud Ahmad was, in another moment of this offstage value-and-decision structure, visiting Washington the very week preceding 9–11, and is known to have ordered that US$100,000 be wired to the lead WTC hijacker, Mohammed Atta before that. These facts do not fit 'the whole new reality' that is officially proclaimed after 9–11, so the global corporate news empire communicates only disconnected trivia dominated by terrorist news to sustain the appropriate audience reactions. What is feared above all in rule of audiences by illusion is a reversal of 'the public mood'. Government investigation of the facts thus remained administratively blocked on both sides of the event.

It would take a logbook more to report the full panoply of failures and stand-downs of standard operating procedures throughout the highly co-ordinated steps and logistics of the 9–11 attack, later described by a former German Minister of Technology, Andreas van Buelow, as 'unthinkable without years-long support from secret apparatuses of the state and industry'. High-level interventions in normal precautionary routine included years of overriding immigration rules for US passports to Middle East 'freedom fighters' destined for al-Qaida, US Air Force training of Afghanistan-based terrorists, non-action on repeated alarms of al-Qaida terrorist activities threatening the United States and New York, airport security lapses, top-down interdiction of investigation of Saudi royal funding of al-Qaida, and ignoring of known floods of puts on affected airline stocks before 9–11 linked to a firm, A.B. Brown, with high-level CIA management.

The money sequences, arms and illegal narcotics connections all bore a familiar pattern. What connected them was their regulating structure, the ruling moral syntax whose portrayed meaning is 'protecting the Free World', but whose last steps on the stage were across the open heavens and difficult to conceal. Although US Air Force interceptions of hijacked planes are normally minutes-long in duration by established and codified routines, there was a stand-down of these automatic interception actions for all of the hijacked planes. The terrorists circled jumbo jets known to be hijacked around the military command's front-yard airspace for over an hour with no action whatever taken that interfered until after all three of the buildings had been dive-bombed.

Yet no disciplinary process nor formal investigation by the Pentagon, the FBI, Congress or the mass media was undertaken despite all the stunning breaches of defence routine which provided a continuously open passage to the long-planned attack. All attention was, instead, riveted on the claimed threat of an Islamic-based plot to 'destroy America'. No sooner had the 9–11 disaster sunk in than 'the anthrax attack' followed. Not even the known genetic signature of an official US source for the anthrax sent to Democrat Senate majority leader, Tom Daischle, registered as a fact over the weeks of terror that followed. Throughout, the inertial acquiescence of the occupied mass mind remained intact. What goes against the grain of conditioning is experienced as not credible, or as a hostile act.

The Unseen Moral Syntax

Once the anthrax scare too had run its course, the disconnection between reality on the ground and proclamations on the media stage was maintained by the orchestrated public drama of one new threat after another with 'no end in sight'. The larger restructuring of the world underneath by the actually regulating value programme of corporate globalisation was all the while kept in motion. There is, as we will see through the study ahead, a fanatic meaning to this order that locksteps with heroic images and flags flying overhead as the fields of destruction behind it grow to catastrophic proportions. The logic of action underneath and justification above are as crimes to alibi, but as a regime of world rule. The taboo that is required to keep well-documented facts unspeakable in public is the ideological cover of the value-and-decision structure that selects for what is suppressed. Together, both point to a wider normative disorder of the 'Free World' itself. This is the global subterrain which this study investigates – the actually regulating moral system of the New World Order.

As a philosopher, I am not interested in 'conspiracy theories', the favoured term to invalidate all questions about 9–11. I am interested in the deeper question of *the life-and-death principles of regulating value systems which connect across and explain social orders*. In the wider lens of investigation of the normative regime of a civilisation, the pattern of 9–11 decisions is linked to a larger historical pattern of policies and an increasingly pernicious value set. This larger pattern included US plans prior to 9–11 to invade Afghanistan for long-stated geostrategic reasons of Central Asia oil, forward military bases, and political axes of control. It included as well the US's successful strategic plan for Soviet Union collapse a decade before that – a collapse which was precipitated by the multibillion dollar strategic, financial and armaments support by the US National Security Agency and the CIA of precisely the same Afghanistan fundamentalist factions and warlords who plotted 9–11, including Osama bin Laden. These 'moral equivalents of the founding fathers', as then US president Reagan called them, were US-supported terrorist rings who were also later involved in training, armed support and narcotics-route partnership with the KLA ('Kosovo Liberation Army') insurrection in Yugoslavia as well as in Russia's Chechnya province. Interestingly, it was only when the formerly favoured Taliban faction suddenly shut down over 90 per cent of Afghanistan's opium production for the global market in 2001, as UN officials confirmed in March 2002, that the Taliban was declared America's mortal enemy and all its known positions bombed for months on end – while the opium that remained growing was concentrated in the areas controlled by the now-favoured Northern Alliance. The underlying connections disclose a system of 'Free World' approval and disapproval across borders whose moral meaning has remained unpenetrated – the actually regulating deep lines of 'the defence of our values and what we hold dear' which evade the detection of analysis.

'Who benefits?' is a standard forensic question which helps to clarify the moral meaning of acts of commission and omission. One of the prime connecting interests of 'the great game' played here is the vast and largely untapped mineral deposits across this entire central world region of continuing crises and wars. *Political chaos* is a prime strategic pattern of this system of world rule – from Latin American death squads through sub-Saharan Africa wars to South-East Asian covert armies and invasions. In this case, there was also the US's off-stage government's threat of a 'carpet of bombs' for Afghanistan before September 11 if the formerly favoured Taliban faction could not or did not expedite the long-planned UNOCAL oil pipelines through Afghanistan to Central Asia's vast oil and gas fields – a prime value objective which was quickly confirmed for construction with the Pakistani Minister of Oil on October 10 after the bombing of Afghanistan had been accepted by the official world. The more the dots are tracked in their interlocking frame across time and place, the more the lines of their connection reveal a deep structure of values, choice and consequence which crosses national borders as the universalising logic of a civilisation's accumulating moral corruption.

Although this underlying structure of values and decision has been, as we will see, distinctively ruinous of societies and innocent lives in its enactment since 1990, it is interpreted as '*power politics*' – a ready phrase whose acceptability consists in failing to penetrate the actually regulating value system to which all of the 'power moves' themselves conform, and in terms of which this global order is itself understood. The deep-structural value set at work is untheorised even in notions of 'hegemony' not only because the life-destructive decision sequence is overridden by the surface language of mass and class propaganda, but because there has been no analysis of socially regulating value sets themselves. They are, instead, reified as 'economic laws' or submerged in mass politics, not critically disinterred and examined as *elective normative constructions*.

Only value-system analysis can penetrate the infrastructural meaning of such patterns, but critical investigation of actually regulating norms of surrounding rule are methodologically ruled out by the known disciplines, including moral philosophy. *Normative systems analysis* is avoided even by critics of capitalism who assume profoundly opposed as well as overlapping value commitments, with little depth inquiry into the actually regulating value systems at work. Instead, this primary level of the modern human condition is repressed from view in scientistic assumptions or idealised accounts. The ultimate question of regulating societal values beneath propaganda is, at one pole, dissolved into the politics of class struggle and power, and at the other pole, etherealised into technical debates about isolated ideals with little connection to social reality. The infrastructure of the absolutist value-set and its *a priori* pre-scriptions actually regulating society's reproduction is, in neither case, laid bare to investigation. Normalised inhabitants of market capitalist society presuppose its ruling values as the inherent structure of 'the real world'. What opens it to question or exposes its destructive consequences disturbs the very foundations of collectively conditioned thought and emotion. Thus the facts of 9–11, as others, are selected and excluded in accordance with a ruling framework of perception and understanding, and critical evaluation and dissent are blocked out at the level of the mind-set itself.

It follows predictably from the complicity of the *rationalising* with the *actually regulating* structure of consciousness at work here that if questions arise to expose the contradictions at the heart of the Free World, they will be ignored, invalidated, or attacked as heretical. Thus with the 9–11 decision chain, there have been administration demands of 'limits' to Congressional inquiries into the disaster's cause as a patriotic imperative, while presidential records of the tell-tale decisions are ordered permanently closed. This process of repression and denial at the institutional level will be generalised, one can predict, to all affairs so long as the actually regulating value set remains assumed as given, and the contradictions between its regulating principles and its public rationalisations remain collaborated in. Moreover, it follows predictably that as long as threshold numbers of the public are bound up with such a clinically disordered framework of value perception and understanding as their own self-identity and moral community, they will be structured to attack whatever exposes its delusion with group-mind certitude and passion.

The Paradigm Case of 9–11

It is revealing of this moral syntax's general hold on public understanding that before this book went to press my explanation of the problem from core sections of it was passionately vilified in selected snippets by two columnists of Canada's national newspaper, the *Globe and Mail*, by Fox Television, and by the *Wall Street Journal*, with subsequent posting on the *New York Times Abuzz* website. The excerpt exposed value contradictions that were perceived as too subversive of final certitudes to let pass. Letters of inflamed denunciation poured in to my university and department with nothing beyond the denunciation thought necessary, including the reporting of me to the FBI and CIA by a physician-PhD couple from Cambridge Massachusetts of Harvard fame. A Darwinist former colleague wrote from Florida to a Canadian paper to announce unilaterally on behalf of my colleagues their moral abhorrence of my analysis. US academics who raised questions suffered national and institutional censure. Ironically, as the mob-mind attacks occurred, the scandal of Enron, the major financial backer and source of the US war administration and its members, began to emerge as 'the greatest corporate swindle in history'. Enron's money-sequencing rule decoupled from value accountability along with its simultaneous occupancy of state offices exactly followed the value system laid bare in this investigation.

The extremes of crisis and depravity may perplex us as they manifest in one shocking ecological and economic disaster after another. Yet underneath these topsy-turvy phenomena, the universal issue which this book addresses is of the *deep value system* from which all of these crises, covert operations and official decision sequences are connected expressions. What is the ground of value at work here? What is the guiding thread beneath a decade of one-sided wars, economic meltdowns and destabilising global ecosystems? It is ultimately at the level of its first principles of value calculus that the New World Order is most deeply understood. Structuring policy and outcome beneath the particular powers and interests that are dominant at any one time and beneath the Byzantine maze of ideological misrepresentations and chaotic facts, system-deciding values are assumed as primitive emotional and moral givens prior to consideration of choice. It is this fundamentalist inner logic that this study decodes. No leader or even state is the basis of these values and the decisions that follow from them, for its regulating value structure is presupposed by leaders and states as their transcendental moral order in terms of which they have their own significance and meaning. Like the rules of the game to the players, and 'the great game' is the language of the ascendant players themselves, the rules of value are not an issue they can think of inside the game. They can only calculate what maximises their places within its political offices and investment returns. The truth comes increasingly to be only an issue of when the cheque clears for the individual, and for world society how much more of the globe is made subject to transnational money-sequencing. This moral syntax governs beneath thought or evaluation, and increasingly rules the world on behalf of an unexamined normative apriorism represented as 'Freedom'. Yet, the ruling imperatives, we discover, entail betrayal of the public interest, mass murder and ecocidal consequence as 'necessary costs' and 'collateral damages'. Catastrophic effects on lives and life conditions not only do not register as issues for concern, they even reinforce the certitude with which the ruling value system is presupposed as the final order of reality.

An illustration explains the closure of the fanatic moral syntax. When the US president immediately identified the 9–11 terrorist attack as 'a declaration of war', his categorical assertion was certain and officially accepted as certain although there was no international law or norm which justified this official designation. Here, as elsewhere, an absolutist group-think rules above the law and beneath it, and it is in terms of this that the law itself is selectively enforced or disregarded. That the saturating declaration of '*war* against America' by an enemy that could not be found, and who came from a different country from the one to be bombed, did not occasion reflection. Nor did the fact that international law requires invading forces to be repelled to justify such an attack across another nation's borders. True to the comportment of this mind-set, the imperviousness to due process or evidence overrode the legal fact that the subsequent US bombing and invasion of peasant Afghanistan 8000 miles from its borders was itself a major war crime. None of these issues can compute to the fanatic value set that assumes itself as final prior to judgement or inquiry. For it is structured to repudiate or deny militantly whatever evidence questions its validity – including the number of innocent civilians maimed and killed by the 'historic triumph' of the superpower's attacks on one of the world's poorest countries.

Official and media representation in such a world operates only to manage public perception to justify what cannot be wrong. That this system is not connected to life interests beyond its commands is not a problem that can arise to its bearers. That the war which followed 9–11 bombed a distant and starving people, that it knowingly stopped food supplies from reaching the rapidly increasing millions of famine victims, that it disrupted planting of the next year's crops, that it terrorised the majorities of the larger cities to flee into homelessness, that it killed far more innocent civilians than were killed on September 11, and that its carpet-bomb invasion caused the deaths of countless innocent children and uprooted millions – none of these facts could be perceived through the lenses of the ruling moral syntax *as* facts. This deep-structural derangement crossed borders and governments with little clear exception.

Inside the Fanatic Mind-Set

Facts were selected out of view by this moral syntax because they do not conform to its regulating structure of perception and understanding. The ruling morality – and all that prescribes universally with punishment imposed on violation is a ruling morality – is locked into its self-affirmation as the all-conquering Good as the meaning of the world. Since whatever it designates as Evil is evil by definition, and since it is identical with the forces of the Good, no mass homicide of innocents or ecocidal practice which it perpetuates can be bad. It can only be right in 'staying the course'. Such a fanatic group-think can be contagious across cultures, and certainly has been across English-speaking states. Those who criticise the actions of the 'world's last best hope' and its 'allies in the battle against the forces of evil' ought, it follows, to be denounced, blocked out or attacked as 'supporting terrorism'.

What is most revealing is that even those whose life interests are violated by such a closed fanatic circle 'don't want to know'. This is because their own moral identity structures are threatened by exposure of the value system they are structured by and express. We have observed the social syndrome of collective denial before. So long as 'the force of public opinion' remains complicit in the denial, the deep structure of the derangement cannot be comprehended. *Lines of force follow lines of value.* It is these lines of value concealed in the sleep of habit and presupposition which form the deep stratum of my inquiry.

Normative diagnosis of a ruling value system identifies its regulating principles which, in turn, enable moral predictions of its response-types. Normative and political circumstances before 9–11 called for just such a response-type as then occurred. Prior to the event, the need for some mobilising shock to restore the legitimacy of the US-led global system in the face of its growing global opposition was quite clear. The quickening undertow of world disquiet at the continuing disastrous results of the New World Order on the majority of the world's people and planetary ecosystems is a matter of record. After the unexpectedly huge demonstrations and violent oppression of protestors in Genoa in mid-summer before 9–11, protests whose 350,000-plus participants exceeded all official expectations and which multiplied the famous 'Battle in Seattle' by more than ten times, the stage has been set for an Enemy which this system is structured to comprehend and respond to – an unfamiliar enemy that can be represented as attacking the people. 'Communism' and 'the evil Soviet empire' could no longer work. The attempts to portray young and socially conscientious citizens in protest as worthy of mass gassings and cagings had failed. It was deducible from the New World Order's regulating values, I wrote at the time, that the New World Order's global corporate governance required 'a dramatic turn to justify the continued imposition of an economic paradigm that is proclaimed as the meaning of "the Free World" but is increasingly resisted by the world's peoples as a disastrously failed global experiment'.

However we may decode the attack on September 11, 2001 as an historic event – whether as an isolated insane tragedy or as a geostrategic pretext for US-led military actions across borders to enforce new levels of transnational surveillance and control for the global corporate system – the deeper meaning is much the same. The 9–11 turn provided the moral, that is universally prescriptive and obligatory, framework of meaning to justify a systematic repression of this world opposition by the global corporate system's most heavily invested-in strength – US–NATO armed force. The magic incantations of 'free market and democracy', 'global prosperity' and 'solution of world poverty' had by August 2001 profoundly failed to enlist support for the 'global revolution of shareholder value'. As global civil and environmental fabrics palpably degraded under the New World Order's never-ending policy prescriptions, economic restructurings, deregulations, and privatisations of public wealth, there were ever-larger citizen movements against still wider plans of secretive transnational treaties to override accountable government control of domestic economies and resources. Yet, escalating police attacks and anti-personnel weapons were not deterring, but provoking, rising citizen disquiet and outrage. Despite pervasive media denunciations of 'violent protestors', increasingly morbid riot-police weapons and unprecedented steel walls across cities, the public protests did not decline in numbers or urgency, but grew and connected across cultures and continents – from the Americas through Western Europe to India, East Asia and the South Seas. Most profoundly disturbing to thinking people across languages and national borders, life conditions themselves were unprecedentedly at risk on ecological levels with no capacity on the part of US-led global institutions to respond to the deepening crises of human and planetary life fabrics. The ruling moral apriorism could only relate to the crises by positing an Enemy which it was capable of defeating. Revealingly, the 'liberal growth ethic' of perpetual money and military expansion which propelled the lifeground crises to begin with were now escalated in fanatic repetition of the failed value programme.

At the symbolic head of the growing collapse, rising questions about the US president's legitimacy itself had become ever more outspoken in domestic and international public opinion. Even the global market's meaning as an *economy* had become open to question. The leading economic faculties in France had begun to wonder whether 'the New World Order' was driven by an '*autisme théoretique*'. Before the imposed amnesia of the 'new war against terrorism', the system for global corporate rule plan was plainly losing its campaign for world legitimacy. It was, in fact, rapidly retreating in the face of citizenries awakened to a bunker rule of state plenipotentiaries negotiating treaties behind wider and wider walls, bigger and more violent riot squads, and ever more transparently false slogans and proclamations. While material interests of more and cheaper access to vast deposits of Central Asian gas and oil by US transnational corporations and escalated revenues and powers for the US–NATO military industrial complex are both gains of America's 'New War', the explanation and understanding in this study move under such material interests as *mute givens* to the regulating order of value of which they are *expressions*. Beneath 'economic laws' and 'capitalism' assumed as ultimate facts which produce inevitable outcomes, this study begins to unmask the regulating decision and choice structures which, in fact, construct and reproduce both through every moment as their underlying and determining value premises and decision ground.

Restructuring Civilisation

As my analysis had tracked the cumulative policies and consequences of this deeper order of regulating value and disvalue for years prior to the 9–11 turn, there was no sense of 'the whole world has changed' since its occurrence. On the contrary, the study shows a clear and systematic connectedness of the ruling logic of decision between the pre- and post-9–11 stages of the New World Order moving towards totalisation by the *carte blanche* of the new war. Underneath the familiar delirium of a designated Enemy and non-stop bombing raids made on it with impunity, the new war of 'Enduring Freedom' expanded to vast proportions. By 2002, the moral logic of the system now not only ruled out all choice of option, but entailed that all opposition to its rule was support for the 'terrorists'. 'You are either for us, or you are with the terrorists', proclaimed the US president in moral ultimatum to the world. As a mark of the totalitarian field in formation, no-one in official circles commented on the absurdity of the claim, or the fanaticism of its meaning. Least of all did media or academic commentary recognise the underlying moral derangement from which all followed. Yet every decision followed from the ruling value set as predictably as the vast new transfers of public wealth to private corporations and the rich once the war was declared. In the meantime the effects on the ground were bound to be ever more disastrous because the regulating value system only deepened in blindness to the life co-ordinates of peoples' needs and ecosystem requirements. The 'globalisation' of corporate rights to control and expropriate across borders was now legitimated by a war which had no outer circumference to its overreach. As Secretary of State Powell said to Congress in mid-February 2002, the new permissions of military forward basing achieved what 'we could not have dreamed of before'. Thus, every step of the world occupation escalated in certitude of its Just Cause, and all was in exact accordance with the moral syntax in its actually regulating and its rationalising levels of operation.

As increasing majority impoverishment, global environmental destabilisation and global life insecurity have spread and deepened, the regime's demand for the one right way of all existence has increased in direct proportion to its disastrous failures. Public institutional capacities to prevent and overcome ecological and civil crises have, in accordance with the imperatives of the same value programme, been further defunded and dismantled, while international trade and investment decision structures have simultaneously become unaccountable to electorates and responsible government. Corporate-front states have been lobbied into the place of the will of sovereign peoples. 'America's New War against international terrorism' has functioned in these circumstances as a *moral shock diversion* from the growing macro incapacity and incompetence of its rule. Projection of all evil onto the Enemy closes the circle. What connects all of these phenomena across their diverse levels of decision and effect is certainly not 'economic laws'. Every decision that is prescribed and assumed by the official regime of thought across borders expresses a fanatic value system *to which economies themselves are restructured to conform.*

A structure of mindless absolutism is easily detectable in fanatic cults to which we do not belong. However, when it is the ruling value set of a world empire and its satellites, such an intersubjective normative system becomes self-evident to its bearers. Official and public perception are submerged in its ruling frame of reference, and so whatever resists its demands is perceived as ridiculous, wrong, and if persisted in, as 'the Enemy'. Just as the German war state of the 1930s was regulated in every move by a fanatical moral programme to rule the world, publicly camouflaged behind self-representations of its values as 'international peace', 'civilisation', 'efficiency', 'national security' and 'self-defence', so similar validating slogans mask the actually regulating value programme of the US-led global corporate system. We should know that any universally prescriptive order for the 'reform' of entire societies by one-formula-fits-all imperatives which are financially and militarily enforced by a faction-led superpower is oppressive of humanity by its very nature. Nonetheless, when it is called 'freedom and democracy' or 'economic necessity' (and it is called both by its agents), such an order is accepted by the ingrained mind-set as 'inevitable', even though all societies' and ecosystems' capacities to reproduce their vital means of life systemically decline as its prescriptions are obeyed.

The Inner Logic of the Value War

'Evil' is a taboo word in the academy except when it is deployed against officially designated enemies. The dominance of such a propagandist structure of judgement in any society measures its moral nonage. If the regulating values of one's socioeconomic order are not open to question, for whatever reason including 'scientific rigour', not even critics excavate their bearings as values. At the same time, no existing methodology selects for such moral-system inquiry. This is the state of the US-led 'Free World' at the turn of the millennium. Its moral non-age becomes mass homocidal when its closure against disconfirming facts becomes fixed and the projection of all evil onto an externalised Enemy justifies armed crusade against all who oppose it. Critical observations which would normally expose such jejune externalisation of guilt onto the Other – for example, 'threatening the world with weapons of mass terror and destruction' – cannot arise within the fanatic mind-set. Since it is the designated Enemy who is by definition evil, the problem must lie with it even if almost all 'weapons of mass terror and destruction' are produced, sold and used by it and its satellites. Although the Enemy is increasingly shadowy forces with few or no capacities to pose the threat attributed to it, this is of no importance to an *a priori* absolutism. It operates independently of the world of fact, and indeed enlists mob fury in its support by this very structure of value which is, by definition, always right. Group-mind moral commitment is in this way inflamed into war against the declared Adversary as the bearer of all evil, with reversal of the evident facts and plans of terror standing as the proof of its justice. When this grammar of delusion becomes a mutually determining culture of homocidal programme *across* armed lines, the underlying moral derangement is reproduced as a sacred war for all. Imprisoned in the intersubjective dementia across the lines of opposition, the only moral foundation is war against the Enemy. If such a mirror-image Enemy is not found in reality, one is constructed.

When a vicious circle of moral absolutism is prescribed across all limits of validity beneath familiar and idealised goods as its accepted message, then the society or civilisation which continues to be bonded by it becomes morally insane. At the level of the life-ground, the profundity of the evil that results is proportionate to the range of life that is degraded and destroyed. The extent of its inversion of reality, in turn, is measured by the opposite grandeur of goodness that is assumed – in the extremest case, self-representation as humanity's and the world's final bearer of the Good, even as its prescriptions systemically deprecate life and life conditions. Since people's self-flattering conceptions of themselves as God's chosen or 'the Free World' motivates acceptance of such a programme, the fanatic value-set can have no pretext of compulsion. It is accountable on the wider moral plane of historical crime. Globalisation of such a disorder of social self-regulation is not, in the end, consistent with the future of humankind.

It is true that an imperial order ruling across continents has powers of collective validation and invalidation which can delude people into a blind complicity of group-mind that knows no bounds of false and vicious certitudes of assumption. If the regulating moral syntax of a social order and its creatures becomes overridingly blind, there is no normal deterrent of social detection and disapprobation to inhibit the disorder's virulence. Only the social system's openness to internal criticism – the great achievement of post-Renaissance Western civilisation – can expose it.

Such a reclamation of moral intelligence occurred with both victorious and defeated nations after 1945 in Europe. Its civilising world turn, however, has been the major casualty of the fanatic value set emerging as dominant in the post-1980 era. Humanity's evolved capacity for life bearings and alternative is repressed only so long as this pathogenic moral syntax is not comprehended. In the period within which the world still lives, ignorance is strength, as Orwell foresaw, it, and truth and freedom are structured as lies and slavery – in precise ways which are defined ahead. It is not a question of 'a monstrous construction with no author', as Jean-Paul Sartre described the problem before the Great Reversal. For any social construction, however monstrous, *is* constructed, and reproduced. This locked sequence of reproduction is the moral cancer at the deciding marrow of the world condition.

Beneath the represented culture of scientific comportment, liberal tolerance and voluntary market exchanges, fanatic religio-moral assumptions steer every step of this system's globalisation – as we will see. With each 'necessary sacrifice to get the fundamentals right', the slow-motion lock-step of value equations structures the world toward ecological breakdown, majority-world dispossession, loss of public life services, and the economic meltdowns of once prosperous countries. With no critical feedback loop-of-life co-ordinates to the ruling value programme's prescriptions for ever more bleeding and shock treatments of societies, the empire's servants of scientific method, technology and armed force together compel the sacrificial restructuring. The continuous war of movement and expropriation across boundaries is the proof of its solution. At the same time, an unseen sea-shift towards reconnection to life values and the life-ground grows within this cumulatively catastrophic global experiment.

An alternative exists. The life economy option is thus the subject of the last half of this investigation. Its organising principles are articulated in constitutional decision paths of supercession of the life-blind moral syntax by which the world has been bound. The resolving value system of the life economy we here re-enter is as old as shared language, communal wells and air, public literacy and the rule of law. Its meaning derives from the depths of the long human social evolution which is epochally at risk at the turn of the third millennium. Within the unexamined deep lines of this hidden 'value war' develop the nature and future of planetary life organisation.

World history has many precedents of ruling metaphysics and absolutist value programmes that presuppose their prescriptions as final necessity. The Nazi and Stalinist interregnums are recent past forms of this failed restructuring of societies in accordance with fanatic commands yoked to military-industrial machines. The global corporate system is their transnational mutation. Once again, opposition against the mutant moral syntax forms across cultures, but the meaning of the new

Resistance remains unclearly connected to its moral ground, and untheorised as the life economy it stands for. Thus the deeper value bearings and public policy structure required to steer through the collapse are slow in recognition. Unlike the structure of prescription which has fatefully bonded Marxian and global market doctrines of 'inevitability' of outcome, and unlike the dominant 'descriptive' and 'neutral' frames of reference which overlook the deep moral syntax in fact regulating their basic assumptions, this study uncovers the system-deciding values which determine the lines of force. Once the human project is released from their invisible prison of presupposition, the constitutional resources to steer out of the accumulating breakdown of life conditions become decisively evident. Here as elsewhere, value systems are destiny, and reconnection to life co-ordinates their lost truth and meaning.

Part I

The New World Order

Inevitability and Terror: The Unseen Pattern

The slogan 'Marxism is dead' was proclaimed almost immediately on the fall of the Soviet Union in 1991. Very soon after, a strange ideological inversion occurred. In place of 'the inevitable victory of the proletariat' which Marx had predicted almost 150 years earlier, there was instead the 'inevitable process of globalisation'.

No-one in the postmodern global order noticed the reversal. Marx's meta-narrative of necessity had been pilloried for over a century for violating plurality and freedom, but the language of 'inevitable revolution' suddenly *shifted sides*. What was once abhorred by liberal theory as the metaphysic of 'Marxist economic determinism' had transfigured into a neo-liberal programme of 'necessary economic restructuring'. What was formerly condemned as a brutal violation of 'people's moral freedom to decide how they live' was now declared a matter in which 'there is no alternative'. From Margaret Thatcher's and Ronald Reagan's 'landslide' 1979–80 election victories with a minority of the electorate, all societies on earth were increasingly issued with one master decree, 'Adapt or perish'. Only now it was from the leaders of the 'Free World' that the ultimatum of history's future was declared.

No longer was it the liberation of workers' lives that was to be won, but the freedom of shareholders' value. Necessary sacrifices were not commanded by Soviet apparatchiks, but by English-speaking leaders of the global market. 'The restructuring may be brutal', the ideologues of the market revolution declared, 'but there is no choice.' As with past revolutionary 'necessity', there is a millenarian ring to the call. But now the revolution is of the rich against the poorer. The expropriations double instead of halve between them, and the *absolute* impoverishment of the poor deepens beneath rising aggregate income figures.[1] Yet, a fundamentalist faith in the ideological opiate of an 'invisible hand' rules out all criticism as 'failing to adjust to the new order'. Non-compliance or resistance are attacked, with 'harsh punishments' meted out to those 'not listening to the market', and bombing of non-marketised societies obstructing 'Free World' access to natural resources and transnational strategic sites.[2]

The Emerging of a Fanatic Mind-Set

Underneath public or learned notice, the traditional liberal conscience against claims of *economic determinism* and *sacrificial restructuring of societies*, always deemed totalitarian before, became silent. In its stead there has sprung from the depths of the historical preconscious a neo-liberal exultation in the demands of 'inevitable globalisation' to which all humanity must submit to 'stay alive in the brutal global market competition'. The livelihoods of millions are discarded as 'uncompetitive'. Life security for whole societies is abolished as 'unaffordable'. Financial war is waged against the welfare state. From the late 1970s onwards, 'necessary Structural Adjustment Programmes' led by the International Monetary Fund and the World Bank stripped social sectors in sub-Saharan Africa and Latin America, leaving these countries paying up to five times more on debt-servicing foreign banks than on public health and education. After the Reagan administration's inauguration in 1980, these Wall Street-driven programmes of social stripping by 'debt reduction' erupted as 'inevitable sacrifices' everywhere else.

The new freedom with no alternative quadrupled stockholders' value, but the majority of workers became poorer and less secure. By the time the 'new prosperity' of the 'world-leading US economy' peaked, the richest 10 per cent had more than doubled their wealth in the last five years, while non-supervisory workers' income had *declined* from 1970 by up to −20 per cent depending on the end-year and statistical co-ordinates. By 2000, the top 1 per cent had more wealth than the bottom 95 per cent of US citizens.[3] In East Europe, the degradation and insecurity of the majority was more dramatic under 'market reforms'. The average incidence of poverty across the region increased sevenfold from 1988 'under Soviet domination', to 1994 with ascension to 'the Free World'.[4]

In the majority world under 'the new economic thinking', the life insecurity of tens of millions escalated as monetised aggregates grew. The global market experiment with the world's peoples became a macro-economic pattern which led to life insecurity and disaster for majorities across the world, but were heralded in official and media circles across continents as 'market miracles'. 'More than 100 developing and transition economies,' reported the 1997 United Nations Development Report, 'suffered disastrous failures in growth and more prolonged cuts in living standards than industrial countries through the Great Depression'.[5] Despite the suddenness and extremity of the unprecedented globe-wide redistribution of wealth from the poor and middle-income to the rich, all was proclaimed to be in accord with self-certifying 'market laws' which, paradoxically, were said to the basis of 'freedom' at the same time. That radical and secretive policy interventions in the market were, in fact, behind every change was a deep-structural fact that none publicly noticed, or dared to discuss.[6]

'Structural reforms' were, instead, celebrated as 'the painful medicine of the market necessary for recovery' – the market theology's correlative of an Old Testament God whose punishments expiate sin. For those not fit to compete in 'harsh market competition – about four-fifths of the population, according to the best-known US Secretary of Labour[7] – 'all must adjust, or not survive'. Those who disagree are 'protectionists' – a term that reveals much – or 'conservative forces' or 'leftists', or, at the nadir of the invalidating predicates, 'afraid to compete'. Manipulation of leveraged money at the margins was, incoherently, supposed as the proof of *vertu*, while – as the protests mounted across the world against the new world disorder – the US head of state spoke for a regime increasingly in trouble by officially declaring 'those not with us are for the terrorists'. On the other side, for there are in the end only two sides in this fanatic metaphysic, are the 'cowardly acts' of suicide attacks on symbols of the global corporate order.

Throughout the world re-engineering by the global apparatchiks, there has been a transformative principle of representation across phenomena and crises: to *invert social values and general facts into their contrary* so that no bearings remain for intelligibility of resistance. For basic example, that a corporate oligopolist system in which over 60 per cent of international trade is between offices of the same firms or interlocked partners is *the opposite of* 'a free market', never arises as an issue.[8] It cannot compute to the locked mind-set. The contradiction is overridden as a problem by endlessly proclaiming it as an axiomatic given. In the manner of the fanatic mind-set, the organising principle of judgement is to rule out any reality that does not conform to it.

The closure of fanaticism is revealed by *the evangelical repetition of certitudes, and simultaneous abolition from view of whatever truth contradicts them* – a closure of group-think which *becomes more dangerous with the unilateral instruments of violence at its disposal*. Considering the pattern as a cultural phenomenon, one can examine any mass media organ from 1985 to 2002 to see if even *once* the evidence against the global market experiment arises as an issue of concern. In fact, the public discourse of the corporate state and the mass media have disconnected from any principle of truth which would expose the reasons for concern. Postmodernism has been the theoretical correlative of this decoupling from the principle of contradiction and confirming evidence, but only as an academic symptom. In the 'real world of the market', mind-stopping contradictions are proclaimed without notice as givens. Oligopoly is 'free competition'. Leveraged money demand with no commodity produced is the 'moral desert of market success'. Catastrophically failed economic experiments are 'needed economic reforms'. Bombings of poor civilians and their life infrastructures are 'humanitarian interventions'.

In particular, one can look to see whether it is ever once mentioned in the official culture's publications that a free society must have a choice as to how its people live, which the command of 'no alternative' excludes. More subtly, one can search in vain for one place across 'the new world order' including its universities where it is acknowledged that growth in monetised aggregates of the priced sectors of an economy do not, in principle, correlate with overcoming poverty or increasing people's freedom as is universally proclaimed as the bedrock premise of 'the new reality'.[9]

The 'Free World' in Reverse

In the chillingly acknowledged reality of administering 'shock treatments' to whole peoples, the certitude that all was 'necessary' and 'inevitable' entailed a sinister consequent which was not observed. The systematic restructuring of societies across the world *has no moral author* of society or elected leadership or even global corporate faction, because all occurs by necessity and economic laws. So throughout the re-engineerings of people's lives in conformity to the grand schema, a global cosmology of determinism by external laws and unaccountability of their prescriptions to the people ruled by them was never questioned within official circles. Even public policy and ethics journals joined the racing bandwagon of triumphal economic fatalism, or remained silent in studious focus on issues whose determination avoided all engagement with the surrounding social revolution in reverse.

A metaphysical switch in officially acceptable thought had occurred, and it permitted the imposition of the new system across continents and peoples as without choice. In startling inversion, an historic group-think operation had turned the world inside out with its effects, but none appeared to notice the mind-set reversal. The moral identity of the Free World had been exchanged with the identity of the sworn Enemy in the dark regions of the ruling psyche.

Before the fall of the 'Evil Empire' no moral anchor was more deep-seated than repudiation of the 'denial of free will' and of 'moral choice' by the doctrine of 'inexorable economic laws' and 'historical inevitability'. No doctrine was thought more objectionable by such cornerstone social ethicists as Karl Popper and Isaiah Berlin than one prescribing belief in whole societies' submission to 'the external forces of necessity'. The heroic story of Western civilisation was finally triumphant, most believed, when such scientistic predestinations of world power had been defeated in the victory over Nazism, and the Communist Other. Hardly had this historic victory of the Free World been won, however, than 'iron economic laws', 'necessity' and 'no alternative' were the leading battery-slogans of 'the new world order'.

Projection onto the Enemy of the US's own strategic methods had long been the mainswitch operation of 'free world' propaganda.[10] But *re-introjection* of these properties as its own was a new stage of the war against Evil. The Enemy's claimed metaphysic was now declared a final truth of the Free World. For years on end the chorus of the 'inevitable restructuring' of one society after another absolved the dogma-delirium of the architects from any responsibility for what was overtly declared as the 'axings', 'slashings' and 'cuts' of the shared life infrastructures of whole peoples across national borders and continents. To acknowledge that the effects were *decided* would have been to concede a deliberate reign of economic terror. But in eerie transmutation of roles, the command of the inevitable was not by fascist or communist bosses. It was carried as the daily given of 'the free press'. Yet the volte-face nowhere registered. The tell-tale indicator of contradictory propositions asserted as simultaneously true was, instead, totalised as global presupposition.

'The new reality' in which opposites are the same, however, requires a massive restructuring of the mind. One reversal after another of social meaning is demanded to unhinge consciousness from its past co-ordinates. Thus, no sooner had life-security programmes across the world been sacrificed to 'face down debt crises', than historically deep tax-cuts took their place to restore the shortfall of government revenues and the public debt as another 'necessity'. Restoration of social programmes were by this double stroke pre-empted, with governments' policy makers as enthusiasts for the inevitable revolution backwards. Sustained by the emerging culture of conditioned mass-mind certain of its freedom, the lion's share of the tax-cuts again flowed to the rich, just as they had the first time in 1980 when they precipitated the deficit crises. Slogans substitute for fact without the inhibiting reflection of thought. The sea of contradictions is, thus, called 'staying the course', and remains publicly and academically unproblematicised. For those not embracing this war on the life-ground for multiplications of money command to the trans-national financial faction, new instruments of 'counter-terrorism' are, over time, constructed to target them as the Enemy in the new moral universe. We will have to go far in history to find a remote match for such pervasive inversions of meaning and documentable fact as the triumphal daily fare of a way of life.

As the world's civil and natural ecologies increasingly unravelled underneath the saturating slogans, the final law of 'global market competition', the moral touchstone of the self-referential doctrine, remained untouched by reality. Indeed as the world entered the third millennium, the global market order was more declared more certainly than ever as a necessary structure determining the future as surely as the laws of nature make objects fall and heat rise. The test now as well as then is to look at any day's chain newspapers or television broadcasts. Has any in a decade doubted the efficacy and inevitability of the new order as former 'miracle economies' have melted down, the weather itself is globally destabilised, and a universal insecurity increasingly reigns? Has the certitude of 'the fundamentals' which every one of these degradations of life-field follows from been once questioned by a government, a business roundtable or a mass information medium during the unravelling?

On the contrary, the ineluctable destiny of all peoples on earth to compete to succeed in serving transnational investors is the ultimate given of social value, and increasingly the regulating principle of life consciousness itself. As in previous dark ages, all must submit to the final value of servitude to the absolute to be intelligible, or safe; and from their depths of the unconscious, the universal insecurity is proclaimed as Freedom. What peoples had long set their soul against – an order imposed on them by wheels of a higher, inexorable power – is now prescribed as every society's final meaning.

Sudden, disruptive restructurings of settled orders, the meanings of words inverted, the properties of the Other internalised as inevitable, laws of sacrifice declared inevitable, militant slogans and wars moving from one crisis to the next, domestic peoples perpetually off-balance and told they are being attacked – the pattern was familiar and undeniable, but the consciousness of it unthinkable.

The Paradigm Case of Britain: From Thatcher to the Third Way

When Margaret Thatcher made the slogan '*There is no alternative*', six centuries of British working-class struggle stood as an historical backbone against the occupation of society by the new order, but operant conditioning of consciousness with no other public message permitted mass reproduction eventually overwhelms the unaware mind. If the mass media's spaces are owned by those who multiply their wealth from the 'necessary economic restructuring', then how can any alternative be *communicated* to the public? In such circumstances of silencing, but with new conditions of social insecurity lurking everywhere as the threat underneath, there are two general pathways for adapting disquieted peoples. Both depend on the new final system-deciders for political survival and success – the conglomerate media and their base, the financial market.

One course for maintaining an order by decree is to finance official and unofficial armed militias to terrorise, torture and kill effective opponents – as US-directed and narcotic-financed operations have done from Indonesia and Chile to Guatemala, the former Yugoslavia to Middle Asia – a campaign of world subjugation that conforms to the master operation of this regime, *to invert the representation of reality into the opposite as its meaning*. Thus 'the rule of law', 'freedom' and 'anti-terrorism' are more pervasively proclaimed as the contrary more evidently occurs on the ground.[11] At the other pole of the decision path, which is confined to the most developed electorates, a leader of 'progressive' aspect can be selected to be presented to the public as the finder of 'a new message'. Here what is sold is a poll-validated image of reassurance which will appeal to increasingly insecure populations who remain uncertain of the new rule within which they could be the next to lose out. There are, as well, various paths in between the poles of 'no alternative' – from orchestrated solidarity of attack-the-Other (as in North America) to desertion of party traditions or election promises by social democrats beholden to financial and media powers (as in Britain and, less so, Europe). What all have in common in the post-1991 era is their willing compliance with the no-alternative order, with the axis of interlocked corporate media, electoral financial funds and threat of social disinvestment silently steering ruling party obedience to the presupposed programme.[12]

Let us examine the case of Britain. To ensure that its inevitably restructured economy continued down the same path after Maggie Thatcher and her Tory successor, John Major, a movement was selected from long-out-of-office Labour. It was called 'the Third Way', a vague slogan recycled from the days of the Vietnam War. The 'Third Way' was led by Tony Blair, who could be precisely counted on *not* to represent any other way. What was specifically required for stability of the counter-revolution was to ensure continuity of the no-alternative order as the democratic choice. This was Tony Blair's condition for achieving office.

Before being trusted by business as the successor TINA regime, Blair had to establish his credibility of subservience to the primary selectors – the corporate mass media and London financial centre. This route of succession was predictable from the given circumstances *if* Blair's leadership was to be counted on to sustain the still ongoing freedom of no choice. Blair inverted the Labour Party to secure the trust. The Murdoch press in ongoing exchange ensured the mass media favour required for public-image sale. The London financial district silently approved by not warning of a severe economic downturn or threatening capital flight if he were elected – the standard blocking tactics against Labour in the past. Again, any doubts that might arise were, as always in the new order, expiated by a new public relations slogan. This was 'New Labour'.

Evidence for the success of these arrangements is not hard to piece together from both ends. Only favourable coverage of Blair – unheard of for an actual Labour leader – came from the Murdoch press empire. No dire forecasts or even hints of economic instability – unheard of in the past – came from London's financial district. The other side of the arrangement proceeded in pattern. Murdoch's giant corporation was not pursued to pay tens of millions of British taxes which it continued (again unpre-

cedentedly) to evade by financial location in offshore banks.[13] Questions
of the legality of Murdoch's growing media and professional sport
monopoly were not raised by the 'New Labour' government, but silenced.

More significantly, the London financial district got what it had been
unable to wrest from any past regime – New Labour's formal and
immediate relinquishment in May 1997 of all control over national rates
of interest and currency exchange to the Bank of England. By this unpublicised action immediately on achieving office, Blair handed over the
main financial levers of sovereign government to lead bankers of the
financial faction. No decision has been more fateful for Britain, or for
European societies subsequently doing the same (a matter we investigate
in detail in Part III). In this way, elected government's control of the
nation's main financial selectors for the common interest are abdicated
from the centre. Disconnection from accountability to the public is the
order of rule.

The anti-Tory majority of England received what it wanted in the way
of an end to 'Thatcherism' in name, but the new foundations of transnational corporate rule were, in fact, deepened by 'New Labour'. Its rule
persisted in every neo-liberal re-engineering of the British economy to
strip the social infrastructure and to disempower labour, and under Blair's
watch went much further than Thatcher in financial and corporate
colonisation of government and public services. The deep-structural
transfer of the responsibilities of elected government to unelected financial
and corporate executives has led the global revolution backwards in the
modern home of democracy, an historic reversal to which his labour constituency appears to have been successfully lulled asleep.[14] The
underlying principles regulating Blair's terms of office are, in microcosm,
the institution of the universal value-set of the corporate fundamentalism which re-regulates societies across the globe.

Beneath the Ideology of New Labour: Dispossessing Labour to Add Market Value

The induced sleep of British public opinion is managed by pervasive
images of ruling party moderation and generalised public lies repeated
as given facts. We may consider one or two synecdoche cases. Blair's
New Labour makes much of securing market prosperity to expand social
spending on Britons' lives from the dark days of the Tories. But a callous
truth underlies the non-stop spin. After a second term was awarded, New
Labour's 2001 March Budget was trumpeted as 'new social spending to
begin the new era'; but in fact was the same public spending as a
proportion of GDP as the Tories spent when Blair represented them as
unconscionable and antediluvian.

At the same time, this 'new public spending' comes from lower taxes on the rich. New Labour's taxes, in fact, 'took *more from the bottom quintile of the population* than the top, and still left 5 million Britons in 'absolute poverty'. Despite the 'booming British economy', 5 million souls suffered with insufficient food and shelter, lack of drinking water and sanitation facilities, and inadequate education and information access, as defined by 117 countries at the 1995 World Summit.[15]

Blairite policies have, simultaneously, increased the subjugation of workers 'for increased efficiency and new prosperity' – not only by campaigns of union bashing and confiscation of former labour rights and powers, but by ballooning compulsory work hours and increasing insecure and part-time jobs. According to the Cambridge University Rowntree Survey, 'New Labour' policies have imposed increasingly longer hours on workers (10 per cent more than the European average), with a full three weeks fewer holidays a year, more job-related stress without recourse, and more work-related ill-health. Blair then further repudiates 'in principle' any compliance with EU Directives to involve workers in 'information and consultation' on their work futures.[16] Although this last position is also in precise contradiction to the 'development of individual responsibility' that is declared the hallmark of 'the Third Way', the value-set driving every step of this systematic campaign of workers' life reduction is neither exposed nor penetrated as its regulating value pattern.

The moral reality is that decent lives and conditions of life do not compute with the fanatic's value-set. Under the moralistic proclamations that are the Blair trademark in policies grinding workers or bombing civilians, people's means of life are 'cost burdens for business' – all the more so if consideration extends to the unprofitable destitute. Accordingly, under Blair's 'Third Way' social insurance and labour taxes have fallen to just over *half* the rates of neighbouring Europe to undercut their social economies on behalf of reducing 'business tax burdens', a reduction of corporate taxes which left them at 50 per cent less than the US itself. Still, Blair was demanding in 2001 more labour concessions to more 'inevitable sacrifices we must make to compete in the global market'.[17]

Already making its people work longer hours than anywhere else in the OECD excepting the rising work week of non-unionised Americans, 'New Labour's 48-hour week limit is claimed to be 'voluntary', which means that it is not enforceable against employers who require employees to sign a waiver to work more than 48 hours a week before they get a job. This is all represented to the public as 'dynamic economic growth', the global market doctrine's magic panacea to all problems – although economic growth means only greater volumes of monetised exchanges. These system selectors for reduction of the majority's lives are then represented as 'new equality of opportunity and freedom for the British people' – in continuing conformity to the silent operations of value inversion which define the ruling character of the universal regime.

Perhaps most sinister is that the New Labour government served the lives of its labour constituency by new instructions from its Health and Safety Executive ordering all inspectors to reduce prosecutions of corporations violating health and safety laws. This commanded abdication of responsibilty to enforce life-protective law had the immediate and unprecedented effect of a 25 per cent decline in enforcement notices, and a 20 per cent increase in serious injuries and deaths to workers in workplaces, the first rise in decades.[18] The sacrifice of people to the new inevitable order typified the value-set of the homicidal fanatic who denies all accountability to others' lives, but the pattern was not noted, or reported in the mass media. It was soon to resurface in international form with the bombings of poor societies as acts of justice on their behalf.

The Market Laws of No Choice

There will be doubt about the disturbing implications here. The abdication of government responsibility and the sacrifice of workers' very lives to lower market prices and increased business returns does not seem to fit Tony Blair's enthused moral sincerity. However, the global market mind-set is self-referential, and so facts – even deaths and maimings – do not deter its certitudes. Nevertheless, common sense may wonder how such an image-conscious Oxonite could truly *say* he believed in the *no-choice* demand to so restructure British society, the modern world's oldest democracy, as an *inevitable* fate – even if the vicious consequences are blinkered out. Surely New Labour could not willingly fashion policies to grind labour harder than Thatcherism under the same slogans of fate's command?

Here we need to let Prime Minister Blair speak for himself – long after TINA Thatcher has been dismissed from office. Thatcher herself is so long gone that she only appears on the world stage when she returns from the catacombs of lost office to trumpet defence for her friend and ally, the Chilean mass-murderer, General Pinochet. Pinochet, we may recall, was the first to impose a 'no alternative' order – on electorally socialist Chile. His first-blood attack on democracy by a rule of terror, torture and death squads initiated the 'market revolution' worldwide, with all the life-depredating effects on peoples everywhere that we have reported.[19] But these connections too are abolished from the memory, and the agenda is now borne by Blair's state from inside the Labour Party itself.

Tony Blair follows the new moral 'disciplines of the market' that Thatcher and Pinochet pioneered as standard bearer for the next servant generation. His exact words on the nature of this new order deserve reflective pause. For they have been crafted to lead the public in the desired direction by the desired means of appeal which Blair embodies. If nothing else, Prime Minister Blair's public relations managers have long proved their mastery of political representation. What Blair proclaims here about inevitable higher powers that rule us reveals the moral metaphysic of 'the Third Way'.

'*These forces of change driving the future don't stop at national boundaries. Don't respect tradition. They wait for no one and no nation. They are universal.*'[20]

We need here to analyse out the inner logic of Blair's revealing statement to understand the programme of power that it urges his national Labour Convention audience to submit to. On first blush, Blair's statement is the political rhetoric of a national leader demanding the recognition by his party of a new reality to which its working-class members must adapt. There is, however, a deeper layer of meaning which goes beyond Britain itself to identification of a cosmic condition to which all people everywhere have no choice but to surrender their self-determination. Blair's statement reveals by its sweep of assertion the invasive global forces which he stands for as boy advocate. His words are very clear. Their structure deletes the subject of every sentence as nameless, inhuman, 'forces' without definition, accountable to nothing beyond themselves. They affirm with no qualifier an occupation of societies everywhere by 'forces' which will stop at no line of national jurisdiction or cultural identity. All that was once secure in historical time and place is here declared powerless against 'the universal forces' that are presumed without meaning as the Good.

Tony Blair discloses without knowing it the nature of what it is he is awed by. The powers of corporate global revolution by which all that he sees have been overwhelmed are, he enthuses, beyond any possibility of control. Even he is helpless in their face as British head of state, for their new commands overrun all limits of law, all values of historical 'tradition' and 'nation'. The referent of his words could be the invasion of Europe by the Third Reich. Here too the 'universal forces' overrunning the rule of borders and laws were adored by state collaborators as triumphal and good. The totalitarian subject is always so submerged in the rapture of submission to higher forces. This is the ground of absolute authority's internalisation by its creatures. The nation-overrunning forces are cosmic, what all everywhere must surrender to in glory as 'driving the future'. The eros is the affirmation of the subjection. The market God, as Yeats' Zeus plunders Leda, rapes the world to implant in her the new cycle of the earth, and those who know the dread gyre's powers submit as infused with its higher mission.

One might think, on the other hand, that Blair's statement is a rhetorical flourish. But is it, in truth, the missing key to every policy of Blair's office? What act in his record of office is *inconsistent* with any part of it? When has Blair *not* acted in conformity to this belief in the higher laws of corporate globalisation – 'waiting for no one and no nation', overriding all who do not move into line with its omnipotent, grander advance. We comprehend both Blair and these forces if we read him as a political *expression of* their value-set. The 'clashes of political will' and 'party conflicts' which provide the narrative framework for historians and journalists cannot recognise the opposite pattern at work here. It is the *repression* of opposition, the homogenising of parties by 'the universal forces' of the final moral programme that rules, precisely *not* the contest of ideas and parties.

As a total programme, it is predictable from it that Blair must denounce and isolate anyone who represents any opposition to it – in particular, the militant resistance within his own party, from Tony Benn and Ken Livingstone to Labour's grass-roots across Britain. We can understand too why Blair like Thatcher has opposed any decision by the European Union if it moves to institute the economic rights of working people, or if its governments seek national tax obligations or human rights.[21] We understand the Third Way only if we look to the actually regulating principles of value to which all its moves conform.

The State and GMO Progress: Reading the Symptoms of the Global Corporate Occupation

One might think from this explanatory standpoint that Blair is especially odious; but one needs to search for evidence of any head of state acting to limit the power of transnational corporations in any of the world's nations since 1990. The prime minister of Canada, for example, is driven by the same programme in his every diplomatic move as leader of 'Team Canada', permanently roaming the globe seeking more contracts for transnational corporations, contracting through the Ministry of Foreign Affairs and International Trade with any violent dictatorship which might buy atomic energy reactors, electronic infrastructure, helicopter engines, oil servicing equipment, or open up mineral deposits for foreign corporate looting.[22]

It is poignantly ironic in this connection that Canada's Minister of Industry and Trade could find no more final defence against parliamentary questioning on exposing the country's public health and education systems to for-profit foreign corporate takeover than to elevate Tony Blair as the time's yardstick of truth and goodness. 'The NDP' (New Democratic Party), said the minister, 'does not want *to move with the times*. It could not even applaud Tony Blair in the House when he said that free trade was good for the poor.'[23] The new moral order crosses all boundaries. Under its global reach into the souls of men as its vehicles, there is a presupposed *norm* of polite exchange to keep order and survive on the fast track of progress: to yield the public interest of the nation as formerly conceived in return for the corporate media spotlight and business support.[24] It is the new age of the global market. All who do not comply are soon publicised in the corporate press as 'nationalist' or 'against change' –

even 'against helping the poor'. Blair's catechism to the higher forces is housed by servant politicians across the globe as their inner credo of life's moral meaning.

The submission to the 'universal forces' includes, we need to recognise, not only the subjugation of the British Labour Party to corporate financial and media control, but far more sinister dimensions. Prior to co-leadership of the aerial bombing of other peoples' social infrastructures – whose meaning we analyse ahead – 'New Labour' has also joined as a junior partner with the US in a globe-wide campaign to assist corporate agribusiness to alter the world's food cycles by uncontrollable genetic engineering under corporate patent control.

The agri-oligopolist war to force the world to eat genetically engineered food whether they want it or not is performed in the service of 'food for future generations', 'feeding the poor' and even making the blind see. In fact, public and university research have both been fund-forced from the highest political offices to serve this fraudulent project of transnational agribusiness corporations for over 15 years. Behind this very profitable takeover from traditional agricultural communities – which rides on the public purse and government-funded higher research institutions and whose scientists are not funded if they do not comply – lies the US industrial-food complex. It has already seized control of the soya and corn markets of North America, and overrides public protests, organic farmers, unbought scientists and anyone else who gets in the way. Even the separation or labelling of genetically engineered food products is prohibited while universities, like my own, run public relations campaigns for genetically modified organisms (GMOs) to get funds. Blair's government has distinguished itself in this corrupt process by politically suppressing scientific evidence against genetically engineered foodstuffs, and by surreptitiously permitting the contamination of non-GMO agriculture by the dominant genes of genetically modified crops.

The regulating order of the corporate absolutism of 'value adding' only becomes evident by connection across the publicly disconnected facts. With the increasing failure of corporate 'space-age' technology in Britain itself – in such areas as rail transit (e.g., corporate negligence by private Railtrack of its rail infrastructure causing train crashes like the fatal Hatfield disaster during a 60 per cent rise in company profits),[25] and corporate factory farming (the mad-cow disease and foot-and-mouth epidemics in which profiteering cost-cutting and poorly regulated mass operations led to both tragedies),[26] the Third Way's response is sustained in obedience to the higher value programme. The corporate command economy of minimum costs to corporations and maximum externalisation onto others, of guaranteed high returns by transnational control of factors of production, and of monopoly-patent technology across economic and state sectors 'cannot be stopped' – even if people are increasingly immiserated and the public are no longer secure in their life goods. Again, facts and consequences do not register to the value-set as relevant to the certainty of its truth.

The case of GMOs is paradigmatic. Corporations do no precautionary research on the long-term effects of genetically engineered food on people who consume these products, nor on the ecological effects of reproducing organisms on the environment.[27] Although GMOs reproduce and colonise other seed stocks (unlike chemical inputs into foods for which the laws are gauged), the danger of chain effects has not been tested by their producers or suppliers before releasing them into the larger ecosystem and food chains.[28] It is therefore no exaggeration to say that both human beings and their life-host are guinea pigs for the GMO corporate state experiment – itself a symbol of the larger global experiment they symbolise.

Dr Arpad Pusztai's research in 1997–98 at the Rowett Research Institute in Aberdeen, Scotland was thus of particular direct interest when it showed, as an unexpected side effect, severe gastrointestinal tract damage to rats eating genetically modified potatoes. Although firmly a pro-GMO researcher, Dr Pusztai, with the Institute's permission, revealed his government-financed findings on a 150-second interview on Granada TV in August of that year.[29] There was an instant response of search-and-destroy. The public evidence, the prospect of further study, and the reputation of its provider were all treated to a scorched-earth response. The data was confiscated, and the laboratory was closed to the experimenter. The 67-year-old scientist was issued with a gag order, suspended from his senior scientific position, deprived of his $1.4 million research grant, and publicly denounced by New Labour's Parliamentary Committee on Science and Technology. As Pusztai declared later (emphasis added), 'I can say from my experience that *if anyone dares to say anything even slightly contra-indicative, they are vilified and destroyed.*'[30] Pusztai's co-researcher wrote me in subsequent correspondence in October 2000 that their research was 'potentially stopped by the highest office in the country, although denied by 10 Downing Street'.[31]

Only connect, in the words of E.M. Forster's epitaph, and much comes to light. The moral template of the global corporate regime is revealed in its 'Third Way' microcosm – but it propagates in wider pattern to the bombs on Belgrade, Baghdad and Kabul citizens – and who next?

Pusztai's research was eventually refereed through three rounds and published by one of the world's most prestigious medical research journals (*The Lancet*, 16, October 1999). The truth of the matter did not occasion any apology, change of course, or policy reconsideration. That an aroused British citizen resistance to GMOs continued to increase simultaneously with scientific support for health and contamination concerns did not deter the magical thinking of 'miracle technologies' and 'market competitiveness' which have only salvational outcomes. On the contrary, a sudden New Labour edict in February 2001 dramatically and unexpectedly *doubled* the number of GMO experimentation sites to 96 as the scientific and public demand for segregation of the contaminating crops grew. Blair's agriculture ministry at the same time declared a 'perimeter' of 90 metres around crops, although seed contamination was already known to exist in practice to over 3500 metres and predicted in much wider range by biologists and ecologists.[32] Since the accompanying fact of foot-and-mouth disease indicated the possibility that air- and vector-borne contaminated pollen could spread by wind over many miles, as the 2001 outbreak had just made evident, it was clear why 90 metres around an open-air plot would be insufficient to prevent aerial and vector contamination by mutant pollen at the very time that the foot-and-mouth epidemic was spreading through 450 miles.[33]

The 90-metre perimeter was known, in fact, *not* to prevent contamination by airborne pollen spread from open fields of genetically engineered plants. As Saskatchewan farmer Croft Woodruff, a victim of GMO degradation of his crops, wrote to Prime Minister Blair on March 13, 2001 from his direct experience (I quote from the copy to me): 'Monsanto [the lead GMO-commodity producer] knew its GE [genetically engineered] seeds would cross pollinate, that gene flow was uncontrollable.' He added what all genetic scientists know – that '*the GE altered gene is always the dominant gene, which means the loss of seed varieties and biodiversity*'.[34]

Since Woodruff like other Canadian farmers had experienced a 50 per cent revenue drop from trying to sell GE food crops to a collapsing international market in which British supermarket chains refused to market known GMO products, there was a deep problem. Demand for organic produce was exponentially growing at the same time beyond farmers' ability to fulfil it. Huge financial commitments had been made to GE food production in prospect of matching or surpassing 70 per cent markets in soya and 81 per cent maize, as US mega-corporations had already achieved. Giant oligopolist corporations like Cargill, Archer-Midland-Daniels and Zoh were now rapidly losing market share to a groundswell international movement of NOT-GMO! An emergency, called 'Threat' in the management lexicon, was therefore evidently declared in agribusiness boardrooms.

That the clear market trend to non-GMO seed stock and crops must be stopped was the premise of the value-set regulating the losing corporate giants, whose chief executives happened also to be amply represented in New Labour policy committees.[35] From the standpoint of their moral set-point, *the rational way* to deal with this runaway loss of market share consisted of two steps. The first is well known – to ensure against labelling of the GMO products so that consumers would not know, an assurance that the WTO still guarantees by its rules against 'process discrimination'. The second step is not known. It is to *continue to allow contamination of the non-GMO crops by the corporately engineered GMOs*. This is not a 'conspiracy theory' – the standard invalidating predicate to block tracking of strategic decisions. Here, however, no complicated tracking is required.

The conclusion follows straightforwardly from the market value calculus. The ongoing contamination of other food crops and seeds would only be a problem if the government banned the ongoing open-sky growth of GMO seeds, therefore exposing the decision to criminal and civil liability as well as loss of reputation equity. Blair's government obliged by not banning GMOs. Indeed, its corporate-led state policy not only permitted the ongoing GMO contamination of other crops, but set boundaries around them not so wide as to prevent GMO contamination.

This strategy to protect collapsing market share plainly follows from self-maximising business decision. It is irrefutably moral within its value-set. The fiduciary duty to maximise the returns of shareholders entails this strategic protection of market share as obligatory. Blair's 'business-friendly government', in turn, is obliged by its commitment not to make a business-unfriendly decision which might cost agribusiness and supermarket shareholders billions of lost future profits for what 'the science is unclear about'. That government does *not* march to the same drum as corporate business because of its sovereign and opposed duty to serve the public interest – here protection of the food chain, small and organic farms, and the nation's ecosystems – is a moral decision that Tony Blair has never shown himself capable of making. Therefore, we can reasonably infer from the facts of the situation, and none before or since disconfirms the forensic inference, that Blair's administration permitted the probability of contamination of British food seeds by corporately engineered open-air crops. All the facts confirm this *explanans*.

In considering the gravity of this evident complicity in corrupting the future food-seed supply of the British people he was elected to represent, we must recall Blair's awe of 'the universal forces' and, more specifically, the powerful corporate interests he has everywhere invited in to chair his government committees.[36] Blair demonstrates in such ways his unfitness to hold public office. Yet the corporate ethic he serves is much deeper than his subjugation to it. When we bear in mind here the undisputed scientific facts that GMOs contaminate with no boundary to their movement, and that their *always dominant genes predictably colonise non-GMO seed varieties with no identifiable limit to this extinction of rapidly shrinking seed-varieties*,[37] we begin to comprehend the heinousness of the value-set behind such effects. We have seen it select for life-devastating outcomes from the deaths and mutilations of British workers to corruption of the food chain itself by 'leaving it to the market'. We may remember here with more resonant clarity Tony Blair's triumphal claim that 'these universal forces don't stop for anything'.

In this way, the world's future food supply still becomes 'more efficiently managed' by corporately engineered mutant food products. Thus Promar International confides that: 'The hope of the industry is that over time the market is so flooded that there's nothing you can do about it. You sort of surrender.'[38] The corporate strategy and the Third Way dovetail in the objective of necessary surrender. Like prime ministerial collaborators of the past with the globally projected power of imperial forces occupying nations, government has become a quisling.

The Political Credo of Collaboration and Abolition of the Moral Subject

At this point, it is instructive to re-examine Blair's underlying cosmology of the global corporate system which is again typical: '*These forces of change driving the future don't stop at national boundaries. Don't respect tradition. They wait for no one and no nation. They are universal.*' Let us deduce the *meaning* of this new order by logical diagnosis of Blair's words. In this way, we may uncover the *regulating principles of value and thought* of the life-destructive value system we track.

1. The forces of corporate global restructuring are *without meaning or value in their direction*. They are external 'forces', not what we care about intrinsically, and they 'drive the future' as the forces of combusted gases drive pistons or the forces of gravity move the tides. They are to be submitted to, not because they are *good* or promote life's well-being, but because they are all-powerful.
2. The forces of corporate global restructuring are *lawless*. They 'don't stop at national boundaries', as all lawful agents are obliged to do. The first principle of domestic and international law, to respect the boundaries of others, is overridden. The sovereign boundaries of nations upon which all other legal boundaries depend must fall before the advance of the higher powers.
3. The forces of corporate global restructuring are *unaccountable*. There is no electorate or public standard or higher authority they answer to because 'they wait for no one and no nation' and 'drive the future'. They are, it follows, above democratic or other forms of social responsibility.
4. The forces of corporate global restructuring are *absolutist*. They 'respect no tradition' – ethical, legal, or cultural. There is no exception. English-speaking traditions of rule of law, past morality and life-values themselves are powerless to resist. They cannot and ought not to stand in the way.

As we unpack the inner meaning of Blair's statement to his working-class party and to the world press, we need to ask whether his position is truly *representative* of the position of governments in the 'globalisation' era. To answer this question, we can pose a general question to reflective observation: What governing political party has not *acted* in conformity to the demands of these global corporate forces? What 'democratic' political leader across 'the Free World' does in fact *stand against, seek to make accountable, hedge in by enforced law, raise the common interest above, or in any way morally question* the transnational forces whose powers Blair proclaims as overriding all past limits of culture, boundary and way of life?

One need only pose the more general question to recognise that it is not easy to name an exception. There are of course exceptions, and the future of civil and planetary life-organisation depends upon them, but these exceptions, whether occurring in Malaysia after the Asian meltdown with successful capital and currency controls, or in Cuba with a still remaining social infrastructure, or Norway which until the later 1990s supported its social programmes with oil revenues, are not reported in the world's corporate communication system. Social values higher than monetary profit are, instead, in accordance with the ruling principle of value inversion, projected as 'dictatorship' and 'harming the middle income and the poor'.

At bottom, there is a meaning which is not exposed. An effective morality of genocide selects for and attacks any form of economic or social organisation that does not conform to the absolutist regime. The value code is not self-disclosing in this genocidal nature of its regulating principles, needless to say. Fanaticism is not capable of self-recognition. Whatever obstructs universal rule by for-profit corporations and trans-national financial institutions is marked and pursued for extinction as a matter of consistent documentable fact over an extended period without notable exception. This general fact can, again, be tested by looking for the exceptions. If social infrastructures provide an *alternative* to for-profit corporate rule, they are as a matter of historical record invariably marked for financial destabilisation and military invasion – not only in such obvious post-1980 cases as Cuba since 1960, Nicaragua under the Sandinistas or Mozambique under the leadership of Juan Marischal, and others too numerous to identify here, but also, as we will see, the destruction of Yugoslavia from the Reagan administration onwards, and the destruction of Iraq's civilian social infrastructure during the same period.[39] Blair's catechism to the final new forces of world power expresses the ruling *mind-set* in its reverent proclamation that they 'respect *no* national border'. These unaccountable forces have thus become *normally* accepted as the changes of season are accepted .

Even those who do not adulate these forces, but abhor them, may submit to the submerged thought pattern that 'there is nothing one can do'. There is perhaps no order of oppression in history that has not depended on this self-dehumanising response for the continuance of its oppression. 'The greatest weapon in the hands of the oppressor', as Steve Biko recognised, 'is the mind of the oppressed.' In the case of the global corporate system, however, there is no moment of its advance anywhere that is not, in fact, people's own doing each step of the way – planned, met over, decided, ordered, accepted, silently borne and obeyed in individual and group action at every level of technological, economic and political constructions and implementations. Yet the contradiction between inexorable economic '*laws*' and the actually *deciding process* of every moment is repressed from view, as it must be for the programme to be perpetuated.[40]

Most repress this conflict to avoid internal distress and social rejection. Many do so because they believe in the regulating order as transcendant and beyond human choice. The latter is the legitimiser of any fanatic system, and must be believed in for it not to provoke revolt. In the end, the economic theology of the Market is the soul of its absolutist world order. Blair's 'universal forces that respect no national boundary' are this modern God's efficient causes, and the final cause they effect is One Global Market Over All – *the* Market, the end-of-history order across all boundaries to which no alternative can exist – even if it is no longer a recognisable market. Beginning with Adam Smith's 'invisible hand' and arcing across centuries to F.A. von Hayek's ersatz 'transcendant order', an unseen deist metaphysic is at work legitimating the imposed order as ultimately moral even as it wages a campaign of war against civil and ecological life organisation itself.[41]

The constructed economic programme of a transnational corporate and financial sect has in these ways been *internalised* as a value-set which is reified as the structure of reality itself. A sign of the collective mind's submergence in global market totemism is that not even postmodernism contests its ultimate meta-narrative, or thinks beyond its desiring-machine images or self-referential circuitries as given. The deepest problem that eludes theory is the locked group-think underlying the permitted frameworks of intelligibility – the preconscious herd submergence in prescriptive demands as laws of collective motion, no more to be questioned than laws of physics, which is by no accident the model of neo-classical economics. This is a mind-set which, it is no exag-geration to say, exceeds in totality stone-age awe before the universal forces demanding the daily sacrifice of human beings to the laws of nature to perpetuate them. Yet, decision-constructed technology and money-demand, not natural laws, drive every moment of every cycle of this system. Economists, not priests, absolutise the order they postulate as independent. Scientific, not religious, superstition reads coerced social uniformities as inviolable laws. The re-engineering of world societies 'cannot be stopped', *because* they are assumed as written into the order of nature as divine design.

2

Return of the Genocidal War

Tony Blair exemplifies the character structure of the global market order. Packaged in the corporate culture of youthful image, he is constructed as sincere, energetic and moral. Like other ruling-party leaders, he has worked hard to be selected by the financial and media axes of power as 'the man to do the job'. He is a moral metaphor of the system.

The Public Relations of Genocidal Morality

US presidents are the prototype, and one thinks these smiling men are better than a Thatcher or a Pinochet. That is their function – to appear cordially pragmatic, while re-engineering the world to serve the 'universal forces driving the future'. They know that 'these forces wait for no man', and that is why they run so hard to serve them. Set these smiling faces of the new corporate order a task of bombing civilians and cities and destroying the children and futures of whole societies which resist the interlocking axes of power they are selected by, and they rise to the occasion with towering moral indignation. 'The cause of freedom' – even the deaths of 500,000 Iraqi children – is worth the 'collateral damage'. US and British heads of corporate states will uphold the armed enforcement of 5000 children dying every month over ten years, and then move on to demand the carpet bombing of a country of starving millions as 'the moral fibre to defeat fanaticism'.[42] The global occupation requires such men as public relations functions of final moral rectitude.

These are creatures who, before all else, seek to stay in group favour. In the limelight they are bathed in by the corporate media, they are historic performers of heroic resolve. Yet the mass destruction they in fact order of innocent Third World citizens and their life-supports have one master theme in common across all their tasks. Like the economic paradigm they stand for, they are *disconnected from the effects of their decisions*. This is the defining feature of the psychopath, but in the case of a social system's leadership is understood by them as the 'necessary' and 'unavoidable' consequences of the system which they represent. Since it is presupposed as the Good, then they who follow its demands too are the leading participants in the Good; and those who oppose the rule they stand for are Evil. This is the group-think of the global corporate regime's political and bureaucratic servants across borders, and it is self-referential. No problem of consequence can compute to its closed circle. As its lock-step of fanaticism is set and enforced as an overtly global programme, it destroys all that 'obstructs' it as without alternative. If it is not understood, it has no outer limit to its triumphal destruction.

The Dramaturgy of the New Wars

The closed circuit of a media-spotlighted 'crisis' with a foreign despot as the villain is the post-1980 format of war. The action always follows a theatrical formula. The *Other* as murderous psychopath is not the Other to begin with. He is one of Us, one who stands against a previous Other who is then 'all evil visibly personified', as Moby Dick is experienced by Ahab. In truth, the later personification of evil is first armed and trained by the US, perhaps as a 'freedom fighter'. Here he is an ally warring against a monstrous enemy in common. Known well and having performed the right functions, the Saddam, the Milosevic, the bin Laden remains out of media sight until he is required for his title role. Then he is constructed as the embodiment of all evil when another war is required.

At this juncture, whoever the new enemy or wherever the new war site, the once-ally despot is named. Although his worst deeds of blood-thirsty mass murder are apt to have been done *within* the alliance with its weapon commodities, he is portrayed everywhere as the wicked Other, the dictator or terrorist beyond dictators and terrorists, the Enemy of all enemies. One message alone is permitted public communication. The personification of evil, whether in Yugoslavia or Afghanistan or Iraq or somewhere else, must be publicly defeated to vindicate the freedom and justice of the world. Accordingly, he is spotlighted in every living room of the people as the Evil One, a face of alien malice for the mob to vent fury at until the mood has risen to a crescendo of moral outrage too vast to contain. Finally, one time after another, the cathartic bombing of Third World civilians and their social infrastructures follows as the morality play climax. In denouement, the borders once protecting the wicked one are 'opened to free capital and commodity flows', and the salvational political-military control of the US-led Free World 'restores order to the tragic chaos'.

Throughout 'the alliance leaders' invoke a moral rhetoric of absolute proportions – always accusing the Other in transcendent indignation of doing what has been or is about to be done by themselves in far greater extremes of terrorising, uprooting, and killing poor and innocent civilians. Nonetheless, somehow the named Enemy always avoids harm during every step of the war preparations, and becomes more invulnerably wicked through all the ascending denunciations and cries of moral outrage and demands for right and justice. He becomes a star, the Villain of the global movie set of the world system, as important to keep alive and flourishing as the hero of the grand morality play, the Free World itself. Thus it has been with Saddam, with Milosevic and – as I write – yet again with Osama bin Laden, all within one decade. The difference is that the poor peoples whose countries are bombed while the essential villain remains untouched to ensure the bombing's rectitude, are ever more helpless and defenceless with each episode of superpower bombing. As 'the war without end' diverts the mob, the new strategic prize is won from what were once inaccessible territories of rich resources and non-corporatised orders.

Always a long foreplay of negotiations or alliance building precedes the climax of destroying the life-means of the poor – the underlying constant of the morality play. In this way, the full savour of the sky-lighting destruction is discharged from the rising bile of the world system. Since the Vietnam lesson, 'the new war' is never risky combat on the ground, but one-sided bombing of peoples without air defences, destroying their infrastructures end-to-end. Always the victory of industrial weapons over a Third World country is triumphally proclaimed a victory of 'Freedom', 'Civilisation' and the 'Rule of Law' over Darkness – although none are free to doubt publicly, and international law is violated at every step from the planning stage on.[43]

The morality play of 'democratic forces' defeating 'dictatorship' and 'terror' plays out around the clock. It works so well to boost the popularity of even an illegitimate and dyslexic US presidency that the third millennium has been promised a non-stop diet of it for 'as long as it takes'. The fleeing and homeless hundreds of thousands caused again and again by 'the universal forces' are severed from the cause as inevitable side effects, while the Enemy is righteously blamed for their terrible plight. This the operation by reverse causation which distinguishes this ruling mind-set's operations.[44]

All is performed with no accountable process of fact discovery, impartial witness, exposure to trial, or even permitted counter-argument to interrupt the event of sanctified society destruction. One side alone presents reality to the fawning lights of transnational television cameras and rising world audiences. The militant group-mind is quickly resurrected across societies as orchestrated Chorus in the Good versus Evil plot. When the climax of the real violence-entertainment comes, all are bonded in glory lost from the future prospects of their lives. There is nothing like a war against a demonised Other to win the favour and admiration of all on our side – or so it seems for a time. If, for example, the peace movement is gaining, the environmentalists are winning, the anti-corporate groundswell is out of control – all true in particular before the Afghanistan War – the time is ripe to unleash the bombers again at the Enemy that has been constructed and set in place. Always a set of favourable consequences follow beneath discussion – more US corporate and covert agency control over global oil and narcotic supplies and routes, and more leverage over citizens' lives by US and allied militaries and armed force factions.

If the economy is going under and the international legitimacy of the president is in rising question, Tony Blair himself has advised us that 'the universal forces stop for no one and no nation'.[45] Enrage the audience, ensure the Enemy is far smaller in size, make sure the perimeters of armed force around the world grow as the blackout within them is secured, set the kill-clock for peak television hours, and then test and market the newest infrastructure-destroying commodities in live conditions.

As we will discover, this format has been followed in exact choreographed sequence for the two 'wars' we will anatomise in detail, the same formula in both. Then, as now, no perception of the resemblance was permitted to break the suspension of disbelief. The third war has followed the same formula again, against still poorer people and further into Asia. It is now the old heartland of imperial centre, and the new heartland of gas and oil. The third war has just happened historically, but the inner logic of the alibi and of the deep meaning beneath it are the same, with each a step closer to the totalitarian pattern that builds across the slain countries of the poor and into the imperial people's society itself. The pattern grows until it is seen.

The Operation of Life Disconnection by the 'Free World'

The key to keeping the audience on side in the total morality play is *the disconnection of act from consequence* – the master meta-theme of this era which defines its fanatic character. This disconnection is necessary because, as the Vietnam War showed, the citizens of the smaller and weaker country whose heavens and earth are rained with fire for weeks on end from above *must not be seen in the agony connected to the bombing* if demonstration of the universal forces is to work. The underlying life-ground of humanity will not tolerate it in the end. The unspeakable programme of destruction of a different economic order can only proceed if the terror and the destruction of peoples' lives is blinkered out from home view. Since Vietnam, therefore, war on the poor has been packaged like a one-way video game. One triumph of power after another by 'our boys kept out of harm's way', blanket control of all news-gathering and reports in the name of 'security', and selection of all media facts and reporters of acts, sustain the total illusion down to the omnipresent TV screen.[46]

Since the home majority never sees the terror and the ruin of poor people's lives by image control around the clock, only those who make it their business to find out – the heroes of the global civil commons – learn the truth. They speak in church basements and publish in non-profit journals what they know – that there are masses of innocent refugees fleeing the real terror, that poor civilians' babies and children are infected with nuclear-tipped weapons (as in Basra, Iraq); that their clean water supplies and home electricity are deliberately destroyed by 'surgical' transnational bombing (as in both Iraq and Kosovo); that children die by the hundreds of thousands in the first year, and continue dying for years by the tens of thousands (as in Iraq);[47] and that the problem that was said to cause the war is first incubated by US-led covert strategic construction, and then multiplied many times over by US–British bombing (as in Kosovo's or Afghanistan's refugee masses).[48]

However, these facts kept out of the public eye do not jeopardise the meta-operation – to destroy the alternative economic order – Iraq's, Yugoslavia's, rural peoples' next to oil – or the rising of one's own awakening peoples against the life-destroying system.

In this way, a feel-good indifference to the terrible consequences of one's actions is *structured into the decision and consequence at every level to block out the linkages between cause and effect*. This is, at the deepest level, the silent engineering of the mind-set that regulates the era – the structure of seeing and judging that is delinked from all responsibility or account-ability for ruining people's lives and life conditions without limit of destruction. This is the moral order of the homicidal fanatic at the personal level, but once inculcated as normal fare and punctuated with righteous anger and smiling pleasantry as presentational effects, the abyss has no base.

This severance of strategic decision from systematic life devastation is *the organising meaning* of the global corporate system. As elsewhere we look for facts to disconfirm the principle of explanation. There are none. In peacetime, the disconnect of mind distances head-office decisions from the ruined environments and livelihood-deprived families their corporate processes and products daily cause. It decouples, for example, oil, timber, and banking operations from the ravaged children and destroyed ecosystems they effect across the majority world from Colombia and Guatemala to Nigeria or Burma or the South Sea Islands. In war, the separation of cause and effect, purpose and consequence, is not spatial or personal, but is systematically constructed by secrecy, censorship and controlled news. Thus, all that was once inconceivable is normalised, and now even the US Congress itself is kept from knowing what is going on.

Between the decision and its implementation, between the plan and its life catastrophes falls the shadow of public unseeing. Self-maximising goal, scientific impartiality, technological distancing and media blocking together organise even the learned mind *not to see*, to become lost in images with no form but what is imposed, to be confident that all is for the best even as the death squads roam and the clinics are bombed. To decouple the intention from its execution, the deaths and disease from the strategic plan causing them, is the master-stroke of the dehumanisation as a way of life. Write such a design large, and mask it in market-tested images of sale, and there is no systemic terror that cannot be perpetrated with righteous equanimity. Reality becomes the management of perception.

Severance of the public image from the despoiled life-ground it draws a veil over is, in fact, the *ground of the system's legitimacy* when no other still exists. Conversely, reconnection of the decision-set projecting the image to the life-devastation trailing behind it is the ground of the system's *de*legitimation. Yet, underneath the operations of images displacing facts, there is the system itself from whose regulating circuits of money demand all orders of the global economy proceed. The 'universal forces' include not only globe-ringing financial assets and controls, world product technologies, and electronic media and information systems centred in US transnational corporations and the state administrative apparatus representing them. Behind them all is the final authority of a globe-straddling system of military terror and kill-power which is centred in Washington, but which joins with Thatcher–Blair Britain as an aerospace and armed-force axis in whatever war ventures are planned next. NATO's $1,200,000,000 expenditures of public tax revenues every day roll the wheels of the kill-and-destroy threat and bombing-edge of the global machine, ensuring final military control over all foreign regions and societies in 'the global free market', including in particular those not yet pried open.

Resistant societies, which could include the US homeland itself, require periodic demonstration of the terror for those 'who are not with us'. The saturation bombing and embargo of Iraq and Yugoslavia in the 1990s were such demonstrations. Their occasion, as we will see, is selected to unfold in the one-superpower era in accordance with proven formulae that none can contest. The morality play of corporate America is as simple in the macro as it is in the micro – Good versus Evil, with the US always the Good, and always against an Other who cannot retaliate. The saturation bombing and embargo of both Iraq and the former Yugoslavia exemplified this pattern, as did the Afghanistan war. The transnational military powers of the most technologically advanced nations together unilaterally bombed small, single countries of the poorer world with no defences against air-bombing. Yet a deeper meaning underlies the genocidal attacks. *The cataclysms replicated corporate 'peace-time' in hyper form.* The operations were borderless and moved to dislodge and expunge all local control and traditional life security. Transnational devastations of planetary ecosystems and social infrastructures by corporate commodities were effected in speeded-up design. Frenzies of public subsidy and new demand accelerated the state financing of the corporate high-tech sectors and transnational sales through all the moments of the product cycles. The system-wide disconnection of decisions from consequences and proclamations from facts operated everywhere as the master structure of illusion. Facts and fictions were more spectacularly turned upside down. The patriotism of the corporate market as packaging for the moving line of appropriation and dispossession across borders became more absolutist in militance and hysterical in delusion, but the inner logic of the life-disconnect was the normal 'way of life' of corporate America in its hidden meaning.

Foreknowledge and the Genocidal Meaning

The apparent illogic of the process at every level, destroying life to save it in endless contradictory variations, is insane from the standpoint of a life-ground ethic; but from the standpoint of the ruling mind-set, everything turns out as it should. There is only triumphal victories of Western technology, law and civilisation over 'the forces of darkness'. Yet to comprehend the structure of the underlying value calculus regulating these wars, one needs to consider the words which express it from the actors themselves. After refugees multiplied to over 1 million homeless people *after* the NATO bombing of 'the former Yugoslavia', the NATO commander of Kosovo operations, US General Wesley Clark. annulled the problem of the massive terror as *'entirely predictable'*. In response to the increase of ethnic massacres which the bombing also caused, Clark clarified that NATO operations *'were not designed to prevent ethnic cleansing'*.[49] UN Ambassador Madeleine Albright, following the same moral order, responded to the concern that half a million children had died as a result of the saturation bombings of Iraq by NATO forces by a very revealing justification: *'We think the price is worth it.'*[50] Gulf War field commander General Colin Powell, later US Secretary of State, characterised the incineration of thousands of young Iraqis forced into battle and fleeing with more rigorous disconnection: 'It's really *not a number I'm terribly interested in.'*[51]

Note that throughout, the mass-murderous consequences are not denied – not by Ambassador Albright, not by General Clark, and not by General and later Secretary of State Powell. Nor are the mass killings of innocent or helpless people at all unanticipated by any of them. *All delink from accountability.* Their morality, like Blair's, *excludes the consequences of their choices that would make them responsible.* For their value-sets, there is no connection of actions to effects on which accountability is based.

When mass terror and killing of innocent and helpless persons by the hundreds of thousands *is* raised as an issue for this mind-set, it is rejected as a matter which *could* affect the choice causing these consequences. The decision to destroy the lives of others even in the millions is serenely reaffirmed. In the latest war, 'the war with no end in sight', an estimated 2 million poor Afghan people, families and children were driven in mortal terror out of their homes. With millions of other refugees who were starving as the UN Food Programme to serve them was closed by US–British air attacks, the 'War Against Terrorism' was terrorising almost the entire Afghani civilian population. They were not the only victims. The UN's mine-sweeping headquarters in Kabul was bombed the first day, and the capital's electricity system was bombed the second. That the designated Enemy was no closer to apprehension than before, and nowhere near the bombing according to the US's own intelligence, was not perceived as an issue. The Secretary of Defense, Donald Rumsfeld, lurching into the question of what next, replied that: 'We're not running out of targets. Afghanistan is.'[52]

The following day after a village was destroyed and hundreds of villagers killed by US bombs, Secretary Rumsfeld replied with no denial but, in confidence of the group-mind's capacity to sustain contradictions as equations, retorted: 'Everyone knows in this country that the US government never targets civilians – but we all know there will be civilian casualties.'[53]

Accountability is thus ruled out *a priori*. Responsibility for war crimes and crimes against humanity under law are not computable to the value-set.

How can others be accused of these crimes, then? Here is where the operation by inversion defined above stabilises the fanatic's closed programme. What we do is Good, and what opposes us is Evil. Therefore all that kills and destroys is the Others' fault by definition. The only problem which can remain is 'communication' of this given structure of the moral universe. As the Madison Avenue 'top gun' hired by the US State Department to ensure the rest of the world gets it right says in response to the challenge of America's 'image abroad': 'The whole idea of building a brand is to create a relationship between the product and its users ... We're going to have to communicate ... our belief system and our values.'[54] Repetition of the self-referential programme more pervasively suffices to justify it.

The fanatic moral logic regulating these decision sequences is sustained because it is nowhere exposed. Not even moral philosophers penetrate or discuss it, yet we have not yet comprehended the full meaning. The *premeditation* of precisely these decisions, actions and effects was years in the making in every case. The Afghanistan case is still not fully plumbed; but it is known that bin Laden and al-Qaida were armed and funded by the CIA (not to mention the $43 million given to the Taliban by the State Department in May 2001); that a former Pakistani diplomat was told in mid-July that the US planned to attack Afghanistan by mid-October;[55] that the CIA was meeting with bin Laden the month before September 11;[56] that Pakistani military intelligence chief Sheikh Mahmoud ordered an aide to wire transfer US$ 100,000 to the leader of the September 11 suicide plot, Mohammed Atta, weeks before;[57] that the deputy director of the FBI resigned in protest before September 11 against the US administration's blocking of intelligence pursuit of al-Qaida as Bush appointees sought a 'big prize' oil route through Afghanistan;[58] that on September 11 the standard interception routines of the US Air Force were not followed for over an hour before the suicide jets hit their targets; that Secretary of State Colin Powell did not deny in his December 18, 2001 press conference that Israeli intelligence officers in the US knew of the September 11 attack beforehand; that vast oil and gas fields in Central Asia and a new oil route out of them was a preoccupation of the oilman US administration and long treasured by US geostrategic policy;[59] and that the new war against Afghanistan opened both the oil and gas fields and their Central Asia pipeline route to new US control.[60]

All of this helps to explain why President Bush Jr. immediately and falsely described the September 11 terrorist attack as a 'declaration of war' in his first press communication to justify the bombing of Afghanistan in violation of the UN Charter – a war crime under international law if not in self-defence against invasion by another state.[61]

In the cases of the Iraqi and Yugoslavian social bombings, they too were not suddenly targeted by the reflexes of moral horror. They too were longer in the making, and in the case of Yugoslavia much longer. Yugoslavia was targeted for social destabilisation and destruction of its 'market socialism' alternative – the original 'Third Way' – by top-secret US National Security directives in the early 1980s.[62] Iraq's region-leading socialised infrastructure, including especially its socially owned large oil reserves, had long been an object of US intervention, including well-known military and CIA support of Saddam Hussein's coup d'état and dictatorship. The Yugoslav and Iraqi societies were not targeted *in spite of* their regionally advanced social systems, but *because* of them. Like Nicaragua and Grenada a few years earlier, and Iran, Guatemala, Cuba, Vietnam, and Chile before that, there is one general cause that invariably provokes the US corporate state to aggressive interference and armed invasion at will. Beneath notice, the one heresy that has not been forgiven since at least 1950 is any instituting movement in the Third World *in which social ownership of key natural resources has been introduced and universal literacy, health and social security systems constructed.*

Both Yugoslavia and Iraq had developed social infrastructures for their citizens which were unique in their regions. Both were targeted long before their bombing – a pattern that repeats until it is seen through.

Both societies were destroyed while their leaders stayed unmarked by legal process and untouched by the bombs. Both were supported by the US in their rises to power and their moves to dismantle their socialised economies. These facts and the decision pattern connecting them are never publicly discussed, even as the same strategic sequence is repeated once more. But if we factor in the control and public ownership of oil by Iraq, the strategic centrality of Yugoslavia and its formerly successful socialist economy in the region, the development of the social infrastructures and working classes outside corporate commodification and command, and the need for demonstration of the forces of 'the new world order', then we can see how this selection process conforms to an unexamined pattern.

Armed attack on socialising or socially controlled economies and infrastructures had always been masked in code phrases like 'communist', 'Soviet beachhead', 'threat to the national security of the United States', and so on. With the fall of the Soviet Union, however, the justification of a 'Soviet plot for world rule', 'Moscow subversion', and 'the global communist threat' was no longer operational as a pretext for destabilisation and invasion. Deprived of the former satanic enemy to justify such interventions in criminal violation of international law – and almost every US intervention in Third World societies has been criminal under international law[63] – other pretexts were required for the dismantling of social orders whose natural resources, markets and militaries were not yet pried open for the 'free movement of capital and commodities'.

Financial destabilisation of social infrastructures by 'debt crisis' and IMF prescription was the normal route, but such re-engineering of societies by foreign bank debt does not secure the decisive dismantling of successfully socialised economies. On the purely geostrategic level as well, the need to ensure the 'projection of power' by the US and NATO makes it necessary to keep its military system in motion, to test and market its billion-dollar weaponries, and to justify military war as a legitimate instrument in globalising the corporate market system in the final stage of colonialism.

These effective criteria were never stated or self-conscious in the lockstep of the selection process for war, which is volatile by the nature of its mass-homicidal operations. It is sufficient that the targeted societies be isolated, small states possessing substantial resource and strategic value, calling themselves by the taboo term 'socialist', and vulnerable to social-infrastructural destruction from a safe distance.[64] With no effective resources of defence against saturation aerial bombing, each could be sanitarily defeated without political risk of dead American or British citizens. Underneath all else, the wars of obliteration against Iraq and Yugoslavia functioned to destroy the infrastructures and public sectors of socialised economies not integrated into the global corporate system as resource basins and markets for unimpeded transnational access.

This is why one of the strongest points of morally conscious critics of these one-sided military operations of social devastation – that there were always far more brutal and murderous regimes available for moral intervention by US-led armed forces – missed the point. In fact, such terms of moral reference were no more a realistic factor in their set-up and execution of these wars than in the previous destruction of the socialist infrastructures of Vietnam, Chile and Nicaragua; but as in any other corporate ad campaign, concern for life is the necessary link to the life-ground to get people to buy the product. Smoke Camels to be attractive to the opposite sex. Bomb despots to save lives. Which 'murderous despot' qualifies for US armed intervention has, in fact, no point of contact with 'saving lives', but is selected instead by the overriding moral criterion of whether the society in question is a *'free market'* – that is, open to trans-national corporate expansion and unprotected exploitation of its domestic markets, natural resources, public budgets, and military national security apparatuses.[65] This is a concept of the 'free market' which is assumed in speech by even critics, but it has deadly implications. Whatever society is not such a 'free market' is slated for extinction as unfree.

Neither Iraq nor Yugoslavia was such 'a free market', and so each was fated for attack by this life-and-death criterion. Each society had struggled and won over half a century the nationalisation of the country's natural resources and publicly funded and managed life-security programmes. These socially owned and controlled infrastructures persisted despite their recent dictators' destabilisation of them – dictators who themselves came to power with the active support of the US security apparatus. These common characteristics are what links them under their different cultures as victim societies, what unifies their real moral meaning. Yet the next war is the amnesia of the past ones, although all conform to one meta-programme of decision. The problem has been that the understanding and debate of the real wars being waged have not penetrated the inner logic connecting them across the diverse phenomena.

The Real Value War

What is not 'open to the free market' is any society, however peaceful, with developed social sectors and publicly owned resources closed to foreign corporate expansion and exploitation. Markets presuppose private property, their exchanges presuppose priced goods, and their corporate formations must expand into new territories by their nature of growth. Whatever falls outside this structure of private appropriation cannot be a function or space for expansion of the global market; yet, who has noticed this general fact across the destructions of the Iraqi and Yugoslavia social infrastructures by corporate state bombing? A developed social sector based on public ownership of basic resources is in principle inaccessible in every moment of its retention to transnational corporate access and control. That is why the Mexican government had to privatise the communal lands of its peasant and indigenous peoples before it qualified for NAFTA, even if it meant rewriting the Mexican Constitution – the silenced reason for the Chiapas uprising since.[66]

The former Yugoslavian and the Iraqi majorities had no desire whatever to travel such a route. After long wars of resistance and decolonisation to achieve public ownership of their key resources and broadly developed social sectors of worker income security, free healthcare and higher education, pensions and other social goods said to be 'unaffordable' in much richer capitalist societies, they were far better off as life economies. Corporate media flagellation for 'inflexibility' and 'protectionism' was not producible in such societies. When the Yugoslavian people had an IMF privatisation programme seconded by Party *nomenklatura*, including Slobodan Milosevic, imposed in 1990, 650,000 Serbian workers walked out and 'worker resistance crossed ethnic lines as Serbs, Croats and Slovenians mobilised – shoulder to shoulder with their fellow workers'.[67] When Milosevic then led the internal Serbian turn towards ethnic scapegoating for the IMF-stripped social economy, a policy of ethnic divide-and-rule already launched and sustained by Kohl-Germany's diplomatic support and recognition of Croatian separatism and later instituted by the US-led partitions of the rest of Yugoslavia, 'Greater Serbia' was not supported even by Serbs. They revolted against his ethnic-diversion rule in worker and student rebellions in March 1991 and February 1997.[68]

Like Milosevic, only for a far longer period, Saddam Hussein was a US ally. He became Iraq's head of state in 1979 by shooting his predecessor in the head at a cabinet meeting, with a CIA office next to his own for years after. In his position, he was encouraged to invade Iran which had just nationalised US-major oilfields. Using US- and British-supplied weapons, he also gassed thousands of Kurd villagers, and ran a reign of terror against all political opposition.[69] However, he was not in a position to privatise Iraq's oilfields which were 99.5 *per cent nationalised* in 1958 by a Communist Party-supported government – which was replaced with US support by the anti-communist Ba'ath Socialist Party through which Saddam Hussein came to rule. Even at the usurped top of this government, the murderous and US-advised Saddam was never in a socially strong enough position to privatise public revenues invested in a strongly developed and popularly based public infrastructure and social sector that had been built with 95 per cent nationalised oil revenues.[70]

In both Yugoslavia and Iraq, in other words, there was a politically immovable 'barrier to free capital movement' and global corporate penetration, especially to the vastly wealthy mineral resources each had, in particular oil – the fixation of the Bush presidencies whose family fortune is in oil. The people were very much in support of their socialised economies and the mass benefits of life goods each provided. Even US-friendly dictators were not sufficient to alienate them from identification with these common and hard-won grounds of their shared well-being. Indeed Saddam's Ba'ath Party was in confrontation with its working class just prior to the bombing over demands for wage indexing, continued guarantees of housing and food, and maintaining labour law standards. Eight years later, Milosevic was in even profounder political rupture with educated Serbians and progressive socialists prior to the NATO invasion.

The real basis of these wars is found in the underlying social conditions of the Iraq and Yugoslavian peoples. Destroying their social infrastructures, and not their dictators who stayed in power throughout, was not an error, but a logistically enacted resultant. The saturation bombings of, first, Iraq in 1990, and then the former Yugoslavia in 1999 achieved nothing else.

The eminent British medical journal, *The Lancet*, reports that before its massive bombing, Iraq as a society had achieved levels of social development near the highest in the Middle East and the Arab world. Its per capita income was US$3510 (now collapsed to $450). Its healthcare training and infrastructure reached 97 per cent of the urban and 77 per cent of the rural population (decisively higher figures than the US's private health system). Ninety per cent of the population had access to safe drinking water. Infant mortality had been reduced to almost a third of former rates over 25 years, and under-five mortality more than halved.[71] This was the rapidly evolving civil commons based on society's shared natural wealth that was not mentioned in media reports of Iraq for ten years, the enemy of an *alternative* to the transnational fanaticism of the 'global free market' which proclaims 'no alternative' as its meaning.

Yugoslavian society had also developed and flourished as a socialised economy for decades, overcoming its age-old 'balkanisation' of ethnic groups by the shared social supports of a developed civil commons, federally supported social programmes, and rich-to-poor transfer payments across its Serbian, Croatian, Macedonian, Slovenian, Kosavar and other provinces, and labour-managed firms and publicly owned enterprises – all in a 'market socialism' that was long thought to be 'the third way' between Soviet and American economic paradigms. Under a planned market economy with social ownership, available low-interest public bank credit, and universal life security programmes, its economy performed spectacularly well in development. By 1986, its per capita GDP had increased to (US)$6262, almost six times its 1947 figure when it was the poorest major region in Europe.[72]

Nothing that can be destroyed by bombing remains of these social achievements in either society. An explanation must be consistent with the known facts. There is no explanation consistent with the facts that accounts for the deliberate destabilisation and laying waste of these societies' social means of life and infrastructures other than to annihilate them. Let us test the contrary, received explanation which blinkers out all these facts from its moral narrative. Each of the claims it asserts as grounds of action – 'humanitarian mission', 'upholding of international law', 'maintaining the world safe for democracy', and 'ensuring the security of a new world order against crimes of dictators' – fails to fit the facts. Not even all put together even remotely *explains* what happened in Iraq.

Consider the internationally documented facts. They include the US and British states continuing with foreknowledge to: kill 5000 children a month over a decade in Iraq by war bombing and postwar embargo enforced by non-stop US and British bombing raids (10,000 in eight months of 1999 alone); hollow out a society's food supplies and medicines years on end; incapacitate its professional workforce and its public education systems so that most professionals in the country have fled or been reduced to street labour and a third of children are no longer in school; destroy essential water and electricity infrastructures by precision bombing and blocking their subsequent repair for a decade by embargo; and persisting in all of these after the society's social standard of living had collapsed to a fraction of its former levels.[73] These are not facts which fit any account but the *deliberate destruction of a society's capacity to reproduce its means of life and the next generation itself*. This is, in fact, precisely the conclusion reached by the British former Assistant Secretary-General of the UN who, after he resigned, explained that he could not continue to collaborate with Allied policies which were 'destroying a whole society'.[74]

Critics rightly see moral insanity; but what they do not see is that it *follows regulating principles of value-set throughout in a pathway of life-decoupled rationality that consistently expresses and enforces its meta-programme.*

Once it is laid bare, the rest follows suit in accordance with its sovereign purpose. The saturation bombing of Iraq specifically increased the control of oil corporations over the world's supply of oil, with Iraq's major market share of socially owned oil under embargo. It decapitated the Iraqi, Palestinian and Yemeni working-class oppositions in Iraq, Kuwait and Saudi Arabia whose leaders and opposition were destroyed by the war.[75] The unrest and widely predicted uprisings of Palestinian and Yemeni workers in Kuwait and Saudi Arabia were pre-empted. Leading members of Iraq's working class opposing Saddam were sent to the front to be massacred by the 'universal forces'. Of 400,000 Palestinians in Kuwait, 360,000 were expelled to penury and disbandment, and 1 million Yemenis were forced from Saudi Arabia. The Gulf War in this way responded in moral type to the transnational oil businesses *and* Saddam's massive growing labour problems, at the same time as it destroyed Iraq's advanced socialised infrastructure. *System-deciding values* select for what is consistent with their principles of preference, and every action by the

US– British state axis expresses the same value-set in engineering these consequences.

Such effective genocides of socialised Third World economies achieve what the ruling value-set selects for from the beginning: (1) privatisation of these economies by command of the terms imposed by the victors to stop the bombing; (2) consequent opening of each's borders to transnational corporate control and exploitation; and (3) removal of the dangerous example of a socialised life economy from the region, and from the world.[76] The Market God is a jealous God.

The Strategic Planning of Genocidal Wars after 1990

No-one can plausibly disagree with the following principle of practical reason. The more successful an economy is for its poor majority, the more attractive its alternative structure will be to other peoples. Conversely, the more effectively it is annihilated and its peoples caused unbearable misery, the less temptation there will be to imitate it. This is the background explanation to the US-and British-led destruction of every such order by every means possible from 1917 on, when these states led armed support of the proto-fascist Czarist Whites to put down the Bolshevik revolution. One might trace this pattern back to the Paris Commune uprising of 1871, when the French and German armies were ordered by their warring governments to stop in the midst of the Franco-Prussian War to jointly and bloodily suppress the Communards' revolt and the first successful experiment with community ownership of modern productive forces.[77]

This underlying pattern continued in multiplied form after World War II with the US threatening and destabilising every socialist movement and government in the non-industrialised world – usually in gross violation of international law, but with little official disapproval – Greece, Iran, Guatemala, Brazil, Cuba, the Dominican Republic, Indonesia, Vietnam, El Salvador, Grenada, Nicaragua; the list is long. These may have been prototype expressions of 'the forces that don't stop at national boundaries, that don't respect tradition' which, as the war criminal Blair advises us, 'drive the future'; but the complexion of these transnational forces, their targets and the justification for their armed invasions of less developed societies changed radically after the financial collapse of the US's opposing superpower, the Soviet Union, in 1991. Now much smaller 'rogue states' were the Enemy, and their declared ultimate crime was not 'communism', but 'terrorism' and 'violation of international law'. That the state leading the attack on 'rogue states' for 'terrorism' and 'violation of international law' was demonstrably the serial author or instigator of the most extreme forms of terrorism and violation of international law over decades, and refused for itself to be bound by accountability to international law, has still not been an issue discussed in international meetings on or media coverage of these issues before or after the wars waged on behalf of 'freedom and justice'.[78]

The post-1990 targets of the 'the US world policeman' were, without much notice as in the previous 75 years, societies which threatened 'the free world' with the *example* of an alternative which was said to be impossible – a more successful economic order that was not structured for exploitation by foreign corporations and financial institutions.

The first wave of destruction of Yugoslavia's socialised economy followed the same steps as the stripping of non-profit social sectors of societies across the world. The same global strategy of destabilising them by US-controlled financial instruments went into full effect with the ascension of the Reagan Republicans to power. The US Federal Reserve multiplied interest rates to nearly 20 per cent prime. The US Treasury's international arm, the IMF, immediately demanded economic restructuring of social sectors to pay foreign debts in US dollars, and the transnational corporate media headlined 'government debt crisis' day in and day out.[79] The co-ordinated campaign precipitated a bankrupting of social sectors everywhere, but the strategic plan especially destabilised socialist countries which had accepted the encouragement to borrow new floods of Middle-East petro-dollars after the trebling of oil prices in the 1970s.

In the light of equally extreme tax-cut demands restarting a decade later – which helped initiate the first 'deficit crises' in the 1980s with history's single greatest tax-cut to the rich – one can recognise better the wider strategic construction of the globalised 'debt crisis' which preceded the 'global free market'.[80] The debt-and-deficit crisis achieved the results its financial managers selected for. Reverse and redress of an accumulated loss of real investment and bond returns during the 1970s was the explicitly stated goal of the IMF. The Wall Street Reagan administration ensured the means of reversal. Yugoslavia's original Third Way was targeted for special, destabilising attention. The strategy was not to make room for Blair's unac-knowledged and revealing bastardisation of the term 'Third Way' 15 years later, although this happened. It had a deeper purpose. Yugoslavia's 'market socialism' was covertly targeted by a top-secret National Security Decision Directive for US financial and security destabilisation to force its restructuring and entry into the global 'free market'.[81]

The overall strategy worked globally and, in particular, in the targeted Yugoslavia. The Yugoslavian Federation was compelled into IMF 'Structural Adjustment Programmes' to receive the loans required to pay off its escalated compound-interest debt charges. These IMF 'austerity measures' terminated the government's access to credit from its own Central Bank, and triggered liquidation of socially owned Associate Banks, deregulated and privatised the economy, bankrupted social programmes, liquidated worker-managed public enterprises, abolished the federal equalisation programmes to the regions, disemployed over 20 per cent of the workforce in months, collapsed wages by 40 per cent in six months, and forced repeated devaluations of the domestic currency, while opening the door to lower-priced imports.[82] The results included a –10 per cent industrial growth rate by 1990, and collapse of the gross domestic product by 50 per cent in three years.[83] Again, all the effects have been disconnected from their cause, the inner logic of this regime's mindset, but all at the same time obeyed the ruling value-set which is to annihilate any life-economy alternative as immoral and impossible.

When social resistance erupted, the ethnic politics of the past began again in public for the first time in almost fifty years. Slobodan Milosevic was an unknown chief executive and banker who quickly became famous by a public speech in which he diverted attention from the financial sources of the social unrest, and his and other apparatchiks' own participation with the IMF in the Structural Adjustment Programmes precipitating the crisis. Milosevic blamed Albanians for the economic crisis, whipping up the very ethnic divides which would undermine the political possibility of the cross-ethnic social uprising against the financial stripping by foreign banks and their internal collaborators. At the same time, external diplomatic manoeuvres by Germany and the US, and foreign aid to recognise separatist movements propelled by the leadership of the former Axis Ustasa in Croatia and the drug-funded Kosovo Liberation Army Movement in Kosovo, sustained the declared moral diversion on the ground. Campaigns of armed 'ethnic cleansing' moved the Yugoslavian federation into a chaos of atavistic ethnic war.[84] Because the socialist federation had few resources left to sustain the shared life goods of their federal social infrastructure which had integrated the ethnically-riven Balkans to begin with, threshold numbers of desperate peoples led by unemployed males reverted to the ethnic hatred of their ancestors and its primeval bearings – endless revenge cycles of murderous attacks on out-groups.

Thus ended the market-socialist Yugoslav Federation which had provided the only form of effective government in the common interest that the Balkans had known – a social example that leads in the direction opposite to corporate globalisation. Revealingly, the very ethnic divisions tearing the federation apart after the imposed defunding of its common social base were what the US Rambouillet Accord and the conditions for ceasefire instituted in the region after the bombing – not financial assistance to restore the social infrastructure of the multi-ethnic society that had worked for decades before financial and strategic destabilisation from without. More tellingly, control of Kosovo's rich mineral resources by 'free market principles' and opening of borders to commodity imports from transnational corporations were prescribed as conditions for stopping the social bombing.[85]

The Fanatic Value-Set: Making War on Iraq

The final steps of the destruction of Iraq's socialised economy in another region, again the only one surviving, may have come as more of a surprise to the Iraqi people. They had been previously treated to more than a decade of CIA consultations with its coup d'état dictator, daily counselling and direction in Iraq's war against Iran, intelligence warnings of assassination attempts, a Kissinger-led US–Iraq Business Forum, and US and British military supplying of anthrax and botulism and sale of nerve gas and massive conventional 'weapons of mass-destruction' (later to be what Saddam was blamed for having).[86] Saddam Hussein was known as 'our son of a bitch', our 'love affair' in the in-character humour of US foreign affairs circles. Most significantly, his invasion of Kuwait was preceded by a tacit green light by the US Ambassador in Iraq, April Glaspie – as were the September 11 logistics within the US in the accustomed trap-set pattern.[87] Just before Kuwait's refusal to negotiate over disputed oil-field claims, a similar impasse in negotiations which preceded Iraq's invasion (with US support) of the Hormuz Straits to begin the Iran–Iraq War, Ambassador Glaspie was 'neutral' on Iraq's claims against Kuwait. The oil-rich territory in dispute had historically been divided off from Iraq in the decolonisation process. The US ambassador assured Saddam Hussein shortly before the long-foreshadowed invasion of Kuwait that the US was neutral. As the Jordanian ambassador to Iraq reported later: 'He fell into the trap.' US Ambassador Glaspie's recorded words were: 'We have no opinion on the Arab–Arab conflicts, such as your disagreement with Kuwait.'[88]

Most tellingly, when the UN denunciation of Saddam for war crimes and the US–British aerial bombings led to uprisings against Hussein in Basra and the south of Iraq, US armed personnel forcibly stopped rebels from attacking arms depots, and provided helicopter cover to Saddam's elite guard to escape.[89] Saddam Hussein was not, in fact, the target. The saturation bombing of Iraq and strangling embargo since were not to destroy the dictator, whose presence was necessary to justify the bombing. He was enriched and empowered further, while the bombings and embargo destroyed the social infrastructure of Iraq, removed its publicly owned oil from the global market, and decimated the society's next generation.

As for the invasion of Kuwait, it was a long-known and threatened scenario after years of failed negotiations with the colonially created emirate of Kuwait on oilfield rights. As the threat built, Saddam's military suppliers included all the states that bombed Iraq. Iraq's water and sewage infrastructures were then refused the materials required to repair them after the war, while the countryside continued to be bombed for alleged possession of the very 'weapons of mass destruction' sold to Saddam by the global armaments cartel leading the bombing.[90] The embargo on Iraqi society itself, and continual US–British bombings to enforce it achieved no dint in Saddam Hussein's military dictatorship, but continued the annihilation of the Middle East's only still standing socialised economy and its oil revenue basis. By the end of 2001, the next attack on Iraq was being floated under the guise of 'fighting terrorism'. This time, the pattern promised, it would be to ensure the privatisation of Iraq's nationalised oil wells themselves.

The value-set that selects for the destruction of a human society is based on an absolutist first premise that whatever serves its unilateral globalisation is good, and whatever obstructs or resists its universal advance is evil. No fact can disturb this presupposition if it is locked into the ruling group-think and remains credible to collaborating publics. To comprehend the depth of this mind-lock and its mass-murderous consequences, consider the following sequence of official US policy in Iraq after the official war was over. US Defense Intelligence documents silently released years later in 1995 demonstrate that the global market's first power knowingly selected for the consequences of infrastructural bombing, including the disease-killing of hundreds of thousands of children. For example, a US Defense Intelligence document entitled 'Iraq Water Treatment Vulnerabilities', January 1991, spells out exactly how postwar sanctions against Iraq were constructed to prevent any public authority from providing clean water to citizens.[91] Extensive technical detail then reports that 'with no domestic sources of water treatment replacement or chemicals like chlorine' and 'no desalination membranes', and with water 'laded with biological pollutants and bacteria', 'epidemics of such diseases as cholera, hepatitis, and typhoid' will occur, but 'it will probably take six months [of sanctions] before the system is fully degraded'. One is reminded of Adolf Eichmann's punctilious attention to detail in administering another and less painful form of mass death implementation.

A second document, 'Disease Information/Effects of Bombing on Disease', also dated January 22, 1991, reports: 'Conditions are favorable for communicable disease outbreaks by coalition bombing', with the 'most likely diseases during next sixty-ninety days (descending order): diarrhial diseases (particularly children); acute respiratory diseases (colds and influenza); typhoid; hepatitis (particularly children); measles, diphtheria, and pertussis (particularly children); meningitis including meningococcal (particularly children), cholera'. The third document in the US Defense Intelligence series, 'Medical Problems in Iraq', is dated March 15, 1991. It reports that the US–British-enforced sanctions by interdiction of needed civilian water-treatment resources and bombing [Tony Blair's term, 'humanitarian sanctions', comes to mind here] have succeeded in ensuring that 'water is [now] less than 5 percent of the original supply ... diarrhoea is four times above normal levels ... Conditions in Baghdad remain favorable for disease outbreaks.' The fourth document of May 1991 reports: 'Cholera and measles have emerged at refugee camps' and the fifth document in June, 'Health Conditions in Iraq' is still heavily censored, but can be deciphered as reporting observations that 'almost all medicines were in critically short supply' and 'Gastroenteritis was killing children ... In the south, 80 percent of the deaths were children.'[92]

Observe the repeated use of the phrase '*favorable* for disease outbreaks'. It discloses the pathologically inverted value-set regulating official perception and speech. US and British political and military commands are undoubtedly war criminals under law, and guilty of the gravest crimes against humanity.[93] To conclude they are also '*terrorists*' of the most virulent nature in 'the killing of innocent civilians to achieve political goals' – the official definition – is a conclusion which reason is constrained to admit. In connecting the fanatic mind-set across its expressions, we see the US state's systematic *operation of projection* since September 11, 2001 revealed with breathtaking clarity.

The Fanatic Value-Set: Making War on Yugoslavia

The same pattern of systematically selecting for construction of the conditions which would select for the destruction of a still-standing socialised economy transpired with Yugoslavia. Iraq and Yugoslavia were by 1991, in fact, the last resource-rich functioning socialist resource economies in the world from the Americas to Vietnam. As obstacles to 'the new global market order' and the 'free movement of capital and goods across all borders', the strategic plan to liquidate them followed from the ruling value-set. The global corporate market is a jealous God, and its commands are inviolable and universal.

We have tracked the pattern of determining decisions over 17 years in Yugoslavia. Here too the social death sentence was climaxed by saturation bombings of social infrastructures. NATO aerial bombardment of a small country over 78 days expressed well the first principle of the value-set. Whatever is socially owned limits transnational corporate freedom of access to the assets and markets of another society, and thus restricts freedom itself by the ruling standard. As a 'barrier to trade and free capital movement', it must be eliminated, and so is eliminated.

Yugoslavia, it may be countered, was already destroyed as a socialised economy by the debt, financial destabilisation and the 'ethnic cleansing' culture that had returned. There is substance to this point, but the unravelling of the socialist civil fabric by the ethnocidal turn is not nearly so clear in fact as it has been made to appear. The major claim of the 'ethnocide' was in the *New York Times* of April 4, 1998. It reported as fact that 350,000 people had been murdered in orgies of Serbian massacres. The *New York Times* claim was followed the next day by the

US State Department's more sensational assertion of 'genocide', with now 500,000 Kosovars 'missing and feared dead'. The facts were approximately opposite. International investigations and European forensic teams later revealed that there were no mass killings. The International War Crimes Tribunal itself charged *2108 dead*. It later charged Milosevic, who was said to be responsible for the 'genocide', with 365 deaths. In other words, the principal pretext to justify the two-and-a-half-month aerial bombing of Yugoslavia – the Serbian government's genocide of Albanians – was an historic falsehood. It multiplied the facts by hundreds of times – 250 times by the 'honest broker', the US State Department itself. However, since the staggering falsehood was circulated by the *New York Times* and the US State Department, the big lie could not be recognised. Nor was its atrocity fabrication ever officially connected to what it falsely justified – the armed-force invasion and destruction of an historic society's infrastructure, the homelessness of a million people, and the direct deaths of more persons than were killed by the Yugoslavian security forces in Kosovo – who themselves were reacting to a CIA-supported and drug-financed separatist movement that had several hundred elected federal officials and civil servants.[94]

It was not as if the fabricated genocide story which sparked public support for the bombings was not known to be implausible from the evidence available. German Foreign Intelligence had reported beforehand that 'explicit persecution linked to Albanian ethnicity is not verifiable ... The actions of the security forces [were] not directed against the Kosovo Albanians, but against the military opponent [the KLA] and its actual or alleged supporters.'[95] The Kosovo armed uprising itself, although called an enterprise of 'freedom fighters' by NATO leaders and the press, was known to be financed by heavy narcotics trafficking, served by terrorists trained in Afghanistan, and dedicated to the overthrow of the legal government by terror and armed force.[96] Normally called 'narco-terrorism' by the authorities, the 2108 Kosovars killed in a violent war against the constitutional government in which it had already assassinated 200 elected officials and civil servants was hardly 'genocide'. It was explicable without any ethnic issue entering the account.

The conceptualisation of the Yugoslavia government's reaction to a narco-terrorist attempt to overthrow it as a 'genocide', which justifies, in turn, the bombing of the country's social infrastructure that follows, is a transparently pathological train of perception and thought. It is also spectacularly self-contradictory given the future US 'war against terrorism' whose named 'al-Qaida network' has all along been connected to the KLA (bin Laden holding a Bosnian passport in return for his help in destabilising Yugoslavia in the 1992–95 civil wars there), whose international terrorist operations NATO has backed right to its 2001 terrorisation of the government of Macedonia.[97] As always, fabricated atrocity stories pervasively proclaimed in the mass media provoke the rage of an uninformed public for total revenge, which the bombing of Yugoslavia soon provided. It was prior to these circumstances that the attempt to 'find peace' was led by the US, Britain and other NATO countries. Yugoslavia's refusal to sign the resulting Rambouillet Accords was, with the following reported 'genocide' of Albanian Kosovars, the tinder for the match that ignited the 'humanitarian' bombing of Yugoslavia – its historic bridges, railroads and trains, schools, factories, office buildings, oil refineries, television stations, and thousands of civilians in the terrorised and defenceless population who got in the way of the non-stop aerial bombardment over months.

Once again the facts were not as they seemed. What was not revealed about the Rambouillet Accords was that their Appendices – kept secret from the public – prescribed terms that were impossible to accept – the military occupation of the whole of Yugoslavia ('free and unrestricted passage and unimpeded access [of NATO forces] throughout the Federal Republic of Yugoslavia'). They also prescribed the dismemberment of Yugoslavia by separation of its historic province of Kosovo, and (under Chapter 4a, Article 1) the future foreign control of Yugoslavia's mineral-rich province by 'free market principles' as determined by the Chief of the Implementation Mission.

US and NATO commands for the country-wide military occupation and corporate privatisation of Yugoslavia's principal natural resource wealth went unreported and undiscussed. But they had an unstated function. They guaranteed that not even 'NATO's indispensable partner in the effort to stabilise Kosovo' (as Milosevic was earlier described by a senior US official) could agree to sign 'the last effort at a peace agreement'. Since Milosevic was prepared to sign the very same terms of the *final* Peace Agreement *before* the bombing took place, we can conclude that the Rambouillet Accords were not, in fact, to secure agreement, but to prevent it.[98] As a State Department official later acknowledged: 'We intentionally set the bar too high for the Serbs to comply. They needed some bombing.'[99]

The justification of 'upholding international law' was another defining inversion of reality to suit the underlying morality, just as 'the light of justice' by bombing Afghanistan would be three years later. Throughout the flip-flops of surface events, however, the fanatic value-set remained the guiding thread of their meaning. Money sequences are made more universal with fewer barriers to their expansion, and an example is made of those who incur bombing for being in the way of the global market's free penetration across borders. As the oil war presidency has declared in its most recent manifestation, the world is engaged in a 'monumental struggle of Good versus Evil', and no-one questions who is the Good, because 'you are either with us or you are with the terrorists'.[100]

Once the inner logic of the moral schema is clear, the actions are not surprising. They follow the fanatical structure at every step. Mad behaviour, as Henry Kissinger has long counselled, is instrumental behaviour to meet criteria of achievement. You are with the global market's claims to all that exists as its freedom, with the US as its leader and superpower, or you are the enemy of civilisation, justice and goodness. (As the Bush Jr. presidency again put it: 'We go forward bravely to defend freedom and all that is good and just in the world.'[101]) With all or nothing fallacy as the structure of thinking and itself always *a priori* in the right, it follows that international law is an instrument for realising what is already determined as necessary and good.

Thus in the war against Yugoslavia by NATO, much was made of international law though international law was systematically violated – as it always is when there are aerial bombings of civilian infrastructures. The US–NATO attack violated the NATO Treaty itself as well as the United Nations Charter. Walter Rocker, the American lawyer who prosecuted the Nazis at Nuremberg, described the bombing as 'a continuing war crime',[102] but the final moral goodness of the side doing the bombing entailed its justice – as it would again in Afghanistan less than 40 months later. Behind the scenes, the UN itself was replaced by US–NATO in the enforcement of the justice that was known *a priori* without due process of law. The US government thus 'obtained a hitherto undreamed-of concession: the UN Security Council [the global armaments cabal] entrusted NATO with the task of enforcing its resolution by military means'.[103] As in Iraq, the social death sentence decision followed from the ultimate principle of the global corporate programme – which is to permit no 'barrier', even a society, to 'freedom of movement of private capital and goods'.

As in Iraq too, collateral advantages were secured for specific corporate firms. Share prices of US Raytheon and British Aerospace skyrocketed and the US and British corporate economies continued their upward climb in stock-values (just as, more directly and lavishly, IBM, General Motors and General Electric averaged just under $1,000,000,000 each of tax-revenue handouts as the Afghanistan war was declared in 2001). That international as well as domestic legal expert opinion judged that the massive civilian and infrastructure bombing of Yugoslavia was 'war criminal in design and implementation', violating not only the UN Charter, but the Geneva Conventions, and the Principles of International Law recognised by the Nuremburg Tribunal (i.e., 'planned, instigated, ordered, committed or otherwise aided and abetted in the planning, preparation or execution of [war crime] offences'), such truths of codified law and legal judgment did not and could not obstruct the higher morality of the New World Order.[104]

In all cases, it followed from the fanatic value-set that the social bombing must be Good – of poor Iraqis in 1991, of poor Yugoslavians in 1998, and of poorer Afghanis in 2001. There is no colour bar, legal impediment, or moral issue, because only one side can be right, and so all that it does, including mass killing and disease of civilians and children, is necessarily right too. Prior to *disconnection* from the consequences, they are *irrelevant*. In the certitude of the moral absolutism that it knows itself to be the Good, 'prevention of the humanitarian catastrophe' can be achieved by causing it. For the Enemy is necessarily assigned blame for the disasters. Thus 750,000 Albanians and 250,000 Serbs of 'the former Yugoslavia' were made homeless by NATO's 'humanitarian intervention'. Half the workforce was disemployed. Incomes plummeted still further from $100 to $15 a month. Sewage systems flooded rivers. PCBs, petrochemicals, heavy metals and toxic compounds extended through the rivers systems and ground water. The destruction included 58 hospitals and health centres and 78 monasteries, along with bridges, schools, railways, media centres and thousands of homes.[105]

Within two years of NATO's bomb-devastation of 'the former Yugoslavia', the US-assisted Albanian Kosovo Liberation Army, 'the freedom fighters' connected by narcotics, arms and personnel to the Taliban and al-Qaida of Afghanistan, had moved beyond Kosovo and were invading Macedonia, another province of the once thriving Yugoslavian socialist federation.[106] Canada's former ambassador to Yugoslavia publicly acknowledged in 2001 that 'we created a monster',[107] but in the moral calculus of the incubated fanaticism, all was right in the best of all possible moral orders.

The global corporate system's 'shock treatments' assume various forms to compel compliance. Unwilling societies 'must adapt to the new requirements of the competitive international market system'. The re-engineering of society may be catastrophic, but these are the 'necessary costs' for the inevitable future of 'global market freedom'.

3

Decoding the Global Market Ethic

Since it is everywhere proclaimed by those leading the agenda of market globalisation that the proper *limit* to freedom is 'harm to others', a principle best expressed by John Stuart Mill but consistently purported by free market advocates, a deep question arises. How could the primary value of *freedom without harming others* entail social death sentences carried out against whole peoples and ways of life?

The Historical Blinkers

Such a question goes deeper than the destructions of the societies of Iraq or Yugoslavia. It silently perpetuates 500 years of genocide of First Peoples and, in the twentieth century, socialist societies and movements which have in one way or another lived an alternative to the global corporate system. Non-compliant peoples pay with the destruction of their societies, ways of life and countless millions of their citizens. From the scientific side, this process is silently accepted as the rigours of 'competitive selection', and from the moral-religious side as 'freedom' by the invisible-hand mechanisms of the international market. But still the question which no liberal inquiry asks is posed. Is the epochal contradiction between claimed 'freedom' within limits of not harming others' and, at the same time, sustained genocidal invasions of other societies and peoples' lives explainable by moral reason?

In truth, a *logos* of instituted thought pattern has long regulated such ethnocidal and persecutory effects in the name of 'market freedom'. The most learned thinkers of four centuries from John Locke and David Hume to John Stuart Mill and Friedrich von Hayek have tacitly or explicitly assented to every such genocidal invasion and prosecution on this account.[108] The explanation of such advocacy and complicity in continuing genocide oppression is that the people who affirm it as 'tolerant' and 'liberal' thinkers are in truth regulated beneath their consciousness and communications by a *meta-programme of genocidal presuppositions* – which, while assumed as the very structure of freedom, consistently selects against any alternative as intolerable. Such a mind-set can no more examine or question the assumptions in terms of which it perceives and understands than a Nazi, however academically trained, can experience Jewish or communist community as acceptable forms of human life. A meta-structure of sensation and judgement assumes a value-set as absolute, and its principles read all harsh consequences as 'necessary'. The mind-frame is locked into a simultaneous system of principles which organises perception, understanding and moral judgement more deeply, that is viscerally, than Kantian *a prioris* of the mind.[109]

This is the unseen problem of our epoch. It is a problem of mind-set which is itself not necessary, and increasingly world-destructive. An animal's instinctual repertoire itself can vary, and go into fellow life consciousness in open play, rather than predator-prey division of fear and aggression – as we see even with domestic cats and birds. Similarly, instinct's counterpart on the human plane, the accustomed mind-set, can open past a long re-enforced structure. Even the theoretical autism of global marketeers, as close to a closed repertoire as we will find, can learn to accommodate vital life co-ordinates instead; but the meta-programme is daily conditioned into automatic sequences which reproduce themselves. Indoctrinated classifications and prescriptions sort the world and all its beings into assignable functions and dysfunctions, preferences, limits and infinitudes in strict accordance a fundamentalist moral *a priori* that is never questioned.[110]

Thus, John Stuart Mill's voluminous *Principles of Political Economy* cannot perceive, for example, the problem of mass unemployment in Britain or anywhere else which follows from deregulated mass importation of cheaper goods from abroad by 'free trade'.[111] He sees only gains, although the evidence of the world around him refutes his fixed supposition – a fixity of presupposition he remains confined to by perception through extensive mathematical formulae everywhere substituting for empirical fact. The issue of ruined lives is invisible to him, even though tens of millions of village weavers in India displaced by British machine-made cotton commodities starved during Mill's own life in consequence of the 'free trade' he enthusiastically advocated. It is not a question of referring to where Mill blocks the issue out. *It does not appear to view.* Seeing through the lenses of the ruling principles of his day (and ours), Mill writes:

> Commercial adventurers from more advanced societies have been
> generally the first civilisers of barbarians ... International trade ... is

the greatest permanent security for the *uninterrupted progress of the ideas, institutions, and the character of the human race.*[112]

Mill's closed value-set (emphasis added) is revealing because it indicates how deep the closure of the 'free trade' structure of thinking is – even with the English-speaking world's greatest philosopher of the era. We are dealing here with an unexamined infrastructure of social consciousness and its collective manifestations across a civilisation. On the most general level, it is the common structure of individual and group consciousness which we see in blind prejudice, superstition, dogma and all the other accustomed closed circuits of seeing and thinking which startle us from previous ages. This is the fixity of assumptions we call 'mind-set' or, more exactly, meta-principles regulating perception and judgement as an effectively *a priori* frame behind what appears to the eyes. This is the underlying, organising order of what we also call *group-think* – the lock-step of instituted mental habit which is indifferent to the life-destructions it prescribes, and which silently regulates virtually every endogenous catastrophe of human history.

The hardest question to pose within normalised life-blindness is one of reflective diagnosis. Just what *are* the constituting principles of the ruling order one lives within which are so presupposed that their catastrophic effects are blinkered out as 'necessary'? How can such questions make it through the blocking operations of the ruling value-set of the group-mind?

The Value-Set that Determines Lines of Force

This is the really revolutionary question because its very posing requires that consciousness works beneath the presuppositions of the surrounding social regime which are assumed as normality, and which structure acceptable meaning for the group. Even those who may risk the social contagion of opposing the ruling programme assume its concepts, although they stand meanings on their head – '*free trade*' for oligopolist intra-firm operations, '*globalisation*' for transnational corporatisation, '*development*' for the stripping of evolved life-systems. It is at the level of these presuppositions of *meaning itself* that the meta-programme orders and steers social reality. If these norms are opposed, they must be opposed from what the community understands as *anti*-'free trade', 'globalisation' and 'development'. This places critics in the position of rejecting what accepted language and doctrine designates as the Good.

Once a social regime is embedded as the Good in the language of the community which accepts its categories of self-description as given, then the mind-set becomes instituted in even the opposition. At bottom, these preconscious principles are more primary than the material forces of power which *express* them. They are more primary because they are presupposed *before* and *by* the ruling strategies of class and other power which are steered by them. 'Force rules in the global market system' may be true at the cutting edge of brutality, but conceptualised as 'freedom', which is assumed as equivalent to market freedom, which in turn is assumed as equivalent to the global corporate system, *the apparently primary datum of killing power itself is strictly confined within the value-set it expresses*. This is an extended set of ideas so locked into the mind-set that not even all the NATO civil and military command together could transgress one of the determining principles of its meta-programme – to which, in fact, they more obediently conform than any of their victims. The frame of mind here and its terms of reference can be tested. The testing can proceed by application of any or all of the *system* of principles of value defined below to any or all actions and advocacies of NATO, the WTO, the G-22 heads of state and their retinues, the chief bankers of the OECD, the world's major mass media, and all of the foregoing's derivative functions.

The automatism of the group mind is familiar in history. It is most dangerous when it transmits across privileged and deprived alike as a common ground of attacking outgroups (the essence of fascism). Outgroups, in turn, are preconsciously determined as whatever society, group or individual doubts or rejects in any way the assumptions of the group-mind. Active defence or enactment of an alternative way of life not satisfying these same principles is a provocation to the very *identity-structure* of those participating in the group-mind. *The principles below define the exact lines of social force which result*. The converse also holds. Release from the regulating value-set as given negates the pathologic mind-lock. 'The mind is truly,' say the Upanishads, 'the means of bondage and release.'

However, the meta-programme runs deep. Underneath every step of the Iraq and Yugoslavia bombings, regulating every decision of their construction and, ultimately, every policy formation and implementation of the 'globalisation' agenda itself over 20 years, are a set of principles which are assumed beneath conscious comprehension of even the planners of the 'universal forces'. These 'commanding heights of power' are, in effect, merely strategic implementers of the organising value-set which has become as much their lord and master as the programme of a cybernetic servo-mechanism. As these regulating principles of the global market cosmology are laid bare to reflection, we can test the truth of their absolute command over their bearers by asking which one of these interlocked prescriptions is ever deviated from by any 'leading' global market agent.

1. The human species is properly and finally ordered as individual owners and exchangers seeking to maximise fulfilment of their individual desires. This final meaning of 'freedom' is called 'the free market', and they are assumed as moral equivalents.[113]

2. The free market remains the free market through all transformations of its conditions, even if they do not follow from, but contradict principle (1). These are renamed '*the global free market*', and there is no limiting line to its mutations of the original market structure. The global corporate system remains 'the free market':

(i)   when oligopolist corporations, not natural persons, are the owners;

(ii) when their influence on supply and demand as well as government subsidies, regulation and granting of rights is not ruled out, but is in each case systematic and increasing;

(iii) when consumer desires are not autonomous or need-based, but are planned and constructed by the operant conditioning of corporate conglomerates;

(iv) when control of the means of exchange is not neutral or by savings, but by unregulated money creation by private bank leveraging and control of the economy's credit;

(v)   when in the preponderant volume of market activities the producers are not owners;

(vi) when exchanges are not negotiated by the transacting agents, but are increasingly prescribed from central foreign offices; and

(vii) when over 90 per cent of the volume of global market transactions are not for the purchase or production of any tangible good, but private financial leveraging without any productive function;

3. The free market which has thus been 'restructured to overcome obstacles to the free movement of capital and goods' is throughout and always the final, organising good of social life-organisation, and is superior to all other existing or possible forms of economic organisation through all of its mutations;

4. Any other form of producing and distributing goods for any society present or future is bad or evil to the extent of its deviation from or barrier to 'free trade', and must be restructured or annihilated by the political will of global market agents;

5. Maximum growth and development of the human species demands globalisation of this 'free market' across all of the earth, air and water, and outer space as it is accessed;

6. No privation or death of other human societies, individual lives, species biodiversity, vital capacities, or conditions of planetary life itself can disconfirm the final goodness of the global market system, but can only justify more universal application of its fundamental principles;

7. There is no alternative to this order which can rightly exist, and any existing or proposed alternative is subversive of the foundations of well-being, and rightfully isolated or, if successfully persistent, attacked

by force of arms to extinction as 'a barrier' to or the 'enemy' of, 'the Free World'.

To test the truth of any of these principles *as* the inner logic of this system's general theory, planning, advocacy, articles of prescription, transnational implementation and wars against non-conforming societies or groups, identify *any* moment of these operationalisations – from theoretical promulgation to social bombings – which does not conform to these principles. The field of test includes academic publications across mainstream journals

What is of interest to our analysis of this value-set here is its violently fanatic programme of perception and judgement, which even the avowedly peaceful of its adherents house as their very structure of personal identity. It is this *internal* order that can always be counted on to react in type when the war drums of this value programme are sounded. Yet people do resist, all over the world, and the resistance succeeds when the programme is seen through and the evidence of the mind and senses is restored. Otherwise, there would be no Cuba or European Union standards of labour, non-profit healthcare, or any *other* function than what the market morality selects for – everything that exists to be perceived and understood as, in effect, profitable priced commodities and saleable derivatives. The pedagogical problem with this fanatic value-set, as with any other, is that it has *no feedback loop* whereby its life-destructive effects can register on its bearers to deter still more of the same – much like the mind-set of a fanatic cult, of which it is history's most dominant exemplar.

An Exemplar: The Market Absolutism of Friedrich von Hayek

One can trace the mind's assumptions and organisation of thought by this undergirding meta-structure not only in the secular world, but in the market theology of the global market doctrine's senior champion, Friedrich von Hayek. The passage below expresses in its own way all of these presuppositions, some directly, some by shared false equivalence of corporate and pre-corporate market forms, some by unstated entailment. For brevity's sake, I select typifying statements to disclose the regulating structure of mind which Hayek exemplifies (emphases added):

civilisation depends on the extended order of co-operation known as capitalism ... For there is no known way other than by distribution of goods in a competitive market, to inform individuals in what direction their several efforts must aim so as to contribute as much as possible to the total product ... If *humankind* owes its very existence to [this] one particular rule-guided form of conduct of proven effectiveness, *it simply does not have the option of choosing another* ... The fruitless attempt to render a situation just, whose outcome by its nature cannot be determined by what anyone does or can know, only damages the functioning of the process itself ... For the most part, *only unknown lives will count as so many units* when it comes to sacrificing a few lives in order to serve a larger number elsewhere. Even if we do not like to face the fact, we constantly have to make such decisions ... *We have never been able to choose our morals ... If we ask what most men owe to the moral practices of those who are called capitalists the answer is: their very lives* ... Most of the millions of the developing world owe their existence to opportunities that advanced [market] societies have created for them.[114]

There is one regulating principle, however, that is never acknowledged in any global market representation. The 'transcendant impersonal order' revered by Hayek is not, in fact, regulated by the principle of competitively priced production – although this character is still projected onto even the unproductive instability of transnational financial transactions. The actually governing sequence of private investment and returns which rules the global economy is very different. It is leveraged money demand seeking to become maximally more leveraged money demand through increasingly monopolistic corporate and syndicate investment vehicles which produce nothing at all;[115] but no principle of the regulating mind-set can discern the opposition between reality and doctrine because all are presupposed as finally good and true by prior assumption of the doctrine's universal infallibility.

Getting the Fundamentals Right: The Global Market's Syntax of False Value Equations

The lock-step of the global corporate programme is not easily understood by those who think in terms of human values. Its fixed mind-set that knows itself as the final solution of how peoples everywhere must live is inhuman in conception. Its occupation of public consciousness continues to succeed by what is not seen – a covert structure of *value inversions* that transforms all that it demands into the Free and the Good, whatever its effects, and all that opposes it into the Unfree and Bad.

On the surface, preference for 'the global free market' is dinned into the heads of publics by slogans saturating the corporate media around the clock, and by clubbings, tear-gas and rubber bullets if the slogans don't imprint; but underneath the instituted violence and propaganda, a *primitive syntax of value equations* is always at work preparing the public mind for acquiescence. Freedom is equated with 'the free market', and 'globalisation' is, in turn, equated with transnational corporate rights to all of the world's resources. Thus, the question is permanently made to arise against the opposition to this global occupation: How could any sane person *not* believe in the self-evident principles of freedom and global interconnection? Although the slogans trail in their wake the regulating principles of cultural genocide as their system of meaning, this *way of seeing* masks the destructive consequences as the triumph of freedom.

Those who oppose 'free trade' and, thus, 'the free market', are by the same value-set inversion perceived as *opposed* to human freedom and cross-cultural exchange. The only issue for those governed by this frame of reference is how to ensure rapid acceptance of this 'freedom' across human borders. This is the global marketeers' autistic circle, and nothing breaks into its final certitude – as long as it is acquiesced in. Conformity to the value-set is all the while perfected by media and academic *idealisation*, whose function is to reproduce this group-mind circle, while repelling all facts which expose its life-destructive effects.

Freedom = the Free Market is the grounding equation of this ruling doctrine and the system it legitimises. The further equivalence of the free market to the global corporate system is, in turn, unthinkingly assumed. What is not seen in these *non sequitur* transitions is that the free market is, in fact, the *opposite* of the global corporate system. For the free market in principle rules out *the domination of supply* by corporate oligopolies and intra-firm international trade which now rule trade and investment across the world. Just as foundationally, any true free market rules out *the domination of demand* by oligopolist firms' pervasive advertising, domination of public regulators by political funding and media control, and semi-monopoly of public contract bids. Yet these contradictions between the ruling doctrine and the structure of reality are contradictions that the regulating mind-set cannot discern because it rules out reflection on itself.

The grounding equation of the system thus becomes extended to mean an extraordinary and absurd master assumption: *Freedom = the Free Market = the Global Corporate System*. Conversely, it follows from this primitive regulating equation that those who *oppose* the global corporate system must also oppose the free market and are, thus, the Enemy to human freedom itself. Consequently, the negative corollary of the grounding equation of the doctrine becomes *Opponents of the Global Corporate System = Opponents of the Free Market = Opponents of Freedom*. We have seen the genocidal terror for dissenting societies which this primeval value-set has entailed over much of the last century. The world's indigenous and subsistence farming peoples have been suffering it for over five hundred years.

This primitive assumption-set has, in the surface world of global market ideology, many *elaborations of substitution and reversal which together generate an entire omnibus ideological programme*. In place of 'Freedom', the basic syntax of the doctrine also substitutes for the prime term

'Democracy', 'Prosperity', and 'Development'. One can discern the locks of linkage here by trying to find where any of these declared master values is anywhere publicly distinguished, or conceived as in opposition. Each of these concepts, that is, is substituted for any other in the *primitive set of equations*. The convenience of ideological defence or aggression then triggers this programme of false equivalences into repetitive assertion.

At the same time, the mind-set *inverts*, at will, the order of equations so that the following structure of equations simultaneously becomes the automatic and overriding programme of 'Free World' discourse: *Global Corporate System = Free Market = Freedom = Democracy = Prosperity = Development.* Accordingly, in converse, opponents of the global corporate system become the Enemy of each and all of these goods as invalidation requires, so that the original equation becomes by negation: *Opponents of the Global Corporate System = Opponents of the Free Market = Opponents of Freedom = Opponents of Democracy = Opponents of Prosperity = Opponents of Development.* Interestingly, these ever more deeply worn pathways of automaticised equation and conversion come to be accepted at the most primary level *by even the most vigorous opponents of the global corporate system.* They too astonishingly assume that the global corporate system *is* 'the free market' and 'free trade', and they do this as a matter of pre-conscious mind-set operation regulating their speech acts. In particular, they presuppose even in addresses to fellow opponents the dominant current equation: *Global Corporate System = Free Trade = Globalisation.*

Although opponents may *not* accept the rest of the chain of equivalences generated by the regulating syntax of meaning, they have often internalised these basic equations. In consequence, they assume that what they oppose is, in fact, 'free trade' or 'globalisation' when, in truth, what they oppose is neither free trade nor globalisation, but *corporate oligopoly.* This corporate oligopoly, in turn, is engineered through transnational investment treaties, and prescribes a totalised regulatory control of domestic economies across the world.

Preconscious assumption of the doctrine's foundational false equations has fatal consequences. The opposition fails to target what it opposes in public, so the remainder of the chain of false equations which the public has been conditioned to assume recoils on their criticism. Because they say they are opposed to 'free trade' and 'globalisation', they are assumed by conditioned minds to be opposing freedom and international interconnectedness as such – an impossible position to defend. It is as if the opponents of human slavery were to assert in compliance with the slaveowner's language game that they opposed 'the rights of private property'.

These confusions at the base of the mental frameworks of both global market fundamentalism as well as its ever increasing opponents are not permanent, yet they remain an unseen scaffolding of thought that collapses opposed meanings, and *thereby permits the lines of the value war to appear as 'freedom' and 'globalisation' against 'protectionist' ,'nationalist' and 'backward-thinking' resistance.* The life-and-death war behind the killing fields is not understood until these presupposed moral equations are laid bare in their meaning. Until exposed, those who in fact put their lives on the line for freedom and internationalism are made to look as if they opposed what they stand for. The master operations of inversion and projection are thereby held intact as once slavery too was maintained as the structure of human freedom.

Uprising Against the Global Corporate Regime

The lock-step of the global corporate group-mind is not easily opposed. Its fixed value-set knows its fundamentals as final and good, and prescribes how peoples everywhere must live; it is a totalitarian morality that is eco-genocidal in its systemic effects. Nevertheless, its total occupation of public consciousness can only succeed if its structure of meaning is presupposed by its hosts. In the battles we now enter, the instituted violence and aggression of the global corporate system depends for every step on public acceptance of its contradictions of value-set, which in turn requires that they are kept hidden and repressed from the view of even the global marketeers. Humans are value-bearing beings, and their ultimate ground of value is life itself; but, because the ruling economic order has no life co-ordinates in its regulating paradigm, it is structured always to mis-represent its *life-blind* imperatives as *life-serving.* This is the organising principle of its acceptance. Thus, the freedom of unfreedom, the terror of anti-terrorism, the peace-seeking of war are, like the life-endowing properties of dead commodities, contradictions which are generated by the global market system's syntax of meaning itself.

This is why in the face of the mass public opposition to its coercive pre-scriptions rising up in the streets, the system's advocates are driven to ever more absurd distortions of meaning and fact. In the first instance, they proclaim that the opposition does not, in fact, exist, but is a passing apparition to be closed out of the rational mind. In the second instance, when the opposition keeps growing, they pretend that there is nothing in fact to oppose, since all that the opposition demands – for example, 'poverty reduction' – is what the global market already brings. When the evidence is clear that these assertion are false and the numbers of the international opposition increase, the perimeters of armed force to close out reality and its voices grow wider and wider – until, in desperation at the still imploding condition, a global crisis is declared in which opposition itself is made to withdraw lest it be read as 'supporting terrorism'.

The first notice of the global market system that there was any problem to repress first occurred in American head offices in November 1999. Tens of thousands of people from around the country and the world gathered in Seattle to stand against the secret World Trade Organisation negotiations conducted by corporate trade and investment lawyers to prescribe new rules for the world's domestic markets and societies. None involved in the negotiations could admit what the new terms of trade dictated – still more rights to transnational corporations, and no-one else. Among the new rights to be instituted were the rights to replace the world's public health and education infrastructures with for-profit control, to impose the consumption of unlabelled, genetically altered foods on world consumers, to override national environmental and food-safety laws, and to do all this by a general *modus operandi* of secretive application of legislatively undebated transnational regulations.

From across the country there then arrived 50,000 people who were willing to stand against the effective coup d'état by a transnational corporate regulatory apparatus displacing electorally accountable government with hundreds of overriding plenipotentiary fiats dictated by corporate-state trade lawyers. The politicians and the media were surprised, not only because they had probably not read the hundreds of pages of legal documentation imposing these supranational and extra-parliamentary fiats to the world's peoples and their existing markets, but because the opposition was led by people who had studied their NAFTA prototype over years.[116]

Lacking any ground to stand on, the corporate media did what their professional role as corporate advertising vehicles required them to do. All of the opposition to these usurpations of electorally responsible structures and laws was blinkered out as abnormal or violent without once engaging with meaning of the opposition.[117] On the ground, massive police beatings, tear-gassings, and jailings of hundreds of protesters confirmed the intolerability of the protests to the fundamentalist mind-set. 'They don't know what they are protesting against'; 'They are flakes', 'extremists', 'rich students looking for thrills' – the trivialising abuse saturated the official fields of meaning. The *New York Times* featured a description of the resistance as a 'Noah's ark of flat earth activists'.[118] Washington, Prague, Quebec City and Genoa repeated the social uprisings and the media and police attacks, but with ever more aroused citizens confronting the escalating suppression.

The final recourse of 'a war against terrorists', specifically to include those obstructing 'the means of transport' of supranational trade officials, revealed the full fanaticism of the global market programme for ruling the lives of peoples. After 2001, peaceful resistance to the construction of still more transnational fiats unaccountable to electorates and existing laws was categorised across nations as a 'terrorist act' to be punishable by long years in prison.[119] The pattern of corporate-state repression begun in Seattle had moved very quickly towards police-state laws within 24 months.

From Trivialising to Criminalising Opposition to the Global Market Programme

The most revealing pattern in the unexpected upsurge of 'the battle of Seattle' was that no reasons for the opposition to the WTOs transnational corporate programme were permitted public report. No article or analysis of the articles of these treaties themselves was then, or since, allowed public view. [120] The grounds of the opposition were, in a pattern with many variations, made to disappear. What the NGO representatives, teach-in experts and concerned people from around the world were and remain opposed *to* has, in fact, not yet been publicly understood. The systematic overriding of elected government policies, laws and historically won social goods that the protesters have stood against has not yet been even acknowledged. The *why* of the events is thereby abolished from consideration.

The no-alternative agenda operates on the ontological as well as the ideological level. What the regime overrides *does not exist, or is evil*. The truncheons, tear-gas and rubber bullets enforce the protesters' non-existence on the ground by gassed lungs, clubbed bodies and shot faces. [121] The mass media turn the materiality of tens of thousands of people into a chimera with no acceptable meaning, and what stands in opposition into criminal elements, soon to become 'terrorists'. The long course of history behind the social uprisings is severed from the people's living presence, and collective memory is transmogrified into amnesia and passing violence spectacle. Now you see it; now it has disappeared. Political absolutism's familiar rhythm of fraud and force takes shape underneath the smoke and inversions of meaning.

Follow-up protests against the WTO in Washington DC in April 2000 by tens of thousands of resisters were more systematically denied their existence. To prevent their appearance before the corporate courtiers, 100 square blocks of Washington, the political, business and communication centre of the US capital, were walled off by heavily armed forces. Intermittent spray-firings of tear-gas and rubber-bullet machine guns at passing demonstrators ensured that this time the opposition to the ongoing global corporate revolution of government did not exist as even a temporary spectacle before the corporate state officials. This time, unlike Seattle, the no-alternative order eliminated the international public opposition from the entire negotiation area, their interface with the official delegates, and the corporate media presentation of the proceedings. The armed-force terror behind the scenes by the club-wielding phalanxes was not reported, but congratulated by the media as 'restrained' and 'orderly'. [122]

The Quebec and Genoa meetings of the FTAA (Free Trade Area of the Americas) and the G-8 would open the ruling mind-set to the real, but not yet. The mass media in general ignored the entire event of international protest following Seattle a few months later in Washington DC. The world order's ideologue, *The Economist*, typified the public reaction of the press. It liquidated as every other chain medium in North America the volumes of analyses and proceedings of the resistance and all of its stated historical, democratic and life-protective grounds by one sweeping denial of 'any coherent explanation of why they were there'. The *Wall Street Journal* went further with the next, larger protest in Quebec City against the 'Free Trade of the Americas Summit'. It did not *report* the massive protest and saturation gassing of citizens in even one line. To add condiment to the silencing, the protest of thousands of volunteers from across society who risked their well-being to be in Seattle was headlined by *The Economist* as 'An *Anti-Police* Uprising'. The violence done to citizens was now not ignored, but smirked at in triumph: 'Despite a few photographs of students being clobbered,' *The Economist* concluded, 'the police were widely praised for doing a good job.'[123] A new set-point of the fanatic mind-set was moving into gear – representation of those standing for responsible government and the life-ground not only by first trivialisation and then blackout of their meaning, but by mounting organised state terror masked in a public-relations smile.

Value War: Militarisation of the Market Value-Set vs. Emergence of the Life-Mind

One cannot plausibly assert that this all-levels inversion of reality was merely another media slant. It is a deeper problem than that, one that structures the mindset itself. It is what we might call an *internal totalitarianism* – the subjugation of the psyche as normalised perception. This is what Tony Blair's 'universal forces' finally mean – the occupation of the public mind as the ultimate marketing site. The global market's demands overpower across all borders and cultural sovereignties, including the interiority of the experiencing subject and individual consciousness of choice. What is real and of value *within* is engineered as well as what is without. The ground of human self-determination itself becomes the unseen field of battle. For the future, as the state compradores declare from the inner circle of the great abdication of responsible government, is already determined. What fights against the global occupation is first unintelligible, and then becomes the Other that is 'anarchy' and 'terror' to the fanatic market value-set.

When the Summit of the Americas occurred exactly one year later in Quebec City in April 2001, the tactics for silencing the opposition and its grounds were advanced further. This time the agenda of transnational edicts to the 32 governments of the Americas was kept a strict secret so that there was nothing to be seen to oppose. A cement and chain-link wall ten-feet high was erected to surround the inner city of old Quebec so that the opposition could not be seen, or make its views known with signs and street discussion with passing delegates. During the three-day armed occupation of the old city to protect the corporate negotiations, 6000 helmeted and gas-masked men in black armour carrying shields, truncheons, gas-bombs and guns gassed the crowds outside the ten-foot wall for hours on end so that people's eyes were on fire, organs burned, and people's lungs and skin could not breathe through the city. A 62-year-old woman on crutches who gave flowers to the armed retinues was gassed for her gesture, while a young woman silver-dressed and resplendent on stilts as the Statue of Liberty was, in synecdoche of the new order of intolerance, shot down by water cannon. The large tanker trunks behind the wall directed heavy water-cannon at all assembled citizens in a non-stop barrage, while rubber bullets were shot at seated and unarmed demonstrators at will – 'It felt like we were being tortured for fun', were the words of a weeping PhD student to me. All of this, the corporate media explained, was to 'stop the violence-threatening protesters'.

The emerging walls around the forbidden city of supra-national corporate government had many rings of power. Not only were the new terms of rule kept secret, but the orders for the wall itself were also kept locked within walls, with politicians saying it was the police, the police saying it was a matter for the courts, and the courts declining to become involved – although it was a matter in which Canadians were suddenly prevented from free passage through the public space of the country's oldest mainland city, deprived of the right to assemble peacefully to petition their rulers, and daily threatened with new weapons being issued to attack any demonstrators who might still appear. They were called, in a telling harbinger, 'anarchists' on national television by the Prime Minister's Personal Assistant to make the matter clear, a prelude to crim-inalisation as 'terrorists' within five months. Once the tear-gas, the water cannon and the rubber bullets filled the air outside the cement and steel wall surrounding the city far from the heads-of-state meeting, the Prime Minister congratulated the show of force against 'the violent extremists who were trying to destroy democracy'.

This reconstruction of events into their opposite was not unplanned. The burgeoning security forces spent ever more tens of millions of public funds to intimidate the public beforehand – to prevent their free movement and assembly, to remove all lodgings from the free market, to leave those of all ages who at great expense to themselves had travelled great distances to stand up for their country's homeless, to harass, threaten and refuse entry to all visitors at the borders seeking to stand at the Summit, and to move hundreds of prisoners from the jails to make room for the free citizens the police intended to kidnap, to manacle and to cage. Yet all the chain media would discuss throughout was the *violence of the protesters' before they arrived.*

The forces of the new order, alarmed that the people still found a way to keep coming, next constructed a prototype cell of a terrorist opposition. They planned a cache of weapons to be found the night before the official summit opened – to justify the armed closure of the city, and to prove the uncontrolled violence of the protestors before they had appeared. But reality intervened after the evening news headline story of the 'terrorist plot'. One of those arrested unexpectedly explained in front of reporters that 'the arms cache' had been mainly planned, bought and directed by an undercover police agent – a report that was 'not confirmed or denied by the police'.[124] This was another microcosm of the construction of the 'war against terrorism'.

As the tens of thousands of citizens still continued in the face of the violence projected onto them, another tactic was launched to stem the tide. The most general demands of the opposition – democratic process, reduction of growing poverty and inequality, response to collapsing ecosystems, financial support for failing social infrastructures of health and education – suddenly became the preoccupying public relations concern of the Summit leaders. All of the secret 'free trade' articles and treaty that had brought 32 leaders there to negotiate no longer seemed to be what the meeting was about. Now it was a 'democratic clause' that was their concern, 'development bank loans for poverty reduction', 'mutual support for education', and 'connection of the poor to the internet' – yet the hundreds of actual pages of articles and appendices that were released at the last moment contained no iota of reference to any of these proclaimed concerns.

In fact, none of these concerns found its way into the subsequent text either. There was not one change or addition of binding article, and none that existed even referred to any of these issues. There was no significant new financial commitment. The centrepiece 'democracy clause', in fact, ominously repeated what the US-controlled Organization of American States had already used as a pretext to place internationally illegal trade embargoes on Cuba, and now to isolate Venezuela's land-redistributing President Hugo Chavez.[125]

In the background, the US Trade Representative, academic economists and other shills of the corporate state whispered affirmations behind the Mexican president ('the Fox', as Chiapas leader Marcos refers to him), who played his role of Coca-Cola adman in sweeping slogans of the 'reduction of inequality and poverty by free trade', when no evidence remotely substantiated the claim, and the evidence from Mexico itself showed radical drops in workers' incomes, massive loss of full-time jobs and livelihood security, degradation of working conditions, privatisation of educational and social goods, and haemorrhaging ruin of small farmers. The detailed demonstration of the falsehoods in the alternative summit assemblies, web-pages and letters pouring into editors and par-liamentary houses was blacked out of the corporate press. In this manner, the already determined future could unfold as prescribed by the corporate globalisation programme. But the centre of gravity was shifting underneath the red carpets and court pronouncements. The slogans were becoming unstuck under the public gaze in the long awakening of the citizen mind still narcoticised with inverted images of the world.

A new equation of opposites to confront the opposition movement was now engineered to structure future response: *Opposition to the Global Corporate System = Violence = Terrorism. Imposition of the Global Corporate State By Violence = Anti-Terrorism = Peace and Poverty Reduction.* This is the locked syntax of the fanatic mind-set generating the false equations as instituted public order.

On the ground, the imprisonment of people as creature functions of its global market programme is not ultimately won by jackboots, concen-tration camps or – with notable exceptions – military invasions. It is a totality of rule whose *occupation of public consciousness* is its moving line of advance, its controlled territory, and its base for more comprehensive occupation. Acquiescence in its lock-step as 'inevitable' is its force of social occupation. However, as the programme for the future is recognised – to colonise all that lives and exists as functions and detritus of its 'value adding' – the thrall of empty images and despoiled life conditions comes increasingly unstuck. The life-ground begins to rise within and across the distances and divisions of peoples in ways that that no official force can decapitate. Internal totalitarianism like any other totalitarianism depends on there being no alternative available to consider; but the consciousness of the life-economy alternative is the mind's structure of being human.

Part II

Unlocking the Invisible Prison

4

Property, Punishment and Prisons: The Origins of Corporate Absolutism

Although 'law and order' is never far from the lips of corporate government, a still intact historical memory reminds us that the origins of capitalism itself were in rebellion and violence against rulers who also presumed lordly privileges for themselves at the life expense of others. John Locke wrote the first philosophical justification of this new order of rule, and his views on *private property* and its obverse, *punishment*, set the framework of thought on these matters to the present day.

John Locke and the Founding Principles of the Market Value-Set

Locke's canonical doctrine, on the face of it, asserts and justifies the free security of private property for all. In fact, the regulating principles of property and punishment with which he ends are the opposite in their determination. Their actual meaning is:

1. to *legitimate* private property without limit in the possession of the few;[1] and
2. to *punish* as enemies of society all those who transgress private property right (meaning, in effect, the indigenous and the poor).[2]

These are the two great hidden pillars of law and order of the 'global market order' set in the abstract over 300 years ago. They remain the essence of its inner logic today. The definitive difference is that what was once *real property* has become ever more dominantly *money property* seeking to become maximally more money property; while what was once inherited inequality has become exponentially *multiplying inequality*.[3]

Such an oppressive and unjust structuring of social life cannot be accepted as legitimate when seen face to face. That is why our media, our governing parties and our educational institutions do not face it. This blind eye is not written on the stars. It is not directly enforced. It is sustained by a normality of buying and selling selves and commodities in the consume-and-obey cycle of 'global market competition'. Poverty is the great fear. Prison is the great warning. The instituted mind-set translates both into social normality.

Reversal of Value Meanings as Justifying Logic of the Modern Market

Human norms and institutions conform to *value-sets*. They typically change by their life-endangering regulators being exposed and understood. They change for the better by more life-responsive principles outgrowing them. The cognitive mediation between these moments is exposure of the mind-set that *obstructs social consciousness* by assumptions which block out the life facts.

The regulating idea of capitalist private property was first philosophically explained by John Locke in a treatise which was published the year after the English bourgeois revolution deposing James II in 1688. What Locke argued in *The Second Treatise of Government* was that all right and legitimacy whatever was the *right and legitimacy of private property*. Even 'life' was and remains for this mind-set another form of private property: hence payment for its loss was and remains an exchangeable asset, worth only the sum of money it can be marketed for if still alive.

The *public good* in this system is also conceived in private property terms. It is the property security of property-holders erecting government as their legislative and executive 'deputy'. No other right or obligation exists. 'Political power', Locke asserts (emphases added), 'is the right of making laws with *penalties of death and all less penalties for the regulating and preserving of property*.'[4]

Reason is defined in this world view as *the capacity to obey these laws of private property*. If someone does not obey these laws of 'right reason', then he is judged to have *'put himself into a state of war'* (section 18) with the one whose property he transgresses, or the state representing him.

To understand another as 'putting himself into a state of *war*' with society by transgressing an individual's property right is an extreme position. Its fix on exclusionary possession, which may itself have no ground in work or just desert, is also blind to the needs of life, e.g., the needs of the poor. Consider, in contrast, the redistribution of unneeded property for *life need* – as Jesus, Robin Hood and progressive tax systems have in part stood for. Or consider the first peoples who had their lands seized from them by Europeans. For them, the privatisation of nature into exclusionary private property was understood as a violent offence against both the earth and fellow members of the community.[5] The price that indigenous peoples' paid for these private property rights was centuries-long genocide – a genocide that persists at lower intensity today across the world, and is symbolised by large populations of native people behind bars.[6]

The primitive accumulation of private property in Europe over much the same period was in some ways similar. Violent invasions and enclosures of common and fief lands drove millions of people off their traditional lands by the legal enactments of an absolutist state. After these enclosures, the state punished the tens of thousands who did not work for employing 'masters' by such methods of punishment as public mutilation and hanging.[7]

Such examples have never much disturbed the value-set of the money-property party because the facts are selected out of view. This repression of fact deepens as corporate privatisation of native lands and resources still advances in core regions of Africa, Latin America and South-East Asia.[8]

Locke, who was a lawyer, first systemically expressed the proprietary mind-set that eventually developed into the corporate privatisation of the world; but Locke, like Milton Friedman and many others since, had to conceal the regulating principles of this system under pretenses of constructive individual freedom. By a theoretical shell-game that has been ideologically overlooked since, every one of the property principles he declares as justifications are surreptitiously transformed into their opposite meaning without notice.

Locke *begins* his treatise on property and punishment by putting three sensible limits to private property possession first, which – once reasoned through to win the reader's acceptance – are all reversed by 'the introduction of money'.

1. Private property must be the outcome of 'mixing one's labour' with what is 'appropriated from nature' (section 26).
2. Private property must always leave 'enough and good in common for others' to do likewise (section 27).
3. Private property must not 'be allowed to spoil' (section 31).

Locke then abolishes these reasonable limits on private property by a simple device, *the substitution of money-demand possession for real property*. He says or implies (from section 37 on) that the introduction of money nullifies all three of these provisos of lawful property.

According to Locke and the ruling system his treatise speaks for, money's use expresses the 'tacit agreement' and 'consent' of men to distribute wealth by the possession of money-demand rather than labour contribution. Since money can buy *others'* living labour, the owner's labour mixed with the property is no longer required. The absolute right of the non-producer of property against everyone else, including its actual producer, is thereafter presupposed as absolute. Money possession rather than work contribution now rules the social order, and is subsequently sanctified as 'the cornerstone of human society and civilization'.

Punishment of all who transgress this unqualified money right remains, however, fully intact. Anyone who infringes its claims – even if these are unearned, financially levered and in absentee demand – is still read as 'putting himself into a state of war' with the property owner and the state.

Since money-property does not 'spoil', its possessors also have the right to *unlimited amounts, even if most others have none*. As for 'enough and good left over' for these others, this third proviso of private property right also disappears from view. It is submerged in an argument (section 50) that all inequality of money possession, however many may have none or have more than they need, is rightful since (emphasis added) 'it is plain that *men have agreed* to a disproportionate and unequal possession of the earth' by their '*tacit and voluntary consent to the use of money*'.

This inequality has no bound in theory or law. It is perfectly consistent with it, for example, that a few have exclusive title to dispose of all that exists 'of the earth', while the rest all owe them more money to compound this inequality further. Such a condition is not far off realisation today.[9]

Accordingly, *punishment* of all who transgress this doctrine's absolute right to accumulate limitless money-demand property is imposed on more and more people, who are left with insufficient property to enable them to live. This 'free market', as it is called in the psych ops of the doctrine, has in fact become the opposite to the justifications made for it. Far from protecting a realm of life-security for all, it has become a reign of terror over increasing numbers of poor people. The 2 million people we now see in American prisons, the many millions more who are on parole from it or in danger of it, the exponential increase in prisoner numbers since 1975, and intensification of people's anxiety about their economic future, are downstream effects of this property-and-punishment doctrine in the world's leading market order.[10]

The Moral Unreason of the Doctrine

The doctrine we are ruled by is not, then, based on 'reason'. It is based on misrepresentation bordering on fraud. Locke and his successors, for example, hide the fact that consent to money or anything else requires an option before it is 'voluntary consent'. Neither do they acknowledge that what is justified here means that ever fewer people can have ever more property, and ever more people can have little or none. They do not conceive it to be an issue that the original 'labour right' to property, which is the foundation of the doctrine, has been reversed. Still less does it occur as a possibility to this mind-set that those who transgress against this injust condition are unjustly caged for doing so.

The underlying absolutism here seems greater than that of King Charles I who had his head cut off by the private-property party in 1649. The king at least wondered who would look to 'the people's interest' against the militarily ascendant private-property party when he was gone. 'I shall have the hide of whoever infringes my property', this doctrine secretes as its inward message. 'He has attacked my being, because I *am* my property. Whosoever threatens a jot of it makes war on humanity.' This is, at bottom, the Beast behind the system. It demands caging for those violating its ever mounting demands. It demands illegal embargoes and military attacks against societies which do not subject themselves to its universal rule. It eventually calls 'violent' and 'terrorist' those who stand against it.

It matters not that corporate money-demand has, in fact, replaced personal property right as sovereign, or that this money-demand itself is gained by leveraging it to greater and greater sums with no productive contribution to society by its possessors. Unearned compound interest and land, stock and bond speculation together multiply this insatiable right to tens or hundreds of times the original values with no labour performed. The concept of 'property' with which the doctrine began – a sphere of personal right to enjoy a domain of earth unmolested by all others including the King – becomes in this way completely decoupled from its traditional normative meaning, and indeed turned into its opposite. The right to enjoy private property free from the interference of others becomes the right to expropriate and harm others' property by the force of money right. Yet this mutant right of money property is viewed as absolute, and with no limit to its demand by self-multiplica- tion, as we see elsewhere in this investigation. Most specifically, it claims the right of the state in its defence to cage the poor who transgress against it, a right that is sanctified as a law of God. This is the closed programme of the market value-set, and it is the mental prison behind the real prisons it demands for those who violate it.

The deep-structural fact which is concealed is that corporate money- demand becoming maximally more with no contribution of its owner to any life interest has, at this stage, become the right to command the world in all its levels of reproduction. Far beyond the reach of the divine right of kings, this right not only treats the survival acts of the poor as an act of war on society, but under 'trade and investment regulations' such as the NAFTA and WTO institutes policies and laws to prohibit governments anywhere from exercising even sovereign national rights to regulate domestic markets or control the wealth of publicly owned resources. The corporate financial and industrial complex knows no limit to these ever- expanding imperia of possession, while those who house its value-set bay for harsher punishment for those who do not submit, even if this means the destruction of whole societies.[11] The war against Third World social ownership over half a century is perhaps the most revealing conscious format of this advancing system of global rule.[12]

One domestic correlative of this mind-set is that its bearers demand to be taxed ever less, with the rich proclaiming the market imperative of fairness that they be taxed no more than the poor. Any more than this is 'injustice', 'theft', 'confiscation', 'enslavement' – these words are used even by contemporary philosophers. They express the deep mind-lock of an absolutist doctrine for which any alternative is a heresy against 'freedom'. Any deviation from this market rule by act of public ownership or redistribution to the poor is to be punished by any means available – from prison cages for individual transgressors to the aerial bombing of deviant social orders. The connections are unseen, but disclose the depths of a fanatic metaphysic.

The Prison Regime as Ideal Type of Totalitarian Property

The sovereign right to make war on all who transgress even imaginary proprietary right was, we might remember, once confined to the psychopathology of kings. With the subsequent order of capitalism in its unregulated forms, it became a right claimed by all who had money property beyond need to expect public authority to make war on any who transgressed unlimited rights to acquire more. For, as Locke reminds us, it was the state's sole justification to institute and protect this ordering of society: 'The reason men have entered into society', he states, 'is the preservation of their property' (section 221) – and, what is left unsaid, but eventually follows from the doctrine's precepts, the preservation of the right to acquire ever more without bound to subjugate all that lives.

This is where the right to '*lawfully do harm*' to any who transgress – or, in fact, seek to set a bound to – these totalising demands becomes quite unhinged. It attacks any social life-organisation which does not conform with worldwide vilification and threats of armed intervention, retaining the Lockean language of 'defence of property and freedom' across other societies' borders. At the level of *domestic* criminal law, however, it might be replied, the value-set is historically progressive. The 'lawful harm' to fellow citizens who transgress these escalating rights to 'private property' has evolved historically from the established right to kill or maim these fellow citizens, to caging them instead.

This is a true claim so far as it goes, and it has been brought about by citizen uprisings against the right to kill and maim poor people to protect rich people's property. But an underlying pattern remains still unexposed. Like the captives of war who were once dragged in chains behind the glory of kings' chariots, the real function of prisons is *not* to *deter*, to *reform*, or to *retribute,* as has long been asserted and debated in official culture. These are only the competing rationalisations of imprisonment, and they function to divert critical analysis from the prison's unifying meaning. The true and unexamined meaning of prisons is far deeper, and has always been unspeakable. It is *the right of the ascendant property party to publicly defeat all transgressors by a subjugation so total that only a possessed organism remains.*[13]

The covertly regulating principle of the prison regime is not, then, as is now dominantly claimed, to *protect society.* The hidden and actually ruling goal is to break human beings and life itself into *another form of property.* This deep structure of the prison regime has not been penetrated, but once laid bare can be seen to be at work in every step of the prison's punishment process. Every moment of the imprisonment ritual and ceremony, every overt and covert operation of the police, the courts and the guards, every commanded surrender of the captured body's move and position is exactly regulated by this never-stated purpose: *the absolute defeat of the human status of the prisoner and possession of an obedient body in its place.*

The chain-gang, the woman-in-irons, the execution chamber are the final steps of a wider unseen regime. All express the fundamentalist mind-set of the age, and its compulsion to reduce resistant life to conformity to its ruling framework of existence. What crosses its prescribed lines is annihilated as a form of life, even when doing no harm to any other person. One cannot, in fact, make any connective sense of the vast panoply of oppressions at work in the prison regime until one recognises this underlying ruling principle by which all are unified into a single unstated programme – the reduction of persons to the disposable property of their rulers.[14]

Consider the exactly ritualised procedures which deconstruct the prisoner to a non-human object.[15] *The inner logic of every step is to relate to every distinct capability of being human so as to annihilate and to own it – to manacle the human hands and its opposable thumbs, to reduce the upright carriage to animal postures at command, to control the wide-spectrum eyes and the bipedal walk within mechanical ranges, to forcibly disconnect the prisoner from family, friends and every human relationship developed over a lifetime, to prohibit all privacy from being watched, to abolish the right to human voice and language by enforced silence and obedient sounds, to remove all the clothes and signs of individual and juridical identity, to liquidate all free access to humanity's civilised tools of reading, writing and creative inscription, and, above all, to deprive the human mind of the human being of every normal stimulus, space, time and medium to connect, to self-direct, and to create. Total proprietary control of the human as obedient body is the primeval goal – which follows from the mind-set behind its form.*

It is only in terms of this preconsciously regulating principle that the jail and prison regimes can be understood, that all their constitutive steps cohere as intelligible. Every outlet, choice or relationship by which to live and think as human, every aspect and step of free will around the clock is closed or confiscated across every region of life. The confinement to the 'hole' for any assertion of human resistance to the programme, the living amidst one's body waste as an animal, the ever-present terror of attack or rape from the jungle all around – all of these are the palpable signs which point to the underlying master programme. From start to finish, the regulating design that operates beneath speech or written code is to strip the prisoner of human status, and possess what remains as a subjugated object – the inner code of the system with numberless variations on its life-extinguishing reduction.

The Proprietors Behind the System

Just as the laws of private property were ultimately derived from 'the laws of nature', according to the founders of the doctrine, so the 'right to punish' their violators derived from these same 'laws of nature', which were seen as prescribed, in turn, by God Himself.

In the state of nature, the transgressed had the natural right to mete out the penalty to the transgressor; and since violation of private property right was 'an act of war', it followed that this penalty could be death. In a state of civil society, this right to penalise trangressors of private property was transferred to the government, as the property-holder's 'deputy' acting on behalf of an individual's private property rights, the sole ground of government legitimacy on earth in this hoary metaphysics. In this structure lay the defining nature of 'the public good'.

The arc of moral meaning to the present is clear. Just as protection of private property and punishment of its transgressors constitutes for this value-set the organising principle of public good, justice and law, so the same is true, writ large, of the global corporate programme today. However, so much has changed to absolutise the control of the corporate and financial factions of the economy that the market of Locke's days has been usurped in its meaning. Locke was dealing with an economically pluralistic society of yeomen, small businesses and professionals, long before the dominance of oligopolist transnational corporations. Even Adam Smith a century later ridiculed joint-stock corporations as large-scale economic mechanisms which are incapable of anything but 'uniformity of method – with little or no variation'.[16] Smith saw through to the incubus of the life-blind mechanics of a world system to come.

In contrast to Smith's individual human proprietors, automaticised private corporations today control more revenues than most governments, and a few hundred of their stockholders own more wealth than the total income of most of the world's population – a disproportion that grows more extreme in the aggregate with every business cycle.

Because every round of the profit-maximising money sequence compounds the corporate monopoly of human global wealth still further, and because national boundaries to its transnational occupation of societies have been increasingly overridden, multinational corporate 'private property' is effectively unlimited in its planetary rule. Transnational trade and investment decrees negotiated and adjudicated by corporate trade lawyers in secret, derisorily called 'free trade agreements', are the primary vehicle of this agenda. The public have been diverted from understanding this deep pattern by long-time projection of it onto a demonised Enemy – a role of alien scapegoat now increasingly filled by the disobedient poor, including entire poor societies. On the domestic level, mass prisons are the *terminus ad quem* of this war, and cage millions of dominantly impoverished persons in the US alone.

This is the larger framework within which today's 'justice system' operates. It is a fundamental mutation from the Lockean doctrine of private property and punishment in the seventeenth century, and as the corporation replaced the *individual* in the legal camouflage of 'person', the private proprietor has magnified a thousand times into a non-living appetite for limitlessly more money-demand possession of stockholder collectives. These corporate bodies, accordingly, demand correspondingly more surveillance, control, armies, police, and prisons to cage any person or society which 'puts itself into a state of war' with their unlimited and growing property claims to all that exists – including the publicly owned resources of other societies, human knowledge discovered by others, and the gene structures of life forms themselves.

In the end, the prison regime exposes the *internal prison* of the money-to-more-money property system itself. This regime is driven by the programmmatic compulsion to reduce all that lives to obedient functions of its final regulating demand: which is to turn the money inputs of corporate stockholders into maximally more money-demand outputs with no permitted bound of enclosure and subjugation of life within its hungry jaws. For this reason, there is no moment of international economic policy within the World Bank, the World Trade Organization, the IMF, the US Treasury or the commercial press which does not presuppose this inner logic of the system as overriding all claims of life value. All that does not serve its imperatives is conceived as 'an obstacle' or, if resistant, as 'the enemy' – whether Third World socialist governments, present public sectors, or resisters in the streets of Seattle, Washington, Windsor, London, Melbourne, Prague, Quebec, Genoa, or peasants in Central Asia. This is the larger, invisible prison within which the future is increasingly captive. True to this rapidly extending form of rule, the armed-force perimeters around even domestic citizens have become ever wider, and media blackouts of the surveillance and armed operations inside and outside the latest military encirclement have become more total so as 'to protect society' against ever more shadowy enemies that are declared omnipresent.

At the individual citizen and domestic institutional level, punishment is meted out by legal penalty, or by loss of job or funding of those who do not serve this order. The convicted criminal class is at the physically caged *pole* of this global system. Their members are from the majority class of the world who are poor, without secure jobs, and non-white. There are now over 2 million of this underclass in US 'correctional' cages, even as violent crimes decrease. The prison industry has many functions within the larger corporate order. One is to keep society's increasing human rejects out of sight. Another market function is to profit transnational corporations like Wackenhut, Corrections America and Boeing which lead the human-caging business. A third is to provide low-cost work forces for larger corporations which reap the profits of forced labour.

In a subterranean shift underneath notice, natural psychoactive drugs competing against the patented drugs of pharmaceutical corporations are criminalised, with more and more people imprisoned for their possession alone, while the legal drugs affecting the central nervous system and sense organs have correspondingly multiplied at the same time.[17] Jobless citizens in prison are, in another concealed function, kept off the unemployment rolls, reducing the officially unemployed by a full 2 per cent in the US. The violent culture of the prison system which results from this Byzantine exploitation and oppression then provides a violence entertainment site for the chain media and film business.

Beneath all, the master function is to terrorise the increasingly insecure and exploited majority outside the prison walls with the fate of the cage if they stand up to or violate the money-to-more-money regime which rapidly advances across the US and the world.[18] All of these functions are paid for out of the public purse. To complete the closing circle, evolved public sectors to serve human life rather than to enforce corporate money sequences are simultaneously slashed as state budgets for armed forces, police and prisons steeply increase. Thus major states like California spend more on prisons than on higher education.[19]

The Civil Commons and the Life-Ground Underneath

The life-ground and the civil commons have an opposite logic of security and growth. Their regulating value is *to turn life into more vitally comprehensive life by means of life*, not increase money sequences for the few. They are at work everywhere the corporate system is not – in child and home care, in sustenance economies, in the public sectors of life-service, in protected wilderness and park spaces, and in the still unpriced air and ecosystem cycles. However, because the vital goods of the life-economy are not priced for a profit, the corporate state does not recognise any of its functions as of value in this form. Only what maximises money outputs over money inputs computes to this value calculus.

In consequence, we see every field of natural and public activity which *enable people's lives* being hollowed out and appropriated by for-profit corporations. First, the public sector is *defunded* – schools, universities, higher research, healthcare systems, libraries, public broadcasting and arts, and welfare assistance. Next, simultaneous *privatisation* of functions increases so that the civil commons becomes increasingly dependent on and managed by corporate profit-sequences in a system of expropriation by stealth. The US leads. Britain and Canada follow closely behind. In all these movements of corporate enclosure and stripping, well-paid media demagoguery leads in various guises. In Canada, for example, public universities are now over 50 per cent dependent on private funding, while its once proud public health system approaches one-third corporate ownership despite fierce public resistance from the majority of citizens.[20]

As we know from reliable evidence, for-profit services never work to protect and enable life. This is because that is not their regulating value system. The US private health system, for example, costs $1000 more per capita than Canada's public system, has far higher administration costs, fails to insure over 50 million people, and kills an estimated 100,000 people annually from corporately produced and marketed drugs and pharmaceuticals.[21] These outcomes follow from its single ruling principle, which is to reduce costs and maximise profits for its shareholders, not provide health protection to citizens. The life-destructive consequences are predictable, but the contradiction of value goals is concealed.

With 'correctional institutions', the life-incompetence of for-profit corporations is not a problem on the surface, because prisoners are there to be punished anyway. Big public budgets along with a prisoner-hating majority provide a *carte blanche* for maximally profitable exploitation. Prisons are in this way an ideal target for corporate appropriation, with multi-billion-dollar public budgets and rising demand curves, and with no problems of customer complaint to increase cost inputs. The human cage is, at bottom, the totalitarian corporate market as pure-type structure. This is the innermost secret of the larger global corporate system the prison regime expresses – the compendium of its agenda *to reduce all life on the planet into predictably 'value-adding' functions of profitable investment sequences*. Prisoners are simply at the outer limit of this regime in its domestic order. They are the publicly known example of living death for those who openly disobey the system's commands.

Life Value and Rediscovering the Meaning of Crime

The first step in understanding this condition is to recognise that prisons are structured to cage the poor who do not comply with the rules of the game, converting lack of money-demand in the market into new public monies for the prison-industrial complex. The second step of understanding is to see through the category of *'criminal'* which even critics assume as given. Here the received value-set presupposes that all those who are imprisoned are justly *'paying for* their crime' – 'doing time' as a price for disobedient life by being caged. That the vast majority behind bars have, in fact, committed *no offence against the person* discloses the deeper meaning of the prison system. It is not to protect people's *lives* against harm, for many or most within prison have done no harm to another person. It is to *enforce life's reduction to obedient servo-functions in the ruling order.* The recent corporatisation of prisons as slave-labour pools follows from this inner logic. Thus, it is victimless 'crimes' of illegal substance possession and petty property violation which are the most likely offences to land a citizen behind bars in the world's lead market order. There are, in fact, more people in US prisons for non-violent 'drug offences' than the entire prison population of Europe.[22]

No fact of the official punishment regime is more revealing. Yet here too the value-set blinkers out the regulating bias against life-value *as* value. Even criminologists rank 'high-risk offenders' and 'security requirements' not in terms of propensity to harm others' lives, but in terms of the *will of human life to seek freedom from being caged.* Here the vicious circularity of the 'criminal' category structures even the science of studying crime.[23] The 'high-risk criminal ' is not such by his threat to the others, but on account of his resistance to the caging of his life for non-violent transgressions.

In complete opposition to this deranged moral logic of the prison system, *a life-ground ethic focuses* on *crimes against human life.* Deliberate murder for self-gain heads the list of such individual crimes, while rape, extortion, armed robbery, battery and the rest follow as truly criminal in proportion to the extent and duration of each's harm to the person. The fact that *97 per cent of police-reported US crimes involve no injuries at all to victims, and in 86 per cent no violence whatever to another person is involved,*[24] while the category of 'criminal' continues to draw little or no critical reflection within 'the justice system' itself, indicates profound cultural insanity. Yet its normality blocks recognition. The *interior prison* generating the outer prison reaches across classes, educational levels, and the sciences themselves.

The third step of understanding follows from the first two. The life-ground ethic releases judgement to recognise that the gravest serial crimes of our world are, in fact, perpetrated day in and day out by corporate states themselves. The regulating purpose of the transnational corporate system which current states serve is itself a form of racketeering: to take maximally more money-demand out than what is put in, and to conspire in this direction across all borders and without restraint or respect for others' life interests. The reckless disregard for life that is built into this structure of motivation is, for the life-ground ethic, criminal by its nature;[25] but where anywhere in legal studies, criminology or philosophy of law do systemic corporate and state crimes arise as even a *question*? Again we confront the internal prison which reaches into the public sphere's life-protective, juridical and academic functions themselves.

The instituted intention to acquire ever more money-demand without accountability to life-protective law and persisting at any cost to human and planetary life-security is, beneath mainstream learned reflection, a greater public threat to citizens' lives than all prosecuted crimes together since the Nuremberg trials. For example, lethally hazardous corporate processes and products are knowingly sustained with the consequence of millions of deaths, and corporate and state agents obstruct the recognition of what international life-protective norms and laws exist.[26] Predictably, however, the money-sequence value-set from which this quintessentially criminal pattern follows is repressed as a given premise of 'global market competitiveness'. Systemically homocidal and ecocidal activities are not only abetted by corporate states, but state terror is deployed against those seeking to stand against these very violations of public security.[27] The regulating value-set selects not to protect life, but to punish the poor for resistance, lack of market demand, and petty trans-gressions against monopoly drug laws.[28]

Logically speaking, those who plan, counsel and direct actions which cause systematic destructions of others' lives and safe environmental conditions are criminals of the most dangerous kind. The imprisoning value-set is structured, however, to project criminal intent *onto* those who are victimised. This master operation of inversion criminalises dis-possessed societies too, and it does so in serial repetition. However, the inner moral logic connecting across phenomena remains unexposed.

In the end, the most striking institutionalised symbol of the global corporate system is not the World Trade towers, but as before a past revolution, the prison-cage itself. It expresses the moral logic of the system at its most acceptably inhuman. Poor people are caged in their millions for doing no harm to other persons, while the real capital criminals are selected for success by the ruling morality's first premises.

5

Understanding the New Totalitarianism of the Global Market

Projection of the Terrorist Pattern

The problem with market fundamentalism, the dominant theology of our time, is that it is decoupled from society's life conditions – the civil commons of clean water for all, education of the young to speak and write, rules to protect the life of every citizen against assault or disease, supportive care for all when ill or old, public spaces to enjoy in free time, and vocations for citizens to work for the common life interest. Market fundamentalism is unable to recognise any value to any life condition except as it can be made to serve corporate stockholders.

Since the commitments of a society to safeguard the lives of its members and to ensure they are able to express themselves as human is the measure of its civilisation, this market ethos is not only uncivilised, it is pathological. For if we recognise the real meaning of 'terrorism' – *to instil in innocent people fear for their life security in order to coerce their compliance to an armed party's demands* – we see a terrorist pattern that is increasingly pervasive but unnamed.[29] Under the financial dictates of the corporate market backed by rising extremes of armed force, citizens everywhere – not just prospective prisoners – are subjected to a low-intensity campaign of destabilisation and fear that leaves no aspect of their lives secure.

Even in the world's most well-off societies, the silent terror grows. Their natural resource heritages are increasingly degraded and exhausted, but corporate governments sign their remaining future away to US-engineered trade-and-investment dictates. The minds of the young are so shackled by a culture of violence and demands to buy that their capacity to think is stunted, while their public education is increasingly structured as a marketing site to reproduce students as compliant servo-mechanisms. The rule of law is cumulatively overridden by transnational trade edicts to subjugate all that exists for corporate profit. Riot squads club and gas unarmed opponents, and civil liberties are stripped by Orwellian 'security' machinations.

Always the threat is against life and life-means to coerce compliance to corporate demands. Public sectors are defunded and privatised, while corporate commodities and schemes so lay waste to land, water and public ways that it may be unsafe to breathe the air, walk freely, or count on a forest or aquatic habitat being there in a year's time. The vocation of serving fellow human and planetary life by one's daily service of work is slashed in every life function. Always the command is to turn money into more money for corporate investors, or 'not survive'.

The pattern cannot be plausibly denied once it is exposed. There are two major forms of attack on peoples' means of life used to coerce them to conform to global financial and corporate demands. The first is to defund societies' non-profit social infrastructures everywhere until peoples have no choice but to privatise their management for profit. The second front of attack is more directly violent – to wage one financial and military war after another on the poorest peoples of the world to control their states and expropriate their regional resources. Both these wars on humanity are driven by a fanatic fundamentalism – to produce ever more money for those with most money, with no limit, regulation or higher goal permitted to 'obstruct' these transnational money sequences.

At an useen level, the world has been usurped by a pattern familiar in the microcosm, but not yet decoded at the macro level – a revolt against human society itself. The historical maturation of nations after the world's greatest depression and war was called 'the Great Transformation' by Karl Polanyi, but the Great *Reversal* has not yet been publicly understood. Its meaning is primeval. It is the atavistic return of society to *an unaccountable male gang seeking to dominate the world.*

We see this pattern most recently in the Afghanistan War beginning in 2001. The public phase began when thousands of people of mixed nationalities, mostly American civilians, were killed by suicide bombers of a foreign male gang of Islamic fundamentalists.[30] Each side then duly proclaimed the other the embodiment of evil, each repudiated the rule of law from start to finish, and both killed as many innocent people as got in the way of their war to rule other countries. While the gang leaders throughout stayed unscathed behind walls of armed protectors, both called each other 'cowards'.

There is little difference in moral substance between these atavistic gangs, although a megalomaniac rhetoric of each side proclaims direct backing from God. Both sides are mass killers, and both systematically destroy civilians and their means of life with sanctimonious justification overriding all accountability to truth or due legal process. Both proclaim their mission as the working of divine Justice, and both destroy the lives and human conditions of innocent others with a pathological abandon that takes the breath away. This is, in fact, the function of the demonstration killings and destructions – to command by terror, and seize whatever is wanted. With complicit governments like Britain's and Canada's barking and crouching behind, the real deal is struck beneath public notice – incalculably more innocent people in terror in exchange for incalculably more oil supplies for US-led oil corporations and, as a side deal, $200,000,000,000 in giveaways of public revenues to corporations and the very rich.[31]

There are, however, two reasons why the primeval criminal-gang structure is not tracked. The first is that saturating conditioning disconnects people from reality. 'It is easy. All you have to do is tell the people they are being attacked, and denounce the the peacemakers for lack of patriotism and exposing the country to danger.'[32] These are Hermann Goering's words, and they transmit the code of this the gang form of rule. Concealed under the most ludicrous lies, its coercion reigns supreme. University employees and a talk-show host have been unconstitutionally suspended in the US for pointing out the most undeniable truths.[33] The disorder goes to the heart of the ruling corporate psyche.

Consider the pattern. The adolescent group-mind plots in secret behind the closed doors of secluded forts for control of the rest of society to maximise the gang's private take. Privately multiplied debt issuances are the currency of the global corporate gang's control. Sex and violence are the ruling images of its kingdom of ever bigger deals and attacks on designated outgroups. The gang's ethos of power and control pervades the larger society with a barbaric code of acquisitive stratagem, take-over of others' territories, continuous extraction of gang tribute, and indiscriminate violence and armed force at will.

Throughout, group slogans and tough-talk re-enforce the bonds of male and servant-female bravado in the face of ever greater extremes of life-depredation, confiscation and fear. *The universal insecurity the many feel is, as the resistance grows, played back to them as what the gang is protecting them from.* The logic of rule by force is then openly declared. The US President declares an ultimatum to the world – 'You are either with us or for the terrorists', and after starving Afghanistan is carpet-bombed his administration cries 'Who will be next?' Charles Krauthammer declares the mood in *Time Magazine*: 'America is no mere international citizen. It is the dominant power in the world, more dominant than any since Rome. Accordingly, America is in a position to reshape norms – How? By unapologetic and implacable demonstrations of will'.[34] The extortion racket of the neighbourhood is, in a word, writ large as 'the international war against terrorism' – a war in which those who monopolise terror are licensed to exempt themselves from its meaning.

Lacking the resources of character to compete head-on, the global corporate gang everywhere relies on *controlled images* instead. The image-set loved most by the gang's crowds are performed around the clock – symbolic male gangs in corporate logos attacking one another day in and day out in competitive spectacles, all constructed to glorify the riches of the winners. The never-ending, sudden-death dramas hold the many in thrall, so distracting them from the actual violent struggles of life and death in the wider world. These are displaced onto the sports or war screen as a universal marketing site for corporations and banks.

'Sport', as it is ironically called, is the corporate gang's daily morality play of trained group-think, fanatic factionalism and ever more money for those with most. Defeating others by overpowering monopoly is the heroic display most highly revered. Pistols, bombs, collisions, space thrusts, take-overs, wars, round-the-clock terror, get-rich schemes, endless machines and fast-lane consumption are 'our way of life' before adoring crowds and female bodies. Behind the scenes, however, 'instruments of transnational trade and investment', 'competititive mergers' and 'privatisation and deregulation of the public sector' are the deep booty system. Outside the manufactured conflicts of interest which lie inside the never-ending games to which the many have their hearts and minds fastened, the world is restructured as a pay-on-time system where the payments issue more and more debt for all to pay. As this or that entertainment product wins or loses in the coliseum, the gang's trade lawyers secretly construct hundreds of new laws behind everyone's backs through which only the rich can win. This 'new world order' is backed by iron cages, starvation, rains of gas and clubs for resistors, and genocide for peoples from which the latest declared Enemy comes. Few dare to name the game, and its order is ritualised with ever more one-sided shows of mass destruction and violence discharged on the dispossessed to demonstrate the inevitability of its rule. The world, in the revealing terms of the occupiers, is a 'limitless market opportunity' for 'maximum penetration and control'.

The New Totalitarianism

The deep pattern of the male corporate gang in its global form is, as David Rockefeller put it at the June 1991 Bilderberg's meeting in Baden Germany, a 'supranational sovereignty of an intellectual elite and world bankers which is surely preferable to the national autodetermination practiced in past centuries'.[35] As such a structure of world rule, it is accomplished by the same financial and media system deciders as put Tony Blair into office in Britain and George Bush Jr. into the White House against majority vote. Transnational corporations have marketed and financed these political leaders to ensure that captive states serve them rather than the peoples by whom governments are elected, guarantee-ing through state plenipotentiaries and transnational trade edicts that governments can no longer govern them in common interest without infringing the new trade and investment laws in which transnational corporations alone are granted rights.

All along the corporate media have, as Rockefeller again advises, co-operated with this 'plan for the world ' by a 'discretion' of public secrecy for which he thanks them. 'It would have been impossible for us to develop a plan for the world if we had been subjected to the lights of publicity during those years'. With financial and media selectors ensuring compliant party government leaders, all the requirements for this 'plan for the world' have been set in place for a totality of control of world societies by a centralised global system which is by law not accountable to any electorate.

The meaning of the post-September 11 bombing of Afghanistan may be best understood in the light of this general background. Beneath all the spasms of propaganda of 'America's New War' and 'the forces of Good versus Evil', the 'new war' is a variation on an old theme, but with every step of the preparation and aftermath of this 'whole new war with no end' conferring cumulatively more and unprecedented strategic, legal and military control over the world's peoples from an unaccountable US financial and armed-force centre. It is in its underlying meaning the latest expression of an emergent totalitarian pattern of instituting world corporate rule with no limit of occupation or accountability beyond itself.

However, the 'war with no end' is not just for world dominion and, as it is humorously titled, a 'fight for civilisation'. There is a clear particular strategic objective propelling the undergirding totalitarian pattern as a major prize along the way of this deeper meaning. The grand prize of this specific war in its opening campaign of the 'war without end' is unimpedable control by US multinational oil corporations of the world's greatest oil and gas deposits which are located around the Caspian Sea of Central Asia, formerly the territory of the Soviet Union.

Long-time US strategic adviser, Zbigniew Brzezinski, counselled 'unhindered financial and economic access' to precisely these 'Central Asia natural resources' years ago in 1997, referring specifically to the 'enormous economic prize of natural gas and oil located in the region'. Brzezinski advised that, in the face of domestic resistance, it will become ever 'more difficult to fashion a consensus on foreign policy issues, *except in the circumstances of a truly massive and widely perceived direct external threat*' (emphasis added).[36] Brzezinski's plan is not disconfirmed by any evidence since.[37]

The result of the Afghanistan War is that the US-led corporate regime is becoming more effectively total and pre-emptive of thought or act in opposition to it than any previous totalitarian interregnum – as successive catechisms of 'no alternative', 'globalisation', 'controlling earth from space', and 'the whole world has changed' reveal to connective thought. In Congressional expression of this totalitarian mind-set, US Senator Bob Smith, whose legislation got the US 'Space Commission' for monopoly military control of the heavens passed in 2000 long prior to September 11, prescribes this new world order as the plan of Fate: 'It is our Manifest Destiny. You know we went from the East Coast to the West Coast of the United States of America settling the continent [*sic*] and they call that Manifest Destiny and the next continent if you will is space, and it goes on *forever*.'[38]

This is the supra-terrestrial correlative of the doctrine of total power, and it can conceive of no limit to itself. As earth events interfere in resistance to the unaccountable world rule, military and police links are forged on the very sites of the resistance, constructing and exploiting the new Enemy to justify the sweeping new powers of coercion and terror which the global corporate system requires to rule an unwilling world. As in all protection rackets by terror and financial manipulation, the greatest threat to life comes from the very system of armed force, surveillance and attack which is said to be protecting citizens from it – conceptualised by presidential proclamation after September 11 as one in which all 'in every region – are for us, or are with the terrorists'. US Trade Representative, Robert Zoellick, then explained this meaning to include explicitly those protesting against the WTO's campaign to occupy all the world's economies. 'This President and this administration will fight for open markets. We will not be intimidated by those who have taken to the streets to blame trade – and America – for the world's ills.'[39] Within weeks, US law HR 3005, the 'Trade Promotion Act', was passed in Congress to rule out both debate and ratification of the executive edicts of 'The Free Trade Area of the Americas' blocked before the September 11 turn.

The Omnipresent Centre

Totality of rule is not the only parameter of totalitarianism. In Hannah Arendt's phrase, limitlessness of power also proceeds from 'an *omnipresent centre*'. In the new totalitarian movement, this omnipresent directive force communicates through global financial and media control centres, with Washington and Wall Street the dominant nodes of the interlocked system.[40] The world's *means of life* and *mass media* are the *material* and *symbolic* vehicles by which the flows of goods and demand for goods control populations. The regulating principle of all decisions is to multiply by ever more deregulation and new financial instruments the monetised circuits of power through which directive control of all of the world's means of existence increasingly pass. Whole societies and even continents can suddenly find themselves without enough means of life by the operations of this central system and its sudden strategic decisions for self-maximising change of money and capital flows – as in 'the Asian crisis' of 1997–98.[41] However, with centralised financial, media and back-drop military pressures working across borders and with no limiting condition of imperial conflict after the fall of the Soviet empire, Asian governments as well as governments across the rest of the world's continents have been subordinated to the US-led 'global market'.[42]

As with all totalitarian systems, the dominant instruments of social power are wrested from traditional authorities, and then unleashed with none of the formerly inhibiting mechanisms of law, custom and social norm to limit their use and magnification. The great tell-tale sign of the totalitarian movement is that by its very nature it cannot stop. It careers from one life-destructive crisis and suppression to another in supreme confidence of its limitless power and capacities until its overreach exposes it to collapse or destruction. This is the totalitarian career path we know in previous usurpations of accountable public authority.

Armed terror is not the essence, but the punctuation mark of the new totalitarianism's meaning. The money-and-consumption command channel is the secret of the movement's success because it avoids responsibility for its failures. Wall Street-prescribed market failures to provide for societies are, instead, always attributed to transcendental forces of 'the invisible hand' punishing these societies for alleged sins against 'market laws'. Thus, as catastrophes increasingly befall the majority of the world, the victims are blamed for their new deprivation, misery and oppression. This is a far more effective mode of rule than jackboot terror, which is more overt, but it does expose the system to another form of resistance. Such a regime depends throughout on *keeping knowledge silenced and repressed*. This is its Achilles' heel. As soon as people see through it and flag it to the surrounding community, the collective trance on which it depends begins to lose its power.

The new totalitarianism is, ultimately, an American corporate confidence game which rules the world by images and projections of power arcing over the globe's surface, while limitlessly rapacious financial sequencings called 'free flows of capital and commodities' strip world's peoples and their life-ground underneath. The evidence is all around. The meta-pattern is most globally fatal with the planetary ecosystem, but has played out most catastrophically on the social level in Russia, Mexico, Argentina, Brazil, and South-East Asia since 1990.[43] Never is the private and centralised financial control of these operations raised publicly as an issue, nor is the control of the money used by private investment banks and the financial divisions of corporations whose revenues are generated on the basis of creating over 95 per cent of the world's money-demand. Thus 'the omnipresent centre' of interlocked global finance can deprive hundreds of millions of citizens of their very means of existence or their life-security with no exposure of the foreign private powers behind the control of the world money supply constitutionally vested in national governments. The system's choice paths of value are assumed, on the contrary, to be as given as the laws of nature and as unchangeable as the tides – to which they are sinisterly compared.

The question thus arises. Where is the failed global experiment of this totalising rule by private corporate power ever raised? The ground of the silence in even social science classrooms is that this monopolist programme become *internalised* as public value-set. The omnipresent centre is, in this way, made more invisible and unaccountable as it spreads. The public signifiers and meanings to see it are increasingly ruled out in the steering media to set the public mind-lock upon which this totalitarian system depends. All becomes secret in 'the war with no end' to ensure closure against the public even knowing the lines of this system's world advance.

Rule by Insecurity and Constructed Crises

To sustain acquiescence in the sacrifices it requires, a totalitarian movement must *keep all its subjects off-balance by a non-stop succession of disruptive changes and demands.* Private fear for one's own security is a necessary condition across communicatively isolated citizens for their submission to such a regime. The violation of long-accepted norms presented as *faits accomplis,* and the loss of life-bearings by permanent threat to secure livelihood are the psychological operations which are at work in any totalitarian movement. To keep the majority in a continual state of inner anxiety works because people are made too busy securing or competing for their own survival to co-operate in mounting an effective response. In the past decade, the entire population of the globe has been kept permanently off-balance with one financial meltdown and trans-national trade fiat after another emptying national coffers and overriding rights of domestic self-determination. Populations have been so overwhelmed by the moving juggernaut of economic and environmental crises that a rule of universal insecurity has rendered social majorities paralysed by a low-intensity terror – the necessary condition for any totalitarian movement to continue its advance, for keeping its subjects perpetually off-balance is its *modus operandi.* That is why in the Afghanistan case, the war no sooner seems over than the cry goes up, 'Who is next?'

Again, the two system deciders in the new totalitarianism are *financial and media selectors.* Together they confront peoples with continuous uncertainty about their future, destabilising threats from without, and *images of dream-like omnipotence of success* – the latter of great importance in a social field where grandiose images are all that exists to redeem the increasingly shabby lives of the majority. Orwell describes the phenomena of totalitarianism brilliantly as fiction, Hannah Arendt as reality in their great works of *1984* and *The Origins of Totalitarianism* respectively. However, the mechanics of this ever-shifting world of primary fears and aggressions are not *based* in the new totalitarianism on what Orwell and Arendt's descriptions feature – brutal shows of violence by the state.

Arendt's 1955 study is confined to 'the only two forms of totalitarianism we know' – Nazism and Stalinism, but Arendt warns in words that are not remembered that totalitarianism is 'an ever present danger' grounded in 'the endless process of capital and power accumulation' which erupts past former historical and social limits by its 'alliance with classless masses'.[44] Arendt's far-seeing overview of 'endless capital accumulation' mobilising as overwhelming social force by 'alliance with classless masses' is revealingly silent in even scholarly texts on Arendt's work and in complacent analyses of totalitarianism as only existing elsewhere. The agenda of thought is, rather, distant 'rogue states' and shadowy foreign 'terrorists' which are ever ready as new pretexts for more mechanisms of social repression.[45] 'The negative solidarity of atomised masses' which remains is a mental pulp incapable of mutual life defence, and manipulatable by any new scheme of war fever, attack-the-poor populism, or civil self-destruction. Totalitarianism is thus always accompanied by a public communication culture of formulaic discourse and bizarre extremes.

Beneath communication, totalitarianism is a pathological solution to insecure and atomised life bearings which it appears to remedy with a homogenised unity – as we saw in the 1930s, or after the 9–11 crisis. In the latter case, orchestration of patriotic fervour overrides popular awareness of a collapsing internal economy, an illegitimate presidential vote, and rising forces of life-ground opposition. In fact, however, the new unity is false-bottomed. The civil vacuum is not resolved, but exploited to be occupied with the restructuring of democracy by the 'new order'. Demagogic images are then sold at will to demoralised populations. When there is security for life, people claim life freedoms, as we saw at the acme of the 'golden age' of the postwar 'welfare state'. The transnational Trilateral Commission, the Bildersberg Council, the Bank for International Settlements and other interlocking corporate–financial–state bodies that were functioning before the turn to the 'no alternative' future did not fail to observe this general fact. The Trilateral Commission is now known by scholars for its 1976 'Crisis of Democracy' report on 'the excess of democracy' and 'entitlements' for 'previously passive and unorganized groups in the populace, blacks, Indians, Chicanos, white ethnic groups, students and women'.[46] In other words, *fear of the people being free* was the ruling motive of the world's corporate CEOs, US presidential candidates, and Harvard concept-setters leading the Commission's strategic recommendations. What eventually came – global capitalism with no 'barriers' of democratically accountable public authority, life-protective regulations, or social ownership – was constructed in accordance with their strategic plan. External wars then become saleable again behind new veils of total control of images. If spectacularly one-sided, they can be sold as patriotic events to a population whose conditions of life freedom no longer ground demands for an alternative order.

The campaign of life destabilisation was continuous and many-sided – 'the global terrorist' scare to justify the reversal of the Carter 'human rights agenda' and genocidal armed interference in El Salvador, Guatemala, Nicaragua and Grenada, with every citizen made to feel the suspicion frisk at airports from then on; the arms race to bankrupt and thus conquer 'the Soviet conspiracy to rule the world' while testing the new 'low intensity warfare' against poor populations seeking land reforms who were labelled as 'pro-Soviet communists'; the interest-rate constructed 'debt crises' across the globe which broke the institutional backbone of social spending and stripped social and welfare programmes across the world; non-stop globe-roaming currency attacks continuing to 'hold governments' feet to the fire' whenever they were perceived as deviating from the global 'fiscal and monetary reform' experiment; and transnational 'free trade' regimes imposed across continents with massive firings and casualisation of labour forces, rise of part-time and insecure livelihoods for more and more peoples, and the return of the world sweatshop and mass unemployment in the industrial North.

The permanent war against 'terrorists' of the Third World is the cap of a continuous and historically unprecedented financial deregulation of markets and haemorrhages of transnationally mobile capital in and out of nations, leading to meltdowns from Brazil and Mexico to Russia and Asia. The pace of 're-engineerings' of societies' economic bases has been dizzying, as required by all totalitarian movements to keep destabilising expectation. Within a decade, the world has been made to serve the only legitimate value-set now permissible in public discourse: 'private investor value', a condition overtly celebrated as 'the brutal global competition to survive'.[47]

The Inner Logic of the Big Lie

The most notorious characteristic of totalitarianism is '*the big lie*' – *a pervasive overriding of the distinction between fact and fiction by saturating mass media falsehoods*. In the familiar forms of totalitarianism, 'the big lie' occurs in a moving, *ad hoc* form – typically targeting an internal group for systematic attack by brutal persecution, and filling the news with false portrayals of an external enemy. The traditional form of the big lie *targets* a highly symbolic event (the Reichstag fire or the World Trade Center attack), or a claimed enemy of the populace ('communists' or 'Islamic extremists'). Global corporate totalitarianism, however, is not plausibly distinguishable *as* totalitarian in this way – although the targeting in the

US and its Latin American 'backyard' of falsely alleged 'Soviet-led communists' to justify the violent persecution of hundreds of thousands of people by death squads and orchestrated military pogroms was certainly a lead-up to the present corporate system. What interests us here, however, is a more routine and pervasive form of 'the big lie'. The big lie – in the sense of *omnipervasive lie* – is disseminated by round-the-clock, centrally controlled multi-media which are watched, read or heard by people across the globe day and night without break in the *occupation of public consciousness instead of national territories.* Group-think, not soil, is the breeding ground of the new totalitarianism.

On the micro level, the omnipervasive lie operates through a total conditioning apparatus – not only through continuous television, newspaper, car-and-home radio, disc and film mass-programming across private and social life, but increasingly against the citizen's will by unstoppable phonecalls and messages, ad mail and corporate flyers occupying mailboxes and home entrances, and round-the-clock invasions of fields of sight and hearing by demands to buy corporate commodities – eventually compounded by corporate security-state systems to 'put people in jail simply for participating in a political protest'.[48] What is in common among all these saturating occupations of citizens' sense-organs is that all their statements and images are false and misleading as a *form* of communication. Typically they are voluminously trivial with no meaning beyond their occurrence, or repetitions of mind-shackling misrepresentations in high-decibel certitudes.

Questions do not arise in such a total sign field. Indeed there is no ground of truth from which to raise them. *For no criterion of truth or falsehood exists within this 'knowledge economy'.* A boundless field of corporate images and voices that has no standard of knowledge proclaims itself *to be* knowledge by self-definition. This collapse of the distinction between truth and fiction opens the way to totalitarian occupation of consciousness. Across the increasingly invasive occupations of all attention fields by corporate ad-vehicles, the ruling value-set demands only more sales for more profits and the abandonment of any root in evidence or internal coherence. In the old totalitarian culture of the Big Lie, the truth is hidden. In the new totalitarianism, there is no line between truth and falsehood to embarrass the lies. The truth is what people can be conditioned to believe.[49]

In a cultural field where corporate symbols and roles, commodities, ads and PR campaigns dominate, what used to be called 'lies' are no longer an issue. Ronald Reagan is a cultural icon of this *fin de siècle* politics. He said trees caused acid rain, and as his office directed war criminal operations against Nicaragua he proclaimed: 'We have never interfered in the internal government of a country – never had any thought of that kind.'[50] Reagan later denied he knew what he signed from one hour to the next. No bearings remained in the world's leading public office to care about false proclamations because lies require standards of truth to name them. Reagan's media triumphs for eight years set the stage of the new culture of no line left between truth and falsehood. Postmodernism then played its unwitting theoretical reflection.

The learned professions of health and education would seem to be institutions structured to hold the line against this collapse of the distinction between knowledge and fabrication, but whatever operates as a 'barrier to trade' has no recognised right to existence in the market value-set. Success is determined by stockholders' bottom lines, not people's needs, including their intrinsic health or learning. Under proposed WTO law, therefore, the GATS (General Agreement on Trade and Services) prescribes 'General Obligations and Disciplines' that override professional standards themselves as 'domestic regulations, rules, procedures' which 'discriminate' against foreign 'service suppliers'. Only the 'least trade-restrictive practice' is permitted to regulate 'services' as a matter of binding trade law – with the least costly practice defining the 'most efficient'.[51] In this way, regulatory plans to expropriate authority from the long-evolved learned professions themselves are instituted as multi-billion-dollar market-sites, consigning any other regulating standard to the protectionists status of 'impediment to free trade'.

Outside the law, willingness to pay for commodities becomes the norm of truth. A pervasive propaganda system of 'demand stimulation' then operationalises this epistemology by appealing beneath reason to conditioned desires. The conditioned desires, in turn, become the sole input of citizens in the regime's expanding circuits of money capital rule in which politics itself is a sales function – the 'democracy' of the global market'. Thus, the distinction between truth and falsehood which was overridden in past totalitarian systems by a pervasive field of force to suppress dissent is *ruled out from within*. The annihilation of civilisation's line between truth and falsehood is not experienced as a violation, but follows from the ruling value calculus whose measure is manufactured desires generating shareholder profits. Totalitarian success is to have the abolition of this line built into the fabric of everyday life.

Totalitarian rule's familiar aversive conditioners of clubs, guns, tortures, beatings and murder on the streets are thus replaced by a directive field that occupies all the organs of perception and co-ordinates of paying consumers who have replaced citizens in the regime's everyday lexicon – with overwhelming force in the background for perceived system transgressors. As the traditional distinctions between truth and lies, knowledge and falsehood are overridden as 'uncompetitive', the totalitarian system moves to another plane of possibility. The macro level of the big lie is one in which the big lies through repetition are *built into the mind as generic presuppositions.*

The Regulating Big Lies of the Global Corporate System

As the advertising and public relations industry knows well, upbeat slogans ceaselessly repeated across the mass media can make unthinking people believe anything. Thus, in the prototype presidency of the 'new world order', the Reagan administration called drug-financed war criminals invading Nicaragua from the US , '*freedom fighters*'.[52] Although the 'freedom fighters' burned rural schools and clinics as their primary *modus operandi*, and although their narcotic-financed operations were arranged and protected by the President's men, no mass medium ever exposed the equation of *value opposites* at work – fighting for people's freedom, *the value*, while systematically destroying the most basic freedoms *in fact*.[53] The generic big lie consists in such a contradiction brought to the level of *perfect generalisation*: a lie that goes beyond space-time co-ordinates to a universal given applying to all places and times without any qualification by spatio-temporal facts.

In this world regime of consciousness occupation, one generic big lie accompanies another. We return again to our example. A generic big lie which the Nicaragua case instantiated is more specific in the value claimed, but more explosive in the normalised contradiction. As with 'terrorism', the US security state proclaims its enmity to 'drug trafficking' – a 20-year tandem crusade since the Reagan administration, calling the drug-financed Taliban in Afghanistan and Contras in Nicaragua the 'moral equivalent of the founding fathers'. Here again, we see that the proclaimed value of the US state is to stop what it, in fact, everywhere leads. In the words of the former chief of an elite US Drug Enforcement Administration unit: 'In my 30 year history in the Drug Enforcement Administration and related agencies, the major targets of my investigations almost invariably turned out to be working for the CIA.'[54]

The big lie does not stop so long as it is not opposed. In 2001, it is repeated again with a different country, a different president, a different 'national security' personnel, but the same saturating field of declaring the opposite of fact as timeless reality. Underneath the attack of 'Operation Enduring Freedom' on Afghanistan (first called 'Infinite Justice'), there is another full-scale attack on a poverty-stricken peasantry that is not talked about. The people living in the oil region of Colombia are being terrorised and killed by death-squad proxies with heavy US financing, merely for seeking self-determination outside the assigned corporate-military oligarchy's subjugation.[55] Wherever the killing fields occur, the generic big lie is the field of its possibility, and the public's complicity with its inverted moral meaning, its political enabling act.

Big lies grow bigger as they are instituted through time, and one big lie builds onto the next, restructuring the cultural fabric as a tissue of lies. Without public exposure, what was once a breathtaking falsehood becomes by repetition *an accepted assumption* of everyday thought. The communication field becomes permanently deformed by them. We have seen the equations of opposites become standard assumptions of thought on such a pervasive scale that they are not noticed – the key to maintaining public consciousness in paralysis. Only when they are exposed do their bizarre contradictions emerge out of the hypnotic field of images and slogans in which the mind has been submerged. How can big lies be sustained over time? Only by accepted repetition. And one after another they have. '*Conservatism*' means sacrificing conservation and traditional vocations and practices. '*Family values*' means insecure jobs and depriving poor mothers of income. '*Getting the fundamentals right for increased prosperity*' means massive job lay-offs and slashed social services. The '*nation's survival*' means dismantling social infrastructures and life-protective labour and environmental laws. '*The information highway*' means ever more pervasive propaganda. '*Economic growth*' and '*efficiency*' mean eco-service depredation destroying the conditions of life themselves. The '*global free market*' means escalating oligopolist control. '*More competitiveness*' means an economy of bigger mergers that reduce competition. '*More democracy*' means prohibition by transnational trade law of elected government control over their own economies.

That all of these mind-stopping contradictions are daily repeated at every level of authority and public communication without explosion of hilarity reveals the totalisation of the mind-set as normal.

The Master Big Lie

The notion of '*the* market' lies at the base of the mind's syntax for repressing alternatives of thought. What is not noticed is that the concept itself abolishes from possibility any other kind of market except the one that rules – not as superior, but as the necessary structure order of the world. There is no other market before *the* market, as there is no other god before Yahweh. But the traditional Judaic-Christian theology is here exceeded. It recognises that there are indeed other gods, but declares that they shall not be worshipped before God. *The* market, in contrast, does not recognise that it is one market among many – the community exchange market, the traditional public market, the non-monetised barter market, the socialist market, the local exchange-currency market, and so on. It presupposes that it is the one and only market, and that whatever is not it does not exist, or ought not to exist. The totalitarian mind-set is not imposed by an Orwellian rat-cage around the face, or fear of the fire for heresy. It is assumed by the mind-set throughout which the world is seen. Alternative is 'impossible' or 'unreal'. The metaphysical assertion of 'no alternative' is declared *prior* to choice. All alternatives are liquidated as non-existent by the meaning of the fiat. It *is* 'reality'. Thus the tell-tale slogan, 'the end of history'. Afforded no right to exist as thought, alternatives are banned in reality. What is not '*the* market' is void by definition. That all this proceeds without notice reveals the mind-lock of meaning beneath thought.

When abolition of an actual, living alternative is 'necessary', as with the original 'no alternative' order of General Pinochet, the liquidation is revealingly declared to have been a defence of 'the *free* market'. The Other is here recognised (otherwise there would be no need to destroy it), but a categorical value assertion has been added without explanation or justification. It is not just 'the market' which exhausts all fact that exists – the total market as a given. It is 'the *free* market'. Yet once the claim of freedom enters the equation, the big lie must become deeper. For a monopoly-tending system is the opposite of the free market in Adam Smith's own meaning.

The generic big lie is here at the level of first principle. Its carrier and enforcer has long been the economics classroom. Economic textbooks typically begin their teaching by declaring their 'positive economics', their 'value neutrality', and their 'science', but with no scientific scruple of notice, economists also lace their texts and speech the normative slogan 'free' before 'market' as if they meant the same thing. This is the collapse of meaning at the level of the given even in science on which the totalitarian value-set depends. The issue does not arise because every issue is already settled in the inevitable and no-alternative system. There are only the given facts. The sweeping value claim which has been *added* escapes the received value-set's lenses of perception because it can see only what fits within it.

Nevertheless, the truth that is abolished from the mind remains true. For, in fact, the oligopolist corporate market within which most trading is intra-firm flatly contradicts the meaning of the term 'free market', which entails that all agents in it are free to produce and to sell with none of them in the position to influence or control the market's supply or its demand. The global corporate system is oppositely structured. There is no sector of its industrial, financial and service system that is not dominated by an interlocking oligopoly of transnational corporations, from the oil, automobile and aerospace industries to food processing, pharmaceuticals, software, and news and entertainment media. There is also no sector in which this oligopolist dominance is not becoming *more* extreme every quarter by mega-mergers into which ever more accumulated funds are invested instead of into life-capital renewal and formation.[56]

In fact, the global corporate system is hardly any longer a *market*, let alone a free one, since its transactions are dominantly within the same command-structured oligopolist firms which are massively state-favoured and subsidised at every level. The global market becomes in this way a total dominance of transnational financial pools lavishly subsidised with attendant government infrastructures serving them, escalating tax write-offs and subsidies, and using armed force enforcement wherever they seek defence or expansion at the cost of other economic agents or majority populations. Since they effectively control supply and demand across borders by central command operations of chief-executive prescriptions, they are the transnational nodes of a global command economy although representing themselves as the opposite, 'the free market' – with no exposure of the contradiction in public discourse. Increasingly, in consequence, only dependent subcontractors, temporary labour, and financed state parties remain to 'attract' and 'partner with' transnational corporations whose agents simultaneously prescribe laws to further access, occupy and control existing domestic markets and resources with no accountability beyond themselves. This system of world rule can only claim legitimacy by not being remotely understood, but reconstructed by false equations regulating minds to assume the opposite.

Corporate Freedom = Your Freedom: The Closed Structure of Fact–Fiction Inversions

The lock-step of the global corporate programme is not easily opposed. Its fixed value-set regulates perception and judgement prior to understanding, and knows itself as the final solution of how peoples everywhere must live. No feedback loop can modify or correct this closed circuit because it is self-referential in all its indicators, with social and environmental life co-ordinates blocked out as 'externalities'.

On the surface, acceptance of 'the global free market' is dinned into the heads of the public by slogans saturating the corporate media around the clock, and by clubbings, tear-gas and rubber bullets if the slogans don't imprint; but underneath the instituted violence and propaganda, a *primitive syntax of contradictory value equations* is always at work structuring the group-mind to be the willing host of the programme by which the programmers are themselves programmed. The set-point of perception and cognition, as we have seen, consists of two master equations. The first is: *Freedom = the Market*. The second is: *Globalisation = Transnational Corporate Rights.* Since these slogans trail in their wake the effect of cultural genocide as their meaning, this way of seeing establishes the ideological confusion which is required to mask the invasion so that societies do not know what is happening to them.[57]

Those who oppose 'free trade' and, thus, the 'free market', are by these same regulating equations perceived as *opposed* to human freedom and globalisation. The only issue for those governed by this mind-frame, then, is how to ensure the peaceful acquiescence of this 'freedom' and 'globalisation' which are, in truth, the opposite of both. This is the global market system's big-lie circle, and nothing breaks into its final certitude – as long as it is collaborated in. Conformity to the mind-set is thus effected in the face of its contradiction with reality by legal, academic and media *idealisation*. The career function for the journalist is to reproduce without knowing it the group-mind circuit with political dramas and human-interest stories *which always conform to these equations*. For the academic and the judge, the same conformity of value-set is ensured by *methods of exclusion of social facts* which structure professional identity itself. You are for freedom and us, or you are against us and therefore freedom. The Bush Jr presidency has *expressed* this mind-set in pure form at its zenith of delusion, but its inherited frame of reference mind has long been advancing and has been penetrated by such thinkers as former US Supreme Court Chief Justice, Felix Frankfurter. Those his observation refers to include not only judges, but philosophers, economists, political scientists, and indeed official culture as a whole. 'The controlling conceptions of the Justices', he says, 'are their *idealized political pictures* of the existing social order.'[58] The function of what is then called 'rigour' – strict adherence to this idealised model – serves to close the mind to any connection to the facts outside the acceptable framework of conception. Eventually the system becomes self-referential and closed to any other meaning.

Freedom = the Free Market is the grounding equation of this ruling mind-set and the system it legitimises. The further equivalence of 'the free market' and 'globalisation' to the global corporate system is, in turn, autonomically acquiesced in. This primitive assumption-set has many elaborations of *substitution* and *reversal*. In place of 'Global Market' = 'Free Market' = 'Freedom', the basic syntax of the doctrine also substitutes for the prime term 'Democracy', 'Prosperity', 'Development', 'Progress' – and, when threatened, 'Civilisation' and 'Justice'. One can discern the locks of linkage here by trying to find where any of these declared master values is anywhere publicly distinguished, or thought not to be in mutual entailment. All are affirmed as one, as in a catechism but without the formalisation. For the structure is one of group mind operating as its *a priori* regulator of sense and meaning. Each and all of these concepts is substituted for any other as the occasion triggers the repertoire. At the same time, the mind-set *inverts*, at will, the order of equations so that any who oppose it become by its operations the *enemies* of freeom, democracy, civilisation and therefore, eventually, 'terrorists' – as we have observed with the institutionalisation of this value-set by wars.

Yet this repertoire of ever more preposterous inversions of meaning, value and fact exposes the Achilles' heel of the dominant system. Once these inversions of meaning are seen through, their legitimacy implodes at the level of the *mind-set itself*. The unseen scaffolding of thought which ritualises absurdities is not stable, but it is the internal structure of legit-imation without which the system loses its human basis of reproduction – the mind itself. Thus from Paris to Seattle to Washington, Prague, Quebec, Genoa, and Afghanistan the ever more pervasively instituted violence and aggression of the global corporate system against its own citizens depends for every step of its legitimacy on public acceptance of the big-lie structure of meaning. Conditioned speech habits which carry the Trojan horse within our concept structures themselves are the complicity within upon which the occupation depends. The ultimate big lie of this regime is metaphysical, its claimed identity itself.

As Hannah Arendt long ago observed, the big lie occurs by overriding the line between fact and fiction as a matter of normalised routine. The set of fact–fiction oppositions below provides us with *the inner framework of the generic big lie of the* global market order. As we move through its tiers of unexcavated and anti-dialectical contradictions, we can see that every transformation of fact to falsehood is regulated by *fanatic moral operators* – inverting idealisers of reality that are closed to all rebutting fact. These alter reality to its opposite by the lenses of inversion through which their bearers perceive, understand and act on the world.

Fiction 1   *versus*   *Fact 1*
The global free market is constituted of legally responsible, individual market agents.

versus — The GSC is constituted of non-living, corporate entities protecting individual shareholders from legal liability for their offenses against others and violations of civil and criminal law.[59]

Fiction 2   *versus*   *Fact 2*
The global free market is a free and open competitive market.

The GSC's dominant corporate agents both control the supply and create the demand for most and increasingly more of the world's goods and services.[60]

Fiction 3   *versus*   *Fact 3*
All in the global free market are free to consume the market goods of their choice with ever fewer barriers to their consumer sovereignty.

No-one can normally consume any market good without having the money demand to buy it, and the processes of production of the commodities they can buy are prohibited from label exposure by transnational trade law.[61]

Fiction 4   *versus*   *Fact 4*
All in the free market are free to offer for sale the good or service they choose to produce or exchange.

Every business quarter there is an increase in those without the means to produce in land or tools, the vast majority of all market agents.[62]

Fiction 5	versus	Fact 5
All are free to transact with whomsoever they choose in the free market as buyers or as sellers, with no-one forced to buy or sell what they do not choose to.		*Sellers* of labour are not free to transact as sellers when the option is starving or where there are no buyers; where the terms of employment are not negotiable but imposed; and where employees are forced to work with unknown lethal toxins and under hazardous conditions in performing their work.[63] *Buyers* are not free to choose what they buy when the market of commodities they must select from is dominated by interlocked transnational corporations, when they are systematically prevented from knowing the nature of these commodities' production, and when responsible government policies against public purchase of commodities made by criminal methods are prohibited by overriding WTO trade law.[64]

Fiction 6	versus	Fact 6
Societies are free in a newly democratising world to choose by electoral processes whether or not they participate in the global free market.		The majority of voters in most countries have voted against parties advocating transnational 'free trade' and for parties opposed, and in no country in the world have the centrally binding terms of these transnational regimes been publicly reported and debated.[65]

The Total Field of Meaning

These are generic 'big lies' which have been built into the everyday conditions of life and thought as a totalised *field of meaning*. The individual or institutional mind-set that hosts them is, in turn, the living vehicle of every step of the global corporate system's legitimation and advance. The *materialisation* of the system, however, requires a total organising structure to implement and carry the ruling corporate money-sequences on every level of space-time. This total organising system is, in turn, the interlocked mega-order of *scientific method, technology and money capital as one master structure of meaning and value regulation.*[66] Together this steering mind-set *actually* commands the world life-ground as an underlying and interlinked programme which, if it is not discovered, the new totalitarianism follows with 'inevitable progress'.

6

The Master Regulators of the World System: Science, Technology and Money Capital

To Control and Predict All: The Scientific Method Behind the Totalitarian System

Scientific method is a primary instrument in human evolution, but like any set of dominant ideas which is totalised beyond its domain of understanding, scientific method can become a reductionist and closed metaphysic. If it locks the mind within a programme that cannot see beyond itself, it ineluctably becomes blind to all that does not fit its categories. It can become a totalitarian metaphysic if – like neo-classical economics – it purports a certitude of natural science and inexorable laws of how humans must live in society. It is, as well, a false science when its investigations are not of repeating phenomena, and its evidence is in fact prescribed by external interventions.[67]

The Cult of Technological Miracles

Scientific technology is not, in fact, 'neutral' in its meaning or value, but is a a vast global system of moving parts that materially reproduces the transnational corporate order as a totalising mechanism to serve an absolutist value-set of turning money into more money for money investors. Although widely fetishised as omnipotent like the Sky Gods of the ancient past, technology is constructed by man. Nonetheless, magical powers of protection and deliverance are attributed to it – not only by the masses, but by the dominant thinkers of the era. Philosophers and science fictionists have indeed coined complex literatures which not only ascribe the properties of their human creators to computers, but can no longer tell the difference between them. Popular film culture correspondingly fantasises about cybernetic machines taking on autonomous lives of their own, reproducing their kind and ruling the earth as anthropoidal calculators and sensor mechanisms.

Underneath these cultural phenomena, a dominant corporate economics posits technology as a *deus ex machina* which permits its 'value adding' agenda for a dominant financial faction to proceed as if by the laws of Fate. Any disaster that results is also assumed to be resolvable by 'technological and product substitution'. Technology has in this way become to the global market system what divine intervention by Yahweh or Indra was to fundamentalist patriarchies of the ancient past. It is the Providence of the market which produces technological miracles on price cue.[68]

If, for example, cancer is caused by the countless toxins and carcinogens with which industrial production and commodity consumption pollute our bodies and environment– an estimated 75–90 per cent of cancer afflictions are now environmentally induced – governments, pharmaceutical corporations and cancer foundations invoke the limitless powers of 'medical science and technology' to intervene with an externally priced solution. This solution does not relate to cancers' *preventable environmental causes*, because this would call the system into value question. So a millenarian 'conquest of cancer' is projected as a certitude of the future – a miracle cure for all its terrors – although a single cure for what invades cellular life-organisation in radically different ways is not, in fact, scientifically plausible.

As in other faiths in miraculous intervention, belief in the saving forces of Technology substitutes for having to understand and respond to the actual conditions responsible for the affliction – as once self-flagellation for sins or invocations of divine intervention were thought to cure plagues while the filthy conditions that bred the rat vector were ignored. Man-made chemical or environmental carcinogens are similarly ignored as an issue in recognising, researching or preventing cancer,[69] while market fundamentalists demand 'sacrifices for market competitiveness' by budget reductions for what environmental and workplace regulations there are to control human exposure to carcinogenic substances. The facts which are ignored are:

- since 1940 the industrial manufacture of synthetic organic chemicals has multiplied 600 times;
- countless toxic effluents, pollutants, workplace toxins, commodity ingredients and additives, household cleaning agents, industrial solvents and byproducts are not pursued as preventable causes of cancers;

- ongoing weapons-related environmental radiation produces tens of thousands of cancers annually;
- precautionary bioassays are performed on only an infinitesimal percentage of the tens of thousands of industrial and military chemicals in daily use around the world.

Yet all of these realities together constitute a massive causal structure of carcinogenic distrortions of organic reproduction. which is blocked out of view, with the magical thinking of a 'miracle cure' substituting for causal understanding.

Worship of the market's invisible hand materially intervening by production of ever new wonders of technology thus sustains the meta-programme of the system as it continues to deprecate human lives and ecosystems. Technology and its genius of scientific discovery, it is assumed, will save us. The systematic disconnnecting of cause from effect is built into the decision structure of the global corporate system at many levels. Another 'technological miracle' has long been believed as an article of faith – that 'new technology' will transfigure 'the starving millions of the Third World' into universal nourishment. The first such miracle was high-tech inputs of the 'Green Revolution', but this 'Green Revolution', in fact, simply redistributed more agricultural lands to large-scale farms producing for foreign export and out of the hands of the subsistence-farming billions. This systemic effect was, as usual, overlooked because the regulating value-set pushes out of sight whatever does not conform to it. That the locals called it the 'greed revolution' was not reported.

In the most famous success of the Green Revolution, India's total agri-cultural yields were marginally increased from 1.71 per cent to 2.68 per cent per annum in food grains. This marginal production gain was achieved by a system of labour-displacing mechanisation, the genetically homogenising use of hybrid seeds which do not breed true, massive use of priced petrochemical fertilisers and pesticides, and large-scale irrigation schemes paid for by state loans favouring the big plantations and mechanised agribusiness.[70] The destructive results remained unnoted by World Bank and US development experts who had prescribed this solution to 'solve the world's food problem', while the mainstream of economic and social science studiously ignored the pattern, except to report higher output numbers.[71] This is the fanaticism of the market value-set at work in the social sciences.

The 'miracle of the new agricultural technology' was then proclaimed to the 'international community'. In fact, the concealed outcomes were systemically disastrous. They included intensification of extreme inequal-ities and violent conflicts in the countryside; steeply increased dependency on priced inputs marketed by transnational corporations; selection against independent small cultivators, increasingly reducing them to bankruptcy, wage-labour and unemployment; sharply escalated toxic poisonings of the poor; the rapid enrichment of an agribusiness oligarchy who increasingly controlled national political policy; a significant increase of debt-slavery of families and their children; greater siphoning of rural wealth to the moneylenders and middlemen who permeate India's social fabric; and a macro result of about half of the population still hungry for most of the time.[72]

Beyond Magical Thinking: The Moral Meaning of Technology

Dostoevsky's Grand Inquisitor asserted that humanity wanted magic to awe them, power to humble them, and the promise of bread to keep them. The global corporate system depends on the same ideological trinity; but what passes it through the gates of reason is that it is robed in the vestments of '*scientific technology*' rather than revealed religion. In *The Question of Technology*, Martin Heidegger argues that at its deepest level technology's '*Entframing*' rules as a danger beyond any that man knows, both reducing humanity to an instrument ready for use, and confining the truth of Being to an oblivious partiality of Being's disclosure. 'Everywhere', he says in a moment of direct statement, 'we remain unfree and chained to technology.'[73] With similar pessimism of reification, Jacques Ellul construes technology in his classic, *Technology*, as a self-propelling system of uniform, hierarchically organised, and exactly detailed commands subjugating humanity to its mechanical rule, remaking the human subject as an assembly-line object – 'I call', he says, 'for the sleeper to awake!'[74]

What unifies these very different philosophical visions is that capital-T technology is made to appear as *the self-acting author of its effects*. No form of *human responsibility behind and using it* is discerned or investigated. We see here, at a more learned level, a resemblance of thought-pattern to the awed stupefaction of Tony Blair analysed in Chapter 1. Blair sees vast and irreversible forces 'driving the future' which operate as if there were only efficient causes at work deciding humanity's fate by external prescriptions which cannot be disobeyed. The important difference is that Heidegger and Ellul ask us to open to a wider vista of consciousness and meaning, whereas the popular worship of technology is a phenomenon *from* which they urge us to awake. At every level, Technology is projected as imposing its demands on humanity as an external and autonomous power. The deeper meaning is that it is *another category of the epoch's official standpoint that blinkers us to the regulating value-set behind it.*

This is the basis of the new totalitarianism as Global Machine whose self-acting powers are 'universal forces which cannot be stopped'; yet organising and regulating every construction and advance of technology to greater and more overwhelming powers is a *value-set* which selects every moment of technology's growth to more monstrous capacities to serve a final moral goal of which it is an instrument – to reduce cost inputs of corporate investors, or to increase their monetary returns in the higher rule of 'shareholder value'. Even state mega-projects of every kind serve this ultimate system selector to which all other aims are subordinated, as the countless billions of taxpayers' dollars thrown at private corporate contracts for military commodities, while citizens are left homeless and starving, bear public witness.

Yet scientific technology does not, as it may appear to do, 'maximise efficiency of production' even where it is constructed to reduce production costs. Indiscriminate waste and life depredation by corporate technology's extractions, effluents and inhuman regimes are, on the contrary, profoundly uneconomical and inefficient. However, because technology is normally researched and selected for development within the system only insofar as it reduces money costs to corporate investors to increase their returns, this function of efficiency is all that is seen through the prism of the ruling value-frame. Technology is, in fact, typically introduced *to reduce company expenditures on people's means of life* – their wages, social services, and environmental conditions. This underlying and systemically savage inefficiency from the standpoint of life-value is ignored because the regulating value-set is life blind.

Because of technology's successes in reducing costs of life in commodity production, as well as in designing destructive powers to terrorise perceived enemies, scientific method impresses the mind with its awful feats, and has become instituted underneath the economic order as the species' godlike capability of materially transforming power. As it has become dominant as a social institution, a presupposed metaphysic of the true and the real has been erected as capital-S Science at every level of world existence. Science serving money-sequences defines reality itself. It does so by a rigorous and universal obedience to three master principles.

Principle 1: Liquidating Life that is not Externally Observable and Quantifiable

The first master principle of scientific method is so standardly presupposed at such a high level of generality that its organising idea is not spelled out to conscious understanding. While for these reasons this first master principle is not normally specified in scientific texts, but rather presupposed as a regulating assumption of every claim of all of texts, it is an unexamined truth within the realm of science itself. Thus, every scientific text and practice assumes as a ruling principle of perception and understanding that *only externally observable, quantifiable data count as valid information*. This principle is not and cannot be a *finding* of science because it is already presupposed; but it is an invariable presupposition *of* each of its forms, whose scientific findings, if not thus validated, are repudiated as false or illusory.

This regulating assumption of modern scientific method is a *transcendental* principle insofar as its claim is *not itself verifiable* by observation or evidence. As a transcendental principle, it is always a necessary condition *of* science's method, which demands repetitive confirmation to compute its judgements. This first meta-assumption of science is also a *dogmatic* principle insofar as its idea is not open to critical discussion or question. We need to keep these considerations in mind so that the very impressive instrumental powers of scientific technology do not bewitch us.

The first primary presupposition of modern scientific method is epistemologically beneficial as long as it is not believed to be the ground of *all* knowledge and truth-value; but if it is believed that *only* what is externally observable and quantifiable is real – a view that is widespread – then a momentous implication follows. *Whatever is not externally observable and quantifiable is judged as false or illusory.*

Is it empirically verifiable by others? Can you quantify its effects? If not, commit it to the fire for it is nothing but sophistry and illusion. This is a mind-set most famously expressed by David Hume, and it has become standard in our scientific age.[75] It certainly has rid us of many layers of ignorance and superstition about how the material world works. As long as we are dealing with uniformly constituted phenomena – that is, as long as we are *not* dealing with non-re-aggregatable life – we can learn much about the redundant patterns of the world from this method. The physical sciences rigorously report these law-like patterns.

However, if we shift the existential field to the *non*-uniformly constituted phenomena of human history, or of people's internal lives, or of the expressions of creative art, or indeed *any* phenomenon whose properties are qualitative, then scientific method is beyond its realm of competence. Free life itself cannot be scientifically understood, because its nature is to be self-directed within the wide ranges of possibility defined by natural laws. Birds' flights conform to physical laws, but individual flights cannot begin to be predicted. Human beings choose often against their past inclinations, and so more clearly frustrate subsumption under covering laws. One could go on. People's *internal* lives are not externally observable in principle. Beauty, despite the Pythagoreans, is not truly measurable in number. Historical decisions are not adequately construable as matter in motion in accordance with causal laws.

The profound metaphysical error – so commonplace that it is not recognised – occurs when the believer supposes that whatever is not validated by scientific method *does not exist*. This is a dogma which has penetrated the very grammar of modern thought. The long-dominant school of 'behaviourism' in the social and human sciences, for example, presupposes this *ontocidal assumption* as a requirement of its method. Nothing qualifies as real which is not directly observable by others, including one's own thought processes. Second-order knowledge such as I know *that* I am thinking even less can compute to this model. That a person can know most deeply that he or she can choose to forgo a reward as well as seek it, or be conscious, or not, of this option, is ruled out *a priori*. B.F. Skinner widely promulgated this position, but he only represented a general structure of thought that moved freely across the divide of the Iron Curtain from Ivan Pavlov in the 1920s to the subliminal conditioning of the corporate media today.

These implications are not widely recognised; yet, eliminate choice at this *a priori* level, do so as a given principle of scientific method, generalise its structure of understanding to market demand and state policy formation, and you have the master assumption of the totalitarian value-set – that *no real choice exists*. All that is required is to control the conditions to get the outputs central command prescribes. Here an iron cage of social rule can come to be supposed as the structure of reality itself. Since only observable behaviours are real, and these behaviours can be made to follow predictable objectives by the recurrent re-enforcers determining them – the unstated assumption of market consumer and management theory today. Thus, a totalitarian order follows step-by-step from what started as a regulating principle of physical science in the controlled conditions of the laboratory.

With 'the consumer' conceived and operantly conditioned as a malleable resultant with no limit of desires for commodities, and the assumption of this premise by contemporary economic science and policy, the room for choice is essentially liquidated. Since science cannot verify or quantify what is not externally verifiable, it follows from this logic that what is not so publicly replicable must not be real. Since what is not scientifically validated is illusory, it also follows that anyone's reflective decision to, say, *reduce the self's desires* is outside the capacity of the doctrine to compute, and thus delusory. Again, we observe a principle of scientific method turned by an underlying lock-step of thought into a presupposed metaphysical dogma. 'Behaviourist technology' formally institutes this methodological prison. The systematic control of human beings, first explicated by Machiavelli, then becomes a scientific regime. The industries of psychological, sociological, management, and military research into the technology of behavioural control here dovetail with the industries of corporate studies into conditioning human choice to profitable outcomes of product advertising. The underlying, unifying principle for the predictive control of human subjects which runs as a master theme through 'the scientific literature' is mind-stoppingly simple: *all behavioural outputs are determined by conditioning inputs.*[76]

This principle of control is now assumed by corporate and state strategists, behavioural scientists and realpolitikers as the given structure of the world, and all there needs to be known about animal or human behaviour. The principle is not put so transparently. That is how it continues as a given regulator of the mind – with scientific comportment as its warrant of 'value neutrality', and – revealingly – rats and pigeons as its demonstration cases. Such a prison of conception does not occur as a problem to the mind-set. Rather, the operational concern is to construct exact schedules of behavioural re-enforcements to govern scientifically aggregate consumer and voter behaviour in accordance with profitable objectives or, in times of confrontation with a designated Enemy, to blanket-condition home populations with affirmative slogans, and distant populations with bombs.

At the more impressionable level of infants and children, operant conditioning of humans into compliant functions of global corporate order is now proclaimed as a regulating corporate norm. 'The consumer begins to develop in the first year of existence ... We at General Mills follow the Procter & Gamble model of "cradle to grave" ... We believe in getting them early and having them for life.'[77] Scientific method as operant conditioning research reliably establishes the re-enforcers required to 'drive loyalty in the desires of toddler-age consumers'; to condition 4–12-year-old US children to spend and influence over $500 billion of consumer expenditures; to sustain this scientifically researched control in homes and schools ('the ideal time to influence attitudes') for the $150 billion more of the teenage market ; and to carry on the process of blanket conditioning people in their adult years to believe that cigarette and oil corporations 'really care for our people' as they cause their diseases and deaths in many millions.[78] Throughout, the scientific management of desire and perception is the regulating form of reproducing citizens as desire and obedience functions of the global money-sequence machine.[79]

Principle 2: Liquidating Life that is not Uniformly Repeatable

Such predictable conformity for scientific management requires that all that is scientifically recognisable be duplicatable to count as verified, so that a second defining principle of the scientific method is simultaneously at work with the first. This second master principle of scientific method concerns the precise *sequences* which life decision and behaviour must *redundantly* assume to qualify as 'scientifically valid'. Again, here, the principle itself is not open to scientific question. It too is presupposed as necessary to yield knowledge or truth status. Again, too, it is not an axiom that is normally stated in scientific texts or statements. It is a meta-principle whose rule, like the subject-verb order of syntax, can govern without being understood by the behaviour expressing it. Reflection on any set of cases will demonstrate that Principle 2 regulates all of the accepted experimental results, statements, laws and theories which science and scientists accept as valid. If any claim, however otherwise compelling, does not satisfy this unstated principle of validity, it is rejected.

Principle 2 may be formally stated as follows: *Nothing can be known, count as true or proven which does not assume the form of uniform, invariant sequences which are always and everywhere exactly reproducible by others.* An experimental finding which cannot be 'replicated' elsewhere is, therefore, rendered void. An event which happens but is not verifiable is suspect or void. Any succession of phenomena which is not repeatable by others across time and place is 'unconfirmed'. Strict compliance with Principle 2 yields science's famous capacity to *predict*. A claim or theory that fails to provide predictability is deemed false or useless.

Knowing the future is the nature of omniscience, but it requires '*control* of the variable to be certain'. In the 'science of economics', macroeconomic fiscal and monetary recipes are continuously prescribed for governments to act on. As they are acted on from one steering decision to the next over years in succession, a remarkable but unseen kind of predictability results. Expected results are, in fact, *enforced* by state and corporate apparatuses which possess life-and-death control over incomes for survival, and armed violence if these re-enforcers do not work. An unnoted but scientifically scandalous problem thus arises. *Economic explanations and predictions are confirmed by coercing people to conform to them.* This closed circle of 'value-free science' reporting the confirming results of what is, in fact, a consequence of mass indoctrination and coercion, is not recognised as an issue. On the contrary, because the regulating mind-set confuses prescriptions which are sustained by coercive mechanisms as 'economic laws', it perceives only confirmation of them. This is how the system remains locked. Its ruling doctrine is verified by social constraints enforcing its prescriptions. Science then confirms what is prescribed. The mind-set begins and ends the closed circle.

Over time, mathematical equations are first superimposed, and then decoupled from the results. Manipulations and deductions of the delinked equations then increasingly substitute for observation in research and findings, and society's reproduction and growth are understood in terms of the monetised command-system of thought which regulates them throughout as 'laws'. 'No alternative' becomes the inherent structure of the regime, with Economic Science as its legitimating order, and Technology as its material proof. This system-bound pattern was revealingly described in its 'scientific' character by social economists who are awaking from it at the 10th Annual Congress of Social Economics at Cambridge University in 2000 as 'neo-classical 'Stalinisation'.[80]

Reduction of life for prediction and control of it runs deep in the origins of scientific method. In the first formal expression of the *knowledge = power* value-set that was to become the totalitarian construct we analyse now, Francis Bacon conceives of the scientific method in his famous 1620 *Novum Organum* as an 'inquisition' with 'no part interdicted' which 'puts Nature on the rack to compel her secrets from her', deploying 'the mechanical arts' to 'make nature man's slave'.[81]

Generated beyond Nature to include human society itself, ruling over human and environmental life by 'the mechanical arts' of world-restructuring technology, and driven by the money-sequence imperative of reducing costs and increasing revenues for private corporate powers, the totalitarian system grows up behind the back of conscious value understanding. 'Economics' is its theoretical nexus and paradigm. Scientific method is its omnibus structure of understanding, constructing and testing its mechanisms of prediction and control. Maximising money-demand returns to investors is the value-set imposed as universal law.

Blake and the Cogito: Life and Thought Beyond the Invisible Prison

On the one hand, a William Blake may regard the redundancy requirement of scientific method as a world of repetition expressing the 'mind-forged manacles' of a fallen human imagination. 'We live', says Jacques Ellul two centuries later, 'in a world ringed round with hoops of steel.'

On the other hand, every law of chemistry and physics is a variation on this iron-law format, and every engineering achievement of the modern epoch conforms exactly to its uniform schema. Who is right? The answer is neither, and both. Inanimate matter in one way or another complies with invariant sequences – gravitation, laws of liquids, gases and solids – across places and times. To recognise and apply modern scientific method in this realm is the constructive foundation of the material achievements of contemporary civilisation.

This method of positing, discovering and testing universal laws of construction and occurrence even lays bare the blueprints of living matter whose cellular or organic sequences remain invariably repetitive across confined spatio-temporal co-ordinates. To assume, however, that these requirements of scientific understanding of uniformly redundant phenomena – 'what science tells us' – are all we know is the profoundest imaginable *non sequitur*. To think, further, that if science does not validate it, it cannot *exist* is quite insane, yet this regulating metaphysic is normalised in global market culture. *It is a mind-set which projects onto all that is alive the characteristics of what is lifeless.* What does not fit is illusory, or is forced to conform.

Blake did not recognise the proper place of science, what establishes the redundant patterns of the biophysical universe which we have to know to be able to understand and co-ordinate natural forces to serve vital human needs (e.g., from laws of physics to microbial behaviours). In consequence, Blake went to the other extreme, and denied the inner truth of the natural creation which *is* law-like and redundant, valuing only its transfiguration by human imagination, 'the bosom of God'. The engineering mind-set of neo-classical economics, industrial technology and the transnational corporation goes to the other extreme far more dangerously and aggressively. Its outlook increasingly structures the world into a global mechanism of dehumanised functions as 'development'.[82]

Since the standpoint of iron laws and uniformity of character is a dominant metaphysic of our era, we need to to call to mind the most evident phenomena that do *not* fit. Consider all that is real which does *not* follow invariant sequences. This is the inexhaustibly field of *the living moment* which is continuously new. It includes human thinking itself, the felt side of being alive of any being in whom blood runs, and the infinitude of the internal universe of images and thoughts to which awareness at any moment can open. Heraclitus once said that 'there is no limit to consciousness, so far and deep in every direction does it extend'. We can test the *truth* of his claim by inner witness. If we are not in the state of pathological reiteration of thought, there is no invariant sequence within oneself even, let alone uniformity of sequence across individuals. There is, in truth, no more verifiable evidence of what we know more directly than this experience of our thinking. There is no quantification or number which can be intelligibly assigned to *any* lived experience or reflection or internal vision. Even if thoughts could be counted, there is no predictable uniformity of their order across time unless their life-host is insanely fixated.[83] Thus, limits of scientific method become self-evident to the most immediate fact of the awareness being alive; but it is the mark of the meta-structure of thought within which conception has been confined that science's predictable external sequences have come to be assumed as the limits of reality. Life is thus sacrificed on the altar of fanaticism at the level of 'science' itself.

The world we live in and are aware of is not experienced or valued in its presence as the redundant, law-like phenomena laid bare by scientific method. This is a very powerful but limited device of understanding, but it is properly restricted to the inorganic world, and what is infrastructurally homogenous in the life-world.[84] The 'real world' for humanity is the directly experiencing world of being alive as human, whose subjecthood of 'who I am' is boundless in possibility.[85] Everywhere, however, we find corporations, governments, and academics calculating all that exists in the terms of formulae of separated repetition – describing, prescribing and locking humans into isolated, predictable sequences which are assumed as the nature of existence itself.

This is the invisible prison from which life-ground ethics releases the human subject.

Principle 3: Enforcing the Uniform Sequences as Technology

The third master principle of scientific method follows from the first two. It is the *technological extension of scientific understanding into performance mechanisms altering the world.* The knowledge constructs of scientific method are *materialised* as predictably behaving systems restructuring regions of the world by uniform sequences – from the technologies of auto-manufacture and agri-industry to media programming and genetic modification. It is on this account that the scientist Ursula Franklin calls these scientific extensions 'designs for compliance'.[86]

Like the first two principles, this third meta-principle of science is not stated in particular scientific technologies or their description, but all that we know as *'modern technology'* conforms to it in countless constructions and operations. This third principle is explained in profound detail by Marx's account in *Capital* of 'productive force development' from handicraft manufacture to machine industry. But it is not a principle that is consciously reflected upon as a *normative* regime. He presupposes technology's progression and subjugation of material production across the world as a biological process which no society can change except in its mode of ownership. Indeed Marx conceives of this 'productive force development' as the ultimately determining 'law' of historical advance.[87]

In fact, this third master principle now goes far beyond Marx in its totalising regulation of the world without itself being understood as an *organising idea*. It has come to be presupposed as an law-like *necessity* which rules humanity, rather than an instituted organising format which has been reified as a *structure of command*. Scientific technology has become in this way a totalising method of the global corporate system subsuming all that exists as more raw process to subjugate to its order. This third master principle regulating scientific-technological organisation of the world may be formally stated as follows:

Every form of production and reproduction whatever is (i) to be progressively analysed into its constituent phases with (ii) every step standardised and fixed into place in exceptionlessly invariant sequences.

The factory assembly line is the epitome of this organising meta-principle of the world system and its subsystems – a lock-step regime which hundreds of millions of humans must follow to earn their means of life. To achieve ever greater economies of time and motion, the successive phases of these assembly-line sequences are broken into ever more exact and confined steps of prescribed function. Every manufacturing system follows the rules of this technical paradigm of 'efficiency', and even the professions of medical care and education are increasingly made to follow suit with the monetised sequences of corporate 'value adding' their goal.[88]

The world is thus turned into a vast hierarchy of assembly lines with ever more far-reaching impositions. The 'soulless mega-machine' that Lewis Mumford spoke of is not an aberration, but *follows from the principles of scientific method as organising technique – constructing ever more cost-reductive technological and consumer commodities for the final ruling end of profit-maximising sale*. The overarching pattern is, at bottom, the constructed metaphysic of the global corporate system, yet its regulating value-set is by its nature eco-homocidal, for it commands the universalising disaggregation of world-life, and reorganisation of it as functions of mechanically ordering money sequences.

The Military Model of the Industrial Group-Mind

The inner logic of the global corporate system has as its prototype the military institution. Its nature is to *de-life*, to control and gain from others. This is a mechanistic value-set whose common instrument and metaphysic is scientific technology. Long before the industrial assembly line, there was the military structure of subjugating free life to redundant order and obedience for more efficient systems of killing and maiming other human beings.[89] This was and remains the proto-industrial paradigm mechanism of behavioural and material control upon which the systematic alienation of people from previous life-productive tasks, the separation of every individual from their roots and right to self-direction, the depersonalising uniformity of lock-step function, the assembly-line method of co-operation, and the strict hierarchy of top-down command of the modern industrial corporation.[90] As a macro-organisational structure, this system invades and mechanises planetary and social life as its opposite.

The parallel structures of organisation of military and industrial forms of rule are seldom disclosed – the rank-ordering and chain of command, the progressive division of labour to organise and sequence specific tasks and material resources in specialised functions and exactly ordered sequences, the strategic plans of engagement with strictly designated adversaries in battles for resources, tactical advantages and territories, the demand for precise punctuality, unquestioning obedience, uniformity of dress and blind loyalty expected from the troops and officers of the *corps*, the techno-fetishism which elevates the machine to the master paradigm of the organisation as well as its awesome and globe-girding apparatus of material power. Finally, there are the hypnotic slogans, logos, acronyms and symbols as the reflex-ordering content of the *interlocked group mind*.[91] Shop, and kill, are their defining poles of value meaning.

The transnational corporate system is, in fact, as military in its nature as a global system, overriding the market enterprise's early roots of producing for people's needs in free exchange, so that today it dictates the terms of the world's economies by unexposed military means – transnational *treaties* negotiated in foreign sites by state plenipotentiaries over which societies have no participation in even by parliamentary representation, armoured riot squads of thousands to suppress citizen voice when it arises, and since September 11, 2001, a globally organising police-state format for neutralising opposition as 'terrorist'.[92]

The military–corporate interconnection is intuited at many levels, but the systematic homologue of ordering life into mechanical uniformity, maximisation of total power over resisting limits, and mass-destructive consequences remain blinkered out. The thanatic value-set by which they are structured cannot see itself. Even the human officers and monetised beneficiaries of this global corporate system are transient and mortal functions of its *non-living organisation*. As the law of their motion, they analyse every process into ever more transient constituent phases, reduce free-life input towards zero, fix all living and extracted matter into rigidly circumscribed functions, and subsume all that is thus subjugated into the controlled sequences of inputs, outputs and detritus of the mega-machine *as if all this was dictated by physical laws*. So the order marches on with the necessity and measured tread of an Aztec sacrifice, rapidly extending its organising fiat-structure into all opposing peoples and territories, inside and outside, with no limit to the lines of advance. Only consciousness of the system's inner logic is not computed into its controls.

Once military and corporate systems are interlocked as one mega-structure and unified command spanning the globe itself, a NATO-armed transnational corporate order uniformly regulated by the World Trade Organisation centred in the mind-set of the 'Washington consensus' is set to seamlessly rule. That is the meaning of the post-September 11 US law HR 3005, the Trade Promotion Act, by which Congress rules out its own House debate and Senate ratification of the omnibus FTAA, running the master plan for an irreversible imperial corporate economy for the Western hemisphere behind the moving armed-force lines of 'America's New War Against Terrorism'. Here the military–corporate axis becomes one in the war of movement to impose the global corporate system anatomised below.

There is one condition. The public must remain captivated by the media-saturating programme which represents it all as 'global freedom' – held into place by a totalising system of conditioned desires and illusions which is set beneath the awareness of it. Preconscious acquiescence is the inner linchpin of the system – without which it cannot be reproduced, which it has no weapons to destroy once understood, and the exposure of which its closure cannot deal with. 'Satisfied consumers' are the trance of the system, and war its group-mind aggression.

If we step back into the vantage point of historical perspective and long-term regulating mind-set sedimenting and universalising over generations, we see that this lock-step programme of increasing planetary domination has become articulated through centuries of scientific technology as the *instrumental* mechanism of its advance, to finally stand as the ruling truth of the epoch – step-by-step division of all that exists into micro-managed elements organised to maximise a single aim. Everywhere this meta-system moves, its organising format has one absolute and overriding value-set that is taboo to question – the final imperative of serving the money-sequences of dominant private stockholders and their growth as the touchstone of 'freedom'. Everywhere too it depends on this prescribed law of human motion not being understood for what it is, even by those in command.

The WTO and the FTAA: The Meta-Programme for Global Corporate Rule

The advancing rounds of the World Trade Organisation (WTO) and the Free Trade Area of the Americas (FTAA) are the new 'world government' of which David Rockefeller spoke to the press in 1991, and to which his longstanding Trilateral Commission initiatives led with no 'glare of publicity'. Both of these ongoing institutional processes for codified world rule by transnational corporate rights are in keeping with self-maximising traditions of systematic planning and secrecy, and both articulate in countless overriding and binding regulations a single master purpose – secure and unlimited occupation of the planet by a world system calling itself the 'global free market'.

Like all preceding steps of this historic campaign for world rule under 'the trade and investment rules of a level playing field law', this planned rule of oligopolist corporations over all domestic economies, resources and public sectors does not respond to resistance, or move beyond dictation of more of the same. This is because its programme is structured to be life-blind. Propagandist deferral to concerns for 'overcoming world poverty' emerge as the resistance grows, but only as a further justification for the 'economic growth' that is presumed to follow from this plan. That more monetised growth, even were it to follow, has no demonstrated or real relationship to satisfaction of the basic life needs of the poor is not a consideration which can compute to the ruling value-set. In fact, this consideration is irrelevant to it. Only the rights of non-living corporations are recognised. Only further extension of these corporate rights is implemented. Whatever the latest propaganda about 'consulting civil society' or 'overcoming poverty' or 'concessions to the Third World', it is only new public relations packaging to expedite the same meta-programme regulating underneath consciousness of its meaning.

With increasing numbers of people across the world waking up to the slow motion coup d'état unfolding, there have been two steps of response. The first is standardised. The corporate media block out the life-and-death issues at stake, focus on the saleable spectacle of a large public confrontation, blame and trivialise the thousands of opponents who are blamed for the violence, and return to selling other images and distractions once the assault entertainment is over. The second response has been to distract the people with another war against a constructed Enemy – after September 11 a war declared to have no end.

Meanwhile the deepest and most systemic threat to civil and planetary life the world has ever faced persists and increases. Behind the unfolding disasters of regional economies and planetary ecosystems melting down, the threat to global life sustainability is driven by an *underlying meta-programme*, in terms of which every decision, every policy, every regulation and implementation is demanded and instituted by servant governments. The meta-principles constituting this mind-set are robotic, much like the mind-set of a fanatic cult. However, because they are presupposed by the corporate party and its media and political servants as 'necessary' and 'the basis of prosperity', what opposes them is repudiated *a priori* as 'naive', 'protectionist' or, eventually, 'terrorist'. This is the invisible prison of the ruling value-set. Although its connected meaning is *terra incognita* as a fanatical moral absolutism, we can decode its regulating principles into the following meta-frame of value premises which every demand and prescription of the corporate world agenda pre-consciously expresses.

1. The ultimate subject and sovereign ruler of the world is the trans-national corporation, operating by collective prescription and enforcement through the World Trade Organization in concert with its prototype the NAFTA, its European collaborator, the EU, and such derivative regional instruments as the APEC, the MAI, the FTAA, and so on. Together these constitute the hierarchical formation of the planet's 'rule-governed trade' by extra-parliamentary and transnational fiat.

2. Individual transnational corporations are the moving parts of this global corporate system. They are non-living aggregates of dominant private stockholders who, as individual persons, are protected by 'acts of incorporation' from liability for corporate harms done to societies, to other individuals, and to the environment, as well as from accumulated corporate debts or offences against national and international law. This is the legal armour around the agents of the global corporate system which affords them with unaccountability to domestic populations and governments for the 'external' damages caused to individuals, societies and environments around the world.

3. Transnational corporations acting in concert through the WTO and its related supranational constructs prescribe to and are represented by financed national government parties which act in these matters solely on behalf of transnational corporate access to foreign markets and resources with 'no barriers'. This private corporate rule over governments everywhere is understood as 'necessary to compete in the global market', and all must do so to retain 'market share'. Consequently, no binding regulation yet protects any right but that of transnational corporate investors, and not one article of any already signed international covenant or treaty protecting human rights, labour or the environment is binding on any part of any one of these 'agreements'. The Kyoto Treaty on climate-altering gases,

the Montreal Protocol on ozone-depleting chemicals and emissions, the Basel Convention on transboundary pollutants as well as the body of established international solemn agreements and covenants on human and labour rights are all excluded or overridden, in the last instance by final judgments of WTO trade-lawyer panels.

4. Trade and environment treaties and agreements obliging compliance with transnational corporate rights are proposed, negotiated and finalised behind closed doors and wide perimeters of 'security' by armed force, with police pepper spray, shackles, harassment or sur- veillance for those who protest publicly. To prevent 'populist distortions', public participation in or appeal against their decrees by anyone except corporate or state representatives are ruled out, and all disputes are adjudicated in secret before unelected authorities and tribunals with no public or elected observers of these proceedings permitted, and with no record of their proceedings published for public view. At the same time, populations across the world are obliged to pay all the costs of negotiating, instituting and enforcing these overriding prescriptions to the world's nations, and are obliged to pay all the fines and trade penalties imposed on their elected governments for legislating democratic or environmentally protective policies which are deemed to conflict with this unac- countable transnational regulatory authority. This Orwellian arrangement is known as 'investor-state dispute resolution'.

5. All executive authorities *within* individual corporate bodies are all the while bound by the 'fiduciary duty' to maximise monetised returns to their corporate stockholders as the overriding obligation of decisions and actions, thereby compelling them by corporate charter prescription to minimise all expenditures on protecting human and non-human life by worker pay, social benefits or environmental regulation. In this way, it becomes a violation of legally binding corporate morality for any of its operations to take account of the life interests of employees, surrounding communities and environ- ments, or even the future life of the world at the monetary cost of shareholders' continuous maximisation of money profit.

6. The system's universal principle of 'rationality' is, in consequence, to *externalise* all costs onto other individuals, societies and environ- ments so that no form of human existence or responsibility such as 'citizen' or 'person' or 'respecter of other life' is recognised by the market value calculus or its state servants in order to be 'efficient' and 'reduce cost burdens'. Only self-maximising 'firms' and their 'consumers' exist to this value-set. Its form of life is then everywhere prescribed as 'inevitable' for all peoples, and is proclaimed by its agents to offer societies across the world 'no alternative' and 'free' at the same time.

7. 'Consumers', in turn, are not co-extensive with human beings or even the majority of human beings. This is because only humans with *sufficient money-demand* to purchase corporate products are recognised by this global system as possessing any right to access *any* good – from food and water to housing, healthcare and whatever else can be privatised for profit. What can be 'privatised', or in reality, corporatised for profit, is accordingly assumed to include ever more of the conditions of planetary existence without any limit. Genetic structures, the body's most basic means of life, the elements of nature, and publicly funded knowledge are all thus being rapidly disassembled, restructured and appropriated by transnational corporations for their maximum returns in 'the shareholder value revolution'.

8. Any *alternative* mode for production or distribution of any priceable good – socially owned or controlled, publicly subsidised or assisted domestically, self-sufficient or co-operative, or declared without genetic modification or corporate additive – is a 'barrier to trade', 'inefficient' or 'discriminatory' and is made illegal under transnational trade regulations. If any society or government 'does not honour its trade obligations' or repudiates these arrangements themselves, it is deemed to be 'non-competitive', 'protectionist', 'monopolist' or 'communist', and attacked on the ground by every means available, including transnational trade embargo and armed invasion to 'prevent a threat to US interests' or 'the Free World'.

9. Consumers and investors with sufficient money-demand to exchange within the global market are, in fact, the *only* bearers of freedoms recognised by this system, and are axiomatically assumed to have no upper limit to their commodity consumption or their demand acquisition, even if an increasing majority of their fellow citizens or humanity have few or no means of existence. This is the *'non-satiety'* principle of neo-classical economics. It is also the unstated meaning of 'equality of opportunity' in global market doctrine and practice – the equality of money demand for those who have it, and not for any person, community or life form 'not competing efficiently in the new global market order'.

10. There is within the global corporate system no requirement of any kind, theoretical or practical, to recognize any *life need* of any individual (e.g., nourishing food) or society (e.g., non-toxic air) as rightful, or as a priority, or as an issue of choice within this system, however massive and extreme the gap between life-deprivation and over-consumption grows. Otherwise there would be 'ruinous state intervention in the market'. As a few hundred 'investors' exponentially increase their money demand to more than the total income of the majority of the world's population with their 'investments' irreversibly stripping the world's ecosystems at the same time, no policy

is even mooted by the UN to regulate this planetary disaster. The UN Secretary-General, on the contrary, instituted in 2001 a UN 'Global Compact' to require all UN agencies to enter into 'corporate partnership' with the world's richest transnational corporations.

11. Whatever pollution, degradation, overloading, exhaustion or destruction of local or planetary ecosystems occurs, and however irreversibly devastating in consequences to human and biodiverse life these damages from corporate extractions, effluents, and commodities prove to be, there is *not one binding article in any transnational trade treaty or agreement* (excepting intra-European) which protects or seeks to protect any human or environmental life condition or good. These are judged by the value-set to be 'not trade issues'. All 'scarcities' thus arising are assumed, with no scientific evidence to substantiate the assumption, to be correctable by market price mechanisms and technological substitutability alone. This is why the US Congress refuses to comply with the Kyoto Treaty until it makes all pollution abatement measures conform to a system of saleable pollution credits – which have never reduced pollution, but which accord instituted corporate rights to pollute which can be sold as new and free equity, and which can be profited from at another, new level of the global market.

12. However many millions or billions of society's or the world's human population are misemployed, underemployed or starvation-waged with not enough to live on, and however life-destructive and chronically debilitating their hours and conditions of work are – a majority of the world altogether – there is no principle, norm or standard in neo-classical market theory or global market practice which recognises or can recognise any of these depredations of human life *as* an issue or a problem. On the contrary, this life-blind paradigm can only compute these strippings of most of the world's people as a new 'flexibility of labour supply' and a multiple 'opportunity to reduce the costs of labour' by exercise of new transnational corporate rights to produce in the lowest-cost zones of the world and sell in the highest-scale markets with no 'barriers erected to trade'.

13. Any public or government intervention in the presupposition and implementation of any and all of principles (1) to (12) in any way is attacked as 'an interference in the free market'. Any prior cultural, historical, or democratic achievement or institution limiting the systematically life-destructive effects of their unrestricted operation is deplored as 'a distortion' or 'impediment to the market', and targeted for elimination by transnational trade and investment instrument. This is a cumulative and always advancing line of demand by endless transnational regulatory 'agreements', and it moves across national borders and domains of life like a sustained military campaign in its

relentless uniformity of prescriptions to target populations, while blind to the destructive effects as non-existent or unavoidable.

14. No *autonomy* of domestic market in any good or service, strategic use of any natural resource or necessity, protected public utility or social sector, product-safety, quality or licensing standard, local procurement practice or grant is consistent with the 'rules-based international trade'. Such market 'distortions' are, therefore, slated for challenge and elimination by trade prescription or scheduled regulatory assimilation. This is a pattern everywhere documentable, but does not register as an issue to the ruling value-set of politicians, the corporate media, and former corporate employees who negotiate the agreements. What remains constant through the cumulative momentum and volume of these trade and investment decrees is that every article of tens of thousands is constructed to guarantee that dominantly transnational corporations can exploit and increasingly control domestic economies and public sectors across the world with no curtailing limit permissible in law.

15. Local, national and global *management of the money-demand drivewheels of this system is over 95 per cent controlled by for-profit corporate financial and banking institutions* which have covertly appropriated control over almost all government bond issues and investor and consumer lines of credit from government currency creations, national bank loans and state statutory reserves. With no gold or other non-paper standard remaining to control it, corporate bank and financial leveraging has become effectively limitless, with central bank interest-rate raises in the new regime applied only to decrease workers' rising wages and social-sector spending. This is the always *hidden* underside of the system's propelling domestic and transnational force, why covert financial deregulation of money-demand supply is the secret to its every advance, and why no deep limit can be drawn against world occupation by corporate financial mechanisms until the creation of money demand is constitutionally reappropriated by public authority as its essential basis of sovereignty and investment in the common interest (a major concern of the next chapter).

Together these underlying principles of the global market system constitute its fixed and largely unseen meta-structure of perception, understanding and judgement in accordance with which all its policy formation and enforced regulation of societies and economies across the world proceed. There is no principle of 'the free market', 'investment', 'competition', 'comparative advantage', 'efficiency', 'fiscal responsibility', 'labour flexibility', 'inflation control', 'growth', 'sustainability', 'social welfare', 'national prosperity', 'justice', 'civil society participation', 'poverty reduction', or other old or new slogan promulgated by global market institutions and advocates that does not conform to all of (1) through (15) in doctrine and effect. Whenever it is claimed otherwise, one may *ask for the evidence* from any 'free trade agreement' on the planet. The response will always be silence, diversion to another topic, and, if the question is pursued publicly, surveillance by the police.

The Life-Economy Turn

As any life-grounded standpoint can discern, this is a mind-locked value-set, and perhaps more extreme in its fanaticism than preceding totalitarian structures of command. It threatens to usurp every level of social and ecological life condition still existing. Given its self-referential absolutism and history of overrunning and re-engineering whatever life form or organisation stands in the way, we should not be surprised at the trajectory of development to the cumulative catastrophe emerging today in the third millennium. The deepening contradictions between this system's demands and human and ecological requirements requires a response which is as systemic in bearings, but is reconnected to the life-serving institutions of society and its planetary host. Into this apparent abyss of no alternative, the repressed life economy emerges.

The life economy is not a theoretical construction. Its own value-set and institutions have evolved over centuries. In the case of language, the prototype of its infrastructure of production and reproduction, the 'civil commons' of universally accessible life-value reaches back to the origins of the species.[93] As with all the subsequently evolved institutions for protecting and enabling shared human life and environmental conditions, the regulating ethos of the civil commons provides the value bearings to steer the way out of the species' greatest ever crisis. Although this life economy embraces all of the social constructs which society has developed across epochs and cultures, each distinct realm of the civil commons' evolution is defined *by the life means it enables universal access to* – whether the words of language, clean water sources, the rule of life-protective law, universal education and healthcare, breathable air and biodiverse environments, the shared music, arts and public spaces of different cultures, or the *meaning* of all of these as society's deep life economy. It is this shared but repressed ground of the real 'common-wealth' whose realms of serving life connect underneath the pathologic subsystem of money capital organisation of the world for price and profit. Here we move to the bearer of the *life capital* of human reproduction and development and, in the end, the organising value ground of the human project itself.

In the analysis to follow, our focus will be on excavating and putting into play this life economy's instituted system selectors for social life defence against the global corporate occupation which is structured to strip world-life organisation. Throughout, the regulating value-set of the life-ground ethic selects for means of life capital growth, not means of money capital growth, as society's properly regulating principle of governance across generations. As our step-by-step movement through the primary determinants of the global market system advances, we will discover that these repressed civil commons institutions together provide or point to the national and international framework of life-serving bearings, a world common cause, to reconnect humanity to its shared life foundations – by a truly 'rules-based international economy' rather than a preconscious war waged by a fanatic financial-military programme on human society and planetary life.

Part III

The Paradigm Turn: The Life Economy Principles from Where We Stand

7

Regulating the Money System for Life Capital Gain

The Constitutional Life Economy

The general problem confronting those concerned about humanity's civil and ecological life-ground in the face of the global war of occupation analysed in the previous chapters can be formulated in one meta-principle. *The ruling economic paradigm is structured to grow the money-demand of transnational investors rather than the lives of peoples and their life conditions.* Societies and environments are understood as means of corporate stockholders' profit-maximisation, rather than stock markets as means of promoting the shared life good. The world of value is in this way turned upside down. Human and planetary life are subjugated to become disposable means of a global financial faction's market command, rather than being constitutionally subordinated to the sovereign common life interests of societies and their environmental hosts.

In the previous chapters, we have seen this meta-pattern systematically at work in the politics, crises and wars of the global market as well as in the distorted scientific, technological and trade regimes which have become servo-mechanisms to the global corporate market. While this world system has been officially represented as bringing the world 'humanitarian interventions', 'new market freedoms', and 'economic growth to solve the problems of poverty', the opposite has occurred at the level of reality. Destruction of social infrastructures, oligopolist control of economies, ecological collapse, unprecedentedly rising extremes of income inequality, and pervasive insecurity of livelihood have, in fact, rapidly hollowed out life economies across the planet.[1]

Behind the armed repressions, economic melt-downs, opinion polls, political struggles, new governments and wars there lies a regulating order of life sacrifice which holds the world in thrall like a ruinous mass superstition. A life-disconnected economic paradigm assumes that 'invisible hand' allocation of the world's life resources by self-maximising money-capital gain necessarily and optimally serves the life requirements of societies and their citizens. A sustainable economic order, in contrast, moves to the regulating framework of *life economy standards* which: (1) select for fulfilment of the vital needs and capabilities of citizens; (2) re-establish constitutional control over unaccountable debt-issuing of global money stocks, lawless degradation, exhaustion and despoliation of human and environmental life systems, and (3) reverse the corporate usurpation of responsible legislative government at local, regional, national and international levels.

These are major reorientations of governing value-set. However, the point is not the impossible conceit 'to build society anew', or to overthrow the constitutional common ground, or to forfeit the stage of productive powers which have developed – all known dead-ends. Rather the act of life-grounded social intelligence is to recognise that the evolved public bases of modern civilisation have been repressed by a delusional and failed economic paradigm. The primary step is to think beyond its life-blind value-set. This requires recognition that its pseudo-market model is structured to transmute all that exists into more money for money sequencers with no remainder, propelled by millenarian fantasies of 'necessary sacrifices' and 'market miracles', and ruling the world with the most widely propagated magical doctrine in human history.

Responding social organisation cannot rely on an apocalyptic reaction to this disorder, which substitutes a counter-utopianism promising an equally fanatical reinvention of society. The first premise of value to guide life-grounded judgement is straightforward, but it is sufficiently decisive in restoring life-value to sovereignty. In contrast to global market absolutism, the life economy paradigm subordinates money-demand as instrumental, not the other way round. Once this first premise of value is clear, the institutionalised instruments of the existing economy are understood as *means* of the life economy – in particular the money system itself. The point then is to know what *ranges of possibility* are available to the life economy which are *consistent with developed means of material production and constitutional rule.* These are the already evolved common ground of society's shared life interests, and the historical ground of any viable and enduring social system.

The Four Determinants of the Global Market System

Let us penetrate beyond competing doctrinal mystifications to core in on the indisputable general facts that together steer the global market system as its primary determinants in the current era:

1. that *money demand* drives the wheels of the system;
2. that *investment direction* is the determination of humanity's economic future;
3. that *corporate commodity cycles* are in aggregate the materialised outcomes of the global corporate system's restructuring of the world; and
4. that this or any other economic system is governed *by binding laws or rules* external to its processes.

These determinants are *structuring orders* of 'the economy' through time, with cultures and ideologies at one end and genetic codes and ecosystems at the other. What needs above all to be clear is that for any life economy, *the regulating goal is the fullness of life of individual humans and social and natural life-hosts, not the increased value of its instrumental determinants.*[2] Every step of the economic manifesto provided here follows directly from this baseline understanding.

In Place of Market Fanaticism: Life Standards as Economic Selectors

The life economy standpoint is distinguished from the fanatic standpoint in a straightforward way. The fanatic assumes that an economy is there to serve something other than the lives of its members, and is not deterred from this master assumption, of whatever kind it may be, by the systemic harm done to people's lives by its imposition. Adoption of the life economy rather than the fanatic standpoint means that the co-ordinates we inherit of money-demand, its investment, and its product and commodity cycles are *not* presupposed as ultimate frameworks of value *in themselves*, whatever deprivation they may cause to humanity or despoliation they may visit on life conditions in general. They are *instrumental* formations, and do not prescribe to the world independently of human beings and social policies what must be obeyed with no alternative.

Since economic orders do not fall from the sky as ready made 'laws' of existence, but are decided in some way, a thought-through value system – which any economic paradigm should be – seeks whatever alternatives better satisfy vital needs and enable individual and collective life capabilities by doing so. That is the regulating value of any sane system of production and distribution, as distinguished from a need-disconnected, money-sequencing system which cannot realise it except in the delusions of magical thinking. On the other hand, we must play with the hand we are dealt, the conditions of the historical world as they have developed to this point. The age-old dream, most famously repeated by Marx, 'from each according to ability, to each according to need' *may* one day be generalisable beyond healthy families without money as the exchange medium; yet a principal property of any economy worthy of the name is *non-waste*, and the money exchange medium is not at all 'the root of all evil' insofar as it promotes *this* end, while also enabling universal exchange. On the other hand, the money medium is not good or necessary in any final sense, and we have seen how it comes to be the vehicle of world-destructive waste where it has been inverted into an end-in-self. Production and distribution for life need, and that, in turn, for life capacity and experience in more comprehensive enjoyment and expression – this is the only *ultimate* value on earth. Any sane economy is there to serve it in opening horizons of life worth.[3]

Working with the life-value principles defined through this study, the analysis which follows builds from what is known *within* the ranges of institutional possibility. On the one hand, such unpacking of the given's possibilities lacks the exhilarating uplift of a total revolutionary negation, which many of us are driven by. Such visions of complete liberation, however, 'gang aft agley', not least because they cannot think through the parameters of going from here to there without foreclosing what is most humanly distinctive – unpredictable choice, on the one hand, and habit inertia, on the other. There are also the limits of knowing beyond the past that has been learned from. Perhaps most interestingly, there are *far wider horizons of life-serving possibility on the basis of the given than are recognised.* Even the codified civil commons of developed contemporary 'market societies', as stunted as they have become, is an open arch through which possibility grows as we comprehend their long evolution.

Working with the at-hand historicity of an epoch's economic config-uration of *money-demand, investment, commodity cycles* and *the codified rules of the game*, we now open the envelope of the given to see *the pathways of choice for a life economy.* The *life-value parametric* in terms of which explanation of every problem and solution here proceeds is one in which *satisfaction of vital needs* as defined, *to enable universally compossible enjoyment and expression of human life capabilities* (of thought, experience and action), is the regulating frame of value reference in every matter. Thus, as we will spell out in detail ahead, it follows from these *regulating life standards* that the performance of an economy – that is, a non-wasteful system of production and distribution of goods for life – will select for nourishing food, clean air and water, stable and pleasant housing, and so on for its members, whether the *method* is market ordered, or a mix of public and market production, or socialist. The premise here is that an economy that is not dysfunctional selects for non-wasteful production and distribution of life goods otherwise in short supply, however it may do so.

Given that life standards guide an intelligent as opposed to a supersti-tious economic ordering, I will now focus on the *constitutional system-deciders* which are available to steer the existing economic disorder in life-serving directions to which its paradigm is blind. The ground and guide throughout will be what it has been throughout this study, and what is most lacking in the great 'globalisation' debate – *exact principles of value base and judgement applied within the built frame of the constitutionally possible*. Although the notion of need for a 'moral compass' now frequently emerges from well-intentioned observers, the life-destructive value-set of the ruling system remains mostly unrecognised, and its constitutional options repressed. There are many surprises when one lays bare the unseen possibilities of the life economy which have already been codified in distinct institutions, but remain unconnected across them.

Money

Reclaiming Sovereign Authority Over Society's Money Creation

The money-demand that propels the contemporary world economic system through every moment of its sequences and exchanges is not, as so widely assumed in market culture, a 'universal force' or 'what makes the world go round'. Money-demand is a social construction, and is recognised by every sovereign government as its constitutionally inherent and exclusive powers over the *currency, coinage and credit* within its territories and jurisdiction.[4] These social powers, in turn, are held on condition of the more basic and ultimate constitutional obligation to promote the common interest of the people bound by the laws of that government.[5] This is the first and foremost *general fact* of money demand's legitimacy and accountability under law.

'End of the nation-state' and 'keep the economy independent of government' doctrines are, in contrast, amnesiac opiates. These and other ideological performatives provide the room required for private financial institutions to seize control of society's money-and-credit powers without a public outcry. Once seized, the public pay all the bills and banks extract all the credit and interest back from governments and citizens. This process has surged back and forth since the American Revolution, which – in another cultivated amnesia of public memory – was in large part fought to reclaim this power for the thirteen colonies from the private Bank of England.[6] Despite the American Revolution itself and, later, the Civil War in which Lincoln confronted the same rule by the banker faction now in New York rather than London, governments have been returned to their original financial subjugation under imperial rule. The public via their governments not only pay all the costs of instituting and protecting the currency for private banks and financial institutions through all its exchanges, they also end up paying compounding interest debts to these private banks to provide the very currency-and-credit powers which these banks have, in effect, stolen from the sovereign authority of governments beneath public notice.[7]

The constitutional prerogative over the creation of currency and credit is a very basic and general fact of sovereign peoples which the most distinguished heads of state have emphasised as a first principle of lawful government in the common interest for centuries – from Thomas Jefferson to the longest-serving Prime Minister in the British Commonwealth, W.L. Mackenzie King, from Abraham Lincoln to Franklin Roosevelt.[8] Yet this general fact has been everywhere repressed from view as private banks have winched back the powers they were compelled to yield when their policies of self-serving credit creation and reduction bankrupted the productive economy and brought on the Great Depression and its consequence of World War II. Since 1945, after *public* control of money and credit creation had both ended the Depression and resourced the World War against fascism, the amnesia has been recultivated with the take-back by private banks of public currency creation powers. Constitutional government credit and currency creation by central banks' lending to governments as their sole shareholder has been slowly surrendered by finance ministries behind the scenes. The surrender of public power has been silent, and pushed by the incoherent banker dogma that government currency and credit creation are an 'interference in the economy' and have perilous consequences of 'inflation'.

The first allegation sets itself into opposition to the constitutional powers of public authority. The second provides justification to wrest these economy-steering powers away for banks' unbounded private profit. Yet in paradigmatic expression of the corporate 'system of big lies' analysed in Chapter 4, banks accuse governments of doing to the economy what *their* multiplications of speculative and compound-interest bearing credit do at a furiously stepped-up rate.[9] The fact is that dominant private banks and financial institutions have wrested away over 95 per cent of existing currency and credit creation for ever-expanding private returns, and have increased both public and private indebtedness to higher levels than in 1929.[10]

Reclamation by public and elected governments of control over society's currency and credit can be gradual or rapid. In either case, it proceeds by exertions of constitutional process which have worked in past achievements of public prosperity over centuries, and across continents. The first method of effective currency demand in an economy, with a pedigree long prior to Keynes, is by the direct device of exchangeable notes issued by instituted government in amounts corresponding to productive means – as was very successfully done by five US colonies in the form of colonial script prior to the interference by England which led to the War of Independence. It was later done by Abraham Lincoln's government when faced by a 17 per cent interest demand by New York bankers in 1861 when his historic administration printed $300 million in 'greenbacks' to finance the Union during the Civil War.[11] It has, in fact, been done by government credit creation, minted currency or non-tax government bonds held by citizens during most productive growth periods when bankers have not controlled society's economic lifeblood for their private profit.

Joseph Huber and James Robertson estimate that the private banks' appropriation of government's credit-creating authority presently loses £45 billion to the United Kingdom public treasury a year, costs the overall British economy £66 billion a year, and confers super-profits to these banks of £21 billion a year.[12] Although Prime Minister Blair has specially distinguished himself in handing public power over the Treasury to the banks in return for London financial district ('the City') support, the money-siphon regime of private banks directs hugely costly and counterproductive transfers of public and market wealth across the entire global market system – at an expanding rate of take across national borders with 'global financial deregulation'. The key lever as elsewhere is the cultivated ignorance of the public and the intellectual class who know nothing less than the mechanics of these operations. The fate of pariah for economists raising the issue is instructive. Clifford Hugh Douglas, a pre-Depression advocate of the idea of public credit creation, was labelled a 'crank' by every newspaper that banks advertised in or lent to.[13] The still-remembered John Maynard Keynes reintroduced the idea in a different form (public spending rather than individual credit) in a period when people knew the regime now in place had catastrophically failed and had only recovered by the public spending on war; however, Keynes' own eclipse since 1980 indicates the pattern of instilled mind-block across generations. Concealed behind well-tailored suits, conspiratorial silence and obscurely contradictory dogma, corporate banks are an epitome of the reigning corporate disorder.

Currency Reserves to Control Inflation, to Discipline Banks' Predatory Money Creation by Debt-Issuance, and to Fund Non-Debt Public Loans

Credit creation is not the only sovereign instrument which has been covertly appropriated from society's commonwealth by the financial legerdemain of the private banking faction. The further resource of currency and credit available to elected governments is the *currency reserve*. It has been and can be a primary lever for the public interest in making credit available to governments interest-free, as well as in controlling inflationary compound-interest debt loads and billion-dollar credit speculations by banks which produce no value for the vast new inputs of demand they put into market motion to serve their private capital accumulations. Behind the corporate bank take-over of society's credit creation, private banks have been and can be obliged to deposit hard-currency reserves with the central bank to back their loans and speculations. This curtails their inflationary demand inputs which now have no public inhibitor. The reserve has long been 'fractional', and the fraction becomes ever smaller over time towards zero. There is no good reason that a 100 per cent reserve requirement for money loaned is not a mandatory requirement of public financial management, leaving currency and credit creation with constitutional authorities required to represent the public interest and not solely their own. That the idea is never spoken in public discourse on government financing indicates the transgenerational pattern of concealment and fraud at work. Loaning money that you don't have to others and collecting compounding interest on what you don't have to lend in organised off-set arrangements with others doing the same to avoid detection of short funds would be a major criminal conspiracy for all other agents in the market, but private banks control society's currency creation powers by precisely this method.

It is not 'inevitable' that governments permit this systematic fraud at taxpayers' massive expense. Required bank reserves can be reclaimed from the now near-zero levels banks have silently manipulated. The reclamation of society's money-creation powers would be more successful than a revolutionary assault on legislatures to replace governing parties, and it is constitutionally lawful. Recall that it is on the fractional or zero-reserve basis that private banks print limitless billions in compound-interest loans for the debt-enslavement of nations, poor householders and students, ever more gigantic oligopolist and monopolist mergers, transnational corporate take-overs of domestic and foreign economies, pervasive stock-market manipulations, and tides of currency speculation money hollowing out developing countries – with governments all the while bailing them out at public expense whenever they are threatened with the insolvency of fleeced debtors. The Long-Term Capital Management Fund that boasted Nobel Laureates and rich Washington dignitaries on its vast speculation operation and hedge-fund that was bailed out by the US Federal Reserve when it over-pyramided is only a symptom of a system of financial looting that rings the globe with predatory money-leveraging at the rest of the world's expense – often the starvation and death of millions whose governments have been caught on the hook, and increasingly the debt servitude of citizens. Arrangement to recover the unseen base of this macro-parasite depletion of societies' life resources is not only lawful, it is obliged by fiduciary trust to the citizens and the public interest that governments represent. The pivot point of private bank control of currency creation is the cloud of public unknowing concealing it, which includes political economists of the left.

It is not just a question of lost economic resources and the confiscated futures of societies and individuals that the for-profit *creation* of society's money-demand causes. The *licence to print money* is expropriated from public authority by private financial powers to charge double and more for and freely speculate with across borders. If inflation is caused, the solution is always to charge more for the money-demand the banks create

by debt-issuance, thus ruining small businesses and escalating unemployment. If banks get caught out by squeezing their debtors too far or
speculating billions on stock market prices, mergers, buyouts, and other
unproductive money-sequence schemes, servant governments bail them
out with the taxpayers' money. These taxpayer-funded bail-outs began
very noticeably at a public cost of $500 billion with high-interest US
savings-and-loan banks in the 1980s after the first major wave of
'financial deregulation'. They have continued with public-coffer bail-
outs of Wall Street and other predatory investment banks and syndicates
from foreign economic melt-downs brought on by these very money
sequence speculators. This is a primary determinant of the slow-motion
depression the world economy enters from the confiscated trillions from
public and private economies across the world which this deregulated
money-sequencing regime has predictably propelled.

Raising currency-reserve requirements for banks begins from the 0–4
per cent down to which they have covertly whittled their loan reserves
can move rapidly or by degrees to 100 per cent. All money that is spent
by banks in compound-interest debt issues and stock speculations can
only be spent once with full reserve backing. The 100 per cent reserve
requirement is not only a necessary and constitutional instrument for
controlling the economically destructive money creations and exits
transnational banks they now unleash across borders which have
escalated to more dangerous and socially debilitating levels than before
in history. It is not clear how any *less* than 100 per cent cash reserve for
privately loaned money for profit is reasonable from a market standpoint.
Lending to others beyond savings one has or has been entrusted with for
investment is not a right that one can discover in any constitution or
legal property right. Moreover, the primary importance of an economy's
currency creation requires management by accountable public authority,
not private market agents whose only instituted interest is to expand
their own money stocks. Unlike Adam Smith's market agents, they do
not produce consumable goods, or sell what they have at the lowest price.
Unlike other property holders, what they benefit from has no basis in
right but only from the debts they issue without savings. Unlike
governments, they have no legitimacy in their control of society's credit
from its track record of production.

That is why banks' proper currency reserve for the money they loan
and invest was long ago proposed to be 100 per cent by the economic
conservative, Milton Friedman, and before that by the distinguished
Irving Fisher and the most outstanding economist of his generation,
William Simon.[14] That these striking facts too are not known indicates
the closure of silence around banking activities, which now lend and
speculate with no required savings reserve, and with no regulatory limit
on their private money creation in official denominations. US President
Thomas Jefferson long ago said what has been reiterated in different form

by statesmen since (emphasis added): 'I believe that banking institutions are more dangerous to our liberties than standing armies. Already they have raised up a monied aristocracy that has set the government at defiance. The *issuing power should be taken from the banks and restored to the people to whom it properly belongs.*'[15]

Despite all that has been reported by the most unimpeachable witness about banking interests and the public interest over centuries, history and learning have been silenced in the corporate culture with incalculable damage to the public interest. The complete repression of *constitutional accountability for money creation* reveals the depth of the disorder. Whatever does not fit into the usurping rule of the financialised economy is abolished from view. This unexposed structure of censorship regulates captive societies into their most fateful blindness. While it locks individuals and governments in permanent and rising debt servitude, it simultaneously rules out governments' creating public credit and spending new money into circulation in accordance with productive means to serve the common life interest. Public treasuries instead pay increasing debt and interest tribute to ever richer private banks which bankrupt their resources, and abandon their spending on social assets as 'unaffordable'.

There is no fraud in history that remotely approaches the monopoly expropriation by private banks of the public powers of money creation and dissolution. Its invisible chains bind and imprison the lives and life economies of peoples across continents. Yet how does such a regime endure? The inner logic is always the same. Understanding which exposes or conflicts with the interests of its rule is blocked out by the official culture. When it persists, the cry of 'nonsense' or 'subversion' goes up from the profession of economics which is trained to assume the given order as physical law. The larger group-mind follows suit. Now, some may think the reign of public silence is a coincidence, or that to observe the pattern is merely to succumb to 'a conspiracy theory', but such readings simply reveal the power of a ruling value-set to confine the mind within its frame. The test of the mind-lock is to find an economics text that ever mentions the issue, or a history book that tells of its long history.

The requirement of *bank reserves* for the money banks to lend and speculate with achieves two restorations of financial order. First, it would reduce the private banks' currency and credit-creation which is the leading edge of corporate *control* of the global economy. Reserves do this *in proportion to the reserve requirement.* Remember that even apparently non-financial corporations reap more profits from their private credit-creating operations than they do from merchandise sales. Here at least tangible consumer commodities are exchanged in return for the debt-charges. However, this arrangement too provides currency creation that properly belongs to accountable public authority, with private financial interests creating new money demand for commodities of which it may not be in the public interest to produce ever more (e.g., private leisure machines that burn non-renewable fuels and pollute the air and atmosphere). Bear in mind as well that whatever interest charges these commodity-producing corporations must themselves pay for their own debts provides tax write-offs, thereby fractioning the cost of the credit compared to other market agents.

Reserve requirements also reduce *inflationary* pressures. This is because they reduce the supply of money to the market, setting an upper limit to what money-demand can be put into the economy by loans and interest charges. Without savings back-up or reserve requirement, banks only need to enter the loan in their ledgers to set new money-demand into motion with no upper limit – as long as debtors can pay back.[16] That the anti-inflationary lever of bank-reserves is not used by governments – whereas interest raises on the public and governments are, and that continuously – is a telling indicator of how private banks control governments themselves – or, perhaps more accurately, how a group-think mind-set regulates both with even the debt-enslaved public assuming the inevitability of the enslavement.

The required reserve for debt-issuance costs the banks the use of the money-reserve they would rather be speculating with or lending out again, but it sets a limit to what money-demand they can leverage. That is why the reserve requirement is repelled from bankers' view as an intolerable cost burden even if it reduces inflation far more efficiently than interest-rate hikes for their coffers. Yet the private interests of banks do not explain why governments follow in line, and approve interest-rate rises instead of higher bank reserves for the money they lend. Central banks are run by bankers with the banker's value-set, but they remain by law subordinate to elected governments. Rather than the public paying vastly more to increase the debt revenues of banks for doing nothing, the proper 'austerity' to 'wrestle inflation to the ground' is not to bankrupt small businesses and put millions out of work by high debt-charges, but to restore bank reserves for the money banks to limit their multiplication of their own money stocks with no productive contribution to the economy.

A third way in which reserve requirements serve the common interest is that they are available to *governments to borrow* at zero or nominal interest. The money is thus borrowed without the extra compound interest charges to private banks for providing governments with the created credit that properly belongs to the public sector. This is why Huber, following Friedman, who in turn followed his teacher, Irving Fisher, with each of them reaffirming long-existing and central civil commons practice, all propose 100 per cent currency reserves for private bank loans so as to leave accountable public authorities to create all new public currency backed by the public.

The American Colonies, the American Revolution and Abraham Lincoln – not to mention the governments of revolutionary France and Russia – all depended on this public money creation to relieve themselves from financial parasite classes. Japan's Ministry of Finance did so as well in arranging long-term, low-interest loans for the development of an automobile industry.[17] Every one of these diverse success stories has had an economically successful characteristic in common. *They all managed new debt-free money into productive circulation for purposes accountable to their citizens and the common interest of their societies,* rather than abdicating control of society's money creation to private bank monopoly. They succeeded because all reclaimed their constitutional authority, blocked the financial faction from determining society's future, and achieved the economic efficiency of eliminating hugely depleting and non-productive bank charges.[18]

Money Creation by Public Authority in Accordance with Life Capital Accounting

In this way, societies everywhere can reclaim their constitutional freedom from servitude to banks by pursuing their sovereign path in strict accord with *life capital principles*. Reserves for loans simply require that banks confine themselves to lending the currency or savings that they have under law, and that all new credit and currency creation is vested in the publicly accountable authorities where it constitutionally belongs. The mechanics of reclamation of public authority over money creation are not obscure. Central banks simply issue the exchange notes into the accounts which they hold for their governments, which then *spend it into circulation in the public interest which they are elected to represent and to which they are accountable by the policies they have sworn to uphold.* Public authorities can certainly be corrupt, but they are accountable to the electorate and the public interest as defined in any legitimate democracy. In contrast, private financial interests are sworn or obliged to *no* common interest whatever, serve only their shareholders' enrichment as their final fiduciary duty, and pressure governments *into* corruption by these money-lever controls. What is most important to society in any monetised or market economy – its medium of exchange and public credit lifeblood – must return to public control as a fundamental condition of responsible government, as the greatest statesmen have long understood.

Return to the public of its public medium of exchange which is, in turn, solely sustained by common belief in it – thus the term, 'credit', *whatever all members of a society accept in exchange* – is thus cleanly achieved by constitutional means.[19] With society back in control of its central constitutional instrument in a market economy, the common interest can be served instead of ruinously defrauded by a shadowy faction producing nothing. Those private agents who still conspired to *create currency denominating itself as public exchange* would be subject to prosecution for criminal violation of the law as has long been the case with other forgery or counterfeiting.

Once we understand the general fact of money demand's lawful control by public authority, and its effective use by note issues, credit and/or reserve drawing rights, as well as regulatory authority over the currency-and-credit creation policies of private banks, we can see, more clearly, that *public control of money stock creation as a medium of exchange is the hidden, primary layer of responsible government's fulfilment of its defining obligation of serving the public interest*. Superstitious diversions to 'the invisible hand' or 'banker impartiality' are incantational spells which, if they had been believed, would have left the thirteen colonies in the control of private London bankers, bankrupted the United States of Lincoln, left the world in the Great Depression, made the fight against fascism an economic impossibility (as indeed US corporate heads proclaimed it was), and ruled out Asian automobile manufacture as a violation of market laws.

Life-economy principle 1: **constitutional public accountability of all currency-credit creation by requirement of 100 per cent legal tender reserves for interest-bearing loans**.

Investment Direction

The Life Disconnection of the Money Capital Paradigm

Since money demand in the form of credit turns the wheels of all new investment, the obligation of responsible government is to ensure that *new investment* works for the economy and not against it. The self-evident, however, is heresy in the corporate culture where the causal relationship between investment and society's economic well-being is suspended by inviolable faith in monetised numbers and the magical hand. Thus, the corporate market system allocates resources in mindless disregard for long-term economic sustainability or satisfaction of life needs because it is the first article of final faith that all must come right by the optimum of equilibrium driven by monetary and consumption maximisation within the market's self-regulating, perpetual-motion machine.

Consequences follow from a disconnected economic paradigm. They include unmoored money creation and speculation in ever greater volumes and velocities, profitable manufacture of life-destructive weaponries at a billion-a-day cost, worldwide strip-mining of publicly owned natural resources, and saturating corporate propaganda to borrow and spend more even as debt increases and wages decline. In this universal rule of corporate money-sequencing as end-in-self of the 'economy', *no accountability of investment to the public interest* is permitted to be raised as an issue. This prohibition of accountability to life requirements and common interest is called 'the free market', and – in its global phase – 'the Free World'.

There are two types of investment in the world of neo-classical theology, although they are not distinguished in its doctrine. Both adopt the money-sequence form. The first form of money-sequence investment is in material commodity production, to be discussed below as 'The Commodity Cycle'. The second and increasingly dominant form of money sequence is not really investment, but money sequencing without a produced commodity between its money input and profit output – as with bank loans and speculations for profit with no mediating production. What is not recognised is not only the delinkage of these money-sequence investments from any life-need in their commitment solely to more monetised returns to private stockholders, but their *a priori exclusion of any investment in any public life good* (e.g., social security, public transit, or keeping the air breathable). Investment proceeds solely by the principle of netting maximum monetary gains for private market agents by (1) production of private commodities for individual consumers, or (2) money sequencing producing no consumable good. Investment outcome will, for the universal true faith, be optimal by a doctrinally postulated equilibrium of the deist mechanism that is assumed as the 'regulating hand'.

The logic here is not economic, but anti-economic – one might say culturally insane. The question we raise here, however, is more focused: *what is ruled out* by this atomised structure of resource allocation and consumption? Since nothing which is not an atomic money sum or priced commodity *transacted between two market agents* can register in this paradigm's terms of reference, then *no shared life good can exist for it*. Such an instituted mind-set can only be coherent within a small isolated market with all social responsibility and costs borne by an external authority, as with small feudal markets outside the domain of ruling lords, which is the market's prototype structure. However, this closed frame of reference is in principle incapable of selecting for investment in even *public goods*, let alone life capital or goods which don't return a competitive profit. It is true that the 'collective needs' of armed protection of private property and business infrastructures are assumed by this value-set as unavoidable *costs* by tax imposts, but only what protects and provides infrastructure and inputs for *business* investment counts as acceptable government costs with, moreover, most of these costs borne by non-business taxpayers.

Beyond the Blind Eye of Market Allocation: The Life Economy Turn to Investment in Public Goods

Public expenditures and collective goods *beyond* these are repudiated. They are 'wasteful', 'unaffordable', or 'socialist', and publicly attacked after 1980 as 'government on our backs' (e.g., debt-free higher education or communications for understanding rather than market propaganda). This structure of human life's reproduction and growth is, absurdly, assumed as 'allocation of society's resources for efficient production and distribution', yet the fatal disorder of assuming that only what serves money sequences is of value, does not occur as a problem. This is the marker of a totalitarian value-set. It follows from its closure that this value calculus necessarily leaves out of account what, in fact, contemporary society most evidently needs in its economic production – public investment in life capital and goods. These are, in fact, society's common life-ground of the future, from higher education, universal healthcare and non-partisan media to public transportation, renewable energy supplies, pollution-eliminating systems, the defence and recovery of arable land, management of carbon and hydrological cycles, and public employment and life security for those productive lives increasingly excluded by a global corporate money-sequence system.

No large-scale contemporary economy can afford this systematic lockout of the life economy, least of all a global economy. All of these public goods must be produced for its reproduction as a system of social life-organisation. All must be distributed as interconnected economic subsystems. It follows that all require financing and forward investment in them; yet even as their need becomes a life-and-death choice, all are *blocked out* of the ruling investment regime at every turn. For only what is produced and bought by market agents for a price and profit exists to the mind-set as a valid investment. The value calculus is deranged, but this does not deter its universalisation. That is why the world economy comes at the turn of the century to be in a foundational economic implosion across its subsystems, including corporate money-sequencing itself; yet through the regulating frame of reference, the meaning of the crisis cannot be comprehended. Incantations of 'stimulating consumer spending' and 'raising investor confidence' seek to restore symptoms of past prosperity.

Investment in the shared public goods required to reproduce the lives of society's members and the sustainability of their environment has never been more needed. An economic doctrine that cannot compute them as essential investments because all it can compute is what money-demand signals to the market to supply at a profit for private buyers, is not fit for the investment management of an economy. As corporations now move into public budgets like education as well for money-sequence management and profit (as Blairite Britain does as I write), the ruling parametric cannot accomodate life requirements at the new level of reality. Rather, even public goods are subordinated to money-sequence rule with public funds. The deadly closing circle is not seen.

The list of public goods requiring public investment for the sustaining and developing of an economy that serves the wider life-systems of society and its environment is long. It exceeds by far the civil commons institutions that have evolved. It includes the public goods that have been produced and developed, but abandoned or confiscated since 1980 by the corporate financial occupation – public housing, social transit alternatives, higher education without debt slavery, adequate healthcare distribution, and infrastructure for family farms. It includes such needed public life *services* as systemic environmental clean-up, old-age residences, dental care, day care and home care; and such public life *products* as non-fossil-fuel energy infrastructures, alternative social transit, scientific pollution monitoring and abatement instruments, up-to-date disease-preventative information kits and basic foodstuff advisories for all citizens, and vehicles that do not burn non-renewable fuels. What *connects* all these is that they are all *life-economy formations.* Yet they are all collective life goods that are not, by their nature, invested in by corporate capital, however vitally important they may be for peoples' lives and the future of the planet's life conditions. That investment in such life-and-death goods is read as *'not economic'* by the market calculus reveals the *reductio ad absurdum* of its value-set.

The lethal blind-spot of the doctrine is not tempered by the disasters it causes because they are 'externalities' for its closed calculus. It cannot conceive value beyond priced goods for profit in two-party exchanges. Instead of recognising its confinement to a parody of economic reality, the paradigm is made mandatory for all nations to obey. Societies across the world are then made to conform to its dictates on pain of embargo or invasion. The consequences of mass malnutrition, illiteracy, depression and natural capital devastation are read as the 'tough medicine required', like bleeding to restore health with an earlier paradigm of scientific management by experts.[20]

In consequence of its 'liberal reforms'which abolished public management of food surpluses, for example, the people of India began to starve to death in poor states like Maharashtra, Rajasthan and Orissa.[21] At the same time, further 'liberal reforms' overriding local protection of forests and hillsides allows their stripping by foreign corporations for timber and minerals. Along with aggregate global corporate pollutions causing weather destabilisation and forced invasion of corporate-constructed mega-dams on the people's lands in the same areas, disastrous consequences beneath the market value-set's computations follow the ravaging of the common life-ground: increasing flood disasters which ruin the homes and environments of increasing tens of millions of people who, in the 'new international order', are without food security or social security. This is the larger *meaning* of the 'global market' model. Beneath its monetised co-ordinates, terror and destruction of the world's life economy reign as 'new market freedoms'.

Ending the Public Subsidy of Corporate Unsustainability: The Case of Agriculture

The issue of '*sustainability*' does not inhibit the model's prescription, but rather provides another market opportunity to recycle disasters through its value-set to generate new sales and profit sites. 'Sustainability' means what people want it to mean in the new order of inverted meanings, but its meaning for corporations is exactly the opposite of its normal sense. 'The problem', say the market's corporate planners, 'is *how to tap the large reservoir of value locked up in sustainable development to translate it into shareholder value,* how to embed sustainable development through the corporation's operations and use it to *give life to the Corporate Purpose.*'[22] When people's lives or ecosystems are at stake, the market's calculus of value can only comprehend a stimulus to convert non-corporate life to corporate life, a formula of systematic predation. Governments then subsidise 'the Corporate Purpose' of feeding on other life-organisation while purporting to sustain it.

Agricultural economists David Andrews and Raymond Burke incisively summarise the problem not for distant Third World India, but in the increasingly desertified rural America:

> What we all oppose is the [government-assisted] industrialisation of agriculture and animal factories, and the policies that depopulate the countryside, erode security regarding our food, gamble with our food safety and food production, put our family farmers out of work, and despoil our environment.[23]

Wes Jackson identifies the state money-fuel that propels this system's stripping of the human and environmental life-ground by urban-based corporations with no connection to it.

> In the past five years, farm subsidies have increased 300 per cent [but] 75 per cent of the subsidies go to corporate farms and 72 per cent of agricultural production is controlled by the wealthiest eight percent of farms. The primary beneficiaries are the suppliers of inputs [fertilisers, herbicides and pesticides, patented seeds], and the agribusiness companies who in the year 2000 spent $58 million on campaign contributions. ... Pathogens – inorganics and toxics – and pesticides impair the rivers ... shorelines and watersheds.[24]

The food-processors, Archer-Midland-Daniels and Cargill bear the proper names of the main corporate electoral bribers of politicians in the US in this life-attack cycle; yet the pattern of systematic *public subsidy* for large corporations to occupy the land and dispossess the people on it, to industrialise agriculture with deadly cost externalities of chemical pollutions, to receive free research in corporatised universities for cheapening 'food' commodity production costs by genetic alteration, radiation, sugar and oil adulteration and process pulverisation is assumed as 'necessary for growth' and to 'feed the hungry of the world', although they lack the demand to buy the product. Armed force disciplines resisters as 'subversives'or 'communists'. The meta-pattern can be analysed into three moments of converting the world into the feeding cycle of corporate investment and growth:

1. forced conversion of communally-held lands and subsistence plots into privatised corporate farms or mega-energy projects – as in the corporate Mexican state rewriting the constitution to push subsistence farmers off the land, triggering the Chiapas Uprising; oilfield occupations across continents from Latin America to Burma and the South Sea Islands; or the billions of rural China and India as they enter the WTO;
2. secretive government trade deals opening borders to heavily subsidised, contaminated or genetically engineered industrial-farm commodities to undersell home-grown organic produce – since 1988 across North America by state-corporate 'partnerships' subsidising urban money sequences, and in the European Union following the 1991 neo-liberalisation of East Europe and the former Soviet Union, the marginalised and war-destroyed societies in the Balkans, all of black Africa, Palestine, Iraq, Afghanistan, and most of the Americas;
3. military or paramilitary death squads attacking and killing indigenous or subsistence farmers to seize their land with internal and external corporate state assistance and with taxpayer-financed armaments, training and direction (as across Latin America over 50 years, continuing in Colombia beyond 2000).

The unseen selector for this 'needed global investment' is elected public authority itself. The enormous revenues required to keep the jaws fed are produced by taxpayers. A cautious approach to analysis is appropriate here. It is not the issue of '*private property* in the means of production entitling the private owners to do as they choose so long as consumers pay for the products'. Marxists and capitalists concur with this explanation of the logic of the situation, with the former confronting the capitalists' private ownership as the problem, and the latter conceiving of it as their desert. Both miss the deeper point that it is *the public* paying for a lion's share of the costs of the private money sequencing throughout. The public policy selectors can as easily be reversed, and with overriding constitutional right.

The principal block of the intelligentsia is not moral corruption. Beneath this is the nearly universal assumption of 'greater efficiency of production' by the regulating economic model. The assumption is that industrial agribusiness 'improves agricultural productivity, and hence supply of food and nutritional standards' – to cite a mass-produced economic text on the matter. This is not a strange belief. It is shared by Adam Smith, the European Union, every orthodox economist, and even critics who lament the 'sacrifice of humanity to standards of efficiency'. However, as we have seen in Chapter 5, the efficiency is *illusory*. Industrial agribusiness is an abysmally inefficient food production system *once the costs are factored in* – not only life costs from environmental externalities and industrially adulterated food, but investment costs as well. That is the focus here – the direction of investment by public revenue sources which systematically favours and selects for corporate recipients of lavish aid that is falsely thought to *be* maximally 'efficient and productive' for society, when it is neither.

We have two levels of failure here in efficient allocation of resources to investment. The first is that the received paradigm blinkers out the value of public or collective goods that are not bought by single consumers and are not required to serve the market – at the very historical conjuncture when these life goods are most needed. The second failure is that even for the production of atomic consumer goods, government is everywhere externally assisting corporate producers with costly supports paid for by the taxpayer – hidden selectors of state subsidies, credit, interest rates and taxation subsidies to displace far less costly production for need.

From Money Capital to Life Capital: The Paradigm Turn

The failed paradigm of economic investment requires a sounder alternative, one that 'has the fundamentals right'. A functioning life economy consciously selects *for* life goods, rather than against them. At the most basic, it selects for *life capital – means of life that produce more means of life*. As discussed earlier, all life is a process, and this process always follows the pattern of the life sequence of value, *life → means of life → more life* (e.g., child → food, care and housing → healthy and developing child). *Life capital*, in turn, is like any capital, wealth that can create more wealth – with the wealth in question as *life capabilities and their enjoyments* in the individual, the bio-regional, or the planetary form. Means of life that sustain life may be understood in the immediately *consumable* form (e.g., food and water) or, over time, in the *capital* form (e.g., the economic and ecological capabilities to reproduce and develop food and water supplies and their distribution).

We know what consumable means of life are – what the individual organism needs to consume to survive and grow, and without which vital life capabilities are reduced. Means of life as life capital are what can produce these means as a productive base that is *not* consumed (e.g., the fertile soil), providing what is used to create more in reiteration so long as the capital is not depleted or destroyed. *Life capital* can then be defined as *the generic and non-consumed bearer of means of life in an economy's overall life sequence of value through generations.* Thus life capital *includes* physical capital, natural capital and social capital, as well as money capital, *so far as each serves this macro life sequence of value*, and is not spent away.

The movement to understanding capital as more than merely a reified subsystem of *money* capital is centuries old. Jane Austen's male characters were characterised as so many pounds per year, the heyday of money-fetish capital. Even Karl Marx, the greatest critic of the money sequence, assumed that this form of capital was *all* of capital, and so was left with only the counter-intuitive alternative of *anti*-capital. The consequence was a revolutionary project without an existing life-base. Marx thought that part of the base of a life economy was all of it – waged workers self-governing industrial productive forces. Ever since, Marxists have variously been trying to broaden this base to include regions of what is here called life capital (e.g., subsistence farm and women's domestic economies as well as environment production and services), but have failed, in principle, to fit these subsystems of life reproduction and growth into an industrial labour-value theory.

This is a problem that is greater than ever in the twenty-first century. *Human, natural and social capital begin to be recognised, but remain subjugated to money capital as their criterion and their end.* For example, '*human capital*' is still understood as a subsystem of money-sequence capital, as are 'natural capital' and 'social capital'(if they are recognised at all). Human capital here is understood as investment of money into education so that students turn into producers of net higher revenues. This 'value adding' property qualifies the bearers of this sequence as 'human capital' because they *too* are transformed into money sequences producing more money value than what their training costs. On the basis of this upside-down logic, education is the middle term between money inputs and more money outputs. This aim of education is now proclaimed from political and academic pulpits as the key to 'human capital growth' – and thus 'economic growth', which is assumed as the panacea for all ills.

The same subjugation to money-sequence capital has occurred with natural and social capital, and they are only spoken in the same breath as capital at the *avant garde* edge of economics – which in its orthodox vestments does not recognise *any* value ground other than money sequence capital as the one God of all value *with no other*. The concept of *life capital* superannuates money-capital fetishism, understanding money-demand and accumulations of money-demand as merely instrumental claims *on* life wealth, the only real wealth. Money is not repudiated as such, but is valued as a *society-wide exchange medium, a subsystem of social capital*, whereby different forms of life-value can be distributed by a government-backed currency with commensurable units of 'exchange-value'. Social capital, in turn, is a subsystem of life capital.

The challenge of any fetish system is to bring the value attributed to the fetish object into line with what is, in fact, valuable. So it is here. In a terrestrial setting, the only general value of which all other values are variations is life value. That is the baseline. Life capital is the store of life value that can produce more life value, holding its yield through time, at best increasing it with each round – as with fertile soil that is sustained, undepleted aquifers, and education systems. Accordingly, *investment in each and all is to be selected for by the life value they yield and grow as forms of life wealth*. The selection of *what* life capital and goods to invest in is then decided by what is needed, with life need, *what life capability requires to continue and grow*, being the general selector.

Yet it is precisely life need and the capital required to serve it that is most blocked out by the market's delinked value calculus, with public goods and civil commons formations being the main forms of life capital that are systematically suppressed. In response, government economic selectors for investment which are now structured to favour fetishised money sequences, require redirection towards investment in life capital and its failing subsystems. These instrumental financial selectors are *currency creation, bank reserves, interest rates* and *taxation*.

Once we reground in life capital rather than an absolutised subsystem of one subsytem, we can understand that *investment* serving only this subsystem's unihibited growth under oligopolist corporate possession is not just uneconomic. Its consumption and destruction of life capital is a disorder which is quintessentially carcinogenic in its nature.

Investment or commitment of resources to non-consumed value, is the system decider of any modern economic process, its moving line of capital development through time. In a healthy economic order, public commitment of resources is directed towards life capital sustainment and growth, and not ever more growth of a money-sequences as an end in itself. With money as the primary exchange medium for economic investment in capital in today's world, its investment in life capital is required for any economy to survive and develop over the long term. As an economic system becomes more productive and interconnected, *public* investment in all forms of capital becomes more, not less required, for reasons we have discussed. Civil commons formations which enable access of all members of an economy to life goods (e.g., non-polluted water to drink, air to breathe, universal education, open greenspaces and old-age pensions) are the core *life-capital formations* of an economy, but not the only forms. Private life-capital remains central in a market-dominated system; but here too investment is best understood as of economic value only so far as it produces and distributes life goods. Since market mechanisms do not distinguish between need and conditioned desire, food that enables life and junk-food, public investment in life-security and weapons of mass destruction, public investment has to keep in view not only the *collective life goods that do not appear on the market screen*, but also the fact that *corporate market commodities produced for consumers may not be means of life at all, but pollutive or addictive commodities degrading life by their manufacture and end-products.*

Here government in the public interest has not only a *regulatory* importance, with corresponding public institutions for monitoring and enforcement of life-protective standards. Less understood, government representation of the common interest is of primary importance in currency creation, credit, interest rate and taxation policies to select for *investment in life capital* that produces life goods of all the kinds the market selects against, depletes or pollutes.

Only when we adopt the wider view of *life capital* – the *life-ground in its economic form* – are the bounds of the economic structure adequate to the real world. Even without theoretical recognition of these wider bounds of the economy, civil commons institutions and public investments have still evolved as a very complex and largely invisible life economy infrastructure. Yet this deeper economic base and its still more fundamental ground of natural capital are blinkered out by the dominant economic paradigm. The existence and the value of both – almost the entire life capital base – are implicitly denied at a level rarely observed – *the accounting systems of governments themselves*. Because no capital except private monetised capital is recognised *as* capital in the ruling economic calculus, governments blindly follow suit. Incredibly but invisibly, *the values of all public goods requiring revenues have long been systematically excluded from capital-cost accounting, consumer commodity bundles, cost-of-living calculations, and inflation indices in government accounts.* All revenues invested in public goods and their capital bases have, instead, been classified as 'current' or 'operational expenditures'.

In this way, all life capital formations which are publicly invested in, the undergirdings of any economy, have been abolished from the ledgers *as capital*. No value is recognised in the very basis of the economy beyond the costs of debits by 'operating' revenues expended on them. Thus, public goods of the most durable and economically foundational kinds have been classified in public accounts where their presence appears at all as *negative values – cost liabilities rather than capital assets*. The market inversion of meaning in public capital accounting itself discloses the paradigm's deep disorder. *With no public capital accounting* for human or natural or social capital or even public physical capital, preservation or development of their capital value is ruled out *a priori*. The consequence of this market-warped calculus in government accounts themselves has been incalculably destructive of social, human and natural capital. On the individual level, it has confiscated countless individual life-futures of public-service jobs. For the public-sector economy and the vocation of public service as a whole, the effects have been effectively genocidal –

depredating and liquidating the civil commons that define a people as more than a market of atomic self-seekers.

The exclusion of public and natural capital from public accounts is an abolition by presupposition of their right to existence. This is bad for life capital and the larger economy, but it is *inversely profitable* for the economy's money-sequencing sect, since their economic rule is guaranteed only if money-sequencing capital counts as capital, and only its products of priced commodities count as economic values. This is the unseen meta-basis of the corporate occupation of society. It is also the unseen ground for continuous attacks on the life-services of nature and the civil commons, which are not recognised as of value at the system-steering level of public accounts themselves. Since no investment in life capital – human, social or natural – is counted *as* an investment in these accounts, they are judged as 'wasteful government spending', and are cut to 'save costs'. Thus, education which is the basis of the knowledge economy, public health which enables people's capabilities to produce, and public expenditures on life conditions which make citizens' lives livable are all 'lost revenues of government expenditures' for this black-hole value calculus. It is difficult to conceive of a more deformed value system, but it still rules public budgets. The paradigm turn begins with emancipating the meaning of capital itself.[25]

Because only corporate and privately-priced goods count as value in the money capital paradigm, systematic miscalculations of *inflation* in the economy also follow in train as a consequence, with further slashing of public spending to counter the miscalculated inflation. For inflation-indices include the *costs* of producing and supplying all public goods as expenditures, but do not factor in the *value* of public goods to consumers in their calculations. Thus, an inflationary push automatically registers by public expenditures on life capital and goods because they are not factored into consumer values: for example, massive public expenditures on citizens' health, education, environment, and life-means security. The results are bizarre in more ways than one. Public expenditures on protecting people from disease and death, for instance, do *not* count as an investment or a good, but expenditures on HMO for-profit hospitals in which 80,000 Americans are killed a year by malpractice count as one of the most successful capital investments in the world.[26] This meta-bias of measurement ensures that whenever there are government investments in public goods for people's lives, the taxes that must pay for them *raise prices, but do not produce goods for this false metric*. Therefore, government expenditures for unpriced public goods are, in a sweeping *non sequitur* based on the warp of the calculus, counted as *lost 'operating costs'* without life capital gain and therefore '*inflationary*'.[27] Again when we peel back the life-blind blinkers of the market calculus, we discover how its absolutist monopoly of investment and capital value radically deforms the nature of human life itself.

The inner logic of this value calculus is, however, hidden. The life economy calculus of capital and goods corrects this value blindness. It counts rather than abolishes investments in the life-capital base of the economy. Once investment in the economy is liberated from the jealous God of private-profit capital, it rediscovers its life and ground.

Interest Rates: Selection for Life Capital Gain and not Enrichment of Financial Factions

Interest rates are a primary investment selector in all contemporary economies. While 'intervention by government in the market' is a taboo in the market theology, interest rates prescribed by a central authority external to the market have been a continuous intervention in the market's operations for generations. As the constitutional responsibility of governments or their central banks, base interest rates have long been set, in fact, by central command. Those setting the interest rates, in turn, are accountable to governments or, in the case of the European Union, intergovernmental authorities and, ultimately, to the electorates these authorities are pledged to serve. It is a telling sign of the private corporate take-over of public institutions that elected government control over interest-rate and monetary policies has been recently surrendered to central banks and, thereby, to chief officers typically selected from IMF administrations and Wall Street banks, who presuppose private-banker dogma *as their right* to central command. Yet these central banks are under sovereign law *accountable to* the public, not bank stockholders.

The chief problem has been that beneath public notice, interest rates for two decades across the world have been raised and lowered *entirely in accordance with serving a systematic transfer of wealth from productive and public sectors to transnational banks* and *corporations*. For example, compounding interest rates were raised in the 1980s to a quasi-criminal high of 20 per cent-prime by the world-leading US Federal Reserve, thereby serving the dominant corporate interest of stripping public sectors of their funding across continents, and, simultaneously, privatising their infrastructures, assets and services for corporate profit, vastly enriching Wall Street and other major bondholders with usurious interest rates which multiplied their private fortunes, and indebting governments so deeply that many became debt-enslaved – at best competing to stay in favour for lower rates, and prevented from public-sector spending (a meta-strategy into which the $1.35 trillion Bush Jr. tax-cut going mainly to the rich is a recent major wealth transfer); and at worst, sliding into social and economic ruin (as in the case of most of sub-Saharan Africa).

In the 2000–01 period, in a dramatic reversal of the interest-rate rises of the 1980s which impoverished public sectors, small businesses and workers' livelihoods, rates were just as automatically *lowered* instead of raised one time after another to near-zero real rates by the US Federal Reserve and satellite central banks across the globe. This reversal of policy kept vastly overvalued stock markets from losing too much for private investors, while keeping credit available for private consumer purchase of mass-produced commodities so that corporate manufacturers and retailers too were cushioned from revenue falls. The pattern is strikingly one-sided in the beneficiaries and losers it selects for prior to their economic performance. It is absolute, but concealed. Through all the extreme rises *and* the extreme falls of interest rates, money sequencers are subsidised by cumulative trillions of government policy revenues, while public treasuries and investment, workers' wages and smaller business are sacrificed or ignored. This destructive bias is, however, built into the instituted presuppositions of the regulating decision structure, and not observed or connected across phenomena.

In accordance with this ruling bias, the lionised Chair of the US Federal Reserve, whoever it might be, has structured all decisions to assist the money-sequencing faction in first gobbling up public treasuries and assets, and then keeping the ballooned conglomerates afloat in the subsequent demand crisis. That the earlier, sky-high rates disemployed and wage-lowered tens of millions of workers and bankrupted public sectors and tens of thousands of small and medium businesses across the world during the 1980s was not the issue. The inner logic of interest-rate changes was to select for record boom-profits, and then for safety rafts for the vastly enriched financial sect of society whose members have been permanently entrusted to set national interest rates. Banks in particular were royally served by these banker-made policies, because their holdings had vastly expanded under financial deregulation, from money-holding and lending in the 1980s to portfolio stock holding, massive merger servicing and global speculation by the mid-1990s. The public sector of social services and constructive jobs and vocations for people could be stripped by high interest rates, as happened. That was 'inevitable' and 'necessary' so as 'not to spend beyond our means'; but a stock market fall for corporate and bank-held stocks that had inflated their value exponentially in the past decade with price-earning ratios far beyond past records was for this calculus of value an emergency to treat, and so interest rates were ratcheted down towards zero to 'save the economy'. Underneath, the unmarked pattern was the same over 20 years – interest rates set by public authority which invariably (and unremarked upon) selected for corporate and bank money-sequencers, and against life capital and the common interest.

The life-economy paradigm regrounds in life-value which has always been the meaning of any real economy. *Its selectors for capital growth are used to favour means of life that produce means of life, and selecting money sequence growth for private investors which deplete life and means of life.* Accordingly, interest rates set by life-capital standards would never rise and lower, as now, to keep down wages and reduce and strip public-life goods, while redistributing public wealth and market control to transnational corporations and banks. Credit and interest-rates would be stable and affordable for secure production and distribution of life goods. 'Inflation fighting' would proceed without 'blood all over the floor', but by the precise anti-inflation instrument of reducing unproductive money creation by banks through targeted interest-rate rises and reserves to inhibit their merger, take-over and stock market loans and speculations with no life gains for society. Consequently, the continuous life-value losses we are habituated to by government selection for corporate con-glomerate growth would not result in the long menu of endless job cuts, loss of domestic sovereignty, and livelihood instability that are now prescribed as 'necessary' by the ruling market calculus.

Productive credit would, instead, be the system selector of interest-rates and loans – with debt-free or nominal rates to maximise life-serving investment. As soon as the *regulating principle of value judgement* ceases to presuppose the alchemic value of ever more corporate money sequencing as society's final necessity and good, investment in human life and its advancement can be favoured instead. Because the system-deciding principle selects for means of life for life gain for the economy, rather than money gain for money sequencers, economic 'investment' and 'growth' are no longer a threat to people's livelihoods, or a private-sector offer that cannot be refused. The economy recovers by serving its life sequences of growth, rather than a faction's money sequences delinked from their life-ground. *There is no economic decision that is not re-oriented by this paradigm shift.* It restores life value to sovereignty in the economy, and exchange-value back to its instrument. One would think the matter as obvious as the mind's movement beyond idol worship, but the purpose we know to be self-evident is nowhere yet desubmerged in any economic textbook, or explanation of interest and monetary policy.

As the turning of the conventional mind-set right-side up opens horizons of thought, paths of resolution correspondingly open to view. Whether we consider long-term or zero real interest rates or public investment as the tools of selection, or both, *rates, credit and taxes are steered by the rudder of advantage to life capital.* If we bear in mind the critical yardstick of society's life-capital gain rather than money-profit for some as the regulator of economic investment, then policy paths shift. Instead of financial stripping of social sectors, the *value turn* of the economy selects for life capital investments which reverse the world deflation. The options are as numerous as the problems of the real economy – for example, home-building co-operatives and mortgages for the less affluent; public support for family farm, fishing village and other endogenous life-means production systems in rural communities (now all confiscated by the corporate money-sequence occupation); job-creating enterprises in environment-protecting products and services (currently ignored in vast subsidies to non-renewable resource extractions and non-enforcement of environmental standards); municipal infrastructures for recycling systems for all wastes (now widely defunded by the corporate state at provincial and local levels); small-scale producer and worker-owned enterprises in such major areas as organic farming where product supply cannot keep up with demand (systematically selected against by corporate state policies subsidising and protecting life-blind factory farming); economic activities serving the aged and disabled in other ways than warehousing or inhuman indigence (now pre-empted by subsidy and cutback selectors against public investment in what is needed); non-profit public communications and fibre-optic cable systems (where ever fewer transnational conglomerates are now subsidised to induce a global dumbing-down by unconditional government giveaways of public electromagnetic spectrum bands); funded local enterprises of communications, arts and international education (another region of public investment confiscated by the corporate state in the global era when it is most needed); tuition-free education at all levels (now debt is imprisoning the next generation from primary schools in Africa under IMF loan terms to university students in the developed world); and intergovernmental co-ordination of large-scale investment into water desalination membranes, low-cost renewable energy, and other life-and-death technologies (to steer transnational corporate looting and pollution of public resources towards technologies that corporate investment is structured against investing in by rampant cost externalisation allowed by corporate governments).

Taxes: Paying for Life Capital Gain, not Corporate Free-Riding
Tax levels are not less important than public investment, credit and interest-rate policies, but the bias towards serving money-sequencing taxpayers is so one-sidedly instituted into national tax forms as to be exposable in a one-sentence formulation. The master principle by which government taxation is increasingly ruled *is to maximise taxation for working lives, and to minimise taxation for money capital.* The tax-credit vehicles by which this unseen fiat rules societies are numerous, from lower general rates for capital gains to deferred taxes to large corporations to investment and loan insurance abroad. If taxation is to serve the common life interest rather than a faction's private money sequences, it follows that the requirement for life capital formation and production of life goods must restructure a system which increasingly expropriates the incomes of the poorer to give to the rich. Policy in the public interest, instead, stops tax-subsidising corporate money-sequencing and invests in life capital which has been recklessly depleted and degraded.

All the life capital spheres identified can be invested in by tax-rate selectors as well as public investment, credit and interest rate advantages. A constitutional correction of the deep-structural fiscal and monetary biases of government towards private money-sequencing and against life capital preservation and development is the first priority of any turn from the death to the life economy. Its urgency is evidenced by every trend of environmental and social life indicators. The same generic principle is foundational throughout. *Economic system-deciders in the public domain select for life-value production for the economy, rather than money-value appropriation by the financial faction and its clients.* However, just as money creation, investment and interest policies have been covertly restructured towards unprecedentedly serving money sequencers with every new state initiative and crisis, so too have tax-rates. The underlying pattern is universal. Tax burdens across the world have seismically shifted and continue to shift from corporations and high-income recipients to wage and salary earners and the poor, and – less observed – *away from public investment in life-serving functions to life-destructive powers serving transnational corporations* – global-control weaponry, subsidising of invasive oil extraction and burning, and assisted corporate take-over of public health and learning infrastructures. The US state's policy constructions since September 2001 exemplify the pattern – floodgate tax giveaways to US corporations and hand-outs to the oligopolist and environmentally destructive jet travel sector, escalation of the $1000 million a day of public revenues to the military–industrial complex and its subsystems, and lawless carpet bombing and destruction of the world's poorest country to clear it for new oil-field installations, dangerous mountain pipelines and massive new extraction of foreign oil by the ecocidal oil oligopoly.

All the while, the globally regulating value programme is ruled out of media communications, and a regime of state surveillance and dissent-suppression for 'an indefinite period' is instituted in the name of 'anti-terrorism'.

Structuring taxation to invest in this programme is key to its invasion. From the imperial centre to the peripheries, the domestic pattern is constant: to shift tax loads onto working populations and away from unearned income, while simultaneously stripping public life-capital investment. In the place of lost means of life are slogans of 'attracting investors', 'lower tax burdens for business', and 'the need to be globally competitive', the shadows on the cave wall. The master economic regulators of which all are images are not connected beneath their phenomena, although they reach from rejigging tax-return credits to bombing unarmed villages.

Redistribution of wealth from the poorer to the rich is evident in all corrupt orders through history, and operates in this era through servant government policies all tending towards the same end. The selectors are not related if they are seen, and so it is worth exposing their hidden framework of bias for money sequencing and against life-value – relentlessly reversing progressive tax rates and imposing ever more flat taxes on ordinary consumers; simultaneously dropping, exempting and deferring corporate taxes from past levels of 50 per cent of tax revenues towards subsidised net-gain levels; increasingly fractioning taxes on unearned capital gains revenues, and instituting permanent and exclusive loopholes for business expenses and revenues; appropriating full tax-rates at source for wage and salary earners with no interest for the year remainder, while deferring taxes on unearned revenues indefinitely or to year-end; shifting public support of universal old-age pensions formerly used for public loans to tax credits for high-margin incomes spent on corporate stock-conglomerates and registered stock funds; official and unofficial toleration of estate and foreign haven tax evasions and encouragement of foreign speculative investment by tax regimes; transnational policies of zero tax on financial transactions including continuous ruinous attacks on domestic currencies with bank-created credit; and systematic expansion of tax evasions, credits and subsidies to non-productive speculative and portfolio tides across borders opened by transnational trade and investment regulatory apparatuses; and increasing blanket write-offs of money capital investments and gains, but never life-capital investments and gains in taxpayers' education, life need provisions for others, or reduction of natural capital consumption. Every one of these tax subsidies for money-capital free-riding can be reversed, and the revenues saved directed instead to the life-capital formations defined above.

This is the concealed pattern of the Beast's feeding cycle through public-tax selectors. All of the factors that make up the pattern conform to one underlying trend – the tidal movement of wealth from the middle-income and the impoverished to the rich, and from public life-service to subsidisation of money-capital consumption and pollution of the world. All of them, more invisibly, follow from the unmarked organising principles of a regulating value-set which governments themselves have *internalised as their own*. As elsewhere, the resolving path is an about-turn of public funding by tax policy and other system deciders – away from money capital that consumes and destroys life capital, and towards public revenues for investment in life capital. The *pro*-select principle is decreasing taxation by credit for whatever is invested in life capital. The *con*-select principle is increasing taxation on all revenues gained by depleting life capital in the ways known, steeply rising in proportion to life-disabling effects. For the neutral zone of taxation, the principle is reversal of discriminatory rates favouring unearned income, speculative transactions and unneeded consumption to favour earned income and need-object purchases, in a cumulative cascade od economic justice adjustments that select for life-productive equalisation.[28]

Life economy principle 2: **government allocation of public investment assistance, loan credits, interest rates and taxation levels to select for life capital production, and against money sequences consuming or degrading life capital and conditions**.

8

Preventing Ecocide: Making Commodity Cycles Accountable to Life Standards

The International System of World Ecological Devastation: An Anatomy

Once investment allocation is determined, the global market's next system-deciding phase is the re-ordering of the world's ecosystems and consumers by *corporate commodity cycles* (CCCs). The commodity cycle is constituted of the following subsystems whose cumulative costs to and depredations of life are *not factored into the market value calculus*. These are:

1. the totalising extraction of 'raw materials' from the world's natural ecosystems and the earth's crust and surface to commoditise, with a fraction of what is stripped from the evolved world remaining in the raw materials and the rest left to waste (99 per cent of the natural materials appropriated now becoming waste within six weeks);
2. processing of these raw materials into the finished dead-matter of the commodity, with a still smaller fraction of the increasingly disaggregated conditions of life retained in the final product (about 1:25 ratio of product: biomass tonnages in volume now retained);
3. living labour appended to large-scale machines to dismantle natural life-systems and formations at the lowest cost for maximum volumes and profits in commodity sale;
4. progressively pervasive pollution and degradation of the means of natural and human life by accumulating toxic inputs and polluting effluents, non-biodegradable wastes, and genetic contamination of commodity cycles;[29]

5. long-distance transport and resource-consuming packaging reiterating steps (1) to (4) of using ecosystems as loot-sources and pollution-sinks across global ecosystems;
6. saturating advertising of corporate commodities to operantly condition market demand for these commodities (at a cost that exceeds expenditures on research and life-protective measures);
7. exponentially increasing consumption of corporate commodities with unregulated throwaway packaging and contents, effluents of use and dissemination of toxins which synergistically increase human and natural disease and disorders.

The Causal Problem: Business Efficiency by Cost Externalisation onto Others

All of these moments of commodity cycles for corporate profit that impose increasing and systemic harms on life and life conditions are normally excluded from corporate costs, tax or other liabilities. There is a single, universal principle of 'cost efficiency' regulating production and distribution throughout the operations of this CCC. The system-deciding principle regulates economies without being identified, codified or connected across *all distinct phases.* More primarily, 'cost efficiency' is not exposed as the opposite of efficient in life-capital effects. The unstated but ruling principle of business 'cost efficiency' is *to externalise all possible costs of for-profit commodity cycles onto those who do not profit from them.* The systematic, global and accumulating costs are, by this formula, displaced from their perpetrators and borne by the disease, degradation and death of human and natural life and life conditions (ecological, species, individual organisms, and human beings). The 'market freedom' at work here is, decoded, *freedom from responsibility for harms imposed on others by corporate commodity cycles.* There is no avoidance of responsibility in society more destructive but, prior to corporate media screen-out of cause–effect connections, non-accountability is structured into market accounts.

The Case of the Fossil-Fuel Vehicle

At the macro-level, aggregates of harm are ignored by business associations, corporate round-tables and governments themselves. In consequence, even ecosystem depredation that threatens planetary life is blocked out of view as a connected structure. For example, the facts are that there has been over a tenfold multiplication of automobiles since 1950, and a well over 100-fold increase of leisure motorcraft, with these multiplying units typically increasing in horsepower, mileage driven, non-renewable energy consumption, fume effluents (tons per vehicle annually), pervasive noise pollution, and fouling of the elements. At the same time, each high-income consumer appropriates a total of 85 tons of natural resources annually through their overall CCC feeding cycle;[30] yet the global resource exhaustion and pollution caused by these corporately manufactured and globally sold commodities are disregarded as issues of governance or corporate accountability. On the contrary, more massive CCCs are continuously subsidised by taxpayers at every phase of their resource depletion, pollution, and waste. The richest corporations are the most environmentally destructive. Thus, seven of the top ten corporations in annual revenue in the global market in 2001 are oil and auto conglomerates.

'Development' means doing the same at higher levels; yet already the degradation and depletion of resources and the fouling of the life elements of atmosphere, air and water by unregulated CCCs impel crisis deteriorations and scarcities of natural resources and life conditions. These, in turn, underlie the increases of civil conflicts and armed warfare over dwindling resources and means of existence across the world.[31] Such insecurities themselves, meanwhile, are compounded and repressed by armed force through *military–industrial production* – the single biggest source of world pollution and environmental destruction, whose victims are over 90 per cent civilians.

None of these general facts is challengeable, but their overall cause–effect structure is blocked out even by ecosystem analysts, while the single main culprit, the oil-driven moving machine, is assumed as 'our way of life'. Only disconnected symptoms remain when seen through the lenses of the ruling value-set. At the transnational level, trade and investment treaties prescribe this negligence as something illegal to discriminate against or to label in receiving markets. The instituted decision-structure selects for planetary ecocide with no connection back to the master value programme determining every step.

If and when the externalised costs of the CCC *are* recognised as direct consequences of this or that step of the commodity cycle, they are disconnected from the chain sequence of (1) to (7), denied, legally obstructed, deemed accidental, represented to the public as a responsibly resolved problem, and continued in causal sequence with no resolving action in fact.[32] The *Exxon-Valdez* is only one example of a general pattern. As the Burson-Marseler code of blocking out causal comprehension explains: 'The role of communications is to manage perceptions which motivate behaviours that create business results.'[33]

Ecosystem Defence by Cost-Internalisation and Regulatory Prevention

The primary *economic* issue which arises is one in which corporations normally have a supreme interest. It is the issue of *recognising costs of production* – but there are instituted blocks at work here to structure for unaccountability for the external costs of corporate activities. Again, the disorder follows from the value calculus of self-maximising rationality, which is always supposed to produce the best of all possible worlds, the optimum of efficiency and outcome. The externalisation of all life costs onto others follows strictly from this calculus, with the magical thinking of an 'equilibrating optimum' ruling out real effects. The blocks against recognising and assigning costs of damages by corporate commodity cycles are so systematic in consequence that a genuflection category sweeps all of them out of account as '*externalities*', or 'not a cost of business'. The solution to this built-in blindness of market accounting is, then reconnection to reality: to prohibit them by law, or to make externalised costs internal to the businesses imposing them.

Neither goal is remotely achieved by parallel markets in 'pollution credits', which merely reiterate the closure of the paradigm to life beyond its single measure. Pollution credits grant new equity in licences to pollute, free of charge, to the polluters, and do not reduce pollution, but redistribute its sources by profit-led transactions. 'Scarcity rents' for environmental resources and sinks, the leading edge of market solutions proposed by Herman Daly, are far better because they assign direct costs for depleting extraction of resources and harmful discharges into public life assets,[34] but they still provide licences to deplete non-renewable resources and to pollute. Only when polluters are *either* made to pay the costs of restoration of life conditions (or a multiple to deter repeat violation), *or* prohibited from the outset by enforced law (as with criminal assault), can their calculus prefer life-responsible choice.

The Inner Logic and Idealisation of Corporate Impunity

On the other hand, another market dogma blocks resolution by a *deus ex machina* device – the article of faith that 'the market knows best', that 'there is no problem that market mechanisms do not best resolve', and that therefore 'government must not interfere in the market'. Thus, recourse is left to private lawsuit of tort which only the rich are entitled to under market mechanisms. Captive governments meanwhile strip public enforcement mechanisms of what environmental laws exist. The Bush Jr. administration goes further, planning a law to regulate against class action lawsuits as 'litigious division of Americans'.

Reinforcing these blocks against responsible life behaviour is the corporate charter for limited liability. It provides legal protection to corporate stock owners from any civil or criminal liability pursuant to the acts, negligences and malfeasances of the corporation. This legal device removes the reason for corporate money-sequencers to be concerned as individuals for the damages of disease, death, misery and cumulative world ruin that are imposed by their joint-stock corporate vehicles.

At a third level, the corporations themselves are reconstructed as 'persons' under law with constitutional rights of citizens, but with overwhelmingly more financial and legal resources to ensure that even unfriendly publicity is stopped, reversed and financially punished – hence the acronym of *SLAPPs* for corporate 'strategic lawsuits against public participation and protest'.

This overall process is represented as '*freedom*' – from accountability. It is also represented, in corollary, as 'cutting bureaucracy and red tape' – ensuring that no accountability remains. The depredations and destructions of individual lives, societies and environments by CCCs (e.g., oil extraction and mining and transboundary pollutants) is absolutised as '*the imperative of globalisation*'.[35] In the background, a plan to abolish every government's capacity to do anything to modify or resist the programme is instituted by transnational trade fiats, which are co-ordinated and enforced by what is, in fact, the most sweeping and unaccountable bureaucratic structure in history.[36] Laws or policies which 'deprive investors of expected profits' or which 'discriminate against' their commodities 'process of production' elsewhere, or which specify 'performance requirements', are outlawed. These transnational regulations override past and future domestic legislation protecting environmental life or assets which are inconsisten with them. Huge fines by secretly meeting trade tribunals are also imposed if any government's laws are deemed 'trade restrictive', 'incompatible', 'failing to provide national treatment' or 'tantamount to expropriating future profits'.

Transnational corporate traders are in this way placed above the law, but their unaccountability to any life standard is not rejected by the public or the official intellectual class because the connective inner logic is presupposed as the structure of market freedom. Only emergent manifestations are seen, not the *regulating value system from which they all follow*. This value calculus itself is structured to block out all such grounds for doubt. All paths thus lead back to the instituted mind-set which organises market perception and understanding. We can formulate the causal structure at work in the following law of proportionality. *Every environmental disaster follows in direct proportion to the increased money-value of corporate commodity cycles which are now unaccountable to law through their phases of life destruction.* Yet no market society even keeps public accounts of their life-capital depletions, but only monumental details of day-to-day money prices and aggregates. In fact, corporate lobbies have obstructed public resource inventories – as with timber resources from Chile to Cameroon and Indonesia, and coal reserves in the US.

Regaining our Economic Bearings: Natural Capital Accounts and the Well-Being Index

In general, the concept of natural capital is banned from public budgetary accounts. There could hardly be a more basic demand of economic reason than to keep account of life resources and capital, what is used to produce more life without consuming and destroying life's conditions. However, few inventories of natural capital stocks are kept as they are polluted, depleted and made scarce, and almost no law prevents their maximum extraction. 'We can always find another source', say the corporate extractors who have presided over the decline of 16 of the 25 eco-capital providers of life means by agricultural, coastal, forest, freshwater and grassland eco-services, and the 30 per cent drop in the earth's forests and waters in a single generation.[37] Annual budgetary statements of depletion and waste loads by all major sources is the minimum baseline of *economic science itself*. Assigning and enforcing costs to steer towards preservation of life conditions is the most primary form of rational allocation.

Even then, we have not fully penetrated the need of a life economy. There remains *the intrinsic life-value* of lands, waters, geoscapes and subsurface heritages prior to their priced extraction and pollution – their life value as enjoyed bearers of life. At the downstream end of economic accounting is its ultimate product – *the rising or declining life welfare of its members*. We have seen their exclusion from the market-value calculus, yet we know at the level of experience and valuation that organic well-being normally matters most of all to everyone. Perhaps the single most telling blind-spot of market societies is that even at the public level there is *no set of life indicators to confirm or disconfirm whether the economy is working*. This is a study in itself. An index of life measures is excluded from public accounts, finance ministries, political debate and media discussion.

Underneath official econometrics, however, there are signs of an emerging life-indicator consciousness and measures to match – the United Nations Human Development Index (HDI), the Index of Economic Well-Being (IEWB), the Genuine Progress Indicator (GPI), the Calvert–Henderson Quality of Life Indicators, the Index of Social Health (ISH), the Ecological Footprint (EF), and the Statistics Canada System of Environmental and Resource Accounts, for example.[38] Yet most of these are non-governmental, and underdeveloped. The UN's HDI, for example, has only three indicators – national averages of income (GDP per capita), educational attainment, and longevity indicators – three variables which exclude most of the life indicators identified in this study, and whose averages exclude inequalities and bottom-end deprivations.

In contrast, any minimally adequate measure requires the life-co-ordinates which register life well-being or ill-being. These are avoided by lack of criteria, unthought-through assumptions, and symptom reporting.

The life measures required are straightforward, although revealingly absent as a life-value index in both official and unofficial worlds. Their basic minimum parametric of life means is an eight-member set:

1. air quality
2. access to clean water
3. sufficient nourishing food
4. security of habitable housing
5. opportunity to perform meaningful service or work of value to others
6. available learning opportunity to the level of qualification
7. healthcare when ill
8. temporally and physically available healthy environmental space for leisure, social interaction and recreation.

This is the *Basic Well-Being Index*. Each of its means of life is a vital need in the way defined, for *none can be deprived without reduction of vital life capability.* Together as a set, these vital means of life form the *measure of any society's true economic performance.* An economy succeeds or fails to the extent to which it provides or does not provide its members with these means of life severally and as a whole. Much is made of the market's achievements as an economic system, but almost no market society has ever achieved a satisfactory BWI for all of its citizens, and, more fatefully, market societies become increasingly *inefficient* by life standards as their production and distribution of goods are deregulated and privatised. The Basic Well-Being Index exactly exposes this degrading economic condition, whereas the market's GDP measure wholly conceals it.

This may explain the fact that governments of market societies have long avoided any life accounting system, and thereby any life account-ability of their economies. Despite some life-value accounting initiatives, no nation or group of nations has an official measure close to the adequacy of the Basic Well-Being Index. The most deep-structural blindness of economic calculus of value here looms to view. *For without ongoing objective well-being profiles of a society's population, it is not possible to tell whether an economy is, in fact, improving, declining or even working as a system.* This wide blind-eye is necessary for a mind-locked culture averse to understanding its own effectiveness. It permits the magical thinking of market fundamentalism to run free with slogans and propaganda of life flourishing which are nowhere connected or accountable to any body of evidence to verify or disprove their claims. This is another marker of the market's inbuilt unaccountability to any life requirement or measure.

Instead, voluminous statistics of the money idol alone are punctiliously and endlessly observed and recorded in momentary changes – for-profit commodity sales, exports and imports, hourly stock-value changes and other figures serving the security and growth of *money sequences.* The market-value calculus is in this way a concealment of the economy's defining function. The figures kept indicate nothing about the actual well-being or ill-being of peoples and their life conditions. As we have seen, such indicators as GDP can all rise as life and life conditions decline. It is here that the closed value-circuits of the global corporate system are most systematically disconnected. What an economy is supposed to produce, reproduce and distribute for a society – means of life and well-being for its citizens – are things the received market order does not have any account of.[39]

The defining paradigm shift is *to reground in means of life and what produces means of life as the baseline co-ordinates of the economic calculus.*

The Non-Fraudulent Global Market: Sale Transparency, Cost Accountability, and the Property Obligation of Recycling

'Getting the fundamentals right' in the life economy begins with calculating the costs of commodity cycles which are externalised onto all but the corporations privately profiting from them. The moments of commodity cycles (1) to (7) above expose the nature of these costs. Correction of the costs begins with *institution of conditions of market sale that internalise rather than externalise life costs.* One level of accountability is already instituted – the transparency requirement of posting ingredients of mass-produced consumption goods on them. This is a familiar condition for sale in the mass market, but even here there are gross exceptions – such as the sulphur and lead contents and source of extraction of gas not stated on commercial tanks, or known toxins and carcinogens on cigarettes, or genetically modified organisms in foods. There is no reason whatever why regulatory consistency, protection of human health and consumer sovereignty should not bring these exceptions into line in any rules-based market.

The Case of Food

There is no reason why a constructive label requirement of *certified nutritional value and safe consumption* should not also be posted on every mass-produced commodity for human organic consumption as a condition for market entry, particularly across borders. This labelling could be administered by already qualified and evolved institutional agency, the UN Food and Agriculture Organisation. The lion's share of 'foodstuff' product-value crossing national borders is made up of US-made junk-food and beverages. Whatever does not have any nutritional value or contained poisons needs to be able to be distinguished from what does, or the market becomes a carny vendors' game of suckering consumers. Since knowledge by the market agent of what is being bought is already presupposed in market theory, refusal of access to such knowledge is, in truth, a *violation of market principle itself.*

By itself this labelling requirement would significantly transform the market to 'the knowledge economy' it pretends to be, the 'sovereignty of the consumer' in more than propaganda, and a 'choice of goods' that can select for well-being rather than ill-being (e.g., obesity, cancer of the bowels and other organs, and generalised life degradation). There can be no doubt that nutriment-leached, processed, sugar-saturated, genetically engineered, and chemically contaminated junk-food and drinks are flooding urban and rural markets across the world against all claimed market values – forced in by transnational trade edicts, state subsidised by First World states, putting local food growers everywhere off the land, and systemically depleting the health of humans everywhere. One might truly say the world is having its food forced down its throat until there is transparency of product contents and a choice of healthy good. Clear certifications of nutritional value as well as toxic contents or residues by independent, internationally qualified assessment would significantly correct the deliberate mass adulteration of the globe's very food supply, and favour responsible food production now overrun by corporate contamination.

This is one downstream moment of the commodity cycle, but its logic of accountability is applicable at every moment. In all cases, *the life economy standard is to secure people and their life conditions from degradation or destruction by corporate agents now above accountability for what they extract, manufacture, waste and sell.* One form of accountability is the basic market inhibitor of cost increase. Since the principle of cost reduction has caused the problem in the first place, cost is an *internal* market selector. An orderly process of public authority adding costs proportionate in size to externalised costs caused by corporate commodity harms and public nuisances thus achieves the rational objective of *internalising these costs in the commodity cycle which causes them.*

The market's required internalisation of commodity cycle costs admits of many forms. At the level of the individual consumer or set of consumers, it can operate by choice to buy only those products which have ruled out externalities by the nature of their production and price. *Fair Trade* is a significant movement in this direction, making major headway in Britain with labels which indicate that the good for sale has met the following conditions: democratic organisation of production by worker-owners, co-operatives or independent unions, the exclusion of child labour, safe and self-directed work conditions, environmental sustainability, consumer price that pays the cost of production, social premiums to improve conditions, and long-term relationships between Fair Trade purchasers and their producers.[40] *Small-scale organic production* typically includes organic working conditions resembling Fair Trade, but by ruling out food production with no chemical inputs and no factory-farming methods. It too prefigures the life economy turn. That in both cases growing demand far outpaces supply is a pattern that indicates a trend. The limitation of these important movements in commodity production are that they are generally limited to foods, still have small market share, and are typically bought up by conglomerates as they achieve more. The life economy requires the rudder and keel of public authority to turn the ship.

Cost Accountability in Sales Price

At a more general level, government acts in the common interest by *building restorative costs into the commodity price as a condition for its entry into the market the government represents*: with internalised costs assessed on the basis of costs incurred to clean up or restore, and deterrent steering of firms to more life-efficient production. Types of impostment and sites of application vary with the life harms they target. The market is, however, forced in the opposite direction by trade and investment fiats which make it illegal to 'discriminate' against any foreign-made commodity selling tariff-free in domestic markets because of its 'process of production' (e.g., by child-slave labour or by genocidal occupation of indigenous lands). We meet this problem in Chapter 9. Most of the life-damages done by commodity cycles in any society are, however, caused *within* them by the processes of harm identified from moments (1) through (7). Costs to life of the pollutant wastes left by consumer commodities themselves – for example, throwaway containers and exhaust fumes – can be built into their *cost of purchase* (e.g., waste-taxes on all throwaway containers or commodities, and strict pollution removal requirements on all gas-powered vehicles licensed in the jurisdiction). These are known and perfectly enforcable resolutions, but are blocked from public policy discussion and implementation by the market value-set, even at the level of ecological economics.[41] Yet their application across CCCs would single-handedly reverse the largest uncontrolled aggregates of resource depletion and ecosystem *pollution*. There is no question of 'scaring away investors' or 'jobs', since the application is at the *sale* end of the CCC, not the investment end, and the measure would create good jobs at no public expense.

Property Responsibility for Manufacture and Use of Commodities

The generic resolution of *conditions of market sale* not only includes application of increased costs on life-insulting commodity cycles. Accountability can be restored by another principle well-known in the market, *the private property principle*. Since every commodity on the market has belonged as private property in part or whole to the corporation manufacturing and profiting from it, they are accountable for its effects. If their manufacture does systemic damage to others and to their life conditions, it is reasonable to require that responsibility for such harms extends back to their producer who has made the product. For simple example, *all* corporations can be straightforwardly held accountable for recycling of all the containers, packagings and durable commodities they input into *an economy's life cycle as a strict condition of their entry into any society's market.* Corporate externalisation onto others of costs for retrieval, treatment and disposal of these registered inputs is like an extortionate gang being permitted to defecate everywhere in public with impunity, with others required to pick up after the violators, dispose of their waste, and generally adapt to their continuous fouling of society's life conditions.

This is, incredibly, society's condition today. It is as reversible as the analogue. Recycling of all waste produced by corporations as a condition of the sale of their products in the society's market that hosts them is, again, *a generalisable principle which follows from life economy standards.* It is, in fact, a requirement of any sustainable civilisation. It cleans up the waste, and recovers wasted materials. It thereby selects for recyclable production and packaging, and so reuse reduces demand on natural resources. It also costs no jobs or public revenues, but creates required economic activity at the cost of the vendor who wants the market.

This accountability principle is generalisable to all durable commodities as well – appliances and gas vehicles, for example. Throwaway housings of appliance functions and gas vehicles are far more hazardous than other throwaway corporate containers in the wastes they impose on society's life conditions. They too can be systematically redirected for recycling to the manufacturers responsible for them. The motivator for compliance can again be continued sale of the product in the host market. The costs again are borne by the market agent imposing them, not the host society. This basic principle of market justice is also applicable to any society, or to all at once by binding article of world trade.

The same principle can be applied to *consumers*. The toxic fumes, wear and tear on public roads, and accident causation consumers produce at others' expense by their usage of motor vehicles can also be tracked and paid for at the consumer end by cost-restorative levies on all fossil fuels purchase, satellite tolling of road use, as well as preventative safety regulation. The *life-cost accountability principle* throughout does what the theoretical infantilism of the market model cannot achieve – has not internalised as a life requirement – connecting back systemic aggregate effects of life harm and costs to their cause, and building restorative costs and safety regulation into future production and consumption.

In civilised conditions of market entry and individual consumption, long-term tooling for reuse of used products by market manufacturers becomes a preferable strategy to recover their obliged expenditures on non-polluting and resource-wasting products. At the consumer end, their added price for depleting use and waste can only be avoided by consumers through not buying the product, or paying in full for their consumption. Preventative regulation in all cases targets those externalising costs at the expense of the life of societies and environments. All life-damages that cannot be properly restored by these extra charges are, in accordance with this same regulating life standard, prohibited as crimes against the person and property are prohibited now.

Everything connects, but not in the market calculus. *Only reconnection across the phases of the commodity by a life-value frame of reference can restore the bearings of life organisation to economic judgement.* In such ways, a life-blind market calculus whose universalisation chokes the world with its pollutants, toxins and wastes is made accountable to the common life interest upon which any human society is based, and that any market requires for the transparency of exchange itself.

Life economy principle 3: **labelling of all consumer items with transparent indicators of contents, including UN/FAO-rated nutritional values of foodstuffs and drinks;**

- **internalisation rather than externalisation of commodity-cycle costs at all phases of extraction, pollution and waste by strict conditions of market access;**
- **absolute ban on weapons of mass destruction from market sale, and application of precautionary principle to untested commodities;**
- **natural capital inventories and well-being/ill-being index to both measure and achieve true efficiency of national economies.**

9

Global Regulation by Life Standards: A Rules-Based International Life Economy for Planetary Survival

Despite the magical incantations of marketeers about 'market miracles' conferred by the magic of the invisible hand on 'self-regulating markets', no free market has ever existed or can exist without continuous government regulation and subsidising resources. Not even fundamentalist fantasies of a free market can be imagined without *a public authority external to it to institute, codify and protect its property relations, to guarantee its medium of exchange, and to provide its social infrastructure and security of agents.* That is why market fundamentalists demand police, armies and prisons to protect their private property as well as well-ordered power and transportation infrastructures for their market activities. The market's complete dependency on a regulating public authority for these supports is doubly true of the global market which requires vast state tax revenues to represent, subsidise and protect by armed force the interests of transnational corporations. Global corporations' investment and commodity entries and exits from economies across the world would not last a day without these vast extra-market subsidies and coercive mechanisms to impose them on foreign populations.

The Carcinogenic Logic of the Global Corporate System

We have argued that the deepest threat to world and civil life is systematically caused by this publicly subsidised transnational oligipoly, because it is *unaccountable to any life standards at all in its increasingly economic activities.* The disorder of this economic paradigm runs much deeper than the greed of the system's lead money sequencers because, whether they live or die tomorrow, the regulating logic of this value system is to select for maximally more transnational corporate control over world investment and money returns, with no limit to the appropriation or despoliation of civil and environmental life organisation in this 'fierce global market competition'. We have observed the life-blind compulsion of this exponentially multiplying, merging, invading and globalising corporate growth throughout this study. We have found that the regulating structure of its disorder is an instituted value-set that bridges individual and sect, sect and culture, and eventually culture and world as a presupposed framework of perception, judgement and decision. The non-living vectors of this disorder are, at the same time, transnational corporate vehicles which are now structured to have no life-value terms of reference in their command structures.

When any system of life-organisation is stricken by a carcinogenic disorder, the hollowing out of its life resources and conditions proceeds because life-hosts fail to recognise the rogue code of the invasive growth. The metastasising moment is the take-over of nodal selectors to convert the resources of life-hosts into uncontrolled growth sequencing of the invader code with no commitment to any life function.[42] What I have analysed elsewhere as the 'social immune system' has in this manner been fatefully compromised, with the failure of social nodes of finance and trade ministries of national governments to regulate economies on behalf of their social life-hosts. Societies' domestic wage and tax revenues, market demand and natural resources have been increasingly appropriated by the mergings and growths of oligopolist, transnational conglomerates structured only for multiplication of their decoupled stock-values. At bottom, at the level of individual organism or social life-host, the system of life organisation suffers from an *increasing collapse of life-sequence regulation.*

At the social level of life-organisation, the counterpart to the carcinogenic code at the cellular level is the blind proliferation of undifferentiated money-sequences which by the self-expanding nature of their reproduction aggressively increase their demand on and occupation of social bodies with no contributing life-function; but here it is *a ruling value-code* rather than *genetic code* that regulates the invasive sequences of self-multiplying demand. It succeeds, in turn, by penetrating social borders and defences through three avenues of uncontrolled occupation of local and national economies: (1) the electronically instant transmission of its financial demands moving in tidal flows across borders; (2) deregulated freedom of its electronic and exponentially leveraged capital to enter, strip and exit societies at will; and (3) simultaneous abolition of protective walls of resistance by US-dominated state terror against non-conforming individuals, communities and social orders.[43]

The prior investigation of this study has mapped the co-ordinates of this global occupation. We now confront the ultimate problem – *the overwhelming of social and environmental life-organisation by financial growth sequences which move ever wider in their feeding cycles on social and environmental hosts with no committed function to any.* Debt-based pools of life-delinked capital moving in and out of societies to maximise the money-demand accumulation of a dominant fraction of 1 per cent of the world's population are the ravenous appetite of this financialisation juggernaut, and its greatest triumph is to have subjugated the rule of law and responsible government to a transnational command apparatus forged and adjudicated behind closed doors to protect them from any accountability to any interest other than market corporations.

This apparatus of rule is entirely unprecedented in history, unapproved by any electoral process, and has been allowed to override any law or standard beyond itself; yet its occupation of societies across the world is masked as 'globalisation', while its feeding on life economies to become ever more money is called 'freedom'.

The Constitutional Alternative: Civilising the Justifiable Revolution

The United States Declaration of Independence states:

> Whenever any Form of Government becomes destructive of these ends [for which it is formed], it is the Right of the People to alter or abolish it ... When a long train of abuses and usurpations pursuing invariably the same object, evinces a design to reduce them under absolute Despotism, it is their right, it is their duty, to throw off such Government, and to provide new Guards for their future security.

There can be little doubt that, when the facts are reviewed in the light, this globalised regime of rule by financial value-set has imposed far more dangerous abuses and usurpations on the world's citizens and their conditions of life than ever suffered by the thirteen colonies; yet, with no clear or viable alternative in mind, rather than moving to justified revolutionary rejection of this usurpacious system, prior thought should be given as to what *is* the alternative. In fact, there are many alternatives, alternatives which are known to work but, if we move to the plane of *transnational economic regulation* to which nation-states themselves agree to be bound, what are the alternatives here which can provide the 'new Guards' for people's life security and freedom?

Many thoughtful people think there is no *global* alternative, that markets are properly local and self-directing. This position is branded by propagandists as 'wanting to return to the past' or 'protectionist'. Others reason that capitalism itself is inhuman by its very nature, and that only a revolution to rebuild society anew can release us from its chains. The latter view is called by the hate-term, 'communism', or 'Marxism'. A life-ground ethic does not reject either position *a priori*. It considers first what is possible as an international economy within *a constitutionally governed, democratically accountable framework*. It is certainly possible that no viable alternative can succeed within the oligopolist and life-blind global market that has been imposed. Even if this is so, *any* alternative will still have to take into account the nature of what exists and what is possible within the most widely consented-to framework of contemporary society – a constitutional and democratically accountable market order. It is *within this framework of possibility* that this study concludes. There is no pretense of the realisation of humanity's life-ground project at its higher levels of creative possibility. Rather, what follows is understood as a map of the constitutional market way to a national and international life economy.

The key question from within this historically grounded standpoint is not whether a 'rule-based international system' across borders is desirable, but what *kind* of binding rules should exist. The binding rules can continue to enable speculative money capital to enter, consume and exit life-hosts across borders with no conditions by home societies permitted. Or it can be a rule-based system for movement of the world towards corporate accountability to the requirements of human and environmental life. That is the real issue, the choice that is ruled out by the totalitarian cult of 'no alternative'. In fact, there is not one binding article in current transnational trade and investment agreements outside intra-European trade (whose life-serving infrastructures are themselves under corporate attack) which limits this omnibus set of absolute 'investor rights'. On the contrary, every article is dedicated to instituting corporate 'investor rights' as global, unqualified and overriding all life requirements of evolved societies and ecosystems. Underneath rhetorical frills of 'labour and environmental side agreements' with no binding force (the NAFTA), or a 'democracy clause' which forecloses alternatives further (the FTAA), or looney-tunes claims of 'poverty reduction through growth' by New Labour theorists and the WTO, the sole rights protected in any of these regulatory apparatuses have been those of transnational corporations against any accountability to governments, publics or prior international covenants.

The Failed Global Market Experiment: The Case of the United States and its Satellites

The global corporate coup d'état by militarily and financially coerced economic restructuring has a hidden meaning. The binding obligations of its transnational trade fiats compel massive capital and commodity *deregulation* society at every life-serving level, and simultaneous *re-regulation* of all societies by overriding corporate rights at the transnational level. The consequences are disastrous, but not connected. Consider the leading and only surviving 'market miracle' of this failed global experiment, the United States. It is constructed in market images around the clock as the world's 'superpower economy' and history's most triumphant economic model and success. However, tracking the evidence rather than presupposition of the image reveals another profile – a once near-life economy in financialised free fall. $2.6 trillion of unaccountable documented damages a year are imposed on its citizens by their own corporations, whose Fortune 500 do not create but reduce net American jobs. American workers labour the longest hours in the industrialised world, now 3½ weeks longer each year than the former lead taskmaster, Japan. Taxpayer subsidies to these corporations are at least $135 billion per year and growing in the weapons business, while New Deal laws protecting the poor have been repealed. Average wages have fallen by 12 per cent since 1980, while the average work week is 60 hours a year longer, and one man, Bill Gates, doubles his financial holdings to more than the GDP of Bangladesh.

Yet the multiplying national trade and capital deficits of the US, by far the largest in the world, feed on the external world's commodities and savings as the corporate mergers of US and satellite nations grow by 50 per cent a year. Every 12 months 245,000 people are killed by air pollution, corporate hospital malpractice, and toxic exposures in corporate workplaces with only moves to reduce private litigation countenanced by the corporate and oil-ruled government. Repression of labour organisation and violation of labour laws increased even when the economy was on an 'endless boom', as 90 per cent of the economic growth was appropriated by 1 per cent of the population.

At the bottom, 2 million poor people and parents are in corporate state cages, while infant mortality rates are higher than Cuba and longevity is near the worst of all OECD countries. US Amnesty International charges that the US 'has abdicated its duty to lead the world in human rights – no wonder it was ousted from the UN Human rights Commission'. In 2001, the world's and history's most heavily weaponed nation by any measure planned to spend the most it ever has, not to protect the lives of its own people or anyone else, but to 'defend its *investments* abroad'. At the same time, the same corporate-ruled administration unilaterally repudiated signed agreements for international arms control, environmental protection, child rights, and rule by international law, while it simultaneously led its next carpet bombing of a non-colonised society.[44]

The real world underneath this 'global market order' is more life-oppressive outside the US: societies which were only recently heralded as 'market miracles' have been melted down despite 'having the fundamentals right' according to the IMF, the World Bank and 'economic experts' just prior to this fate. These societies were melted down by 'financial liberalisation' which enabled vast currency and uncommitted capital speculations to liquidate their economies almost overnight. This 'free flow of capital' in 1997 Asia transferred $100 billion to currency speculators from their domestic banks, doubled unemployment in leading Korea and bankrupted 90 per cent of its construction companies, destroyed the economy of Indonesia so that vectors of its 220 million people are now widely plundering the world's most species-rich rainforests in desperation, and occasioned the buy-up of the assets of the Asian tiger 'market miracles' at bankruptcy rates – by the very Wall Street investment banks whose lending facilities collected the public money loaned through the IMF. It was private New York banks, not the Asian people, who were, in fact, 'bailed out' by taxpayers. The IMF loans in US dollars went around in a circle to pay debt charges to these private banks.[45]

No change in the capital or financial rules of the 'global market order' followed. Suddenly discovered flaws of the former 'miracle economies' were, instead, identified as the problem – 'crony capitalism' and other slogans substituting for explanation. The problem, in reality, was that the global experiment of deregulated money capital had failed catastrophically for the societies which were pried open by it. Variations on this foreign financial stripping of domestic societies occurred across the world from 1994 onwards as US-led banker recipes reordered the world in accordance with a deranged market value-set – Mexico in 1994, Thailand, Indonesia and Korea in 1997, Russia and its former territories in 1998, Brazil in 1994 and 2001, Argentina and Turkey in 2001, Africa throughout – with resource-rich Congo being looted as another US-brokered 'peace' prescribes the same financial and trade deregulation.

Who will be the next to be hollowed out? The same pattern of effects follows from the same structure of causation, but their connection is blocked out. *In 2001, as the world enters a global crisis of life* and *market demand depletion – by unprecedented market debt, degraded and low-paying jobs, disemployed social sectors, universal insecurity, and ecosystem collapse all occurring together across continents – the reality wall is being hit –* but, still, only slogans and magical market thinking rule policy and opinion. As I write, the corporate servo-mechanism of Tony Blair's British 'government' is preparing to demand that the European Union itself embrace a radical programme of still more 'financial liberalisation' as well as 'removal of barriers' to 'private management of public services' and 'investment of pension funds'. With no 'miracle' left to declare to the world, the fanatic value-set of the global market's finance and media-heads of state keeps driving the world over the cliff of their unknowing.

The Black Hole of Third World Debt: Its Cause and Solution

A poignant harbinger was the heroic 'Jubilee 2000' campaign for can-
cellation of poor countries' debts. Publicly celebrated after years of
growing international concern when the Cologne Summit of world
leaders finally proclaimed a 90 per cent forgiveness of the debts of 'Highly
Indebted Poor Countries' in 1999, a new turn towards a life economy
seemed possible. But the disorder runs to the regulating centre of the
market calculus. In fact, debt payments from Highly Indebted Poor
Countries *increased* during the height of international campaign pressure
in 1996–99 by 25 per cent; only 21 countries of the 187 indebted
developing countries qualified for debt reduction; and the hidden
conditions turned out to be more financial stripping of the societies bound
to them – privatisation of communal lands, abolition of public subsidies
for basic survival staples, pricing of public education and healthcare to
the poor, non-progressive tax rises, dismantling of home-industry
protection, and the selling of public firms.[46]
    What alone changed was the name for the social death-sentences.
Structural Adjustment Programmes were depolluted by incantations of
'Debt Forgiveness Plans' and 'Poverty Reduction and Growth Facilities'
to ward off the contagion of reality – just as WTO and FTAA fiats were
simultaneously conjured as 'plans to reduce poverty'. The clear pattern
of the regulating economic programme remained to impoverish and
casualise social majorities of populations across the world, and confiscate
the lands and resources of subsistence communities by country-sizes
every year. As social intelligence comes to learn, even the deepest social
ethical tradition of the Judaic-Christian's Holy Bible can be sworn upon
before tens of millions of uplifted voices while, all the while, transnational
bank feeding on the poor increased.
    Since the transnational financial system is systematically responsible
for one structural disaster after another with deepening catastrophic
effects and incapacity to adapt to economic reality, a turnaround is needed
as a life-and-death priority for the world. A 'rules-based international
system' to serve human life and life conditions requires *life standards*.
These life standards must restore to all economies the right of production
and distribution of their means of life, rather than ever more exposure to
foreign capital predation of their bases of existence.
    Awakened social intelligence begins with the *transnational debt regime*
for bankrupting governments and public sectors. This mainly post-1975
system of financial stripping societies has ruinously replaced the public
loans, national self-financing and low-interest government-to-
government lending which lifted the developed world out of the
Depression, financed the defeat of Axis fascism in the Second War, and
rebuilt Europe and Japan from 1945 to the 1970s; but the new debt

siphon of private banks and bondholders into public treasuries given free rein in world economies after 1980 did not fall from the sky as a commandment of economic laws. It evolved in subterranean pattern through known determinants which remained unconnected:

1. global money supplies vastly escalated by windfall oil profits cycled through Wall Street and industrial-world banks, unilateral US refusal to honour its debts under the gold standard, the substitution of its nationally controlled dollar as the world's exchange-value base, and the rise of the external 'Eurodollar' currency market;
2. decoupled money tides of unproduced wealth then released into the world to be lent and leveraged to approved Third World dictators for their luxury, US armaments to repress their people in favour of foreign investors, and expatriation of the loaned money back (including rising narco fortunes) to the Wall Street and private transnational financial sectors which encouraged the loans; and
3. debt-service charges far exceeding borrowed sums from then on extracted from the world's poor societies locked in dictatorial poverty – with their citizens seeing little or nothing of the debt money which they have ever after been forced to pay back at compounding interest up to over 20 per cent annual charge.[47]

Two central facts in particular are repressed here which nullify the legitimacy of the debts and their continuing 'service charges'. The first is that *the debt-service payments have already exceeded the loaned sums.* The second is that the US's own doctrine of 'odious debt' and the principles of national sovereignty itself justify *the legitimate repudiation of debt contracted under oppression or against the will or the consent of the people indebted.*[48] The combination of these two general facts justify the general and lawful dissolution of all debt-load obligations now imposed across the majority world. A first precept of a 'rules-based international economy' must relink with life standards of economic governance by a formula for indebted nations' recovery:

Life economy principle 4: **repudiation of all debt of societies without the consent of the indebted people and/or already paid by debt servicing.**

Ending Predation of Economies by Currency Attacks: Continuing the Life-Economy Turn at the International Level

The next step of a legitimate 'rules-based international system' must confront a more sudden predation of human societies. Again it is by international financial instruments with no accountability beyond themselves.

Here debt is created by the involuntary mechanism of external currency attacks on societies' very means of exchange by speculating financial syndicates.

Currency attacks not only expropriate other societies' wealth by non-productive attacks on their very means of exchange, but they also thereby increase all external debts owed by its government and people with no debt voluntarily undertaken by them. The effect is the reduction of the livelihoods of majority populations overnight with none negotiating, exchanging or being accountable for their reduced market and life position.

These systematic life harms, a grave crime under law in the past, are preventable. An international clearing house for foreign currency trans-actions to protect against currency destabilisation is more viable than trade laws now imposed to protect corporations, and was long ago proposed by John Maynard Keynes.[49] Following the logic of currency-clearing processes already followed in domestic societies, an international clearing house for currency exchange is, in fact, achievable as soon as G-7 finance ministers choose to become responsible for a rules-based system in international currency trade as well as all the other commodity trade regulations their corporate governments have prescribed to the world's markets during the last decade. Control of money speculation instead of domestic societies, to be sure, is still an inaccessible policy option for the fanatic global market programme now in motion. Because currency attacks are by leveraged private money stocks, they are presupposed as 'market forces', and approved because they force governments to privatise their public revenues.

In the case of the now financially colonised European Union, for example, the terror of currency attacks has induced collaborator states to abdicate the central monetary and fiscal policy instruments of government to a new European Central Bank run by bankers and locked off from all accountability to electorates and their representatives. The surface explanation here is that only in this way could EU governments protect themselves from the financial terrorists – an explanation which reveals the extent to which governments have been subjugated by lawless transnational financial syndicates with little notice that anything is deranged. Although it is perfectly within the power of governments in concert to regulate financial terrorists at the world's six major trading nodes far more easily than the armed 'international terrorists' they are diverted by (who do a small fraction of the damage), the market mind-set is locked against whatever is perceived to be a state intervention in the sacred operations of 'the market'. The fanatic value-set selects instead for the expropriation of sovereign states' financial levers by market forces to serve transnational corporations and banks rather than the citizens of Europe.

As with all else in this world financial web, it is the internalisation of the ruling value programme as given which which keeps the people in its chains. The disorder by which they are afflicted has, however, no legitimacy even in neo-classical economic models. On the practical level, an institutionalised international currency-clearing system would be far less cumbersome than current operations of the World Trade Organisation to enforce copyright across continents. Currency stabilisation also promotes the productivity of the world's markets, rather than, as copyright law, creating monopolies to obstruct Third World societies' economic development.

What most of all obstructs the institution of an international currency clearing-house are the walls of dogma internalised even by the public and its government as laws of nature.

An option which has peeked through these thick walls of stupefaction over a decade of building pressure from the socially intelligent is the long proposed 'Tobin Tax' on all foreign currency transactions at source. Its imposition is just as feasible as are these attacks themselves. Consequently, much intelligent analysis has been written on this policy option first proposed by a Nobel Laureate economist over 20 years ago, but it has met with little but evasion and blocking by finance ministries. These ministries are by mental habit the doctrinal satellites of the US Treasury which, in turn, is directed by Wall Street bankers. In such ways, a fanatic cult's value-set is instituted, but there remains, in truth, no counter-argument to the Tobin tax which still remains standing.[50]

Although a financial bit-tax targeting large currency exchange volumes for speculative gains can and would certainly deter their occurrence and reap wealth for public use at the same time as long as the speculative attacks persisted, the resolution is not as structurally sound as a clearing-house for exchange stability. Consider a domestic comparison. Imagine a small tax on speculative gains in an open market in interest charges on all banks which happened to be short of currency at the end of the day to meet their deposit liabilities for customers, rather than the stable and unproblematic clearing system for all that is now instituted.

The argument for a international clearing house for currency exchanges is similar, and is required for the very existence of an international market. For it is a necessary condition of the integrity of any market to have *security of the medium of exchange itself*. With different media of exchange used in a global market in its various regions, there therefore must be some order in convertibility across transactions, or the market itself collapses *as* an international market into chaos – as has happened repeatedly over the last decade with feeding frenzies by speculators and banks on the differentials between exchange mediums. This is why the speculative 'constituency for market instability' – as former Federal Reserve Chair Paul Volcker recognised once out of office – is at a deep level the profoundest enemy of an international market order there could be – a parasitic force that intentionally causes and then feeds on the international market *dis*order it has created. Even the world's leading currency speculator, George Soros, acknowledges that such financial speculation 'requires regulation' to avoid social ruin.[51]

Although Soros does not seem to penetrate to the ultimate reason why, the global market requires strict currency exchange regulation to ensure that there is, in fact, *a medium of exchange without which a market ceases to be market*. What has happened here is typical of the post-1980 market's loss of even market bearings. So fanatical and greed-crazed has been the rush to 'deregulate' everything that the *market itself is no longer ordered as a market*. The first requirement of any market is a stable means of exchange able to mediate among its products and services for sale which its agents can transact *in terms of*. Otherwise it is not a market at all, or even a casino, but a global shell-game in the most precise sense. If one is also interested in theoretical coherence, a shell-game without a stable means of exchange violates the meta-premise of all neo-classical doctrine – knowledge of prices prior to rational exchange in terms of them.[52]

Life economy principle 5: **priority institution of international currency clearing house to prevent forced debt creations, speculator predation and destabilisation of price system.**

We now move to the systematic war of movement by transnational money capital to control the legislatures of the world by a supranational corporate authority not accountable beyond itself. Here the subjugation of the world's peoples is not by the single-track methods of public debt servitude or national currency attack, but by a step-by-step campaign to subjugate all of the bases of self-government to transnational foreign corporate bid, purchase and control – domestic markets, labour forces, local natural resources, and public services themselves. The life-economy turn is systematic in repealing these expropriations of society's very grounds of sovereignty and self-rule.

The Decolonisation of Global Society: Restoring the Accountability of Foreign Capital to Sovereign Legislatures

Short-term and unproductive capital movements are a third predatory financial mechanism raiding societies to and from sites outside their borders. As with currency speculation, productively uncommitted capital seeking only returns without investment in employment or useful production is not, in fact, 'capital investment'. It produces nothing, and seeks only more money claims for its possessor. Its mask as 'capital investment' is a foundational illusion of the global market.

Adam Smith defined capital as what gave men work, what produced tangible goods, and what increased the material prosperity of its home country. None of this is remotely true of money 'capital *flows*' across borders. These are not geared for any economic activity but raiding the capital stocks of other societies. Dominantly under four months of duration, 'foreign investments' are now structured for maximal exploit-ation of margins at maximum velocities and volumes, with no commitment whatever to the society or economy hosting them. Yet these short-term predatory 'capital flows' are systematically prescribed by the US-led IMF and World Bank 'conditionalities' to majority-world societies on pain of financial embargo for disobedience. They are the financial correlative of the Opium Wars on China. The difference is that the financial lootings by private banks and portfolio raiders which are thus permitted are far more damaging than an opium-addicted sub-population. 'Freedom of foreign capital flows' are forced into the veins of economies across the world with all the catastrophic effects documented in this study: every nation in the world is destabilised by their unaccountable rights to expropriate and liquidate domestic firms and resources, access public treasuries and budgets, and bid down labour, social and environmental standards. That these overriding rights of foreign powers are proclaimed as their inviolable and higher 'market freedoms' reveals the fanatic logic of the value-set. It assumes all that exists as properly its object of coloni-sation and rule even as its imperium of rule devastates the grounds of civil and environmental life wherever it invades.

Consider the fact pattern. Of the 'free capital flows' which enter and exit societies at the beginning of this century, 75–95 per cent do not, in fact, invest capital in *any* productive enterprise. Their defining behaviour is short-term exploitation of margins and vulnerable takeover assets to strip, with no commitment to any new productive function, or any productive function at all. They are not, in truth, even *capital*, but expro-priators of domestic capital in a carcinogenic growth pattern. Speculative foreign capital can hollow out economies more lethally even than odious debt and currency attacks by confiscating the value of domestic productive assets through payroll slashing, alienation of resources, reduction of established function and, most infamously, overnight liquidation and abandonment. These consequences of 'free capital flows' can put the livelihoods of a quarter of the population into jeopardy overnight through no fault of their own as the raid exits are suddenly consummated.

We have seen the ruin of hundreds of millions of people and their life conditions across Latin America, South-East Asia, and the former Soviet Union by these piratical money-sequence raids on and flights from national economies with no life function and economy-degrading effects. Indeed, even when societies are not bled dry, there is no committed productive function by short-term capital cruising, misnamed 'investment'. Their set-point is to siphon monetary value out of economies by externally *created* money-demand to enrich foreign stockholders, nothing more or less. Behind every decision moment regulating raid entries and exits is the ruling value-set to seek the growth and multiplication of money-demand holdings delinked from *any* social host. That this system of imperial financial confiscation of societies' means of life can be still called 'foreign investment' and 'capital' is a marker of the derangement of the paradigm.

In its industrial build-up, South Korea successfully made it a offence punishable by death to remove capital from the country in which it took profits, and all countries had protective controls to safeguard domestic economies from such predation – a system that brought far greater economic prosperity in even monetised terms before the capital deregulation regime (1950–80) than after it (1980–present).[53] A very dumbed-down social intelligence has not yet seen through the money-sequence feeding on their societies, public sectors, the working majority and the poor as not, in fact, 'the Free World' at all.

Consider Brazil. It followed the financial sect's prescriptions of 'staying the course' of its 1994 Real Plan of 'economic stability' – again the life-sustaining term for what depredates life, the inner meaning of all corporate market representations. The magic formulae to extract the favour of the market gods were familiar. First there were the paradigm recipes of raising interest rates to 'fight inflation' and 'attract loans' along with the 'necessary stimulus to foreign investment' by ensuring domestic stock-market profits. In reality, both inducements enriched productively uncommitted capital at the cost of spiralling public debt charges and no assured productive development. Measures therefore followed to deal with the rising public debt by 'austerity measures'. These were prescribed to 'slash government expenditures', but in fact meant stripping the country's economy-supporting investment in public infrastructure and services. When, as usual, none of the prescriptions remotely worked, but incapacitated Brazil's domestic investment and economic base, the government still stuck to the neo-liberal cargo cult advised by its US-trained economists and depreciated its currency by 40 per cent in 1998, and then another 25 per cent in 2001 – to 'better attract foreign investment', and effectively stripped its own domestic economy and public infrastructures.

Predictably, Brazil's economy has not succeeded by following the global market's remedies for 'foreign capital investment', 'reduction of debt', and 'market growth'. It too has been hollowed out, another sign of a more general consequence to come. Brazil experienced a tenfold public debt rise (62 billion reals to 554 billion reals by April 2001 and still growing), a dramatic fall in domestic investment, and – the effect of its infrastructure being stripped to pay the rising debt – a threatened energy and electricity blackout in three of its five regions to sabotage its very capacity to conduct economic or other activities.[54] Ever attendant to the calls for 'getting the economy going again' by obedience to the ruling formulae for self-destruction, Brazil's response – as this work goes to print – was a 'great development project' – to be precise, a $40-billion government-backed tidal wave of assault on its remaining Amazon ecosystems to crank out the debt money and, as always, 'new national prosperity', by stripping it too – to reduce it by hired foreign corporations to '5 per cent of its ancient growth' within 20 years, and '42 per cent of the rest denuded or degraded', according to Smithsonian Institute scientists after an intensive study completed in 2001.[55]

The world's largest food processors, Cargill and Archer-Midland-Daniels are setting up to control the transportation stations and processing of the deforested-floor produce as long as it lasts. They are further enriched by the formulae for 'economic recovery' by cargo-cult miracles, and so are the oil and mineral extractors and land speculators who can siphon vast wealth out of the economy by the 'globally competitive' mega-project. The 'foreign investment has been attracted', so where is the problem? There is none that the market value-set can see.

Despite this, social suicide by 'anti-inflationary interest rises', 'reduced public spending' and 'incentives to foreign capital' to expropriate the productive domestic economy is not a law of nature. Some countries break out of the invisible prison. Taiwan protected itself against the Asian melt-down by forbidding its banks to lend currency to foreign banks and requiring all corporations to report any large sums being taken out of the country. Malaysia, which recovered far better than its neighbours, required the repatriation of its currency notes within one month for its continued exchangeability in Malaysia, and set limits of law on any of its currency going out of the country. Chile, the least affected of the main Latin American economies by 'foreign investment' predators, imposed a stiff tax on any foreign capital removing its money within less than one year.[56]

However, policies which connect with social life reality do not sit well in 'market circles'. In consequence, what worked well for Taiwan, Malysia and Chile is *exactly what FTAA and WTO regulatory apparatuses seek to prohibit*. For 'the market is agreed' that a global free market must not permit protectionist rules against 'free capital flows', and, in particular, negotiation of 'performance requirements' of foreign corporations in return for their access to domestic markets, public service budgets, and natural resources as an inherent right of 'national treatment'.[57] There is no concern that the latter blanket right to financial hit-and-run across borders unlocks every society's evolved public wealth to unlimited takeover and squandering by foreign corporate interests.

This is called 'market freedom to promote growth in struggling Third World societies', and it is promised to 'solve the problem of poverty'. Not only are every society's markets and factors of production pried open for transnational capital to have its way with no condition permitted. Every society's *public* wealth of social infrastructure and the tax revenues to pay for it (including healthcare, education, and the electromagnetic spectrum of communications) are, with WTO plans, unconditionally exposed to 'financialisation' too, along with natural resource licences for all that can be extracted and sold for a profit (including oil, gas, forests, fish, precious minerals and – ever increasingly – water to drink).[58]

At this moment, a silent campaign is also under way to convert 'licences' for corporate exploitation of public natural resources into long-term 'leases', which effectively remove public ownership title and right to regulate them during the term of the lease-control, because any regulation which reduces 'expected profits' is 'tantamount to expropriation' under the new laws. This extension of private market right to public resources ends society's right to control any of its own life resources against corporate takeover, including water.

The blanket entitlement of transnational corporate powers to access and appropriate not only all societies' natural resources, but also 'government procurement markets' of every type paid for by public taxes, discloses the clear totalitarian design under the slogans of 'freedom'. What democratically accountable governments have formerly been entrusted with the protection and stewardship of, what has formerly been society's evolved shared wealth of public education, health, pensions, and all of its social services sustained by tax-revenues, is being unconditionally opened to transnational corporate appropriation *along with* all society's natural life resources – perhaps the air next. This unlimited entitlement of foreign private power to exploit and expatriate for profit every society's natural and earned wealth by transnational decree collaborated in by servant state officials, is more total in dimensions than any past occupation by armed force. Here also an ascendant position within the invader's hierarchy as a high public official is the reward – along with the new inducements of media limelight and future board-of-director sinecures in perpetuity. Former 'plots for world rule' are parochial in comparison.[59] That is why a universal 'terrorist threat' from all who set their lives against this process is constructed to provide the armed-force backing to the economic and financial occupation.[60]

The resolving regulatory principle of international trade is not mysterious or unknown. It is an undergirding principle already instituted in the terms of the United Nations Charter of Economic Rights and Freedoms of States, but is unlawfully overridden by every US-led trade and investment treaty since 1988.[61] The reverse of the rolling global coup d'état by trade fiat is straightforward, but concealed in the official culture of the occupation.

Life economy principle 6: **repeal of all transnational trade and investment rules which abolish rights of sovereign peoples to (i) foreign capital controls, (ii) negotiated performance requirements on foreign capital use of domestic resources, and**

(iii) retention of their ownership of public service budgets and natural resources.

Just as the corporate colonisation of human societies is structured to strip them of self-government and their evolved grounds of life for foreign exploitation, so even more ruinously has its fanatic-value programme stripped environmental life-organisation for its money-sequence feeding cycles of 'free capital flows'. This systemic threat to ecosystems and the planetary host requires an *international* level of life economy response to connect across national and regional responses already mapped in Chapter 8.

Reversing Global Ecocide: Binding Environmental Standards in all International Trade Regimes

The best-known pattern of transnational corporate capital is one not yet responded to – *the race to the bottom of labour, environmental and tax standards by corporate money-sequences seeking the lowest cost inputs possible.* The deadly incoherence of this 'efficiency' has been exposed in earlier analysis. Here we formulate the general life economy principle which identifies this false concept of 'development' by a categorical proposition. *No society ever develops by having starvation wages for its people, loss of public revenues for its collective life security, and increasingly stripped natural resources*: yet this is the regulating logic of transnational 'capital investment' across the world at the beginning of the third millennium.

The corrective standards required to reverse this systematic cheapening of human, social and environmental life across the world have been well researched, painstakingly implemented, and long evolved by case law. The European Union has developed and articulated in fine detail codified terms of 'rules-based international trade' over a period of 50 years which protect labour, social standards and environmental life and resources more effectively than any other region on the face of the earth. There remains much to do to develop a flourishing life-economy, but the postwar half century has achieved a bridge to it in Western Europe. Its 'rules-based international trade' rules out *by* terms of trade what is elsewhere proclaimed as unavoidable. The world's most ethnically and linguistically diverse region does not have starvation wages, 80-hour weeks or no-benefit and no-holiday jobs *in even its poorest regions*, because the rules of the EU, as distinguished from the WTO or the NAFTA, have codified standards and monitoring mechanisms to *rule them out as a condition of movement of capital and commodities across national borders.* As we have seen, there are immense pressures to dismantle this entire achievement, led by the Thatcher and Blair governments, and counting on race-for-the-bottom corporate costs outside the Continent to drag down the mainstay French and German social economies to compete by the same rules of life-cheapening to reduce corporate costs.

Here I attend to environmental and labour standards. With regard to the environment, there is a regulatory regime in place which more or less effectively proscribes the earth-razing corporate methods still permitted elsewhere – strip-and-abandon resource mining which has destroyed 80 per cent of the old-growth forests of the world (most in the last three decades), emptied fish stocks across oceans, and eco-genocided indigenous communities across the planet by the oil oligopoly alone. Merely extending the rules-based extension of 'good oilfield practices' and terms of clean-up already required in Europe would be a release of millions of peoples and their life-environments from the lawless destruction and looting by oil conglomerates like Shell and Exxon-Mobil across the Third World and native areas of the First World. Any rules-based international trade without these enforced rules is, in effect, a licence for continuing eco-genocide as well as environmental devastation (whether in Alberta Lubicon reserves, the Quiche highlands of Guatemala, the Karen region of Burma, the southeast of Brazil, the Ogoniland of Nigeria, the Marshall Islands, the south of the Sudan, or the oil-opening region of bombed Afghanistan).

On a more general level, the UN Charter of Economic Rights and Freedoms of States already obliges all governments both to co-operate in the achievement of 'the restitution and full compensation for the exploitation and depletion of the natural resources of developing countries', declares 'the sea-bed and ocean floor – the common heritage of mankind', and prescribes that 'all states have the responsibility [to] ensure that activities within their jurisdiction do not cause damage to the environment'.[62] Nevertheless, all of this already existing rules-based structure of economic order – from known 'good oilfield practices' to this and other international laws and covenants – have been silently overrun in the new occupation of societies by transnational regulatory apparatuses about which almost all affected citizens know nothing.

We have seen enough of the causal structure at work in corporate environmental exploitation in Chapters 2, 5 and 6 to know that mining of natural resources with no effective regulatory inhibition on resource stripping, site degradation, and environmental pollution by emissions to the commodity's consumption and disposal is not sustainable. It not only destroys peoples and their communities in a widening arc of eco-genocidal effects which are not connected back to the value-set prescribing them. Its countless pathways of ever larger-scale despoliation are the cumulative destruction of planetary life-organisation itself as 'increased development' and 'market freedom'.

Few still connected to reality would disagree that *life-protective regulation of natural resource extraction, processing and end-commodity standards* may be the single most important constructive achievement of any 'international rules-based economy'. The importance is equal to the desirability of a human future. However, because global ecosystems are interconnected and do not obey national borders of division, and because the race to the bottom by transnational corporate cost-cutting seeks the ideal of no enforced environmental standards to minimise stockholder costs, the problem *seems* inherent in the 'rationality' of the market paradigm itself.

On the other hand, international rules, perfectly enforcable if market access is dependent on compliance with them, can *prevent* the problem to the precise extent that they are *codified and binding in accordance with impartial scientific standards attested to by qualified research institutions independent of corporate funding and control.* If dominant corporations are not to hollow out and poison the world as an 'externality' of 'efficiency-led growth', a transnational regime of *binding* environmental standards must be instituted. Without obligatory world standards as the priority of international trade, there can be no doubt of cumulative ecological catastrophe. It is already well underway, as this study has documented. *Yet all of the effects follow from the ruling value programme.* Its calculus and instrumentation together *entail* these disastrous consequences over time. Unregulated by life-protective standards, they are predictable in kind over the longer term, and are already confirmed by known fact, but the internal logic of received neo-classical economics is disconnected from these consequences as 'external' to its regulating value-metric.

The clear *causal structure* of wilfully reckless resource extractions, processes and commodities polluting the atmosphere and exhausting the elements, forcing indigenous people and subsistence farmers off their land into cities without life function, re-engineering and homogenising genetic structures and desertifying environments, pumping caustics and acids from wood-pulping and metallurgical processes into adjacent lands and waters, and dumping the growing wastes of oil, phenols, arsenic, mercury, lead, polychlorinated biphenyls, insecticides and herbicides into the world's ecosystems without regulation – all connect across levels and regions of the global biosphere. The *command responsibility* belongs to the conglomerate corporations performing all of the large-scale ecosystem extractions, disaggregations, pollutions, depletions and degradations; but the *value-set* they lock-step to is value-adding to money sequences alone, while intergovernmental trade treaties have not one binding article or standard across thousands of pages of rules to oblige even one form of environmental protection.

Since the causal trains at the biophysical level are scientifically understood in their direct harmful effects (despite corporate denials), and since each systemic environmental damage is traceable back to processes under corporate command responsibility, there should be links between them in public policy comprehension. However, the links are blocked out by the granting structures for scientists who are trained and fund-conditioned to presuppose the ruling value-set and not to connect across the phenomena (as we have seen in Chapters 2 and 6). Yet the missing links are is easily comprehended when not occluded by these blinkers. Because virtually every one of the systematic abuses of our shared life-ground occurs *by the wastes and emissions of corporate extractions, processings, and products, it follows then that lines of accountability can be instituted to track and deter their continuance.* However, these connections cannot be seen through the mind-set of the doctrine or of the relevant decision-makers as long as they house it, nor can corporately financed politicians and political and biological scientists funded from the same financial sources expose them without risk. Here most of all *the abyss between cause and effect is structured into the official culture.*

Consequently, systematic evasion of responsibility follows, such as pointing to 'the consumer' downstream to correct what corporations extract, process, produce and mass-market before 'the consumer' exists in the causal chain. However, if we penetrate the evasions and go beyond them, the known method of prevention of all of these assaults on environmental life-hosts has already been demonstrated. Making corporations accountable for what is evaded as 'externalities' is only a matter of structuring the rules of the global market to track environmentally damaging market actions to their known effects. This result is achievable by three measures which are not controversial once out of the mind-box:

1. independent codification and publicising of the known rules of proper extraction, processing and commodity end-products which reduce and remove environmentalal harms;
2. the institution of global monitoring and investigative processes, and hearing citizen, experts and business complaints of their violation;
3. the application of automatic trade penalty for demonstrable violations of the level playing field rules.

These mechanisms are hardly new, and are already developed in many jurisdictions, including across borders in the European Union, using trade law and penalty as the instrument of prevention. It will be said that the structure of motivation in the market makes such compliance with other-regarding law unlikely but, in reality, there are compelling reasons why it is in the interests of every agent with the right to trade and invest within these rules to comply with such disciplines. First, they are motivated to comply so as to avoid automatic trade sanctions which deprives them of revenue or market share. Secondly, they are also further motivated to ensure that all *other* enterprises also comply so as not to gain 'an illegal trade advantage' over them – the 'level playing field' so long trumpeted in corporate ideology, but self-confutingly avoided in fact. Thirdly, such environmental standards are required by any 'rules-based international trade' that is not exposable as a public lie. Fourthly, state or corporate agents who resist international rules to protect the environment while at the same time instituting rules solely to protect the future profits of transnational corporate activities are vulnerable to truthful charges of extreme criminal negligence in endangering humanity and global life conditions themselves. Finally, for all these reasons, continued refusal of accountability for the preservation of humanity's very conditions of future life de-legitimates such a regime and its agents, with all the consequences that then become permissible. Compliance is motivated by self-interest.

Life economy principle 7: **institution of binding environmental-protection standards in all international trade agreements to reduce and eliminate public pollutions and wastes by resource extraction, manufacture processing, and commodities which externalise costs and nuisances onto others.**[63]

We move now to binding life standards for humans in transnational trade treaties, which are no less blocked out of the regulating value-set of the global market system than the environmental conditions for their existence.

Promoting Civilisation Rather than Destroying it: Scheduling Labour and Social Standards

The most astonishing feature of transnational trade treaties since 1988 is that with the exception of the European Union there is no rule or right for *human beings* in any of them. Rights are exclusively confined to corporations, with no right of the lives of individual persons, local communities or national societies permitted anywhere. My previous articles for *Economic Reform* have exposed market doctrine's complete absence of life co-ordinates, and the formalisation of this exclusion in econometrics. We will not retrace any of these footsteps here. We move instead to the repression on the ground of all '*labour standards*' in the NAFTA and the WTO.

Unlike environmental standards, labour standards cannot rationally be blocked out of transnational trade regimes as *external* to the market. The owners and sellers of labour and services are *the most numerous market agents* in international and global trade, and their transactions the *greatest in aggregate value*. One would think, therefore, that any minimally reasonable agreement of international trade would include the great majority of market agents, and those whose aggregate value of goods is greatest. It is here that we find the profoundest incoherence in the world trading system. Those who are most affected by any change in its rules, those who are the vast majority of its exchangers, and those who own the greatest proportion of its priced labour goods are *entirely pre-empted from every one of these international trade treaties.*

Neo-contractarian liberals multiply in the academy; but few connect to the actually existing world because their self-referential discourses express a delinkage of mind from the life-ground. This disconnection is not peculiar to philosophy. Political scientists are structured to blot out the subject of corporations and corporate power in their studies at another level of avoidance. The idea is blocked out of discourse. What is not discussed excludes critical understanding of it. So across mainstream academia – political science, philosophy and economic theory being at the centre of the abdication – there is silence on the subject of transnational corporate power in transnational structures of governance where no other right is recognised. It is, in effect, a taboo topic. The bridge from factor of production to human being is ruled out *a priori* – as it was with the rights of slave purchasers in another era.

In fact, a new rule-book for humanity's material reproduction and exchange which grants rights to the corporate party alone has largely been completed. Yet no liberal ethicist who is paid to reflect on such matters exposes this abyss of anomaly in transnational contracts which entire peoples must obey. In the face of such an anomaly, contractarian thinkers have said nothing. No employer interests can explain this mind-block. The mind-set regulates perception beneath the market interests of social agents.

It could be answered that all market agents are nonetheless '*represented by their elected governments*'. But this reply only deepens the problem; for it contradicts the dominant market premise that governments 'should not interfere with the market' – claiming to speak *for* the market's vast majority without, in fact, consulting them, while all the while rewriting the market's rules to favour one faction alone.

In truth, the sacred principle of 'democratically elected government' which is claimed to give these very transnational edicts their legitimacy has *itself* been violated by stealth in every step of the 'free trade agreements'. Not one of their terms has been public debated since 1990, voted on, or even made available to be read by the vast majority of citizens. Whip-controlled members of political parties in all countries have been coerced to vote for these omnibus commands they have not read. Only *faits accomplis* are rammed through legislatures, all or nothing in every case. This government by covert plan, procedural secrecy at every step, and all-or-nothing ultimatum is as anti-democratic in process as can be. Indeed, not even the majority of business agents – who are not transnational corporate giants – are spared in this usurpation. For they are no better informed or participant in the process. In reality, the free competition among suppliers that the classical market prescribes is nullified by the dominance of a transnational oligopoly, an oligopoly which trade-fiat structures enforce across borders and against prior laws of national ownership, domestic market share and natural resource control.

Most dictatorially, those who are dispossessed by the rewriting of existing market rules to favour transnational corporate oligopoly are prescribed to from *outside* the market's operations by transnational state decrees. They are not even informed of the nature of the changes that dispossess them. What no-one appears to have observed is that none of this is a *market* function. It is all *political edicts overriding existing markets with no voluntary exchange involved.*

There can be little doubt of the dispossessing effects on the majority of market agents by these *extra-market* prescriptions – mass losses of secure jobs, systematic reduction of livelihood and pay, insecurity of employment, de-unionisation, decline of benefits, deterioration of working conditions and unenforced safety-health standards, and loss of social service and security benefits. As absolutist as these non-negotiated attacks on the majority of market agents by non-market means are, one eventually penetrates the ruling design. *The vast preponderance of market agents are abolished as market agents by transnational trade apparatuses, which, in turn, are imposed in every case from outside the market's transactions.*

Compared with this holus-bolus confiscation and expropriation of the entitlements of the majority, past revolutions are merely reshufflings of the deck. Even the twentieth century's nationalisation of a minority's capital properties by half the world's states does not match this global redistribution of wealth and power. Next to the pretence of 'free market and democracy' concealing this transnational corporate rule by decree, the claim of Communist Party apparatchiks to represent the 'democratic republic of the people' is an impartial conceptualisation. The 'New World Order' is, in truth, the most massive and all-levels expropriation and confiscation of the majority's individual and shared wealth and participation in their government in history, most of all dispossessing and disempowering the world's majority poor. All past economic and political entitlements outside the corporate intra-firm market have been cumulatively suppressed and transferred to a locked-in repertoire of expanding money sequences of corporate, bank and portfolio speculators.

This financial-faction-led revolution has been achieved by the most remarkable process of all, the *internalisation* of the ruling value-set as 'inevitable' and affording 'no alternative'. No fundamentalist religion or superstition has been more absurdly closed to life reality. Academic, administrative and political classes crouch before 'laws' of econometric equations of transcendental order none question.

Even rationalisations of 'democracy' occlude reconnection to the actual world. So it is said with solemnity that 'representative democracy' is not *direct* democracy, and elected leaders must make decisions for society which are in response to the 'new economic forces to which we must adapt'. Yet none of the slogan arguments begin to explain why the contractual discussions for the rules of this imposed global system of how to live, the terms arrived at, and the enforcement by secret panels have been kept from public view through every step over a decade of one set of edicts after another. Nor do slogan arguments which the 'opinion-making class' and the academic mainstream repeat explain why the majority of market traders have never had reported to them a single verbatim article of these 'agreements', and have fundamentally reduced and jeopardised their economic position both as market agents and as citizens with no *market* transaction.

That these articles prescribe all of this, including arrangements to reduce or eliminate workers' shared wealth of social benefits, services, insurance, family and child security is not 'inevitable'. It is the financial equivalent of an armed force invasion. Instead of sending tanks and armies to the front, it has advanced through another medium of social attack and subjugation – financial instruments and commands rather than military ones. We might recall the famous declaration of former US Secretary of State, John Foster Dulles: 'There are two ways of conquering a foreign nation. One is to gain control of its people by force of arms. The other is to gain control of its economy by financial means.'[64] There can be little doubt that this mechanism described almost half a century ago has been deployed in the technologically and politically favourable conditions existing since the fall of the Soviet Union.

This worldwide occupation of societies and subjugation of their workers by 'financial means' has largely proceeded through the device of *rewriting the rules* of international trade so that foreign money-capital rights override all labour and elected government rights. This has been the main vehicle of riding through borders – by monetised rather than armed invasions, take-overs and raids. Part III of this investigation articulates the constitutional means for reversing this covert system of global occupation; but the themal structure of recovery is *the institution of binding trade standards that protect the majority's economic rights rather than abolishing them.*

The excuse of the collaborating political classes has been to pretend that this systematic invasion of the majority's rights and livelihoods cannot be prevented any more than the decrees of Fate. In prescriptive divination of the future, incessant incantations of 'necessity' and 'no alternative' have accompanied the invasion throughout. As with tyrannies of the past, rule is maintained by pervasive ignorance, super-stition, and fear of consequences for disobedience; but in the age of 'the knowledge economy', brute force and stupefaction are not themselves enough. The tyrannical requires the clothes of proclaimed 'science'. Yet the 'science' invoked *conceals* cause–effect relationship by a method-ological autism that decouples from the actual economy. Thus, years after the trade deals have been imposed, only researchers who read their corporate-lawyer contents know that not Fate, but covert articles in hundreds of commands to societies are the 'invisible hand' at work. *The 'inevitable' is in fact prescribed, and then reified as a market law of nature.* The vast majority who must exchange their work to live are thereby made more insecure, most poorer, with a growing minority homeless and destitute. The next generation is left to a future with ever fewer vocations in public service and life-serving jobs. This is the world of universal insecurity that the 'war against terrorism' diverts the world from to another cause.

Ever more slogans of 'new freedoms', 'international trade to overcome poverty' and 'global tides rising' are the accompanying chants of the corporate world crusade, as once the pleasures of the life hereafter were hymned in a previous era of religious enthusiasm; but the actual race to the bottom of livelihood security, working standards, and freedom of human life takes place on the life-ground. Yet an insistent anomaly remains throughout. Nowhere does any 'globalisation' advocate explain why the vast majority of market traders, upon which every market is based – along with the unwaged labour that produces them – are *all* uniformly banned from any reference or protection in negotiations between corporate-state plenipotentiaries over twelve years of writing new rules.

The problem of the contractual exclusion of the majority who trade non-financial labour and services becomes insoluble when one recognises that corporate financial agents and support staffs, themselves not elected by anyone, nor representative of any interest but a small faction of money-sequencers, the under 1 per cent of the first world population who derive 90 per cent of the revenue gains of the new order, are themselves *not* excluded from any of these processes, but are invited in to monitor and direct them.[65] This corporate representatives propose and set the terms, advise the negotiators throughout, occupy 90 per cent of public 'consultation' group seats, and preside over the financial and media support systems which elect and remove heads of state and ministers to and from office.[66] The ideology of the order's legitimation, 'democracy and freedom', are ideals that are, in fact, systematically usurped.

A master illusion of the market mind-set, however, normalises the usurpation. Self-maximisation by some employing and disemploying the rest of society, it is assumed, necessarily maximises the welfare of all by the operation of the laws of the 'invisible hand'. Stolen and bought elections and corporate-lobby laws do not alter the transcendant justice of market laws. Its operations are supported with fundamentalist passion even by those losing their livelihoods. Emotions too are selected for and against by the regulating value-set. Market justice cannot be questioned if it is presupposed as the order of freedom and development on earth. Consequently, the fanatic value-set is duly formalised as axioms of *a priori* necessity, imitating past physics, cast in decoupled mathematics, mystified as inconceivable, promulgated in policy demands by elected rulers, and proclaimed as the law of no alternative to which all must submit to survive in the world.

The invisible hand that is conceptualised holds sway over the flux, it is believed, by linear equations from the nineteenth century. Believers nod in reverence across economics and philosophy to the final norms of 'Pareto optimum/efficiency', whose terms are conflated for maximum effect. The perfecters of cant are lost in its elaborations. To paraphrase eminent dissenting economist, Lester Thurow, near the beginning of this regime's absolutisation: 'Instead of adjusting theory to reality, reality is adjusted to theory – or creed.'[67] As in past system-bound delusions, the trance eventually succumbs to the lines of reality, and society finds its bearings in the world that remains. In this case, the alternative has already largely evolved, but has been ruled out from view from by the doctrine.

We know that *the majority of agents in the market, those who work for a living, have market interests with corresponding rights for their protection if it is a market and not a corporate command system.* Workers in aggregate possess the market's greatest interests even in monetised terms, and their stakes, their required freedom and protections of exchange, their proper security of expectation, their safeguarding from disordered violation, and their importance to any economy's productive functioning and stability are all primary rights of which they and their families are being unilaterally dispossessed *as market agents.* The substance of an economy does not disappear by corporate lawyer fiats, corporate media spins and the smiles of coiffed politicians. If an international economic order is desired, it either includes the majority of the market in its terms, or it is a usurpation of the economy by decrees with no negotiation or transactions with the majority of its agents.

It is not as if the current overthrow of the market's established exchange systems had no option in a new international system. On the contrary, the labour and occupational health and safety standards set up to ensure the security of the great majority of market agents have already been codified in the laws of the International Labour Organisation and the transnational trade and investment of the European Union. Only a political absolutism could exclude all these recognised rights of the market's main transacting party when they had been won over two centuries of history. The 'global market' is in this way the overthrow, not the institutionalisation, of a rules-based international economy.

The Repressed European Model

When the issue of labour standards can no longer be suppressed, as at the turn of the century, shift-the-blame pronouncements declare that the problem is 'Third World societies'. 'They want', it has been intoned since the uprisings in the world's streets, '*to preserve their comparative advantage of cheap labour.*' One pretext gives way to another. The majority world, it is averred, now wants limitless hours of work, no life-protective standards of health or safety, near-starvation pay, abusive command, and no security of existence for paid workers. The logic of evil intent is quite clear but, in fact, the European Union has long ago mastered the problem of including differently developed societies into one set of standards by *schedules of accession matched to societies' economic capabilities*. Such schedules of accession define the meaning of 'a level playing field'and 'rules-based system' among differently developed economies that has been proclaimed as a desideratum since 1988. But they include rather than abolish *human life standards* as terms of trade. The 'return to the past' projected onto protestors is, in truth, what is demanded by the global market sect. As usual, market slogans invert facts into images of the opposite.

The real return to the past is to abolish the last 150 years of history, as the global market party has sought to do. Yet the last 50 years are especially instructive. The evolved history of Social Charter standards across the countries of once war-torn Europe provides an evolved base of human standards of life. The living alternative that is denied is to work from them rather than dismantle them by WTO prescriptions. It is true that life-protective labour standards of the European Union and the developed world in general are being attacked by the same lawless trend to the past, with a race-to-the bottom of corporate costs being the financial ratchet for reversing history; but corporate commands levering power inside governments and driving down labour prices by rewriting market rules can only succeed by not being understood. That has been the foundation of the Great Reversal's every step and life-means confiscation from the majority. The global corporate faction operates furtively across nations. It is Protean in forms – Confederations of Industry and Business Councils inside every nation, fifth columns inside governments as Private Financial Initiatives in Britain, the European Round Table of Industrialists inside the EU, the Bank of International Settlements co-ordinating central bankers, and transnational cabals such as the Bildersberg Hotel Group and the Trilateral Commission.

These corporate gang formations have, in fact, no electoral or constitutional legitimacy. They can only operate through unexposed political servants who, in turn, can lead only so long as their constituencies remain blind to their fanatic value programme. More deeply evolved and legitimate as institutions of international government than corporate lawyer fiats and quisling politicians are the articles of the Charter of Fundamental Rights of the European Union, the original Treaty on European Union and the Social Chapters adopted by the Community and the Council of Europe, with juridical institutions forming case law over half a century. So the dismantling of civilisation is not so far advanced or dissolvable as the 'no alternative' faction would have it. Yet the extent of the repression is indicated by the silencing of 50 years of trade and investment history at the most advanced levels of its international achievement. Not a word is uttered in all the transnational trade and investment advocacies about the already developed and historic European model.

The life-protecting terms and instruments of labour rights and social charters are the benchmarks of Western civilisation. After the self-regulating market's colossal failures had delegitimated it in mass joblessness, starvation and transnational bloodbaths across its most developed regions from 1929–45, a social life-connection was evolved by the lead public authorities of Europe. The market system recovered, perhaps only temporarily, by the painstaking evolution over decades of international negotiations in which labour and the rest of society were recognised as market agents *by binding standards of life protection and social solidarity in rights of citizens' capacitation.* The circumstances in which this achievement was won seemed impossible – amidst ruins and tens of millions dead with former enemies as the contracting parties. Yet the historical solution to the ruin unleashed on the world by a failed market order was constructed and successfully applied over half a century, only to be silenced, rolled back and planned for unravelling by 'financial means'.

After decades of trial and stitch-by-stitch construction across languages and nations, the European model remains the only proven alternative. What is not an alternative consistent with social and environmental life is a lawless and life-devastating regime of US-led transnational bank and corporate diktats overrunning the world as its Third Millennium Beast. The bearings of an evolved life economy in the industrial era have been bought at a costs of tens of millions of lives and patient peacetime progression in Europe, but it is a mark of the rule of ignorant absolutism at work in the WTO, the NAFTA/FTAA and their attendant corporate vehicles of command that this work of the twentieth century itself is liquidated with slogans and decrees – rather in the style of the previous Reich plan for world occupation. This last campaign by the corporate allies and subsequent security advisers of US transnational corporations and banks was more overtly invasive in its war of movement, but it was less total in its demands.[68] The international alternative has been already largely evolved, but is in a state of amnesia. It is the silent framework of the transition to a life economy which still stands and is generalisable.

Life economy principle 8: **all trade and investment agreements include binding accession schedules of labour and social charter standards as conditions for cross-border entry of commodities and commodity contents into national markets.**

Meeting the Counter-Argument

The standard repeated justification for not having labour and social standards in international trade agreements is that they would be used as 'protectionist barriers' by the industrial countries against their undeveloped trading partners. The rich countries, opponents claim, would use these minimum standards to negate the comparative advantage of the cheaper labour and production costs of poorer countries. Surprisingly, even activists for the Third World have joined the battle against labour standards for this reason – as I learned from prominent leaders of the opposition movement at the Royal Society of Canada Conference on the WTO in Ottawa on November 17, 2001.

This an a self-undercutting position. If the leadership of the WTO opposition oppose labour standards with no alternative but 'Stop the WTO', they will continue to be dismissed as having 'no constructive ideas'. On the other hand, those propagandising the WTO can continue to take the high ground by arguing that the opposition agrees that 'labour and environmental standards are not in the Third World's interests'. If the street protests persist, the opposition will be pincered. With their most publicly recognised rationale defused, they will be gassed, clubbed and caged for their 'unreasonable' disruptions, using new 'anti-terrorism' laws to fortify the world repression. Nothing but a publicly known and do-able alternative can move the wider public in these circumstances.

Since the European Union model is a constitutional way forward by *what has been proven to work,* the question arises why the EU model not been pressed front and centre by the opposition from the beginning. It is perfectly clear why the corporate side, including the European corporate side, has altogether repressed these historical bearings and life terms of reference. It is less clear why the opposition has been taken in. Complete distrust of the WTO is justifiable, but does not explain why its clear alternative has been so silenced on *both* sides. Strangely, the answers to my questions to such world opposition leaders as Walden Bellow have indicated they have not, in fact, considered the option. Confrontation day in and out may confine the horizons, but there remain unanswerable reasons to back the EU option.

1. The EU alternative cannot be credibly discredited. With an in-place successful history of accession schedules for less developed economies, the stated justification for no labour or social standards collapses.
2. This option calls the bluff of the WTO party with a constructive and proven solution. This is a strategic key since the most plausible position of the dominant 'free trade' faction has been to deny that the opposition has any workable idea of any alternative.
3. The option enables the opposition to pose a dilemma to the WTO party it does not at present have to face. Either humanise the WTO with known life standards of transnational trade regulation, or the corporate programme for a 'rules-based world economy' will be publicly exposed as a lie in the battle for world opinion.

4. There can be no better way of defeating WTO dictates than to agree with a 'rules-based solution', but to demand the life-protective standards of an authentic rule of law which have been completely overridden by every WTO article and negotiating round since its replacement of the General Agreement on Tariffs and Trade. Even if one's sole objective is to stop the WTO as a life-destructive juggernaut, binding life standards are the way to do it.

5. The opposition's battle will eventually be lost by attrition and superior resources if the claim is merely that the WTO 'has too much power', and if the option to this excess of power is not clear and compelling.

6. The unprecedented basis of enforceable international law without armies and bloodshed has been overlooked by the opposition as the very human project it fights for. Instead of jettisoning this base of enforceability of labour, human rights, environmental and other life-protective laws that have *never been internationally enforceable before*, those standing for the life-ground should demand the only international law that has ever been made effective across borders – binding trade rules with market loss as effective penalty.

This is the strategic option that is most of all in the corporate party's interest to keep unseen and unmobilised. Yet it is, ironically, just what the opposition has been co-opted to by playing the role desired – that of refuseniks. What joins the opposition across all its differences, the stand for life standards in a life economy, trumps every pretence that the corporate propaganda machine can generate. One issue is clear. There can be no advance with a mind-set on both sides that prefers propagandist declarations to do-able alternatives that are known to improve the working and social conditions of peoples' lives over half a century.

Instituting Corporate Accountability: The Global Corporate Charter

Life standards can regulate international economic orders, but their violators are entrenched in their 'freedoms' of violation. Corporate agents as well as the global fiat system they hide behind require the discipline of a rules-based life economy.

Peter Drucker is a dean of market doctrine who years ago explained the global market agenda as 'an attempt to defang the nationalist monster'. As we have seen, the transnational rules-based economy of the European Union already 'defanged the nationalist monster'. However, the EU did so by instituting transnational labour and social standards, not by corporate rule with no public accountability beyond itself.[69] Like Milton Friedman, who his former students have advised me says 'Wall Street is a root of all evil', Peter Drucker knows deep down the nature of corporate rule. 'Its power', he says, 'is derived from no-one but the corporate managers themselves, controlled by nobody and nothing and responsible to no-one.'[70]

Since corporations and their owner-managers are accountable to no-one except fellow major stockowners for what they do, public authorities and the public themselves must ensure their accountability if they are not to be subjugated. The currently instituted condition of corporate culture, however, is that the transnational corporation is *above the law*. Legal exemption from liability of stockholders and corporate charters with no public accountability achieve this despotic privilege at the domestic level. Exemption from international criminal law and unilateral right to sue governments by trade regulation achieve it at the global level.

No lords and kings of the past have acquired more unaccountable powers of imperial right than the global market's oligopolist corporations. The difference is that these above-the-law privileges of corporations *are not recognised as a connected structure* so that, unlike past tyrannical rights, there is not a corresponding justification for being above the law, such as a direct and exclusive line to God. Legitimacy of absolutist rule is, rather, *presupposed without reason*. Nor can any reason exist that any intact intelligence would believe. Yet while transnational corporate presumption of being free of all accountability to citizens and governments is not *acceptable*, it is *accepted* because it is not seen. Even marketeers presuppose the market as composed of 'free and responsible individuals', 'subject to the law and normal social obligations' – mantras of doctrine which they endlessly repeat. Not for a decade, however, are the legal 'persons' of corporations included in these recognised principles of obligation.

As elsewhere, the key is silence. Thus economic and political discourse never raise the issue in public places. Not even the concept of '*corporation*' is mentioned from one academic textbook and article to another. Like Yahweh, the word cannot be spoken. Thus, across entire fields of learning whose object is the study of historical, political and economic power and its regulating forms, the Name does not occur. So great a skeleton-in-the-closet of special market privileges and legal unaccountability is required for the regulating mind-set's stability of rule, for once the meaning is understood, it is revolutionary tinder. Prior to the flames, we can observe the deep-structural irrationality of the value-set which sustains this structure of mind and public affairs. It is not held intact by spies and torture chambers, although these exist and grow. Its cornerstone of rule is the captivity of mind.

Nevertheless, a very deep disquiet has arisen across the globe, repressed in the media as it spreads. The license granted to transnational corporations to sell in societies they do not produce in, to control markets and natural resources they only exploit and free-ride on, to siphon public treasuries themselves while paying ever lower taxes, and to repudiate environmental regulation as the world suffers increasing ecological crises

and breakdowns – these tyrannical rights with no obligations are not
coherent to common sense. The Mongol emperor, Tamerlane, at least
stuck to subjugating the bodies and possessions of courtiers and rulers.
The totalitarian project of the Third Reich, on the other hand, was
controlled by mega-corporations with no life-conscience, and these have
traceable connections to still larger mega-corporations today which collaborated with and produced for the Third Reich – from IBM
concentration-camp punch-cards and AT&T ovens to Dupont chemicals
and General Motors and Ford armoured vehicles;[71] but the Third Reich
never got so far as to ring the world in detailed regulations laying down
how peoples and economies must henceforth reproduce to serve corporations' future profits as their ground for existence.

Forbes Magazine, an epicentre of the corporate mind-set, confided in
alarm to its business subscribers in November 2000 that '*the real threat
to big companies isn't coming so much from the Naderites and WTO protestors
as from the populist mainstream*'. The answer is one new demand after
another, keeping populations off balance, mesmerising spins of justification, and systematic reversal of democratic gains – the underlying
pattern of totalitarian rule tracked through this study. After September
11, 2001, this rule by edict went into high gear as oppositions were cowed
by the pretext, but still the life-ground rises through people's increasing
awareness of the massive stripping of life conditions and social entitlements which does not stop. Countless human beings now connect below
the level of corporate ad-vehicle news in self-governed and long-term
opposition across the globe. The movement cannot be decapitated. In the
Spring of 2000, 50 million people participated in major strikes in India,
Argentine, Nigeria, South Korea, Uruguay, and South Africa. In the
Summer of 2001, Italy's convicted criminal Prime Minister has had to
impose an armed camp on ancient Genoa against growing international
public protest against the corporate agenda, while simultaneously a mass
uprising in Ecuador swept the nation for weeks against the usual world
dictates by the IMF. What connects the life-ground movement is not a
conspiracy. It is the human life economy rising against a lethal global
disorder.

The movement has come up from the ground in so many places that
an increasingly mind-challenged central control has only the resources
of constructed crises and slogans to relate to the global economic disaster.
Since all 'market miracles' have collapsed on earth, the transfigurative
magic is sought in new outer-space command weapons to run the world
from on high, in more death squads and bombings of the poorest nations,
and in technical substitutes for the conditions of life themselves imposed
on consumers against their will.[72] Above all, an enemy must above be
constructed to divert public consciousness from the life-ground. 'The
Company', as the CIA calls itself after its transnational corporate master,
strikes at whatever human social movement does not conform. The

billion-dollar-a-day US military is structured to discharge its inventories to sustain the demand for corporate weaponry, and this too requires a never-ending enemy. The discourse of the US command reflects this design. Yet what is always distracted from does not die – the historic illegitimacy of the transnational corporation itself.

What is above all blocked from view in the global market is a set of hard facts which disclose the *hidden financial levers of world command* which are all illegitimate – the private creation of money-demand across borders which propels every transnational market take-over and regional economic crisis, and the ruling charters of incorporation which are imposed across national jurisdictions with no basis but self-issued licenses.

The Corporate charter in History: From Legitimate Public Purpose to Privateer Usurpation

Ironically, corporations began as non-profit organisations for the public good – as they could be again. Corporations were publicly chartered as charitable institutions such as schools and hospitals to ensure their endurance past the deaths of their founders. The constitutional ground of the corporation is the opposite of what it has become, with no charter conditions of public obligation required. Its origin, however, lies in a life economy function, and in a civil commons institution. Here as elsewhere we can see the rogue deformations by the money-sequence sect. Initially small corporations were also chartered for specific economic functions, such as toll bridges, but again depended for charter renewal on serving a public life function. Then after Elizabeth Tudor's reign, 'charters of incorporation' were granted to trade associations. Still, however, they were not permitted to buy and sell their private products. This was to protect the integrity of their public status. These non-profit trade associations did not begin to corrupt society's institutions until – as George Monbiot puts it (emphasis added) – 'a trade association called the East India Company was chartered. It *slowly and unlawfully* transformed itself into a profit-making company of shareholders.'[73]

It is rarely noted today that the founder of market doctrine, Adam Smith, wrote much of his three-volume work, *The Wealth of Nations*, as an argument against the suppression of free trade by chartered private-monopoly corporations. The idea of 'free trade' was directed straight at them, although Smith did not analyse their legitimating foundation as non-profit institutions chartered to serve the public good. In fact, he never conceived of the for-profit corporation we know today as a market agent worthy of the name. The joint-stock enterprise was capable, he said, of 'nothing but uniform function'. Sadly, Smith opposed the national monopolist corporation to make room for what he never saw – the mutation of the free market agent into the transnational oligopolist corporation. There can hardly be any irony greater in ruling ideology than what has happened in Smith's name – oligopolist corporations with no commitment to any society wrapping themselves in the flag of 'the free market' and 'patriotism against terrorists', all the while overriding markets everywhere with the juggernaut of their aggregate operation.

No constitution recognises the corporation. Here too the corporate genome has required an unrecognised vehicle to grow in gang-stockholder anonymity, to control society with no commitment to its life functions. The vehicle the corporations entered into for their constitutional legitimation is almost science-fiction. *The Fourteenth Amendment to protect the rights of former slaves as 'persons' was inverted in meaning to clothe the corporation in the clothes of the former slave and demanded all her rights with ever more dominant teams of lawyers.* This was a move of such startling metaphysical conjury that it is difficult to believe the trick ever worked. Even Justice Hugo Black of the same Supreme Court and bound by *stare decisis*, publicly acknowledged the usurpation of the US constitution by the hijacking of the Fourteenth Amendment by corporate-lawyer machinations. 'Neither the history nor the language of the Fourteenth Amendment', Justice Black reports, 'justify the belief that corporations are included within its protection.'[74]

Here again the *sine qua non* of rule by usurpation is the unawareness of those subjugated by it. The fraudulent claim to the constitutional right of the individual person to privilege business corporations against public authority over its stock-gangster operations was pushed through by a landmark 1886 decision in a judgment rendered in the case of *Santa Clara County* vs. *South Pacific Railroad Company*. The court recognised the railroad corporation as 'a person' so as, then as now, to obstruct public authority from regulating its anonymous stockholders from group self-gain at the public's expense. There was no principle or precedent of law to support the rigged court's judgment – not the only usurper judgment by a rigged US Supreme Court, as we know.[75]

Prior to the legally groundless recognition of corporations as 'persons', incorporation charters also usurp the rule of law insofar as they bestow an above-the-law privilege of exemption from common-law rules and criminal law regarding the *personal responsibility* of those belonging to the stockholder group. 'Limited' means 'limited liability'. Above-the-law privilege for corporations' stockholders is, as always, justified as 'necessary'. The presupposition of judges with no study of economics is that larger capital pools are necessary to achieve economies of scale. From this it is supposed, in a *non sequitur* without argument, that corporate investors cannot be held responsible for their investments. Observe the multiplying absurdity. On the one hand, the corporate investor 'takes risks by his investment' to justify profits without any contribution of work. On the other hand, the risks that justify the profit are removed by above-the-law legal exemption from the liabilities incurred by the investment. On the one hand, therefore, corporations are made persons, on the other, the investors to whom the corporation is bound by fiduciary duty are made immune to personal responsibility for corporate actions.

As social intelligence sees through the emperor's clothes, they no longer conceal the lawless and unaccountable shape. The basis of legitimacy then becomes *to keep the illegitimacy from view*. When the naked power becomes palpably incompetent in serving those it depends upon to rule, it is then also superannuated by fact – unless it can divert the people with newly constructed enemies to distract them.

Rebinding Corporations by the Rule of Law

The idea to begin with was that acts of incorporation were legitimate by fulfilment of a prior condition – *discharge of a specified services rendered to society, whose fulfilment is required to retain the charter*. This is a requirement still in the jurisdiction of public authority to prescribe – both to liberate its electors from their oppressors, and to recover rule by the common interest. If corporate charters can be justified at all, it is only on account of bearing charter obligations. These have been disregarded. The extra-ordinary privilege of corporate investors' immunity to liability for the corporation's actions is, then, the next tier of stockholder unaccountability by absolutist right. If it is necessary, and this has nowhere been shown, such immunity from liability all the more obliges precise performance of actions in the public interest in return for this above-the-law exemption.

Minimally owed conditions of performance imposed by law can bring any corporation to heel, as with past kings. The public's treasury and resources are complementary means. It is not for nothing, therefore, that transnational trade and investment fiats *abolish* all 'performance requirements' of foreign investors, as in the law-overriding NAFTA which the WTO would prescribe to the world. The usurpation is already codified, and proceeds in the early corporate march of this century towards the global level. Yet, accountability of corporations on the transnational plane is as lawfully recoverable as it is on the domestic plane. On the domestic level, a time limit on charters for performance to be reviewed before renewal is immediately securable by law – with specified social conditions to fulfil, as with broadcast licences today. Corporations can be made publicly accountable *as* corporations. That is why broadcasting licences in the US are continually the target for further 'deregulation', and for long-term leases in place of shorter-term licences. On the transnational level, the same process can be used, with compliance a condition for continued foreign market entry, as with compliance with any other trade law governing across-border exports.

Since an estimated 25 per cent of a major corporation's equity now lies in 'the value of its brand's reputation', the unused condition of public incorporation within and across borders is not only a legal constraint to bring corporations within the rule of social obligation and law.[76] It is the basis of the intangible of 'public reputation' a corporation must have to provide itself with an official logo and to sell its commodities to the public. This value is far greater in asset significance than the lives of all its succeeding CEOs put together. With public reputation on the line *and* fulfilment of condition of corporate charter required to be demonstrated before a publicly accountable process of renewal, it would be a foolish corporation, however rich, which failed to observe and fulfil its charter or precise licence conditions.

The Case of the Mass Media

The mass media are a crucial case to bring under a rule of public account-ability and law because all other corporate enterprises depend upon them for their dissemination of corporate messages, and the public depends upon them for understanding their shared condition and possibilities. Broadcasting licences for exclusive access to bands of the publicly owned electromagnetic spectrum are the established exchange mechanism for corporate media to be entitled to their use. Thus, there is no reason why binding standards of impartiality and programme balance cannot be a codified and enforced condition for renewal of broadcast licence or charter, just as they are for community and public broadcasters in advanced cultures. In particular, the distortion of facts and silencing of all counterevidence and argument can be ruled out as a violation of licence obligation, with non-renewal as an undefiable deterrent. With current corporate usurpation of public accountability for private control of public airwaves, mass media programming has become a universal rule of special interest propaganda. There is no standard of evidence or impartiality whatever. The known result is a public communications regime of blanket indoctrination and falsehood.[77] There could hardly be a more deeply destructive structuring of human culture.

This is perfectly preventable. Lawful assertions of public constitutional right to regulate publicly owned airwaves and distribution places are a basic meaning of government in the public interest. They are also an obligation under law of those sworn to uphold their country's constitu-tion. Regulation by known standards of truth and evidence is already a requirement of every profession, and the only sense of a knowledge economy that is coherent. The most basic standards of documentation for claims of fact, for example, would call into question most of what leaders and officials of the 'Free World' proclaim about designated adversaries which are transmitted across societies and borders with no right of reply for anyone or need for any evidence. These standards are no less achievable on the international plane than they are domestically for mass publication of news and messages broadcast across sovereign borders with no right or capacity for rejoinder. Under this lawless regime, one special-interest faction controls the world's public communications with no accountability to any standard of fact or balance in flooding domestic homes and other societies with false messages. No foreign occupation by an arms-backed propaganda machine could be more pervasive for the world's peoples.

By themselves, international standards of mass public communication across borders would be a major gain for world civilisation and the human mind but, as elsewhere, the problem is the complete lack of malpractice standards which bind other gainful services for the public. The next Congressional sitting or international trade negotiation is empowered to institute such standards. No-one can reasonably dispute a condition for entry into another society's market that rules out systematic distortion of facts, false charges and propagandist slanting in international news and reports. Nor can any sane mind object to the prevention of subliminal ads which mislead people to take up disease-causing consumption such as teenage smoking – now prescribed by the WTO as mandatory for other societies to accept (e.g., Thailand and Japan in the face of saturating US tobacco company campaigns). The 'trade right' to pervasive occupation and indoctrination of *other* societies' communications bandwidths and public sites by foreign 'media barons' is an imperialist usurpation that cannot be sanely justified.

Few know and no public is aware that corporate media owner-managements now claim their absolute right to use public airwaves and marketing sites as they please as the entitlement of their 'private property' as media capital owners.[78] Nor are people aware of their continuous spreading of demonstrably false representations as a claimed right of this private ownership.[79] Yet more deeply, even critics do not register that *no private property right extends, in fact, to publicly owned airwaves and distribution sites.* They do not recognise, therefore, an all-important entailment. Regulation of what is transmitted through publicly owned mediums is *not* an interference with private ownership right. In particular, no private property right confers on its possessor the title to deny all communication through public airwaves of all images and facts that criticise or expose corporate market structures and practices that endanger or harm others. Yet, it is precisely this right that has been unlawfully seized and exercised across public bandwidths and newspapers sold in public places. Such asserted private right over society's publicly owned communication spectrums and public property sites is a political absurdity that can only be sustained by not being seen.

As anyone else seeking a public license, activity in the exercise of the licence must be in accordance with standards of accountability to qualify for continuance in its entitlement: in the case of public broadcast and distribution in public places for self-profit, accountable to standards of truth and non-bias in return for grant of valuable public licence to publicly owned frequencies and sites. There is no remote issue of 'state censorship' here. On the contrary, such standards *prevent* censorship by unaccountable corporate rule over world society's speech and communications.

Monitoring and enforcement of life standards always protects life freedom – in the broadcast mode as well as the medical or the educational. In reality, the already evolved avenue of this protection of public life is by independent bodies outside state and political interference, such as colleges of physicians or accountants. Such accountability is standard for all who are not corporate persons, but is repressed from view by the corporate media themselves in the case of public licence for mass communications. Rule by professional standards applied by independent authorities rules out the corporate pretext of 'state interference', while protecting the public against the hijack of their communications fields by private and usually foreign corporate powers.

Beyond the Rule of Force Across Borders: From Absolutist Rights to Obligations for Corporate Persons

The principle of obligation to the public in return for rights from the public is a generalisable principle. It only lacks reclaimed charter and licence requirements to rebind corporations to comply with the common life interest, as all others are obliged to do when licensed as doctors or lawyers or teachers or any other responsible role of gainful right granted by societies in return expectation of competent function. Such standards are more exactly definable than doctors' obligations, and far less onerous than corporate rules to bind employees in subjugated service to private money sequences trumping the public interest. At the most general level, corporate charter standards are most uncontroversially required as *binding on all transnational trade and investment activities and products which enter other societies and markets.* Just as copyright and brand-name law must be complied with as a condition of free market entry across borders, far more important public interests across borders are protected by exactly binding obligations of 'rules-based international trade'.

Corporate obligations to accompany corporate rights cannot be plausibly rejected. It is true that human society has always been challenged by rogue factions and practices. But all surviving societies have met these challenges. Even in the US with its corporately cultivated distrust of government, public authority significantly subdued the prototype corporate apparatus – 'the robber barons' – whose power was more singularly overwhelming than today. Thus, when the first corporate Rockefeller tried to evade the legal obligation of size limit by secret and illegal 'trust agreements' with other corporations (observe the value-inverting slogan of 'trust'), public authority upheld the law. Federal law and enforcement responded with legendary 'trust-busting'. Nonetheless, obligations of every sort, including against economic oligopoly and monopoly, have been repudiated by a doctrine of market magic whose hypnosis, as in previous interregnums, holds for a while. In the long adolescent stage of the species, there are many bizarre and destructive gang behaviours on the way towards a reasonable life economy. Meeting such challenges to its life has long been humanity's spur to conscious development. Abraham Lincoln is a well-remembered statesman who saw the rogue strain in banks as well as corporations. He saw it in New York bankers' charging the government 17 per cent compound interest at a time of national emergency, and he responded with the preventative action of reclaiming government's right to create society's currency. More generally, he presciently cautioned before his assassination: 'Corporations have been enthroned. An era of corruption in high places will follow ... until wealth is aggregated in a few hands ... and the republic is destroyed.'[80]

In the era of 'the global market', there is another twist to our story that is not seen. The corporate charter is *not a charter that other countries have issued to it or recognised by internal law*. In consequence, US or European corporate operations in other countries and demands for 'national treatment' have not even distorted US and British law to legitimate their activities. Prior to routine bribery of foreign government officials, assisted by corporate state threat of force of arms in the background, *corporations have no colour of right to what they do in foreign societies*. Even when they strip other societies' natural resources and domestic markets with the backing of state-sponsored death squads and military terror, as across almost all of Latin America and much of Africa and South-East Asia has been by US state-sponsored armed force, corporations do not have the independent means securely to access these goods of other societies. They also have no right under domestic or international law to the rewards of criminal behaviours, in particular in complicity in crimes against humanity which has been endemic along with armed intervention in Latin America, Africa, the Middle East and East Asia with oil and other resource extractions from majority world societies. A basic principle of law is that criminally-gotten wealth nullifies all rightful title to it. This is a main reason why the International Criminal Court will not be ratified by the US government.

Although many may collaborate with such criminal intents and behaviours in fear of retaliation and terror, no criminal activity is *entitled* to the unlawful seizures by it. We may think this irrelevant to asserted violent power, in which the most lethal rockets and death squads are assumed to prevail, but this cynical view does not take into account the eventual fall of such regimes, so many in even the last 50 years as to challenge enumeration. In the end, the lawless regime cannot count on the lawfulness of those it subjugates. When the life-ground underneath and the working majority suffer systemic loss of life capability under such rule, the real basis of this or any other society is already unravelling.

On the level of normative stability of rule, *realpolitik* cuts both ways. What is lawless cannot expect lawfulness – for example, in protection of US corporate installations in other nations. That is why silence, bluff, threat, and diversion onto others cannot work in the end when the life-ground and the civil commons of society are attacked. A narrow absolutism can only work if it is not seen through. Placement of the corporation above the rule of law it expects from others to finish its next minute's business, day in and day out, is not an arrangement that can last for long once its meaning is evident.

The unrecognised condition of the world at the turn of the century is that transnational corporations' money sequences can profit from virtually anything at all by any means whatever without restraint or accountability. Trade and investment regulation entitles them to enter, buy up and control other societies' markets and resources without standard of law or right of performance requirement governing them in relationship to the public interest or existing laws of any nation – including genocidal oil and timber extraction, slave child labour, ecosystem devastation, drug and money laundering, and arming of war criminals against their own peoples. Not only placed above international law, corporations and their commanding agents assert the absolute right to sell the commodities produced by such means in all *other* societies, with none having the right to refuse. Even when criminally produced commodities undersell domestic economy producers, NAFTA/WTO terms of occupation rule out labels or standards visible to consumers. This structure of *force*, not 'free markets', has a hidden meaning. It reflects the ultimate big lie of the system – its coercive structure which has to rely on force within even its 'free' transactions.

Where does the force and illegitimacy stop? Corporate charters themselves have little or no legal title beyond their place of issuance. The US's main corporations, for example, ride around the world with entitling corporate charters sold to them by states like Delaware and New Jersey for fast-buck local revenues. Drafted by corporate lawyers, they are no deeper in legal right than Nevada marriage licences which come by similar means.[81] Even local US governments are lawfully repudiating these corporate rights to trade on US soil. In Wayne Pennsylvania, 'three strikes and you're out' legislation bars corporations with three public-regulation violations anywhere in the last seven years. In Boulder Colorado, a Community Vitality Act puts a city-wide cap on the number of chain businesses. Nine midwestern states representing 30 per cent of US agricultural income, prohibit large corporations from owning farmland.[82] As with corporate empires of the past, this reclamation of the life-ground advances rapidly as soon as constitutional resources of public accountability are exercised.

In 2001, Bush Jr.'s Assistant Deputy Secretary of State proclaimed what the US had long showed its true colours on: 'There is no such thing as international law.'[83] To confirm the position, the American government refused to accept the application of international law to itself, rejecting ratification of the International Criminal Court it agreed to in 1998, yet it demands the prosecution of others for crimes against humanity which pale as a candle to the sun against its own.[84] The US corporate state also repudiated every other kind of international law it originally signed to bind others, from the Anti-Ballistic Missile Treaty of 1972 to the Kyoto Protocol on climate change of 1998. It further refused to sign international laws against the export of personal weapons murdering 500,000 people a year, the UN Convention on the Child, the Covenant Against Torture, the 2001 enforcement pact of the Biological Weapons Convention and the original United Nations Declaration of Rights itself. The US corporate state is in these ways the quintessential 'rogue state', a term it stopped applying to others when it became clear the meaning applied most of all to itself.

What is not a democratically or lawful regime by its very nature never lasts. Although the world remains in unacknowledged subjugation to such a regime, the question arises. Why would any sovereign government rush to build a 'rules-based international order' with an internationally lawless nation which most of all benefits from the financial, trade and resource dominance which the WTO enforces against societies, while at the same time repudiating all life standards? Other national trade missions purport 'national self interest', but in fact they sacrifice their national interests to a foreign power which declares only its own national interest as of value. Thus the US corporate party still reserves to itself the right not to comply with trade rules it prescribes to others.[85] Only the indwelling repertoire of a locked mind-set can explain the abject servility of other governments to this imperial inversion even of market rules.

Unlike enslaved conditions of the past, this programme of world rule has a lawful option. That is why the satellite spinners out front are so anxious to persuade others that there is no alternative. The facts are that the US corporate state itself requires the world to use its currency, import its goods, provide it with endless natural resources, host its investments and military installations, accept its corporations' and banks' predatory capital, distribute its mindless infotainment at the cost of home cultures, accept its multiplying trade deficits, and join carpet-bombing of poor societies' civilian infrastructures as 'allies'. Why, reason asks, do other governments accede to these self-undercutting terms against the interests of their peoples, when even this 'lone superpower' cannot successfully invade or embargo more than small Third World societies at its height, and even here has been defeated on the ground when defied by a people.

The '*projection* of power' that all corporate US geostrategy is based on depends, as the term implies, on others' seeing what is not there. Again magical thinking is the master of reality in the empire.

The question insists. What operation do nations require half as much as the US corporate state does to get through the next month of foreign resource and revenue dependency? Its strength is obviously not civilised intelligence, or peerless technological excellence, or natural resources, or indeed anything any other society's life economy requires.[86] Its collapsing world market demand has been sucked out of public sectors and working majorities into top-heavy financial circuits of mega-banks and corporations decoupled from useful function. The self-referential circuits of money sequencing without accountability to social standard or life function have already taken down one great nation after another in under one decade. The macro-dynamic of cumulative hollowing-out of world society over its 20-year subjugation and destruction by US-led 'financial means' has not been recognised.

The alternative to the world economy implosion is institution of *life standards* across exchanging societies. The alternative will save countless lives and ecosystems, and will generate massive new economic demand now stripped by the corporate race to the bottom of wages and tax-supported public sectors. The standards of a life economy are as much needed to regulate China after 2010 as the US now, and alone can set the framework of lawful corporate agency to prevent global economic collapse in the broadest meaning.

Life economy principle 9: **an international trade and investor account-ability charter binding all parties selling or investing across borders to uphold commodity-cycle, labour and environmental standards, no-free-riding tax obligations, international standards of public communication across borders, community property rights, and strict compliance with international criminal law.**

We now return full circle to the private creation of currency and money demand by which all the wheels of the oligopolist corporate economy are propelled – not only at the domestic level in the denominations of the official legal tender, but also *across sovereign borders* by foreign banks who issue debts without the money, and by foreign corporations who issue credit in other sovereign societies with no accountability.

From the New World Depression to the World Reserve Fund

Behind the corporate and bank money tides submerging human and environmental life across the globe in debt enslavement and life-stripping restructuring is the private creation of money demand itself. We have analysed the mechanisms for delinking money and credit from any base in the life economy, and from any other value than money sequences. The Bretton Woods institutions of the IMF and the World Bank have been servants to this process, but only by deserting their constitutional terms of reference – 'currency stability' and *the promotion and maintenance of high levels of employment and real income*' on a global basis. It is no longer possible to recognise this United Nations purpose in the money sequences which the IMF and the World Bank have prescribed to the world. In reality, they are structured against their constitutional mandate to expropriate economies across the globe. The result is a system of universal life degradation.

The 'financial means' which are used to deprive economies across the world of their livelihood security, natural resources, and public revenues are all propelled by the existing global financial and banking system. We have analysed the concealed license to print money in domestic societies against constitutional accountability in Chapter 7. Now we move to the *transnational* money-capital pools created out of the same thin air to exploit price margins across borders, destabilise currencies, merge oligopolist corporations, speculate in foreign stock markets and derivatives, and in every way possible expropriate the wealth of national economies with minimal productive input or technology transfer. 'The international banking market', observes Jane D'Arista of the Financial Market Centre in incisive summary, 'is organized primarily around short-term financial instruments – increasingly financing speculative positions – with an uninterrupted growth of external credit markets squeezing the space for national governments and central banks to conduct effective macroeconomic policy.'[87]

The Unseen Logic of the New World Depression

The global economic pattern which all this has precipitated is neither seen nor attended to by official economics, trade lawyers or national policies, but is, nevertheless, economically ruinous in the long term. It consists in a hidden dialectic of hollowing out the world's economies: (1) the systematic and growing *inflation* of aggregate money-demand levered and multiplied by corporate and private money sequencers and, simultaneously, (2) the worldwide *deflation* of national currencies, public sector spending, and aggregate demand of poorer and working populations.

This is the unseen crux of the global market crisis which is still developing outside economic comprehension. The role of the IMF led by the US Treasury has been not to prevent but to enforce the crisis-building pattern by all the instruments at their disposal – public sector liquidation, currency devaluation, opening of borders to short-term and speculative capital tides and state-subsidised commodities from industrial countries, removal of all local subsistence subsidies, and domestic sustenance lands redirected to luxury export. These demands, in turn, are demanded *en bloc*. They pyramid loans to pay compound-interest debt loads to private foreign banks, and they force societies' production into channels that serve foreign desires so as to pay more in debt-loads. Sub-Saharan African and East Asian countries like Indonesia and Pakistan now pay up to five times more for debt-servicing foreign banks or military–industrial providers than they do to public education and healthcare for their own populations.

The inflationary path of bank money-sequencers themselves is a more deeply concealed pattern, not apparently observed by anyone. It occurs by private financial institutions' tidal creations and dissolutions of money demand and credit in foreign countries, which has been enabled by financial deregulation as well as by the generalised terms of debt repayment imposed by the IMF. This *structural inflation pressure* is not recognised as a problem because it is effectively *counterbalanced* by corresponding axing of public sector revenues, secure and higher paying jobs, and social and work benefits which together reduce the aggregate market demand of *non-financial* sectors, comprising the bulk of market demand. Production of goods and services for life requirements, especially by public sectors, is in this way systematically deprived of effective revenues to 'save costs' for the new regime of 'global market competition' and 'financial liberalisation'. The world's economies on national and international levels is, in consequence, increasingly and cumulatively shaped to serve the growth of money sequences without any life-productive function, while simultaneously expropriating revenues from the underlying public and life economy. This is why, in a precise sense, we confront an unprecedented pattern of civil and environmental life-grounds across the globe being degraded, consumed and ruptured in one natural and economic melt-down after another.

There is a consequence of gigantic menace even for the supply–demand structure of the global economy, yet the instituted value calculus of the ruling doctrine blocks out every step of the systematic attack on and depletion of the real economy, and cannot see the macro-causation of what rebounds on the demand side of its assumed 'equilibriating' model. Even the *aggregate global demand* required for economies to go on functioning has been blocked out of view by a self-referential calculus with no connection back to the reality of what has been stripped from public sectors and working classes across continents. The theodicy of 'Say's Law' that assumes the transcendental equation of *Supply = Demand* has returned as the pre-Keynesian ghost of the global counter-reformation.

The real world eventually intrudes on fanatic certitudes, and it does so in proportion to their closure. The market level of the macro crisis may be put simply. *When demand from the working and public-service base of the*

real global economy is hollowed out, aggregate market demand is correspond-
ingly redistributed towards the top end and so cumulatively contracts elsewhere.
The ruling paradigm cannot perceive the real-world dynamic because
its armies of devotees are locked into formal equations within which
aggregate world demand does not register. Instead, the global business
world comprehends the growing global economic crisis as 'lack of
consumer confidence' when, in fact, ever more people do not 'lack
confidence', but the money to purchase their necessities of life. The
relentless and worldwide downsizing of secure jobs and unprecedented
debt-loads forced on them by the neo-liberal model have consumed their
once growing market demand. Since decoupled money sequences alone
count as reality to this closed paradigm, the problem is not computed.
Thus, while the shrinking top end of money demand possession becomes
ever more loaded with loose revenues seeking to be maximally more with
no outlet but appropriation of past wealth creation and future claims on
it, the rich investors and spenders and narrowing middle classes are left
demanding more from their money-sequencing while effective demand
from the majority and from social sector employment implodes.

The Fanatic Value-Set: A Short History of Economic Doctrine Since 1929

With the ruling economic paradigm structured against comprehension
of the problem, the World Depression builds in regional lurches of
devaluation, systemic unemployment, long stagnation, and free-falls of
stock values. In place of understanding, the locked value-set coins
personal images that, like stones wanting to meet the ground, provide
just-so stories of explanation. Anthropomorphic mysteries of 'falling
consumer confidence' and 'investment jitters' are the rope of market
image over the abyss. Projections of moods onto unanticipated outcomes
rule the group-mind, and the believers count as always on the magic of
the market to deliver them in the end.

   For the 'scientific' version of this deism, the 'economy' is formally
represented as an externalised mechanism of competing sectoral money
sequences equilibriating towards aggregate effects. Nothing is allowed
to intrude. Class divisions are forbidden discussion. The life economy does
not exist as a concept. All the subsystems and needs of the life-ground
upon which every money sequence depends are ruled out of view. What
goes badly wrong, therefore, cannot be understood. Thus, the tidal flows
of money demand from the public and the working majority to the
financial faction of the market cannot compute as a problem the inertial
mind-set. The categories of the value calculus rule out its comprehension. This is the closed box of market fanaticism.

   Its fundamentalist religion has almost ruined humanity before. The
market, it was believed, would always self-correct from any crisis – until

the Great Depression which led, in turn, to World War II. When only non-market demand from *purposeful public spending by government plan* saved economies, there was an unprecedented period of prosperity based on public expenditures. This was called 'Keynesianism'. Its opening of the other eye to the demand side of the equation of Say's Law held sway until a new ruling falsehood, 'Monetarism', dislodged it. Monetarism asserted that inflation is caused by *governments spending over their revenues and thereby increasing money supply to raise prices.* This new orthodoxy to reverse public spending and wage-hikes and return control over the economy to private money-sequencing held sway despite the facts – the main one being that 95 per cent of effective demand in the real world was by private debt issuance, compound interest charges and stock-value inflation. The understanding of economics, having performed its religious function of killing the heresy of public investment, returned to life-disconnected equations.

Stripping of public and rising-wage economies proceeded for 20 years across the world. In aggregate consequence, the global corporate system was increasingly *inflationary at its financial and corporate top end* and *deflated everywhere else* by the post-1980 value-set of money-sequence growth at the expense of all else, including society's life.

Under the politically driven redistribution of demand from the public and the majority to the corporate and banking rich, however, there is an even deeper principle of the value-set. Its first commandment of 'value adding' is built into the mind by the 'economic growth' principle of '*forward discount accounting*'. Its regulating calculus assumes that today's invested money-value is discounted by an exponential function of future worth in the market. This means, specifically, the assumption of an increase of today's invested dollars by the device of counting today's dollars as worth 10–20 per cent+ more next year, and 10–20 per cent+ more than the already expanded sum the next year, *ad infinitum*. The original baseline of growth is compound-interest-return guarantee, which becomes the *baseline of value expectation*, the new zero-line from which to expect higher, *exponential returns on money-capital invested* – even if it is leveraged out of thin air. This might seem to be a law of madness on the internal side, and carcinogenic growth on the outside, and it is both. But it is presupposed by the ruling value-set as a law of money self-increase.

The first and classical way of riding the perpetual-motion money machine is by business making tangible commodities in larger volumes at lower cost to sell for a maximum margin to mass markets. The form of industrial civilisation is a product of that money-sequence of value and growth. The second and third ways of profiting from perpetual motion money-sequences are parasitic. They emerge as dominant after the crises of inflation and profitability were met by the Great Reversal begun in 1980. Its regulating imperative was deep-structural, covert and pre-consciously assumed as a syntax of judgement. *Deregulate finance to enable credit and leveraging of investor money-demand without government limit, and ensure against inflation by chopping demand from social programmes, jobs and wages.* The onslaught of this undeclared war of 'shareholder value' was driven by the forward expectation *built into* the market value-set of exponentially more money demand returning to passive 'investors' by market magic. The 'bottom-line' accounting system works from this dereanged premise as *given*. The world has simply followed suit of. Deregulate money sequences, tax-subsidise returns, reduce wages and secure jobs, liquidate and privatise social sectors, and globalise corporate rights with no government intervention permitted – these have been the commanding principles of the counter-revolution against evolved social and environmental life organisation themselves.

Under the new regime's prescriptions, the only way an economy can 'compete' is by serving this self-multiplying money demand machine more obediently than others to 'ensure investor confidence'. Since self-multiplying money-demand always seeks 'the best returns', and does so in the 'new world order' in life-overriding tides across borders without any commitment to any society, submission is declared 'inevitable'. Because 'the best return' means gaining maximally more back than what was put in, and that as fast as possible, normal morality and reciprocity is turned upside down. At the same time, the privatisation and deregu-lation creed serving the morality leaves societies, workers and environments increasingly unprotected from hit-and-run predation by money sequencing at every level. What is not known thoughout the globalising blood-rituals of stripping life to increase money sequencing is that the money demand that investors 'invest' is preponderantly printed by private financial institutions.

The Global Money-Printing Machine and its Structuring for Collapse

We explained this pattern above; but what has occurred on the national plane has occurred on the international plane more aggressively. The money-demand lent to debtor nations or students is not money-demand that the Wall Street banks or other banks have in their tills, or have outside their tills in savings deposits by their customers for interest and investment on their behalf. It has increasingly been levered from deposits in ever vaster pyramid schemes of lending and speculating by created money-demand. When the premium above rate is received from poorer countries or people, well and good. If debtors suffer a collapse from the predator money lending and uncommitted raids and exits of these new 'capital flows', then with the moral reflex of the corporate mind-set, governments bail out the private financial operations with public money. With banks now increasingly owning brokerage houses under financial deregulation, the money they increasingly leverage goes into transnational stock market and speculation and mergers instead of lending to productive enterprises or even Third World governments. The transnational banks continue to collect large debt-service charges from Third World governments, but decreasingly lend to them except to pay their debt charges. International financial deregulation provides much better opportunities for bigger flip-returns in a hurry. However, the money demand across borders that turns all the wheels is privately printed, with no required gold or legal tender to back it up, no mandatory savings base to balance it, and only inflated 'assets' as collateral. These latter may seem secure, but even the most valuable real assets can lose 60 per cent of their value overnight, as with Japanese real estate at the height of its world-leading boom.

The global financial system is, in these ways, a money-pyramiding scheme whose base is unmoored, and structured only to increase claims on the world's wealth at the top end, yet the financial faction whose members still run finance ministries, treasuries and trade negotiations proclaim that 'foreign capital investment and trade' will save the poor by 'the rising tide that lifts all boats'. The mind-lock again blocks out reality as the catastrophe builds. Life security and production of the means of life are blocked out by the market calculus. Even the effective demand of the majority to sustain the international market is a macro-requirement that the closed market categories cannot apprehend. There is more money demand created by bank credit cards than the US Federal Reserve keeps track of, and they attach 18 per cent compounding debt charge with a public prime rate of under 4 per cent. The reason CEOs are paid king's ransoms and stock markets can go through the roof, or collapse, is that all the stock options and stocks escalate in value for which the revenues are dominantly created money with no base. The junk bonds that create corporate mergers pay far more for stocks than they are worth, then the merged corporations lay off workers in the tens of thousands to get their money back. The Wall Street firms putting together the hundred-billion mergers walk off with billions in percentage service charges introducing more bank money demand into the system, while the money fortunes they input into ever vaster money sequences is transformed out of workers' livelihoods. Transnational corporate lease-deals and transfer-pricing use deregulated financial conduits across tax jurisdictions to evade the taxes they owe, cheating public sectors out of tens of billions of dollars.

The underlying pattern is the same across phenomena. Virtual-reality vendors who pay no rent and have not produced any commodity at all come to be valued higher than General Motors in the stock market, and peoples' savings are used up overnight in the burst bubble which has enriched the financial sellers. The accounts themselves are increasingly cooked, with corporations buying their own stock to raise their values, and hiding large amortised costs of take-overs.[88] The twists and turns of life-delinked money sequencing across deregulated borders are bizarre in the extreme, but an inner logic connects across the wildly fluctuating phenomena of globalising insecurity and 'loss of confidence'. The publicly instituted and protected means of exchange of societies across the world are everywhere expropriated from stable functions of public service sectors, working majorities and their dependents, and redirected to increasingly unstable money-sequence growths. Decoupled value-sets sooner or later lead to ruin. The South Sea Bubble was an early 'global market miracle', with even Isaac Newton bewitched and financially broken. Its fall-out led to financial regulation. Today there are no official co-efficients of economic reality left to expose the self-multiplying money with no committed life function, and a collapsing global demand base. Even an arranged war that does not stably spend money into the great middle of the market cannot rescue an imploding world economy. The wider economic system has to be understood. The wider system most basically includes the *life capital* of the planetary ecosystem, but it is more stripped by delinked private money printing and sequencing than the human majority.[89]

The Case of Japan

Let us recall Japan as a case study. It rose a world economic powerhouse with ownership of seven of the world's ten major banks – living off its spectacular productive rise as the precision workshop of the world in automobile and electronic machines. All of this rise was *carefully planned and financed though public ministries* in co-ordination with the for-profit sector, which itself was characterised by far lower pay differentials between workers and management, and ensured life provisions and long-term life security security for employees. However, once its land base became inflationarily priced for speculation and its surplus became unregulated foreign loan and buy-up money, Japan's economy unravelled. The breaking of Japan resulted from unearned and uncommitted wealth which crashed into stagnation – first, through a speculatively inflated real-estate bubble bursting, then by high-riding stock values imploding, and finally by foreign loans that could not be repaid because of other societies' collapsing from tides of foreign and speculatively escalated loans and short-term investments entering and fleeing with no committed and productive life function throughout. 'Opening up borders to free trade', artificially altering exchange-rates to appease US exporters, and bailing out big banks and corporations with people's tax money then followed in accordance with neo-liberal orthodoxy to make matters progressively worse.

Shigeyuki Yoshida, the social scientist who translated my *Cancer Stage of Capitalism* into Japanese, concisely explains the Japanese social fabric now (I quote from his correspondence):

The exit from the 'lost 10 years' called after the economic bubble burst has not been found yet. Some of the biggest banks and retailing companies have been bankrupted, and the taxes from the general people have been used for their settlements. Performers in the money-sequence world (money and stock traders), global companies which produce their products in China and South-East Asia, and import to Japan in the name of 'price reduction', are getting more money and people without such ways have lost their grounds even for daily life. The present government and mainstream economists call their policy 'structural reform', and are demanding sacrifices from the general population (like SAPs to the developing countries), cutting their pensions and medical care for elderly people, for example, and firing people from their full-time jobs to part-time jobs and jobless 'recovery'.[90]

The pattern of global market implosion is cross-cultural. Yet Japan's public investment formula for historic economic success is not taken to a new level – public investment in *life capital*. On the contrary, a corporate-media Prime Minister of Japan is set to dismantle the Finance Ministry as advised by Wall Street and the international financial faction, which cannot forgive the *public planning of long-term investment* which led Japan's spectacular rise to industrial leadership of the world. The hatred of market fundamentalism for any public control or accountability of money sequencing is primeval, a hatred that runs deeper than white-heat Republican rage at Roosevelt for the New Deal. *Public investment that serves the lives of the public is the mortal enemy of money sequence rule*, the real ground of the Cold War and the post-1989 world interregnum. System-deciders to strictly prevent this recurrent social pathology is the first requirement of the life-sustainable economy – as important to economies as life-protective laws are to civil orders.

The Means and Co-ordination of the Life-Capital Economy: Control over Global Debt Issuance and Money Creation

Yet the bleeding of economies by money-creation and sequencing is more aggressive and lawless in the *transnational* market than in domestic economies. It taps into economies by money-creating debt issuance across sovereign borders as 'free capital flows'. This control over transborder money-demand creation and debt issuance has no function but to speculate, charge compound interest, take over foreign infra-structures, merge companies and attack payrolls, bankrupt governments, move into public-run sectors, and generally siphon out market demand from the productive economy. Most remarkably of all, it is presupposed as physical laws are presupposed, although its money-printing invasions have no life function. On the level of macroeconomic outcome, deregulated sequences of appropriation and confiscation of life economies by private money power eventually lead to global demand crisis in the market order itself, whose public sectors and working majorities have been so cumulatively reduced by 'financialisation' that they no longer have the aggregate purchasing power to spend the market into reproductive motion – a crisis compounding the others in the melt-down of global life-organisation.

Life-productive co-ordinates are the economic bearings to reground. In this paradigm regrounding of economic paradigm in life co-ordinates, a unseen turn is needed. Global society as well as nations must recover control over issue of the currency of exchange moving *across* sovereign jurisdictions. As we have seen, central bank or treasury note issues in accordance with life-capital standards and productive means are essential to recovery. Differential interest rates and required currency reserves to back up debt issuance are also available to direct public and private investment towards *life-committed productive functions*, and away from inflationary economic predation. On the global level, financial regrounding in life capital standards is more profoundly required. The world economy is well into its melt-down. It has already experienced it without recovery in Japan, the former USSR, most of Latin America, and the 'Asian miracles'. As the turn of the century passed, the demand crisis began downloading in the exogenously money-spiked US where the world's rich protect their money. Recovery of transnational bearings in means of exchange has become necessary for planetary economic survival.

A 'rules-based international economy' can meet the need by requiring all international money loan and credit creation across sovereign borders to comply with regulating trade standards – standards which serve shared life interests, not a private transnational banking faction's limitless demands for more decoupled money sequencing.[91] Again, the problem is not the agreement of reason with what is self-evident once seen, but recognition *of* the unseen. The derangement of ruling value-set is the illusion-maker behind the eyes, with the master inversion of reality being the ruling financial presupposition that private bankers printing the world economy's new money by no standard of creation than their own money gain at maximum velocity and volume must, by the operations of the invisible hand, optimise economic growth and the welfare of all. The absurdity of it would be a cause of hilarity if it did not steer the world economy into cumulative life destruction. A stable global financial order cannot without ruin be grounded on the self-hypnotic delusions of a private sect about the magical effects of its monetised self-expansion. In the real world even of the narrow market calculus, accountability for transactions is required which is based on reserves for debt and credit creation. In a life economy, creation of new money to fund investment must cease to be unlawfully privatised and predatory. Its issuance must be regulated by codified *standards of life capital security and formation.* Recovery of public authority in money creation is the value-deciding turnaround to the life-sustainable international economy.

Reserve requirements for *transnational* debt issuance and newly printed money demand admit of degrees. Long-term, inter-state loans can be the stable public medium of large-scale lending across borders, as with the postwar European Recovery Programme ('the Marshall Plan'). Regional and public representation on a *World Reserve Fund* board can ensure against G-7 banker control. *To ensure life-capital security and development, new debt and credit issue must serve reproducible life functions as a condition for creating new demand.* Regulation by life-economy standards rules out the worst loans for expenditures on life-destructive weapons, large-scale ecosystem damage, and luxury good production. Unlike Keynesian 'digging holes in the sand', its public investment selects for vital means of life production such as organic foods and clean water supplies, land purchase for landless farmers and funds for women's credit organisations, and soil and renewable resource restoration projects. In the end, the problem and the solution meet in the life-capital economy.

Any authentic economy consists in production and distribution of means of life for its members which would otherwise be in short supply. Thus *money-demand creation* in a market order is properly accountable to these standards of an economy by instituted means to regulate debt and credit issuance across borders. The paradigm turn of the global financial system is understood in the first instance by mapping the principle of loan-reserves from the national domain onto the wider international domain. In the global domain most importantly, legal-tender reserves based on savings and productive means are a bridge back to life-economy standards. They rein in speculation. They inhibit inflationary pressures. They provide the currency base for credit creation to investment in life capital.The sovereign liability for note and debt issue which public authority has long borne is balanced by the established right to money and credit creation. So too at the international level. This is the turn of global financial order to a life-sustaining system, and it is achieved first by the reserve control of money creation *across borders* by the international financial institution we call the World Reserve Fund, the overdue replacement of the failed Bretton Woods banks of the International Monetary Fund and the World Bank. In place of their disastrous misuse of 'drawing rights' to strip rather than support majority world economies, the World Reserve Fund would no longer be 'the battering ram' (as US Secretary of the Treasury Mickey Cantor called it) used by Wall Street and transnational corporations to financially disaggregate domestic economies for their predation, but would regulate *them.* In place of predation, they would be required to put up the financial bases of sustainable life-capital investment on the ground.

Life economy principle 10: **all bank loans across national borders be secured by legal tender reserves deposited in a world reserve fund as the fiduciary authority for the administration and the extension of debt issuance in accordance with international loan standards of life-capital security and development.**

The Logic of Action: Self-Organising Life-Space Reclamation

Behind all life-economy demands is a logic of self-determining subjecthood. Each demand is a bridging principle beyond the fanatic closure of the global market value-set. Each demand draws an exact line against its expropriations and prescriptions, and identifies the constitutional alternative that is denied; each makes the global corporate system accountable to life standards; and each spells out the clearly defined alternative which opponents are falsely proclaimed to be without.

Together these life demands are unified by their selection for *self-organising principles of human and ecosystem life* to be defended by binding obligations in all markets, rather than overrun and despoiled by money-sequencing for decoupled corporate stock-systems whose frame of reference has no life co-ordinates or accountability beyond itself. Institution of life-economy standards can stave off the cumulative economic, civil and environmental disasters faced at the turn of the century, and they can do so by constitutional means. Two great crises in particular are selected against.

The first is the world ecological catastrophe to which these demands all directly or indirectly respond with known parameters of prevention. The second is the cumulative socioeconomic crash of societies across the world which have been stripped of the market demand of their working majority and social sectors. These global crises are both driven by the value-set of the global financial faction. Like the Great Depression, the world ecological and economic depression that unfolds has been propelled by a life-disconnected paradigm of money-sequencing as final purpose, and a bankocracy that has seized control of society's money creation itself and society's very capacities to invest in its own life.

The life economy principles spelled out above define the normative and institutional selectors to meet the systemic world problem. At the same time, they restore the resources of self-direction to economies so they can select for their own life-capital development and productive vocations instead of continuing to be subjugated by a death economy structure prescribed by the US Treasury, the World Bank of which it is the majority shareholder, the IMF of which it is the major shareholder, the US Federal Reserve which sets the world's interest-rate policies, and the transnational apparatuses of trade fiat which institute the rights of corporations to control all of the world's wealth.[92]

Against the Fanatic Programme: Joseph Stiglitz's Inside Anatomy of the Death Economy

The nature of the death economy is becoming known by its agents. Joseph Stiglitz once presupposed its pathologic value-set as his own, but the former Chief Economist of the World Bank as well as Chair of the US President's Advisory Committee on the Economy broke out of the mind-lock at the turn of the century, and after finding that reform was impossible from within, has revealed the deranged value programme from within. It is worth summarising his analysis here so as to see the depth of its organised eco-genocide across nations.

Professor Stiglitz explains that the World Bank, the IMF and their majority stockholder, the US Treasury, issue the same four commands from the centre as obligatory prescriptions to every country across the world. His explanation demonstrates that this omnibus four-step diktat is structured to ruin their economies by every step, and to do so systematically. The first step is what Stiglitz calls 'briberisation-privatisation' – a programme of 'market reform' by which corrupt officials (e.g., in the former USSR and Brazil) privatise vast resources like oil, electricity, industrial assets, and water for their own 10 per cent commission on hundreds of billions of sales. The second step is 'capital-market liberalisation' or the 'Hot Money Cycle' in which foreign bank-backed cash speculates in currency, real estate and portfolio funds, flees, drains national reserves in hours or days, and host governments are then required by the IMF to raise interest rates to 30–80 per cent to tempt back the financial speculators who have hijacked the country's capital funds. The third step is 'market-based pricing' or steeply raising prices on basic life means like food, cooking oil and water, to 'squeeze the blood out of' the poor countries (e.g., Indonesia, Ecuador and Bolivia) until 'social unrest is predictably sparked' and the 'IMF riots' bring in the military solution in which Washington is most internationally invested, while the accompanying flights of capital and public bankrupting allow foreign corporations to pick off the remaining assets 'such as mining concessions or ports' at 'fire-sale prices'. The fourth and final step is the so-called 'poverty reduction strategy by Free Trade' or, in reality, forced mass imports and 'tributes' to foreign corporations coerced by 'financial blockade' until domestic markets are open to floods of foreign US imports. By this four-pronged war of financial movement on Third World's domestic economies, people are, in Stiglitz's words – all quoted text remains his – 'condemned to death' by such mechanisms as 'impossible' prices for branded medicines monopolised by foreign pharmaceutical companies and (what Stiglitz does not reveal) forced import of health-despoiling commodities. Throughout, the money loan system has a set of uniform 'triggers' for repayment (e.g., 'for school building') which requires every 'conditionality' to be accepted, with 111 such 'conditionalities' the average of these prescriptions for striopping economies.

None of this strip-mining of societies by foreign financial and corporate restructuring would be possible under international trade complying with *life-capital standards*, yet all remain obligatory in the global corporate system. However, there remain two limitations of the life economy principles so far identified. The first is that even a market regulated by life-economy standards cannot achieve the society of which humanity is capable; for until human life security and freedom of self-government and expression no longer depend on selfish calculation, as the market value-set requires, the human condition will remain less than truly human. Until humans beings' relationship to fellow life and being in the planetary life-host is structured to be consciously non-destructive of ecosystems and their life-niches, humankind will remain the depredatory species, the opposite of its vocation.

The second limitation is related. Each of the bridging principles of the life-economy paradigm is a normative guidepost given the flesh of specified institutional constraint to steer capital investment constitutionally. These binding standards together form a regulating framework which system-atically selects for life-serving economic capabilities rather than life-degrading functions to maximise money-sequence returns (the system-decider of the received market system). Such regulating life-standards are required for *any* industrialised economy; but the *internal dynamic* of self-organising life itself is not yet mobilised as the ground of all action. Life-standards *make room for* the life-space of peoples, but *movement into these life-spaces* is required if daylight is to be gained.

Moving on the Land: The Life Economy Principle of Justice

Self-organising space reclamation is many-sided. One basic level of the life-economy movement is the worldwide *recovery of unused and misused arable lands by dispossessed rural people*.[93] This is a movement already taking place in Latin America, particularly in Brazil, Colombia, Central America and Mexico, East Africa from Kenya through Zimbabwe to South Africa, and India, Thailand, Indonesia, and the Philippines. 'Across most of the third world, we are seeing the emergence of a new source of hope, of new dreams – those of the largely non-violent poor people's movements who sidestep government inaction and take matters firmly into their own hands.'[94] This description articulates well the meaning of 'self-organising space reclamation' which we conclude with as a *general normative standard* of the human transformation that is underway.

Ahead of the curve of theory, the movement is led by communities themselves to reclaim the life-ground across the world. The most basic of these movements is rural peoples retaking *wasted land* for *the growing of life-means for life* – the very meaning of life capital. To do so, they must liberate the land from idle occupation by landlord classes not using it, from misuse in new golf courses and military seizures, from recreational occupation by urban money-sequencers, and from other finance-driven forms of dispossession of small-scale farming by arable land waste.

La Via Campesina and FoodFirst Information Action Network have organised the Global Campaign for Agrarian Reform. The Global Congress of Landless Peasants' Movements has been successfully launched. The 500,000-strong Brazilian landless movement is occupying land for food growth with 1000–3000 families at once occupying idle land and turning it into small-scale productive farms. India's Chipko movement is a legend for defending its lands against flooding for an urban-based power project. The Coalition for the Defence of Water and Life has been launched in the same horizontally organising form against globalising corporate privatisation of water and seeds. Russian farmers fight beneath news for retention of farmland from the omniverous real-estate market. The Zimbabwean reoccupation of white settler lands stolen from them by colonisation is followed in Kenya and South Africa as the most politically explosive of the worldwide land reclamations.

In some cases, the government assists or recognises the land take-overs by the poor, as in Brazil and Zimbabwe, but in both cases with mixed meaning. In Brazil, there is still systematic discrimination against the poorer by exclusion of title, and in Zimbabwe there is a conflict between seizing land for family farming or for political loot. In most cases of movements onto expropriated or wasted land, the response is armed attack by landlord killers (with more people murdered in Brazil by landlords farming only 50 per cent of their land than by army death-squads during the military dictatorship of 1964–85), or by US-financed or armed militias and rule by terror (as throughout Central America in the 1980s and in Colombia since 2000). In all cases, the market media response is expressed horror at all actions where homeland people needing land act to farm for means of life against absolutist claims of corporate states and foreign land occupiers to non-productive property, waste and unneeded export crops – all for the money-sequencing of the already rich. In the background, corporate-servant academics like Ronald Seavoy call for 'police and soldiers to suppress peasant dissent' and demand more 'armed forces as one of the most productive investments that governments of peasant nations can make ... to enforce commercial policies on peasants with the maximum amount of violence if necessary'.[95] One cannot underestimate the vicious virulence of the global market value-set confronting humanity.

The *life economy criterion* clearly resolves these opposed claims by its principle of justice. For the just value-set always selects for life capital formation and protection over money sequencing – in farming as in all else. It follows that land take-overs are justified and desirable if they turn unused, wasted or non-food soils into life capital – *means of life for people which produce more means of life*. This ethic of the life-ground, conversely, clearly militates against landlords who occupy unused land, or charge 50 per cent-of-crop rental fees which starve small tenant-farmers, as in India; but the just value criterion also cuts against land take-overs in Zimbabwe or elsewhere which expel productive farmers with no effective use of the land for local family farmers growing foodstuffs, but only arms-seized loot and more wasted arable land, which is increasingly depleted and scarce – a major problem in the first decolonisation process.

World reclamation of the free, small-scale family farm also has just results for the life-ground beyond poor families: biodiverse and less mono-cropped and exhausted soils, less chemically destructive farming, better foods without herbicide, pesticide and other toxic residues, and more life-efficient use of increasingly depleted land – consequences which serve the lives of all. If over $100 billion of direct and indirect subsidies to industrial corporate farming is discontinued, biodiversity requirements instituted across farmlands, and externalised costs to societies *internalised* by corporate agribusiness (as spelled out in Chapter 8), the small-scale farm with endogenous inputs is clearly *more efficient*, all costs considered.[96] Small-scale organic food production is more marketable too – as sophisticated world consumers are showing with their expo-nentially rising demand for organic produce which now far exceeds global supply. Reclamation of the life economy, in short, generates effects of life service and restoration across the world – systematically reducing pollution and conserving groundwater, clean air cycling, and civil commons landscapes for all. The market calculus, in contrast, cannot even compute any of these life-values within its price metric. Justice at every level is best served by life scales.

Self-organising reclamation of life capital is specially applicable to the land, but *forests and fisheries* as well as arable soil are included by the same principle of life-space reclamation – from local Amazonian rubber-tree tappers to Canadian East-Coast villages, from biodiversity-creating indigenous peoples in forests to fishing peoples across the bioregions of the world. Everywhere the land, trees and waters can be appropriated as life capital, means of life to make more means of life for people and their environments, organised action is *justified in proportion to the life capital reclaimed*. World resource reclamation becomes the more entitled the more it converts what is being hoarded, wasted, degraded or destroyed into the life-base for more flourishing and biodiverse life. This is *the life principle of justice* which bridges life-ground morality, economics and the rule of law.

'Just war', in turn, is a struggle to the end in which deadly organised force is stopped in a struggle to preserve life that would otherwise be destroyed.[97] There can be no question of which side is right, life or life-destruction, and the only side that serves life is the one that protects or

produces *more needed and vital means of life as its regulating sequence of value*. This is the inner moral code of the global movement to reclaim life space at every level, including take-back-the streets festivals, policy marches and sit-ins across continents. The world movement of the life-ground joins the landless and the poor, the unwaged and the waged, the professional and the citizens of all countries in a universal struggle to liberate the planet from money-sequence absolutism.

Digressions onto propagandist slogans of 'development' with no life co-ordinates, or to the 'violence' of those who resist organised armed attack upon them from outside, are just that, propagandist slogans. However incessantly incantated they are, they are the language of death's party. The return of the peoples to their lands, waters and forests to grow them for life cannot be justly resisted, except by life-serving purpose itself: which, in turn, cannot be told by self-referencing abstractions, but only by the means of life for life it stands for and fights for on the ground. This is the value war of the epoch, and it leads humanity's reconnection to the creation into which we were born.

Industrial workers' movements and social intellectuals have already led the way here for over 150 years, and their instituted gains for human life across generations is inscribed in life standards of labour, social charters and human rights whose global universalisation has been internalised as a global human project. All of these planes of the worldwide movement to reclaim life-space for life are complementary in their organising of life in accordance with its endogenous principles of *vital need satisfaction for life-capability development*, the biodiverse flourishing of humanity and the global ecosystem.

The life economy principle of justice across realms: **self-organising life-space reclamation across unused and misused arable lands, forests and fisheries, safety of urban concourses and coastal waterways, and public education and policy sites in accordance with codified life-standards.**

Codified life-standards have been the work of this inquiry; but they do not spell out the exact parameters of life purpose and action endogenous to every life-space reclamation. The constitutional criterion of academic freedom does this for all places of learning. Workers' unions have negotiated and struck over life-code terms for more than a century. A community's women can be counted on to provide this codification across cultures. The peace movement, the physicians for social responsibility, the constitutional challenge to transnational trade diktats, the leading-edge environmental organisations, the political Greens, the municipal and bioregional activists – all are variations on the life-ground movement, and all advance public understanding, their historic meaning and their bonds of human solidarity in struggle by the life standards they stand for, comply with, and fight for through the distance. The human and civil rights of constitutions that peoples once founded themselves on are just such codified life standards, and are again in the second great decolonisation.

As the tyrannical global corporate programme and its endless weaponries are exposed for what they are by universal insecurity, war, pollution, waste and unaccountability to any life standard, environmental, peace and civil movements for life security and expression develop across all domains of life's kingdom. The emerging global movement of humanity becomes conscious of its meaning through myriad forms and actions not yet connected across their phenomena. Their campaign on the ground is concrete, focused and joins by its stands for created and creating life value in all its forms. It takes back the concourses of people for people, the coastal waters for connection underneath the factory and leisure machines, the classrooms for learning rather than received propaganda, and the public sites of political decisions expropriating the life-ground from the future. Everywhere the problem exists stands the task. Every moment of the long advance of humanity across generations lives through the life-code of value as the metabolism of its becoming. It is a movement that cannot be decapitated, that cannot be fought everywhere at once and that multiplies its spheres of engagement as global understanding spreads through the corporate interregnum across peoples and continents.

If the official 'war against terrorism' declared at the turn of the millennium did not exist, it would have been invented – once again to find an armed and weaker adversary to justify the ascending hidden war against the life-ground which this deranged ruling value-set blindly entails. The repetitive pattern only discloses the end-game. The recovery begins with the seeing through to the other side, and that has begun.

The Life Economy Manifesto

1. Constitutional public accountability of currency and credit creation by 100 per cent reserves for private interest-bearing loans.
2. Public authority's allocation of investment funds, loan credits, interest rates and taxation levels to select for life capital formation.
3. Internalisation rather than externalisation of costs of corporate commodity cycles by conditions of market sale, ban of all commodities of mass destruction, and application of precautionary principle for all market commodities.
4. Natural capital inventories and well-being/ill-being index to measure and achieve the true efficiencies of economies.
5. Repudiation of all debt of societies incurred without the consent of the indebted people or already paid by debt servicing, and institution

of an international currency clearing house to prevent attacks on the means of exchange of sovereign nations.

6. Repeal of all transnational trade and investment rules which abolish rights of sovereign nations to foreign capital controls, negotiated performance requirements on foreign capital use of domestic resources, and retention of homeland ownership of natural resources, electromagnetic bandwidths, and public service budgets.

7. Binding environmental-protection standards and schedules of accession in all international trade agreements to eliminate emissions and wastes by natural resource extraction, processing and commodities.

8. All trade and investment agreements include as conditions of cross-border entry of commodities and commodity-contents into others' national markets binding accession schedules of labour and social charter standards on the European Union model.

9. International corporate charter binding all parties selling or investing across borders to comply with minimum labour and social security standards, commodity cycle environmental protections, international standards of public communications across borders, minimum levels of corporate taxation, maximum levels of market share, and international criminal law.

10. All loans across national borders be secured by hard-currency reserves deposited in a world reserve fund as fiduciary authority for administration and extension of debt issuance in accordance with international standards of life-capital security and development.

Action: self-organising life-space reclamation across misused arable lands, forests and fisheries, urban concourses and coastal waterways, public education, policy and other life-ground sites in accordance with codified life-standards.

Notes

Preface

1. These facts and those in the following paragraphs are most comprehensively documented by Nafeez Mosaddeq Ahmed, Director of the Institute for Policy Research and Development, in his valuable 200-page study, *The War On Freedom: Causes and Consequences of 9–11* (Brighton, UK: 2002).

Part I

1. It is public knowledge that the gap between the richest quintile of the world's population and the poorest quintile has more than doubled since 1970 (now at 89:1). Less known is the fact that by 2000, three people owned more wealth than the total income of the world's 48 poorest countries ('Overview', *UN Human Development Report 1999* <http://www.undp.org/hdro/99.htm>). Not considered in these figures is the further fact that formerly unpriced supplies of drinking water, subsistence farming resources, subsidised necessities, healthcare, education, income security from unemployment, and access to culture goods have been reduced or abolished at the same time, while environmental deterioration and climatic instability have increased. In consequence, the dramatic *relative* decline of the poor's money-demand in the market is accompanied by what the market's monetised metric cannot see, increasing *absolute* impoverishment of life means.

2. In a 1995 Harper's Roundtable discussion, fittingly titled 'A Revolution, or Business as Usual?', Wall Street editorialist, David Frum, urged that the government 'get rid of' Medicare, Medicaid and all other social programmes for children, the poor, the elderly, and the racially or otherwise disadvantaged 'overnight' if possible, while media 'neo-conservative', William Kristol, proclaimed against the Roosevelt New Deal that 'you cannot have a federal guarantee that people won't starve' (*Harper's Magazine*, March 1995, p. 42). President Bill Clinton obliged the new right's revolutionary demand by abolishing Roosevelt's 60-year-old welfare legislation a few

years later, in 1998. The external destruction of social infrastructures by military as well as financial means is analysed ahead.

3. Dean Baker and Mark Weisbrot, *Centre for Economic and Policy Research*, Fall 2001, estimate that for the three-quarters of US workers without a college degree, 'trade may have reduced the hourly wages of three-fourths of the labor force by between 12.2 and 12.6 per cent'. In 1992, the US wealth-distribution figure I cite from the US Congress Office of Statistics was that the wealth of the top 1 per cent exceeded the wealth of the bottom 90 per cent, a figure that has grown to the more extreme, 95 per cent in the years since.

4. The poverty figures skyrocketed from 4 per cent to 32 per cent of the entire transnational population from central Europe to the Urals (Francois Houtart and Francois Polet, *The Other Davos: The Globalization of Resistance to the World Economic System* (New York: Palgrave, St. Martin's Press, 2001), p. 4.

5. Chapter 1, *United Nations Human Development Report*, 1997, p. 2.

6. See Chapter 5 for explanation of this metaphysical contradiction.

7. Robert Reich, *The Work of Nations* (New York: Vintage Books, 1992), pp. 3–8.

8. University of Toronto economist, Kimon Valaskakis, disclosed this fact in 1994, not to be cited again in 'Canada's national newspaper' ('Wanted: A Gatt Agreement That Covers Workers', *Globe and Mail*, April 22, 1994, p. A11).

9. Over 3 billion people in the world live on less than $2 a day, but it is believed by all global financial institutions and the mainstream of development economists that a marginal rise in the *aggregate income of their countries*, if it occurs, is the way to resolve their deprivation of life means. This is an axiomatic premise of ruling doctrine, but it is a radical *non sequitur*. For it blocks out of view *a priori* Third World people's *non-priced* means of life from nature, community and government which are being systematically depleted, polluted and slashed by the very neo-liberal programme imagined to be 'overcoming poverty'. It also nullifies consideration of their free time and self-government as humans while proclaiming their 'increased freedom'. It is here that we see the complete disconnection of first principles from reality which characterises the deranged mind-set.

10. A general hypothesis which one can test over time is that *whatever the US national security apparatus projects onto its designated enemy* – creation of social instability in foreign nations, construction of illegal weapons of mass destruction, terrorist activities by state agents, conspiracies for regional or world rule – *generally reveals its own practices and plans* (a psychological operation which may not be merely psycho-disordered, but also afford plausible justification for US actions to come). In this connection, it is interesting to study the recently released cables from Langley Virginia to covert operatives in Chile prior to the bloody coup overthrowing the democratically elected 'communist' President, Salvador Allende. The key sequence of regulating ideas here is the 'creation of a climate of threat' so as to 'create the conditions and the solid pretext' for 'economic, political and psychological warfare' to combat 'the nefarious evil' that is constructed. 'Create conviction', 'discredit parliamentary solution', 'surface ineluctable conclusion of the inevitable', 'leaving the

indelible residue in the mind that an accumulation of arsenic does' (September 27, 1970, cable sent from Langley CIA office after President Nixon had ordered the CIA to foment a military takeover in Chile, cited in 'Conspiracy Theory', *Harper's Magazine*, April 2001, p. 26, from Peter Kornbluh (ed.) *The Pinochet File: A Declassified Dossier of Atrocity and Accountability* (New York: New Press, 2001)). This set of strategic operations is generalisable to other specific as well as more global plans of covert US international policy.

11. A straightforward documentation of these operations as a sequential whole can be found in William Blum's book, *Rogue State: A Guide to the World's Only Superpower* (Monroe Maine: Common Courage Press, 2000). The Iraq and Yugoslavia cases are analysed in Chapter 2, and the Afghanistan case in Part II.

12. The most striking submission by post-1997 social democrat governments in France and Germany is their silent acceptance of the European Union's Central Bank control (conferred by the Maastricht Treaty in 1996) over government fiscal and monetary policy, with no Bank mandate except to keep public budgets at an historically low 3 per cent of GDP, to 'maintain price stability', and to 'remove all restrictions on the movement of capital', with the explicit prohibition of any attempt by governments 'to influence' the Bank's unelected authority (Article 107). This unprecedented abdication to bankers of control over public expenditures, social infra-structure development, life-protective social programmes, and financial capacity of elected sovereign governments was confirmed without comment or protest by silent incoming socialist parties. A telling symptom of this silent abdication of democratic government and accountability, kept effectively invisible to electorates, occurred in 1999. Germany's new Social Democrat government attempted through Finance Minister Oskar Lafontaine to recoup some of the corporate taxes halved over 20 years during a period of 90 per cent rise in profits. When Deutsche Bank, Daimler-Benz, BMW and other major corporations demanded a reversal of the elected government's public policy, Lafontaine was fired and corporate taxes were cut further, to below US rates. 'Deutsche Bank and industrial giants like Mercedes', explained a senior adviser to the Chancellor, Gerhard Schroeder, 'are too strong for the elected government in Berlin' (Noreena Hertz, 'We Must Stay Silent No Longer', *Guardian Weekly*, May 10–16, 2001, p. 23).

13. Murdoch's News Corporation made £1,400,000,000 from the production and sale of newspapers in Britain between 1987 and 1999, and paid no corporation taxes (*Economist*, January 29, 2000). Far from blocking such tax evasion, New Labour granted further tax giveaways to other rich capitalists, slashing taxes on capital gains from 40 per cent to 10 per cent (George Monbiot, *Captive State: The Corporate Takeover* (London: Palgrave Macmillan, 2001)).

14. No one has better documented the corporate occupation of New Labour's government than George Monbiot in *Captive State*. The pattern I attend to here is an explanatory frame within which all of this documentation works in substantiation.

15. Patrick Wintour, 'Rich Keep More Under Tax System', *Guardian Weekly*, November 30–December 6, 2000, p. 15 and Peter Townsend *et al.*,

Breadline Europe Study, reported by John Carvel, '5m Britons Living below Breadline', ibid., March 15–21, 2001, p. 10.

16. 'Significant Breakthroughs In Employee Involvement Directives,' *EIRI Review*, January–February 2001, pp. 1–3. At the same time as the European Union seeks to lead the Third Way out of the nineteenth century in relations between capital and labour, its own European workers are subjected to continuing *increases* of 'intense noise, painful/tiring positions, handling of heavy goods, and pace of work' (ibid., p. 7). These cumulative deteriorations of work conditions in even the heart of the European Union's 'overprotected workforce that must learn to be more competitive' show the dark lines taking shape on the shop floors of even the world's most advanced labour order.

17. These figures are calculated from the OECD figures reported by Polly Toynbee, 'Stand Up to the Bullying Bosses', *Guardian Weekly*, March 29–April 4, 2001, p. 11.

18. See Monbiot, *Captive State*, p. 345.

19. Pinochet's control over massive cocaine trafficking as well as mass murder and torture – heinous crimes for which Tony Blair's Home Secretary, Jack Straw (who turned in his own son for possessing marijuana) refused to allow his extradition to Spain – is a matter of suppressed record. 'Twelve tons of the drug was trafficked from Chile in 1986–87 alone', reports Hugh O'Shaughnessy, author of the 1999 study, *Pinochet: The Politics of Torture*. 'There can be no doubt that General Pinochet was a party to trafficking. He declared in October 1981, "Not a leaf moves in Chile if I don't move it – let that be clear"' ('Pinochet's Drug Link Comes to Light', *Guardian Weekly*, December 14–20, 2000, p. 5).

20. Madeleine Bunting, 'Stop the Wheel, I want to get off', *Guardian Weekly*, December 2–8, 1999, p. 13.

21. Blair has as I write, for example, successfully resisted taxes on foreign-registered stockholders of British stock, and reversed the French–German project for a charter of human rights to include economic, social and gender rights, and monitoring of environmental protection data. He has done all this to ensure against 'new costs to business' (the sanitised report in 'Blair claims victory on EU tax', *Guardian Weekly*, June 22–8, 2000, p. 8).

22. Prime Minister Chretien is an illuminating case because he has been a Liberal government minister for 30 years since this government's activist role in promoting a national social infrastructure of health, education, social assistance and public broadcasting, national control of oil resources and prices, and foreign investment review. After he promised 'renegotiation or abrogation' of the infamous 1988 'Canada–US Free Trade Agreement' to win outraged public support to defeat the Tories who had instituted the new transnational regime in a victory that left them with only two seats, Chretien reversed his pledge once in office. He has since led the stripping of the social infrastructure, appointed an ex-IMF bureaucrat as the Deputy Minister of the defunded public health system, joked about his Office condoning the pepper-spraying of protesters ('I like pepper with my steaks') at an APEC Summit after it arranged the clearing of blocks of the University of British Columbia so visiting war criminal President Suharto would not have to see protest signs, and devoted his office of Canada's head of state to promoting transnational business interests in Canada and abroad. As the new *CanadExport* journal of the

Ministry of Foreign Affairs puts it, this is 'the one-stop shop, Team Canada Inc' which 'use[s] governmental status to sign and guarantee sales contracts on behalf of Canada [*sic*] exporters' (*CanadExport*, January 2000, p. 16 and Message From the President).

23. I am grateful to the Honourable Libby Davies, Member of Parliament, Vancouver East, for this quotation (Hansard, 19 March 2001).

24. The second-place finisher for Leader of the Conservative Party of Canada, David Orchard, recounted to me on January 16 just after the national convention that Tory leader and former Prime Minister, Joe Clark, had advised him a few days before that if the Conservatives did not join the right-wing Reform Party, there would 'be no Bay Street support' for the party in the future. Orchard replied that it did not seem to him reasonable that 'Bay Street should control all the parties rather than just the government and the official opposition' – to which there was no reply. One year earlier, Tom Aquino, the CEO of the Business Council on National Issues which controls $1.9 billion of assets, had recently boasted in print that he pressured the relevant Liberal Minister Andre Ouellette, to 'get rid of the Combines branch' of Canada's government upholding competition law, and was assured by the minister, 'That's fine. You've got a deal' (Allan Fotheringham, 'Why Lobbyists Should Keep Their Mouths Shut', *Macleans Magazine*, January 4, 1999, p. 114). This structure of political exchange – sacrifice of the public interest in return for corporate support – has in this way become a transnational *norm* which even the respect-for-law traditions of Britain and Canada have succumbed to through corporately funded parties.

25. Keith Harper and Roger Cowe, 'Fury Over Railtrack Profits', *Guardian Weekly*, June 15, 1997. It is important to note that in 1947, the British Labour government nationalised rail services, and that New Labour's support of its privatisation has been without evidence of its superior efficiency or safety, and with increasing evidence of private corporate negligence and exploitation exposed since the fatal Hatfield crash where tracks had been due for renewal for months as profits rose 60 per cent. Such concerns do not compute to corporate investors for whom share-value increased by 13 per cent in the week of the deadly crash.

26. The October 2000 Philips Report revealed that 'at no time at all were [there] calls for research to establish whether pigs, poultry and even farmed fish could carry diseases fatal to humans' (James Lewis, 'Sheep and the BSE', *Guardian Weekly*, November 9–15, 2000, p. 8). With the 'universal forces' of corporate technology now producing 'food' by up to 10,000 factory-animals crowded in a sunless biotic mass with only continuous antibiotic feeding of temporary effectiveness, the BSE outbreak is indicative of a deeper and more pathological value programme.

27. The main reason for this lack of non-proprietary and precautionary research of genetically engineered seed and food commodities is that US and then Canadian and other corporately financed parties in government reversed the conditions for public funding of academic research in such areas from *not* for corporate profit to *only* for corporate profit (i.e., only if a corporate 'partner' co-financed the research). The for-profit take-over of public research funding in biological and biotech research was initiated by the Bayh-Dole Act of 1981 which authorised profit from patented research for University–corporate 'research partnerships'. A declared

'equivalence' between genetically engineered products and natural foods was then assumed as given to avoid the expense and delay of tests, and it became made mandatory under WTO law to accept the genetic substitutes and it was prohibited to label them. Researchers fell into line as a condition for the future funding of their research. An excellent analysis of the generalisable Canadian experience is provided by Professor Ann Clark, 'Academia in the Service of Industry: The Ag Tech Model', Conference of the Canadian Association of University Teachers, Ottawa, October 1999. Once thus positioned, fund-subordinated scientists and directive corporate sponsors selected only for what reduced costs and what increased profits for corporate sponsors as being worthy of research funding, with proprietary secrecy and 'confidentiality' surrounding the process, its results, and its criteria of funding selection. As a former member of a University research protocol committee in one of the world's most research-intensive institutions in the area, I formally identified in committee and in university publications all of this pattern with no response by university research authorities able to disconfirm any of it. For scientists in the relevant fields, however, threats to positions, to funding and to academic reputation are so systematic that closed communications became and remain necessary among those opposing the corrupted research agenda. At the same time, intensively publicised claims of 'rigorous peer review' and 'continuous testing' with little evidence of either are funded by multi-million grants for 'scientific communication of the benefits of the new technology'.

28. A striking example of the dangers involved here is reported by Mark Ritchie, 'GE Release Could Have Ended Life on Earth', *Third World Resurgence*, 129/30, 2001, pp. 2–3. Ritchie's evidence is discussed in Chapter 7.

29. The only interview in which Pusztai's full story was told, interestingly, was in late October 2000 in *The Hindu* of India, from which the following quotations are reported.

30. Cited in Clark, 'The Ag Tech Model', p. 13.

31. Reported in 'At the Edge of a New Dark Age: The Corporate Takeover of Higher Research and Education', *Economic Reform*, January 2000, pp. 14–15.

32. The New Labour edict permitting multiplied GMO trial sites and corresponding contamination risk (Paul Brown, 'Outrage Grows As Number of GM Trials Doubles', *Guardian Weekly*, February 15–21, 2001) corresponded with Russia's intensive GMO field trials spread across 18 regions 'in the absence of any procedures'. At the same time, the Max Planck Institute revealed that the planting of genetically engineered potatoes 'results in changes to the bacterial communities in the soil' (News, *The Ecologist*, March 2001, pp. 12, 13).

33. In nearby France, despite a moratorium on all GMOs since 1997, 40 per cent of maize seeds and crops of centuries of generational selection have been contaminated according to the French Agriculture and Food Safety Programme ('Precautions Fail to Halt Spread of GM Elements in Food Chain', *Guardian Weekly*, August 2–8, 2001, p. 25).

34. GMO contamination is globalising even despite bans. Although Mexico prohibited GMO maize seeds from the country in 1998, the remote native criollo corn regions of Oaxaca were discovered to be contaminated by

Nature researchers years later in 2001 (reported by John Vidal, 'Mexico's GM Corn Find Surprises Scientists', *Guardian Weekly*, December 6–12, 2001, p. 7).

35. Among the relevant corporate inserts into New Labour government offices is the chain-store grocery baron, Lord Sainsbury. See note 37.

36. Monbiot, *Captive State*, pp. 208–20, provides an anatomy of corporate head of government committees whose decisions affect their businesses.

37. Of 75 types of vegetables available at the beginning of the twentieth century, 97 per cent of the varieties of each type are now extinct (*New Internationalist*, March 1991, 1991, p. 3).

38. Surrender of the British people to GMOs has been assured as far as possible by the Blair government in other ways. Lord Sainsbury, former Chair of the Food Chain Group and friend of the US and British GMO lobbies, Monsanto and the Bioindustry Association, with whom he travels, and also founder of the Sainsbury Laboratory at the John Innes Centre for genetic engineering centre, sits in Cabinet as Minister of the Trade and Industry's Office of Science and Technology and directs government scientific funding to, among others, this very genetic engineering centre. While the public's choice for *non*-genetically engineered organic food outstripped domestic supply by 200 per cent and demand for GMO foods was 'approximately zero', Blair-government funding in 1999 was over 30 times greater for GMO foods than for organic foods, and huge propaganda grants from the public purse were simultaneously given to promote GMOs (Monbiot, *Captive State*, pp. 272–75).

39. Further explanation and documentation of this socially genocidal pattern is provided in Chapter 2.

40. See 'The Market As God' in John McMurtry, *Unequal Freedoms: The Global Market As An Ethical System* (Toronto and Westport CT: Garamond and Kumarian Press, 1998), pp. 57–86.

41. F.A. von Hayek's background reverence for the 'transcendant' nature of the transnational market system is analysed in Chapter 5.

42. Blair's 'moral fibre' in the bombing-sustained sanctions of Iraqi society resisted even the 'pleading to the Security Council' of former UN Humanitarian Co-Ordinator in Iraq, Hans van Sponeck. His fuller text as more Afghani civilians were killed by allied bombing than died in the 9–11 plane crashes and millions more were terrorised and made homeless were: 'Britain is a very moral nation with a strong sense of right and wrong. That moral fibre will defeat the fanaticism of terrorists and their supporters' (Michael White, 'Blair Appeals to Public Over Bombings', *Guardian Weekly*, November. 1–7, 2001). The exact figures and sources of the higher number of innocent civilian killings by the US than al-Qaida are the end number of 2772 for the World Trade Center (Associated Press, November 22, 2001) and the rising figure of 3500 for Afghani civilians (compiled from international news records by Professor Marc C. Herrold, University of New Hampshire, Democracy Now Radio-TV, December 10, 2001). Again, we see the operations of inversion which are the hallmark of this regime's representations: *invert mass-murderous and other heinous acts into actions of high morality, and project the nature of these actions onto the designated Enemy as their cause.* This double operation is the inner logic of the system's militant representations across borders, and has predictive power.

43.   In the public sphere, the editor of *The New Republic* proclaimed the general mood of official US public opinion that 'political dissent is immoral' while 'the nation is at war [*sic*]' (cited by Lewis Lapham, 'American Jihad', *Harper's*, January 2002, p. 7). The prohibition of disagreement has more sinisterly spread into US universities. The mildest expression of concerns by university faculty about the US bombing of Afghanistan were tracked and placed on blacklists, while 1700 universities were implicitly threatened with defunding by the American Council of Trustees and Alumni, a Washington-based group headed by the wife of the US vice-president and former Senator Joe Lieberman whose boasted $3.5 billion university fund-base was used as a war chest to attack 'anti-American' speech on campus (Roberto J. Gonzalez, 'Lynne Cheney–Joe Lieberman Group Puts Out Blacklist', *San Jose Mercury News*, December 13, 2001).

44.   See note 39.

45.   The peace movement had become perhaps unstoppable by the slow-motion fall of the Soviet Union, but was instantly faced in 1991 with another Satan, Saddam Hussein, to justify the necessity and deployment of the vast US and NATO military machines costing tens of billions of dollars an hour. Had this war not provided the justification, we will never know how societies would have been convinced that this expenditure was necessary when there was no enemy empire left and when their life-security infrastructures were being stripped at the same time. A decade later, the international environmental movement, the peace movement and the new worldwide resistance to global corporate rule and the WTO, were all in full rise before September 11, 2001, with the new US President, who had lost the American election on votes cast, appalling peoples and leaders across the world with his repudiation of environmental laws, the Kyoto Treaty, the ABM Treaty, and the rule of life-protective law in general, as the US economy went into steep downturn. Again we will never know how the reversal of all of these growing challenges to the legitimacy of the system itself would have developed if another war had not been constructed to make all dissent suspect.

46.   The dramaturgy of the morality play not only structures the representation of 'allied' bombing attacks from the air on Third World peoples, but also the US's unilateral violations of signed treaties to achieve deadly military monopoly of space weapons delivery. As Defense Secretary Donald Rumsfeld declared in the first week of February 2001 to announce this abrogation of the ABM Treaty and movement to attack capacity of any target on earth from the sky, the 'National [*sic*] Missile Defense [*sic*]' programme is a 'moral responsibility'.

47.   The 1991 bombing of Iraq led to the estimated deaths of 500,000 children, while the post-bombing sanctions have sustained this killing of children at an estimated rate of 5000 every month. According to UNICEF's reliable documentation of these figures, the death rate for children under five in Basra province has increased by 1300 per cent since the bombing, and of children over five by 400 per cent. Lethal cancers caused by the permanently radioactive dust of depleted uranium weaponry, and severely abetted by sanctions denying medical supplies, have been a principal cause of 'as many as 500 children a day dying in Iraq' (Report Prepared by Bill Griffin for Bride Rosney, Principal Advisor to the High Commissioner for Human Rights, October 1997). The most exact analysis of child deaths

from the British and US-led economic embargo of Iraq is M. Ali and Iqbal Shah, 'Sanctions and Child Mortality in Iraq', *The Lancet*, May 27, 2000, pp. 1831–57.

48. Refugees skyrocketed to 750,000 Albanians and about 250,000 Serbs *after* the NATO bombing began, a bombing which was itself a war crime under international law (Drs Mary-Wynne Ashford and Ulrich Gottstein, 'NATO's War on Public Health', *Medicine, Conflict and Survival* 16:3 (July–September 2000). According to NATO commander, US General Wesley Clark, this massive multiplication of homelessness by the bombing was 'entirely predictable'. As for the parallel increases of ethnic massacres, General Clark also reported that NATO operations 'were not designed as a means of blocking Serb ethnic cleansing' (Noam Chomsky, 'Sovereignty and World Order', Kansas University Address, September 20, 1999, p. 12).

49. See note 33.

50. Clark is quoted by Noam Chomsky, 'Kosovo Peace Accord', *Z Magazine*, July 1999. Madeleine Albright's full comment was: 'I think this is a very hard choice, but the price, we think the price is worth it' (*60 Minutes*, NBC Television, May 12, 1996).

51. Quoted in the *New York Times*, January 24, 1991, p. 11.

52. US Secretary of Defense Press Conference, October 10, 2001.

53. Ibid., October 11, 2001.

54. 'Charlotte Beers' Biggest Sell', *Business Week*, December 7, 2001, p. 56.

55. *Le Figaro*, October 31, 2001.

56. *BBC News* report by George Arney, September 18, 2001.

57. *Times of India*, October 11, 2001. I am indebted for the sources of notes 56 and 57 to Michael Ruppert <www.covcia.com>

58. These facts emerged in a CNN news broadcast, January 8, in an interview by anchor Paula Zahn with Richard Butler, former chief United Nations weapons inspector, Richard Butler. The term 'big prize' is Butler's.

59. The geostrategic planning for movement onto control of the vast oil and gas reserves of Central Asia for which Afghanistan provides a route out, at half the cost and to the East Arabian Sea with no Russia detour required, was spelled out in former National Security Adviser, Zbigniew Brzezinski's *The Grand Chessboard: American Primacy and Its Geostrategic Imperatives* (New York: Basic Books, 1997), especially pp. xiv, 30–1, 124–5, 130–9, 211.

60. The question put to Secretary of State Powell in his December 18, 2001 press conference broadcast live by CNN was: 'Since there are corroborated reports that Israeli citizens living in the US as members of the intelligence community knew of the September 11 attack in advance, how is the administration going to proceed on this information?' The Secretary of State did not disavow the truth of the report, cast doubt on it, or deny knowledge of it. He replied that he was a 'consular official' working within 'diplomatic channels' and this was 'a matter for the Attorney-General's Office and the FBI'.

61. The requirements for the self-defence argument under Article 51 of the UN Charter to hold under international law are that another nation must have invaded the defending country by orders of its government, and that the counter-attack must be to prevent further military attack. Neither condition is remotely fulfilled by the September 11 terrorist actions. Bush's immediate claim of a 'declaration of war' was thus necessary in order to

sidestep by its allegation the war crime charge that applied with the later US bombing of Afghanistan by his orders as commander-in-chief of the armed forces. (I am indebted for clarifications on these matters by international law experts co-participating in the Science for Peace Forum on the Afghanistan War, University of Toronto, December 9, 2001.)

62. National Security Directives 54 and 133, since declassified, first specifically targeted the Yugoslavian socialist federation in 1982 (Michel Chossudovsky, *The Globalisation of Poverty* (London: Zed Books, 1998), pp. 244 ff.). Although at that time an unexpectedly prosperous and egalitarian society which had overcome the legendary ethnic divisions and 'Balkanisation' of its history, back into which it has since slid as a result of this very US plan of destabilisation, Yugoslavia's extraordinary social success did not deter this foreign intervention. Its success was the trigger of its effective cultural genocide, despite the facts that Yugoslavia was internationally peaceful, not aligned with the Soviet Union, and trading its products with the European Union and the US itself. The value-set at work here abhors any socioeconomic formation not conforming to it, whatever its life-serving nature.

63. In the case of the US mining of Nicaragua's harbours under the Reagan administration, the International Court at the Hague found in Nicaragua's favour in 1986, and assessed $12.2 billion of damages. The US, however, does not recognise international criminal law as applying to the agents or actions of its government, and has refused to be bound by the rulings of the International Criminal Court even as it successfully insists that other nations and their agents, such as Slobodan Milosevic, be tried by it. In 2000, the American Serviceman's Protection Act, published by Senators Jesse Helms and John Warner, went further and sought also to prevent the US from co-operating with the Court in any way. More tellingly, the Genocide Convention, finally signed by the US after 40 years, did so with the reservation stating 'inapplicable to the United States, without US agreement'.

64. The ever greater distancing of the bearers of US military destruction from their targets has become a defining feature of US military policy as it moves into sole military control of space with its Star Wars and Son of Star Wars programmes (in violation of the Comprehensive Test Ban Treaty it long ago signed with the USSR). 'We're going to fight from space – we will engage terrestrial targets ... from space', says former commander-in-chief of the US Space Command. 'That is why the US has development programmes in directed energy and hit-to-kill mechanisms' (Alice Slater, 'The Big Guns Behind the Global War Machine', *The WTO and the Global War System Forum* (ed. Estelle Taylor), Seattle, November 28, 1999, p. 10). The scheduled destruction of social infrastructures from a safe distance in space has been advanced by the increasing confinement to aerial bombing in the Iraq and Yugoslavia social bombings, and reveals a significant step in the inner logic of global corporate market war 'to protect US interests and investments' (to cite the US Space Command's wording in its 'Vision for 2020', ibid., p. 10).

65. Former Shell Nigeria General Manager, Nnameka Achebe, told *Harper's Magazine* in 1996 that 'for a commercial company trying to make investments, you need a stable environment. Dictatorships do that' (Stephen Mills, 'Nigeria Moves Forward, Oil Company Stands Still', Sierra

Club Nigeria Campaign, November 9, 1998). Security apparatuses of the developed world are no less structured to protect transnational corporate interests against their own citizens, even in such places as Labour New Zealand. Its Security Intelligence Service (SIS), like the correspondingly titled SIS of Canada (CSIS), specialises in targeting public critics of transnational 'free trade' regimes, as the author has experienced, and as reported by A.A. Choudry of New Zealand ('New Zealand's Secrets War', *Guardian Weekly*, June 8–14, 2001, p. 13).

66. See Lynn Stephen, 'Between NAFTA and Zapatista: Responses to Restructuring the Commons in Chiapas and Oaxaca, Mexico' in Michael Goldman (ed.), *Privatizing Nature: Political Struggles for the Global Commons* (London: Pluto Press, 1998), pp. 76–102.

67. Chossudovsky, *The Globalisation of Poverty*, p. 246.

68. A level-headed analysis of the unravelling of Yugoslavia by IMF 'structural adjustment' privatisations, stripping of social sectors, mass disemployment, and abolition of worker-managed enterprises is provided by economist Bob Allen in *Why Kosovo? Analysis of a Needless War* (Ottawa: Canadian Centre for Policy Alternatives, 1999).

69. Saddam's mode of entry to power is little known, as is his backing by US state agents throughout – his coup d'état, his $80 billion military buildup (including the sale of biological and chemical war weapons to his regime), air cover and intelligence for his armed forces during the US-advocated war against Iran (which had recently nationalised its US-dominated oil resources), and – least known – protection given to him against internal coups and even the Basra uprising in 1991 after the mass bombing of Iraq. Documentation of the first and last facts is provided in John Pilger's documentary film, *Killing the Children of Iraq: Paying the Price* (London: Carlton Productions, ITN Archive, NTV). For historical background, see Joe Stork, 'Oil and the Penetration of Capitalism in Iraq' in Petter Nore and Terisa Turner (eds), *Oil and Class Struggle* (London: Zed Books, 1980).

70. From 1987 on, Saddam tried to 'impose an IMF-style plan' of social cutback and privatisation in the face of falling oil prices, and completely failed. 'The whole security apparatus depended on the state simultaneously providing for a relatively comfortable standard of living – a distributive welfare state system – advancement to social groups that had existed only on the margins of society such as the rural poor and rural migrants – price restrictions on basic food items. The 1990 budget was designed to be an austerity budget, yet it increased subsidies on food and basic commodities by 113 per cent. The Iraq government could not impose austerity or privatisation without committing political suicide' (Midnight Notes Collective, 'Recolonizing the Oil Fields' in *Work, Energy, War, 1973–92 (*New York: Autonomedia, 1992), pp. 42–53).

71. Ali and Shah, 'Sanctions and Childhood Mortality in Iraq', p. 1851.

72. Allen, *Why Kosovo?*, pp. 8–9.

73. The specifics are detailed in Haroon Siddiqui, 'Canada Must Speak Out on Embargo', *Toronto Star*, September 12, 16, 19, 1999 – 55 per cent without access to drinking water (down from 96 per cent with access), inflation at 5000–7000 per cent, 2 million Iraqis (mostly professionals) forced to flee the country, mass malnutrition of children, a third of children dropped out of school, and so on. Chief of Surgery at Belgrade University, Miroslav

Milicevic, writes in e-mail to friends: 'More than 80 per cent of the bridges have been destroyed, most railroads and roads, both refineries ... 300 schools and university buildings damaged, no gasoline at all ... one million children do not go to school any more ... The whole generation will be crippled ... There is no future any more.' What neither dares to recognise is that these society destructions are not 'collateral damage', as alleged, but known and predictable in advance by military planners operating with the 'surgical precision of contemporary weapon systems'.

74. Pilger, *Killing the Children of Iraq*.

75. The prior unrest and subsequent effects of the Gulf War on Palestinian, Yemeni and Iraqi oil workers is documented in Midnight Notes Collective, *Work, Energy and War*, pp. 50–5.

76. To sustain ignorance of the inner logic of these obliterative bombings of socialised economies, the terms for stopping the bombings are not disclosed. Thes demand their privatisation and the forced embrace of 'free market principles' as a condition for peace. For example, Chapter 4a, Article 1 of the Rambouillet Accords, prescribed to the former Yugoslavia before bombing, reads: 'The economy of Kosovo shall function in accordance with free market principles.' Kosovo, it should be noted, has vast mineral resources, including the richest mines for lead, molybdenum (essential for armament hardening) in Europe (see Richard Becker, Western Regional Co-Director of the International Action Centre, New York (iacentre@iacentre.org)).

77. This story is repressed in most history books, but is reported on most famously by Karl Marx in his *The Civil War in France* (London: Martin Lawrence Ltd, 1933).

78. Even when the International Court of Justice at The Hague has been able to hear and judge complaint of war criminal actions by the US state, as with its unilateral war of aggression against tiny and impoverished Nicaragua in the 1980s, even when it has awarded court-assessed damages (over $11 billion in this case for destroyed harbour and other infrastructures, excluding the 29,000 people killed by its financed Contra war), and even when the Security Council has called for observation of international law and the General Assembly has voted almost unanimously for this resolution, the war-criminally violated country that has pursued these legal channels has been ignored by the US, and all the due process of international law in its favour has been repudiated by the US government. No other government in history has remotely matched this violation and flouting of international law and judgment and done so with impunity.

79. Reagan's Federal Reserve Chairman, Paul Volker, admitted later the domestic side of this strategy: 'The novel theory [that came in with the Reagan administration] was that the way to keep government spending [on social programmes] down was not by insisting taxes be adequate to pay for it, but by scaring Congress with deficits' (quoted by Linda McQuaig, *Shooting the Hippo: Death by Deficit and Other Myths* (Toronto: Penguin Books, 1995), p. 21). Harvard economist and whiz-kid re-engineer of Russian and Eastern European economies, Jeffery Sachs, revealingly confided its central global dimension: 'The IMF is the instrument by which the US Treasury intervenes in developing countries' (quoted by Martine

Kettle, 'IMF Ensnared in Partisan Politics', *Guardian Weekly*, June 21, 1998, p. 6).

80. I pursue this explanation of the worldwide 'debt crisis' in documented detail in my *The Cancer Stage of Capitalism* (London: Pluto Press, 1999).

81. The Reagan administration's National Security Decision Directives 54 and 133, partly declassified in 1990, first targeted the Yugoslavian socialist federation for a 'quiet revolution to overthrow Communist governments and parties' in 1982 (Chossudovsky, *The Globalisation of Poverty*, p. 244).

82. Ibid., pp. 247–52.

83. 'Ethnic Cleansing', *Guardian Weekly*, June 1999, p. 3.

84. The dependency of the KLA on drug-running heroin from the Afghani Taliban was well known in US and other foreign service circles long before the social bombing of Yugoslavia's capital and infrastructures to save Kosovo 'freedom fighters' from the 'ethnic barbarity of Serbs', as even reported by an American military historian at the American Military University in Virginia (e.g., Sunil Ram, 'Nato in Kosovo', *Globe and Mail*, August 9, 2000).

85. See note 60.

86. These facts are drawn from the sources cited and are connected here as co-ordinates of the underlying pattern of US–British construction of the military threat Saddam came to pose which, in turn, was used to justify the subsequent US and British bombing of Iraqi social infrastructure and its decade-long military embargo – an embargo of all that was required to restore the society to normality: reparative equipment for sewer, water and electricity lines, social food supplies to a country 80 per cent dependent on imports, and medicine for diseased children (in particular children most lethally infected by the nuclear contamination of the Iraqi countryside by the 800 tons of depleted-uranium casings of US shells whose radioactive waste cannot be cleaned up because of the same military embargo).

87. See notes 55–8.

88. This widely quoted remark is discussed by Dr Mark Crispin Miller, 'Essay: The Perfect Storm' <www.feedmag.com/essay/es378.shtml>

89. Interview with Said Aburish (Pilger, *Killing the Children of Iraq*).

90. Members of the Security Council protecting the world from 'weapons of mass destruction' have sold Iraq virtually all its weapons, with US and British corporations the world's dominant armaments merchants. The most publicised and feared 'weapons of mass destruction' possessed and developed by Saddam are biological warfare weapons like anthrax and botulism. It is well known that UN weapons inspections to discover these and other weapons have been used by the US as, in fact, an aggressive military spying vehicle for its own purposes; and Iraq's refusal to co-operate with this substitution of US spying for UN inspection are also made much of to substantiate his 'terrorist stockpiles'. In this further pretext to attack Iraq, whose oilfields are still nationalised under public ownership and control, the anthrax scare in the US fits well into a new narrative of fighting international terrorism, instead of protecting Kuwait, as a justification for removal of the country's remaining barriers to foreign control of its huge oil reserves. As this story builds while this work goes to press, the fact that at least 9 of the 14 biological materials for biological warfare Saddam is charged with possessing were supplied by US firms (Item 9, Harper's Index,

Harper's, January 2001, p. 11) is not a fact which is permitted public discussion. See also note 43.

91. Thomas J. Nagy, *The Progressive*, 'The Secret Behind the Sanctions: How the US Intentionally Destroyed Iraq's Water Supply', *The Progressive*, September 2001, pp. 22–5. No mass medium reported the documentation provided by this article.

92. Censored Defense Intelligence Agency documents from which the above figures and quotations come may be found on <www.gulflink.osd.mil>

93. These actions plainly contravene the Nuremberg Charter in their deliberate targeting of civilian populations, and specifically the 'War Crimes' of 'wanton destruction of cities, towns and villages' and 'devastation not justified by military necessity' (Article 2(b)) and the 'Crimes Against Humanity' of 'inhuman acts done against any civilian population (Article 2(c)). They also violate the Geneva Conventions, in particular their 1979 Protocol 'relating to the protection of victims of international armed conflicts' and, specifically, Article 54, which states, 'It is prohibited to attack, destroy, remove, or render useless drinking water installations and supplies – for the specific purpose of denying them for their sustenance value to the civilian population.'

94. See notes 81 and 101.

95. Allen, *Why Kosovo?* p. 16.

96. The KLA were known and reported to be 'narco-terrorists' in even *The Times* of London in March 1999, and by mid-2000 had control of '80 per cent of Europe's heroin trade'. The US Drug Enforcement Agency reported this connection a year earlier in 1998, identifying the KLA as 'the predominant heroin smugglers along the Balkan heroin route' (Sunsil Ram, 'NATO In Bed With A Scorpion', *Globe and Mail*, August 9, 2000, p. A13). It did not report the connection between US state security operations and manipulation of the narcotics trade as a constant over half a century, as Blum, *Rogue State*, ibid., documents across 20 countries.

97. Former Canadian Ambassador to Yugoslavia, Bulgaria and Albania James Bissett, has publicly reported all these facts in the *Globe and Mail* (see note 105).

98. The 'Ahtsaari/Chernomyrdin agreement' which set the terms of the final peace agreement excluded the terms requiring the right to military occupation of all of Yugoslavia, replaced NATO by the UN as armed force commander in Kosovo, made no mention of separation of Kosovo, provided for the demilitarisation of the KLA, and recognised Serbian cultural and historical interest in the province (Allen, *Why Kosovo?* p. 22).

99. Edward S. Herman, 'Commentary', *Z Magazine*, January 2000, p. 15.

100. US President George Bush Jr.'s address to the nation, September 20, 2001.

101. Quoted in Lapham, 'American Jihad'.

102. Cited by John Pilger, 'Moral Sightseeing in the West', *Guardian Weekly*, June 20, 1999, p. 3.

103. Gilbert Achcar, 'Eastward Bound', *Le Monde Diplomatique*, April 1999, p. 7.

104. The text of the indictment of May 7, 1999 by international legal scholars is available from <www.iacentre.org>. It was not just legal scholars who so concluded. Even the British House of Commons Foreign Affairs Select Committee concluded in an undiscussed report published in June 2000 that NATO violated international law, finding that 'the bombing was

illegal under international law' (Patrick Wintour, 'Nato Bombing of Kosovo Illegal, say M.P.s', *Guardian Weekly*. June 15–21, 2000, p. 11).

105. These figures are provided by Professor Michael Mandel, leading the war crime indictment of NATO leaders reported in note 37 and by Ashford and Gottstein, 'NATO's War on Public Health', pp. 6–8.

106. See Tom Walker and Aiden Laverty, 'CIA Aided Kosovo Guerrilla Army', *Sunday Times*, March 12 2000 and Michel Chossudovsky, 'Washington Finances Ethnic Warfare in Balkans' <http://emperors-clothes.com/articles/choss/fin.htm>

107. James Bissett, 'We Created A Monster', *Globe and Mail*, July 31, 2001, A 17. Links between the 'monster' KLA's drug trafficking in Europe and the Taliban's supply from Afghanistan, and the assistance given to both by the CIA continuing into the post-September 11 tragedy, have not been tracked so far as I know except by Michel Chossudovsky of the University of Ottawa.

108. See Chapter 6.

109. The most famous Kantian category of understanding supposes that the world is unintelligible without the mind's *a priori* organisation of it into cause–effect relations. Yet precisely this *a priori* category of cause–effect understanding is challenged by the Carvaka materialist school of India and the Buddhist Madhyamika as a delusion – for the Carvaka, a loss of the bearings of perception which are our only trustworthy evidence; and for the Mahayana Buddhist, what obstructs Nirvana consciousness. Socially constructed categories of thought regulate the practices of life prior to the practices of life determining ideological representations. This is a foundational counter-Marx point to which we return in Chapters 4 and 5.

110. For clarification, a 'moral' position is understood throughout this analysis as one that affirms a principle of conduct as good and obligatory, and affirms as well that its violation be punished. Moral positions are good/evil, the life-ground ethic holds, to the extent that they enable/disable life.

111. I am grateful to my student, Raymond Izareli, for discovering that Mill does not once address the issue in his 1848 edition of *Principles of Political Economy With Some Applications to Social Philosophy* (ed. Augustus M. Kelley) (New York, 1961).

112. Ibid., pp. 581–2.

113. Moral philosopher David Gauthier, who supposes the market to be the ideal structure of moral freedom, puts this principle starkly: 'Appropriation has no natural upper bound. Economic man always seeks more' (*Morals By Agreement* (New York: Oxford University Press, 1986), pp. 108ff). Gauthier's view is grounded in market theory for which the axiom of self-maximising agents is presupposed as both a given and as the meaning of rationality itself.

114. Friedrich A. von Hayek, *The Fatal Conceit* (New York: Routledge, 1988), pp. 6–7, 74, 130–1.

115. My *The Cancer Stage of Capitalism*, pp. 85–270, demonstrates the increasing dominance of this non-productive financial sector. The monopolistic character of both financial and productive sectors in the global market is indicated by Federal Reserve Chairman Alan Greenspan's remark that 'anti-monopoly law is like Alice-in-Wonderland. Now you see it, now you don't.'

116. A more systematic analysis of the terms as a connected system of meaning is provided at the end of Chapter 4.

117. The scope and prescriptive powers of the World Trade Organization are not debated in legislatures, not reported by the corporate press, and not much comprehended by economists or the academy. Nevertheless, since the WTO replaced the 1947 General Agreement on Tariffs and Trade in the Uruguay Round completed in April 1994 with an entirely new 550-page set of universally compulsory terms for its 135 member states regarding transnational trade and soon investment, it has moved very rapidly to impose a permanent economic revolution on the world codified in detailed articles largely dictated by corporate lawyers (e.g., on 'non-discriminatory market access' and 'national treatment' for transnational corporations in domestic economies of 'goods' and 'services' with no prior limitation except in protected military industries). The principles of invasion of domestic and public economies summarised in the text are two of its more striking implications already borne out in planned and ongoing corporate takeovers of public services (for example, 'the $1.2 trillion world education market') and numerous strike-downs of national environmental laws protecting dolphins, sea turtles, and clean air.

118. Cited by Mark Weisbrot of the Centre for Economic and Policy Research in 'Globalism for Dummies', *Harper's Magazine*, May 2000, p. 15.

119. The 'Anti-Terrorist Acts' instituted across the world found their prototype in the USA – the 'Patriot Act' which violates five of the ten amendments of the Bill of Rights, according to the American Civil Liberties Associations among others, and in Canada's Bill C-35 and C-36, known as the 'Anti-Terrorism Act'. The offence and quotation marks I use in the text refer to terms of Bill C-36, section 431, in conjunction with Bill C-35.

120. I published such an article entitled 'The Plan to Abolish Responsible Government' in the *Globe and Mail* in June 1998 prior to the collapse of the Multilateral Agreement on Investment in Paris a few weeks later. The *Globe and Mail* has since refused publication of any text I write. One can examine the media over the month prior to the historic April 2001 Quebec Summit of the Americas to institute the 'Free Trade Area of the Americas' and not find a single binding article or any analysis of these articles once examined or reproduced.

121. Witnesses report the armoury of one-way, life-assaulting weapons carried by the no-identification armed forces in both Seattle and Washington streets as semi-automatic autocockers loaded with plastic bullets, chemical and pyrotechnic grenades, aerosol tanks and hoses, 30-round mag pouches, tear-gas and pepper-spray canisters, and kevlar body armour and gas masks. Use of the weapons on unarmed civilians was, as I directly observed on frequent occasions, random and unprovoked. On-site Seattle physician, Dr Richard DeAndrea, further reports: 'Some of the damage I saw from these rubber bullets took off part of a person's face – [other] people have been treated for plastic bullet wounds. Lots of tear gas injuries, lots of damage to [the] cornea, to the eyes and skin' (reported by Seth Ackerman, 'Prattle in Seattle', *Extra*, January–February 2000, p. 16).

122. Non-arrested citizens reported police running over protesters with motor-cycles, clubbings and beatings, pepper-spaying, tear-gassing and trampling by horses. Citizens arrested for charges of parading without a permit and crossing police lines reported denial of contact with lawyers for 30 hours,

US Marshall threats of rape, assault and murder behind bars, confinement in handcuffs and shackles for up to eight hours, deprivation of dry clothing and heat, violent assaults by wall smashing, strangulation and beatings, and pepper-spray shot directly into the face and eyes. (I am grateful for this report to Erika Shaker, Director of the Centre for Policy Alternatives Education Project, Ottawa, for forewording of the Public Statement of the Jailed IMF/World Bank Protesters, April 28, 2000, signed *inter alia* by <bhale@ic.sunysb.edu>)

123. Unattributed author, 'Today's Pig Is Tomorrow's Bacon', *The Economist*, April 22, 2000, p. 10.

124. These facts appeared in a buried story of the 'Summit Notebook' of the *Toronto Star*, April 21, p. A18.

125. Chavez criticised the so-called 'Democracy Clause' for just this reason, and was made a 'populist' pariah for, since his own overwhelming election victory in 1998, his administration had passed two very significant sets of laws – one for 51 per cent public ownership of new oil ventures, and the other for the turnover of unused oligarchy land to landless peasants. The same mix of ingredients that preceded the US-supported bloodbath coup in Chile in 1973 then began to appear – endless rumours of military coup in the capital, accusations of 'dictatorial ambitions', strategically arranged opposition voices of 'property' and US 'friendship', and hired people tirelessly beating pots and pans.

Part II

1. See notes 3 and 9, this Part.

2. Telling indicators of this pattern are that black women are the fastest growing prison population in the US in a 2 million prison population that is 70 per cent non-white, and that prisoners have multiplied by eight times since the height of the 'war on poverty' began to wind down in 1970. Under the 1995 US Welfare Bill, 11 million poor American families lost income, 2.6 million people and 1.1 children dropped below the absolute poverty line, and 8 million families lost an average of $1300 (US) each in food stamps. (Avery Gordon, 'Globalisation and the Prison-Industrial Complex: An Interview with Angela Davis', *Race and Class*, 2/3 (1998–99), pp. 145–6 and 'Do-Gooders Rally To Plight Of The Poor', *Washington Post*, May 4, 1997.) See also notes 6 and 8.

3. The United Nations *Human Development Report 2000* reports that the world's 200 richest people doubled their wealth in the last four years, despite already having more total wealth than 45 per cent of the world's population in 1996. The result is that the assets of just three billionaires now exceed the GNP of all of the least developed societies of 600 million people ('Overview', *Human Development Report 2000*, Cary N.C.: Oxford University Press, 2000, p. 3).

4. This quotation from John Locke, and those following, are selected from John Locke, *Second Treatise of Government* (New York: Liberal Arts Press, 1953), with the section in brackets afterwards (here, section 3).

5. As Okanagan Jeanette Armstrong puts it: 'We refer to the land and our bodies with the same root syllable. This means that the flesh that is our body is pieces of land come to us through the things that the land is. The soil, the water, the air, and all the other life forms contributed parts to be

our flesh. We are our land and place. Not to know this ... is to be displaced
... a suicidal coldness seeps in ... people without hearts have lost the generational bond to other humans and their surroundings ... [They are] flesh
waiting to die' (Jeanette Armstrong, 'Sharing One Skin', in Jerry Mander
and Edward Goldsmith (eds), *The Case Against the Global Economy* (San
Francisco: Sierra Books, 1996), pp. 466–7).

6. Canadian prisons, for example, house more than eight times as many
indigenous persons as non-indigenous persons, and select for those aged
20–24, almost a quarter of all prisoners *(The Jurisdat Reader: A Statistical
Overview of the Canadian Justice System* (Toronto: Thompson Publishing),
p. 57). At the extreme, 70 per cent of Saskatchewan's prison population
are first nations' people (Felicia Daunt, 'At War With Our Kids', *Briarpatch*,
November 1998, pp. 3–4).

7. Documentation of these genocidal historical moments of the private
property movement can be found in my *Unequal Freedoms: The Global
Market as an Ethical System* (Toronto: Garamond, 1998).

8. In fact, this process is transnational, including such widespread regions
as the Lubicon and Navajo of Alberta and Arizona as well as the indigenous
peoples of the tropical rainforests of the Amazon and Borneo, the
Ogoniland of Nigeria and the Karens of Burma as well as the Quiche
Mayans of Guatemala. This continuing assault on the lives and homelands
of first peoples is still remembered in its overtly genocidal forms in such
works as Sven Lindquist, *Exterminate All the Brutes: One Man's Odyssey
into the Heart of Darkness and the Origins of European Genocide* (New York:
New Press, 2000). The phrase, 'exterminate all the brutes' is from a
London *Times* editorial of 1873.

9. For example, 450 billionaires had more wealth than the total income of
45 per cent of the world's population in 1996. Within a few years, the
United Nations Human Development Report 1999 reported that under 224
billionaires possessed more wealth than 47 per cent of the world's
population. On the national level, US Congressional statistics disclosed
that 1 per cent of the US population had more wealth than the bottom 90
per cent by 1992. By 1999, 1 per cent had more wealth than the bottom
95 per cent of the population. Compounding debt to the rich simultaneously escalates. Average personal debt is now the highest in history –
passing 100 per cent of annual income in both Canada and the US in the
late 1990s. Poorer nations are in a more steeply declining position relative
to the rich. For example, compound-interest demands by private banks
in the rich world extracted $178 billion from governments of the poorer
countries between 1984 and 1990, but the poorer countries' debt was
still rising steeply in 1999 ('How Bretton-Woods Reordered the World'
and 'Debt: The Facts', *New Internationalist*, No. 257, July 1994 and
No. 312, May 1999).

10. Loic Wacquant, 'From Welfare State to Prison State: Imprisoning the
American Poor' (*Le Monde Diplomatique*, July 1998) tracks this pattern up
to recent years, since when the prison population has increased at a
sustained exponential rate.

11. The most recent societies to be destroyed in this way are Yugoslavia and
Iraq, as described in Chapter 1.

12. For a well-documented survey of this undeclared war, see William Blum,
Rogue State (Monroe, Maine: Common Courage Press, 1999).

13. Michel Foucault is no exception. He writes in a summative line of his *Discipline And Punish: The Birth of the Prison*: 'The perpetual penalty that traverses all points and supervises every instant in the disciplinary institutions compares, differentiates, hierarchizes, homogenizes, excludes. In short, it *normalizes*' (Foucault's emphasis) (Paul Rabinow (ed.), *The Foucault Reader* (New York: Pantheon Books, 1984), p. 195). Foucault does not penetrate the prison institution deeply enough. Its regime precisely does *not* normalise. It *de*normalises at the profoundest level possible, reducing the person to the *non*-human. In a mistaken postmodern impulsion to attribute all brutality to universalist scientism, Foucault misses the deeper nature of the prison system – to defeat human identity itself.

14. Some align imprisonment to slavery. But the key difference is that no slave was kept who was not an *instrument* of the private owner's will. Prison reduces persons to animal status prior to and independent of the prisoner serving any instrumental function.

15. The prison begins as a holding place before execution. One could say that the contemporary prison replaces the dead body with the possessed living body.

16. Adam Smith, 'Of the Expences of the Sovereign or Commonwealth', *An Inquiry Into the Nature and Understanding of the Wealth of Nations*, Book V, Chapter 1 (New York: P.F. Collier and Son, 1909), p. 482.

17. See note 22.

18. Over 30 million US citizens – almost one-third of all adult males – were on police 'capture' and 'observation' sheets by 1998 ('From Welfare State to Prison State', *Le Monde Diplomatique*, July 1998, p. 4).

19. In California, for example, formerly the higher education capital of the world, more public money is now spent on prisons than on universities, while a prison guard earns on average 30 per cent more than a lecturer (*Le Monde Diplomatique*, July 1998, p. 6). US military expenditures simultaneously approach $1,000,000,000 per day.

20. 'Public Financing Disappearing', *Canadian Association of University Teachers Bulletin*, October 2000. At the same time, corporate 'education providers' eye the '$700 billion education growth industry' for privatisation (Canadian Education Industry Summit, Toronto, October 7, 1998), while Canada's Ministry of Foreign Affairs and Trade itself encourages privatisation of the '$2 trillion global education market' (*CanadExport*, September 1999, p. 16).

21. Ralph Nader, 'Out in the Cold', *Chicago Media Watch Report*, Spring 2000, p. 2.

22. Duncan Campbell, 'Hardliner Quits War On Drugs', *Guardian Weekly*, October 19–25, 2000, p. 2. Bear in mind that, as federal 'anti-drug' budgets have exponentially multiplied by 3700 per cent since 1970, with over 1,500,000 people arrested on drug charges each year, pharmaceutical corporations have, simultaneously, more than quadrupled their sales (Joshua Wolf Shank, 'America's Altered States', *Harper's Magazine*, May 1999, p. 38).

23. Canadian statistics show that only 29 per cent of 'high risk' offenders are incarcerated for 'a crime against the person', while for 51 per cent of all prisoners there is no conviction for such violence (*The Jurisdat Reader*, pp. 59–60). Once inside, the prisoners who are judged by the system to be

'*high risk*' and, thus, to be subject to more stringent 'security' measures, are far *less* likely to be convicted for 'violence against the person.'

24. These figures are taken from Eve Goldberg and Linda Evans, 'The Prison Industrial Complex and the Global Economy', *Nexus* (June–July) 1999, p. 17.

25. By the mid-term of the Reagan administration, an estimated 500,000 deaths a year in the US alone were 'attributed to occupationally related diseases, the majority of which are caused by knowing and wilful violation of health and occupational safety laws by corporations' (R. Kramer, 'Corporate Criminality' in E. Hochstedler (ed.), *Corporations As Criminals* (Beverley Hills: Sage Publications, 1984), p. 19), with 56,000 dying annually on the job ('10 Worst Corporations of 1996', *Multinational Monitor*, December 23, 1996). These figures are dwarfed by war crimes and crimes against humanity by US and/or allied forces in the Third World since 1945, with millions such deaths commissioned in Indonesia, Vietnam and Cambodia alone between 1965 and 1973 by corporate weapons, and with war crimes or crimes against humanity since from Guatemala to Iraq tolling many millions more non-combatants. With rare exception, there has been no imprisonment of those legally responsible for or instrumentalising these crimes of mass murder and extermination.

26. See note 26.

27. See notes 11 and 12.

28. In addition to those already in federal and state prisons, 3–7 million people are confined to local jails every year in the United States. Although 'the cruellest form of imprisonment', sociologist John Irwin tells us, 'jails operate as 'catchall asylums for poor people'. 'With few exceptions, the prisoners are poor, undereducated, unemployed, and belong to minority groups', are more subject to 'discretionary abuse and intentional meanness', have 'less space and fewer resources and amenities', and are 'sought out' by the police who 'never patrol used car lots ... and never raid corporate board rooms', but 'are always on the lookout' for the poor committing petty offences (John Irwin, 'The Jail', in T.J. Flanagan, J.W. Maruart, K.G. Adams (eds), *Incarcerating Criminals: Prisons and Jails in Social and Organizational Context* (New York: Oxford University Press, 1998), pp. 227–35).

29. The meaning of terrorism I remind us of here retains its linkage with 'terror', unlike the official definitions of terrorism, which have delinked its meaning from public experience, and redefined it as what obstructs official and corporate business. For example, Canada's 'Anti-Terrorist Bill' (Bills C-35 and C-36), defines as 'terrorist' what is 'intended to cause serious interference with or disruption of an essential service, facility or system' (Bill C-35 83.01 (1)(b)(ii)(E)). Much well-taken criticism has been directed at the sinisterly sweeping definition here, but none has recognised the *deeper delinkage from meaning itself* which is presupposed. No connection with terror remains. Only the emotive charge of the word remains – which is then linked to what corporate-led states are set to criminalise and impose right to arbitrary rule over, without normal protections of law. The dis-connection from meaning escapes detection of even those who are opposed to the law. Thus, eminent Professor of Law, Martin Friedland, properly objects to the 'too broad' definition, but seeks to ameliorate it by substi-tuting (like the UK law) 'an electronic system' for 'an essential service,

facility or system' (Martin Friedland, 'Police Powers in Bill C-36', in R.J. Daniels *et al.* (eds), *The Security of Freedom* (Toronto: University of Toronto Press, 2001), p. 270). The Orwellian operation of expanding criminalising concepts into unconnected meanings in the law itself is internalised without demurral – a sign of the totalitarian communications field analysed ahead.

30. The official number began as 'almost 7000 Americans'. Unpublicised counts then disclosed, with no comment on the radical changes of facts, that there were a great number of non-Americans killed, and the official number was revised to 3900. AP News Service then counted the actual deaths, and reported a figure of 2772 persons killed, 40 per cent of the number killed on the basis of which 'America's New War' was declared.

31. This figure is cited by Julian Borger, 'Tax Bonanza for Bush's Cronies', *Guardian Weekly*, November 8–14, 2001, p. 4.

32. I am grateful to Connie Fogel and the Canadian Defence of Liberty Committee for this quotation in their November 18, 2001 newsletter.

33. 'Voices of Dissent Feel the Heat in the Wake of September 11', *Canadian Association of University Teachers Bulletin*, November 2001, p. A7.

34. Cited by Lewis Lapham, 'The American Rome', *Harper's Magazine*, August 2001, pp. 32–3.

35. Cited *inter alia* by <http://freedomlaw.com/coffee.html> which lists among its sponsors the Cato Institute, the Heritage, and the Mackinac Centre for Public Policy. Rockefeller's further words below are drawn from the same source.

36. Zbigniew Brzezinski, *The Grand Chessboard: American Primacy and Its Geostrategic Imperatives* (New York: Basic Books, 1997), pp. 124, 211. Brzezinski's former Trilateral Commission and NATO colleague, Johannes Koeppl, reportedly recalls: 'It was a criminal society I was dealing with ... In 1983–84, I warned of a takeover of world governments being orchestrated by these people [including Brzezinski] ... It was not possible to publish anymore in the so-called respected publications.' The quotation from Koeppl is provided by Michael Ruppert, 'A War in the Planning for Four Years', <guerillanews.com>

37. With any such hypothesis, one looks not only for the evidence confirming it, but more conscientiously, for the evidence disconfirming it. The evidence confirming US and allied security awareness of and possible complicity in the 9–11 attack is considerable, but I have found no evidence disconfirming it. The principal reason against is the assumption that it is impossible that the US national security apparatus would ever permit such a mass killing of Americans on US soil, but this assumption itself is shaky given that Pearl Harbor itself was likely known about in advance, and non-defensive wars since have sacrificed tens of thousands of US citizens (not to say millions of others) for so-called 'foreign policy and national security objectives' (see, for example, Robert Stinnat, *Day of Deceit: The Truth About Pearl Harbor* (New York: Touchstone Books, 2001)). As we will see ahead, these benefits of the 9–11 attack go still deeper than the pay-offs enumerated here. Isolated reports by major newspapers across the world of pre-9–11 links between the CIA, the Pakistan ISI, and bin Laden's al-Qaida network have been usefully documented by Michael C. Ruppert <www.copvcia.com>

38. Quotation is from Karl Grossman, 'Beyond Missile Defense: Bush Team Envisages Space Weaponization', *Economists Allied for Arms Reduction (ECAAR) Newsletter*, June 2001.

39. Cited by Katherine Ainger, 'A Culture of Life, A Culture of Death', *New Internationalist*, November 2001, p. 22.

40. A few global media conglomerates, who 'work together for the greater good', control most to all of the world's mass news, entertainment and publishing (i.e., AOL-Time-Warner, Murdoch/News Corporation, Bertelsmann, Viacom, Disney, Berlusconi/Vivendi). Most of these media firms are, in turn, put together by Wall Street firms, such as Morgan Stanley and Goldman Sachs, which alone constructed media and telecom mergers worth $888,000,000,000 in 1999 and the first quarter of 2000 (Robert McChesney, 'Global Media, Neoliberalism and Imperialism', *Monthly Review*, March 2001, pp. 1–20).

41. Former Chief Economist of the World Bank, Joseph Stiglitz, as good as analyses the Asian meltdown as driven by an 'economic model' followed 'blindly' but also serving 'US financial interests'. He sees the key players here as the IMF and the US Treasury Department who 'pressured' for both the 'liberalization of financial and capital markets in the early 90's' when it was completely unnecessary with 'savings rates of 30 per cent or more' *and* the imposition of terms after the crisis which made 'the recessions deeper, longer and harder' (Joseph Stiglitz, 'What I Learned At The World Economic Crisis', *The Insider*, April 6, 2000).

42. Mickey Cantor, when US Secretary of the Treasury, put the matter directly when he advised that the IMF should be used as a 'battering ram' for US interests (quoted in Devesh Kapur, 'The IMF: A Cure or A Curse?', *Foreign Policy*, Summer 1998, p. 115).

43. The predictable failure of IMF 'emergency loans' to do anything but sink their Asian targets deeper into economic crisis while bailing out Wall Street 'investors' has led the IMF to rename its 'Emergency Structural Adjustment Programmes' as 'Poverty Reduction and Growth Facilities'. Meanwhile 21 million more people in Indonesia alone fell beneath the absolute poverty line.

44. Hannah Arendt, *The Origins of Totalitarianism* (London: George Allen and Unwin, 1955).

45. Before the Quebec Summit in April 2001, the imminent threat of 'terrorism' and 'terrorists' who never materialised except in the form of a police plant equipping and egging on a small group (see note 87 of Part I) was the central public pretext of a steel wall around the city, thousands of riot troops, and 5000 toxic teargas grenades subsequently launched indiscriminately into crowds ('Police Prepare For Terrorist Attacks At Summit of Americas', *Canadian Press*, April 7, 2001). No subsequent comment by the media or government on the false threats occurred. On the more internationally institutionalised level, 'rogue states' and 'foreign terrorist threats' remain the constant pretext for totalisation of US military control of the planet which is recently expressed in official plans to (emphasis added) 'project power through and from space in response to *events anywhere* – with little transit, information or delay in weather' (Commission to Assess United States National Security Space Management and Organisation, 2001, cited by Karl Grossman, 'Bush Team Envisages

Space Weaponization', *ECAAR Newsletter*, June, 2001 <http://www.ecar. Org./Library/News/grossmanspaceweapons.htm>).

46. Cited in Murray Dobbin, *The Myth of the Good Corporate Citizen* (Toronto: Stoddart Publishing, 1998), p. 162. See also Peter Steinfels, *The Neo-conservatives* (New York: Simon and Schuster, 1998).

47. The documentation of this pattern is provided in my *The Cancer Stage of Capitalism* (London: Pluto Press, 1999), pp. 64–85.

48. The words are those of the Canadian Bar Association in response to the Canadian government's 'anti-terror bill', one of numerous police-state bills put into law after the constructed September 11, 2001, 'war' on the US (Daniel LeBlanc, 'Anti-Terror Bill Goes Too Far, Lawyers' Group Says', *Globe and Mail*, October 25, 2001, p. A 6).

49. 165,000 corporate public relations professionals now outnumber the total number of journalists who work for all newspapers, radio and television stations, with 9000 PR firms the source of an estimated 50–80 per cent of the news presented (Jason Plouffe, 'In Your Interest', *Ontario Public Interest Group*, Guelph, Winter 2000, p. 4).

50. US President Press Conference, September 28, 1982.

51. Article 1:3(c) and Article 6 (Domestic Regulation) are especially pertinent here (see Richard Sanders, 'GATS? The End of Democracy?' *Australian Financial Review*, June 15, 2001, p. R.6). Dr Griffith Morgan (gmorgan@uoguelph.ca) who has made a careful study of the text on behalf of the Council of Canadians succinctly explains the regulatory reach of GATS in correspondence: 'GATS applies to professional, licensing, academic and professional qualifications, technical standards, standards of performance, and entrance requirements which are interpreted by GATS [in closed and unpublished proceedings of unelected officials] as affecting regulation or restriction of services and competition.'

52. This information was initially repressed and first published only by hard-to-find sources (e.g., Alan Moore and Bill Sienkiewicz, *Brought to Light* (Forestville, California, 1986)). Its truth was more or less admitted by a Congressional investigation (*Drugs, Law Enforcement and Foreign Policy*, a Report of the Senate Committee on Foreign Relations, Subcommitteee on Terrorism, Narcotics and international Operations, 1989, pp. 2, 36, 41; I am indebted to William Blum for this reference).

53. The consequences of Nicaragua's invasion by US-directed 'freedom fighters' was calculated to be the destruction of half of its agricultural co-operatives, a 60 per cent unemployment rate, and a 40 per cent rise in the absolute poverty rate to 70 per cent of the population (*Tools for Peace*, June 27, 1994). The International Court at The Hague, in fact, found the US government guilty of war criminal violations of international law for its actions in Nicaragua in its judgment in 1986, and assessed damages of $12.2 billion. But this finding was blacked out by the media, and the US never paid the fine. (I am grateful to former Nicaraguan Foreign Minister, Miguel d'Escoto, for this information.)

54. Cited in Peter Dale Scott and Jonathan Marshall, *Cocaine Politics: Drugs, Armies and the CIA in Central America* (Berkeley: University of California Press, 1991), pp. x–xi. See also Alexander Cockburn and Jeffrey St Clair, *Whiteout: The CIA, Drugs and the Press* (London: Verso, 1998).

55. I refer to the $1,300,000,000 being sent under the US Plan Colombia to the Colombian government which is not to assist in the repression of drug

trafficking, as asserted, because none of it goes to close the major nodes of drug trafficing in Medellin, Bogota and Cali. It goes to expensive corporate armaments and US military training to destroy an alternative order of indigenous farmers in the rural countryside of Farclandia, a 24,000- sq.km territory in the south of Colombia (Julian Borger, 'US Sidesteps Its Drug Problem with $1.3 billion Military Fix in Colombia' and Duncan Campbell, 'Colombia's Rebel Republic', *Guardian Weekly*, June 29–July 5, pp. 6, 20). The big lie expresses a long-term pattern of US drug-running across the world, including into US ghettoes. Operating under the cover of 'drug enforcement', its funds finance covert military destruction of sustenance farming communities rising up against the seizure of their lands and resources (see note 45 sources). The projection of blame onto the victims is a standard psychological operation of a totalitarian system whose control of the public media make it apparently immune to public detection. The CIA, we need to bear in mind, was set up with the lead assistance and intelligence data of Nazi SS General Reinhold Gehlen under an agreement of the US military command with the 'Gehlen Organization' at Fort Hunt (Carl Oglesby, 'The Secret Treaty of Fort Hunt', *Covert Action Bulletin*, 35, Fall 1990, pp. 8–16).

56. Ever larger mergers and acquisitions follow from the deregulated structure of the global corporate market whose dominant corporations must have, by the logic of the system, ever more capital at the end of each cycle. Their exponentially growing accumulation of returns are, in turn, most easily invested in buying up other firms and built assets. With no limit of borders, industry or public sector to this acquisitive merging growth of accumulated money command in ever more concentrated centres of control, and with ever larger fees to Wall Street and other investment banks in soliciting and brokering these productively non-contributing 'M-&-Es', this is a world of 'investment' silently and increasingly decoupling from commodity production as well as the real life economy. It is structured to convert money returns most expeditiously into more money returns with no middle-term of producing any good whatever. Financial shell corporations like the infamous Enron, chief contributor to the election campaign of the Bush Jr. presidency, re-sequence money in ever more byzantine paths of diversionary accounting to liquidate assets from productive function into numbered bank accounts. This predatory pattern of investment with no committed function to any life system exemplifies what I have analysed as *The Cancer Stage of Capitalism*.)

57. See note 34.

58. I am indebted to Matthew Stanton for this quotation. Telling examples of this idealisation of market relations to conform to the ruling mind-set are the industry of contractarian analysis in philosophy and political theory and the incentives versus equality literature in which profit without is not considered. Such abstraction away from the dominant social facts serves to sweep them out from view in debate about ideas and formulae which have little bearing on the regulating logic of the actually existing world.

59. US corporations were given the rights of persons by an 1886 Supreme Court decision, and were given more than a person's rights by limited liability rights protecting their shareholders from liabilities for criminal actions, damages to others' lives or property, violated promises, and so on. As the eminent British jurist Salmond put it: 'The corporation is

nothing less than the birth of a new being ... a being without soul or body
... The company may become insolvent [or criminally convicted], but its
members remain rich [or scotfree]' (P.J. Fitzgerald (ed.) *Salmond on
Jurisprudence* (London: Sweet and Maxwell, 1996), pp. 306, 310).
60. As far back as 1973, John Kenneth Galbraith observed: 'Exponents of the
neo-classical system, while they have long deplored the monopolistic and
thus pathological logical tendencies of oligopoly in principle [by
competitive economies of scale, mergers and disappearance of less
capitalised firms becoming oligopolist and monopolist by the inherent
nature of the process over time] have never done much about these
tendencies in principle. There was cancer, but one did not operate. Remedy
became tantamount to talk about socialising, regulating or breaking the
firms that composed the dominant part of the economic system' (J.K.
Galbraith, *Economics and the Public Purpose* (Boston: Houghton and Mifflin,
1973), p. 17). Today, the global corporate market is indeed 'monopolist
in tendency'. The largest 300 corporations, for example, control 98 per
cent of all foreign direct investment, and 60 per cent of all land cultivated
for export (Maude Barlow and Bruce Campbell, *Straight Through the Heart*
(Toronto: HarperCollins, 1998), p. 37). In general, progressively large-
scale transnational mergers in the 1990s, combined with strategies of
manufacture-market integration, have established interlocking oligopolist
structures in the production and sales of, *inter alia*, consumer durables,
mass media products, cars and trucks, food processing, computers,
electronic components, airlines and aerospace products, oil, steel,
chemicals, and pharmaceutical and biotech products. The new legal
vehicles for this corporate 'globalisation' have been post-1980 transnational trade and investment regimes.
61. Under trade law universally in the GCS, it is 'discriminatory' for any
country to allow the 'process of production' of a commodity to be a 'non-
tariff barrier' to entry of it, even by a labelling requirement. Slave-labour,
environmental or species destruction, even toxic contents of products
have all been ruled illegal by world trade law as a ground for their refusal
into domestic markets. See, for example, Stephen Schryman, *The World
Trade Organization* (Toronto and Ottawa: James Lorimer and Canadian
Centre for Policy Alternatives, 1999).
62. There is also the issue of increasing unemployment, now at one-third of
the world's workforce, where even the choice of unfree work for another
does not exist where there are not jobs available – leaving the 'freedom to
produce for sale a good or service that one chooses' false on two levels.
63. In the wealthiest market society, for example, only 10 per cent of workers
in the corporate sector are in unions which provide minimal workplace
protection to workers, and over 100,000 workers a year die from occupational toxic exposures (Ralph Nader, 'US Economy Not So Great By People's
Yardsticks', *CCPA Monitor*, September 2000, p. 14). See also note 61.
64. Prohibition of labelling or other 'discriminatory barriers to trade' systematically conceals from buyers the nature of the commodities on sale,
even if they are made by slave labour or other heinous methods. (See also
note 63.) There is, moreover, the prohibition of buyers' refusal by public
policy to buy such commodities. This was the case, for example, with the
WTO and US federal strike-down of a Massachusetts' government policy
to refuse to buy oil from transnational corporations extracting oil in col-

laboration with the military–corporate dictatorship of Burma. At a US Council on Foreign Relations Conference on Nigeria at which a paper co-authored with Dr Terisa Turner was presented in New York on January 30, 1998, a federal policy adviser referred to this choice to refuse to buy corporate oil extracted under internationally criminal conditions as 'rogue foreign policy'.

65. For the details of this effectively undebated and unsupported imposition of transnational trade regimes on populations, see, for example, David Korten, *When Corporations Rule the World* (Westport Connecticut: Kumarian Press, 1994) and John McMurtry, *Unequal Freedoms: The Global Market As An Ethical System* (Toronto and Westport CT: Garamond and Kumarian Press, 1998), pp. 226–91. The European Union's terms of agreement seem to be an exception, but the central constitutional powers of elected governments which are overridden by even this more evolved agreement have not been publicised or discussed (e.g., the EU's control over national public expenditures and the European Central Bank's take-over of national interest and exchange policies with codified exclusion under Article 147 of any elected government seeking to influence its decisions). For terms of the Maastricht Treaty, see the reprinted text in Stephen Frank Overturf, *Money and European Union* (New York: St. Martin's Press, 1997).

66. I say 'money capital' rather then 'capital' because it is not capital in the Marxian sense – that is, the system decider of the science/technology/money-capital drivewheel of the global corporate system as it has developed in the last decade. An indicator of this new pattern is the fact that in 1995, 95 per cent of transactions in currency volume terms was speculative, and 80 per cent of that with a return time of one week or less (Noam Chomsky, 'The Poor Always Pay Debts of the Rich', *Guardian Weekly*, May 24, 1998, p. 15). Over 96 per cent of money-demand creation in the US, meanwhile, is not by the government's mint or the Federal Reserve, but by private banks and financial institutions (i.e., leveraging investment and creating credit: see my *The Cancer Stage*, pp. 184–9).

67. There are two operations here – treating economic phenomena as redundant as the phenomena of chemistry and physics are, and promoting state policies which control the very economic data being 'scientifically' analysed. Of the first operation, Keynes writes: 'In chemistry and physics, the object of the experiment is to fill in the actual value of various quantities and factors appearing in an equation or formula and the work is done once and for all. In economics that is not the case ... The pseudo-analogy with the physical sciences leads directly to destroying the habit of mind which is the most important for economists to develop' (cited by William Krehm, 'A Fermentation Has Begun That Will Overturn Economic Orthodoxies', *Economic Reform*, November 2001, p. 3). The second operation is more sinister, and is rarely noticed.

68. Technological fetishism was at the centre of Soviet culture as well, almost a satire of the capitalist system out of which it developed and back into which it fell. In particular, the premise that natural ecologies and human souls could be re-engineered at will into obedient functions of 'productive forces' dominated this parody culture of the capitalist factory. For the ground of this ideology in Marx's industrial paradigm as well – itself an oppositional product of its capitalist circumstances – see Chapter 5.

69. George Monbiot reports, for example, that of the 110 research units cited in the Imperial Cancer Research Fund's website records in 2001, not one referred to man-made chemicals ('A Toxic Environment May Be Why Cancer Figures Are Rising', *Guardian Weekly*, January 11–18, 2001, p. 23).

70. Much of this story is told in Vivek Pinto's *Gandhi's Vision and Values: The Moral Quest for Change in Indian Agriculture* (New Delhi: Sage Publications, 1998).

71. Latin America's Green Revolution raised food production more significantly, 8 per cent a head, but as Christian Aid has publicly pointed out, malnutrition increased in the same period by 19 per cent. The effects in India, identified ahead, were more systematically depredatory on the social fabric.

72. Pinto, *Gandhi's Vision and Values*, notes that Gandhians prefer productive employment for members of the rural community where 75 per cent of Indians still live, preservation of the ancient soil, aquifers and countryside from large-scale agribusiness homogenisation and exhaustion, and a steady supply of cheap, nourishing fresh food for rural dwellers rather than ever more to eat for the top quintile of the population.

73. Martin Heidegger (trans. William Lovitt), *The Question of Technology* (New York: Garland Publishing, 1977), p. 4.

74. Jacques Ellul, *Technology* (New York, Vintage Books, 1967), pp. xxvii ff.

75. The principle is now widely revered as 'Hume's fork' in the social sciences, in particular economics, and recurs in the somewhat modified form of Kelvin's dictum which holds that 'When you cannot express it in numbers, your knowledge is of a meagre and unsatisfactory kind.' See, for example, Donald L. McCloskey, 'The Rhetoric of Economics', *The Journal of Economic Literature*, 21 (June 1983), pp. 581–608. Elsewhere we consider the building resistance to the mathematicisation of economics as a form of methodological autism.

76. This metaphysic was expressed straightforwardly by Ross Perot on CNN the night before the US 2000 presidential election in support of George Bush Jr.'s 'educational presidency'. The ideal, he asserted, was to 'programme students like you do computers'. Perot represents the ruling view of official culture which also subsumes students' professors. In resistance to such programming of minds, my own department by unanimous vote repudiated the behavioural reward and deprivation system in favour of the university's declared ideal of the disinterested pursuit of knowledge by a community of scholars with no such private interests impeding it. The university administration acting on behalf of the corporate board of governors in matters of financial management, ordered the department to conform as a condition of continuing to receive the university's salary allocations.

77. These quotations and the figures following are provided by George F. Will in 'School Is No Place to Learn About Consuming Passions', *Washington Post/Guardian Weekly*, May 24–30, 2001, p. 37.

78. As Shell Oil, for example, was explaining by full-page ads in newspapers like the New York Times that it cared deeply for the Ogoni people who had suffered mass murder and a pervasively despoiled environment under Nigeria's Shell-funded and mass-murderous dictatorship, the former head of Shell Oil environmental studies department reported of their concern for

environment in a statement not published: 'They were not meeting their own standards, they were not meeting international standards. Any Shell site I saw was polluted' (Paul Sheehan, 'Corporate Spins and Lies', *CCPA Monitor*, May 2001, p. 11).

79. To understand the extent to which people can be conditioned to comply with authoritative external prescription, it is worthwhile recalling here Stanley Milgram's famous 'Behavioural Study of Obedience' which revealed the power of an accepted legitimate authority to tell volunteer subjects to administer electric shocks on a 'learner' (a professional actor) which were rated Slight, Moderate, Strong, Very Strong, Intense, Extreme Intensity, Danger:Severe Shock, XXX. All of the subjects went to the last degree of Intense Shock, and 26 out of 40 went to the highest level of XXX (*Journal of Abnormal and Social Psychology* 60:4 (1963), pp. 371–780).

80. Quoted in a report on the September 2000 Conference by *Signalling Left*, October 2000, p. 7. Alfred Marshall, who pioneered neo-classical economics, was not so decoupled from reality in the methodological box that has developed since with mathematical calculus as its packaging of 'rigorous science'. *The Harper-Collins Dictionary of Economics* reports: 'Marshall visited the poor areas of several cities and "resolved to make as thorough a study as I could of political economy" instead of continuing in studies of mathematics' (C. Pass, B. Lowes, L. Davies and A.J. Kronish (New York: HarperCollins, 1991), p. 396).

81. See Carolyn Merchant, *The Death of Nature* (New York: Harper and Row, 1980) for a fuller critique of Bacon's analogue of scientific method to the torture of witches. Merchant emphasises the anti-female and patriarchal cast of Bacon's thinking. The broader and more sinister pathology lies in the underlying assumption that *resistant life*, not just female life, is to be subjugated by torture if revealing, and to be enslaved as an instrument for the sake of power as an end-in-itself.

82. Jean-Pierre Berlan and Richard Lewontin argue that the current revolution in genetically modified organisms continues a 'long process of *seizing control of living things* that began when biological heredity started to become a commodity. In 1907, Hugo de Vries, the most influential biologist of his day, and the man who "rediscovered" Mendel's law, was the only person to realise that in an applied science like agricultural genetics, economics took precedence over science' ('Menace of the Genetic–Industrial Complex', *Le Monde Diplomatique*, 8 January 1999, p. 1). This seems a late starting date. Jerzy Wojciekowski argues (in personal discussion) that 'Western civilisation is the first ever to seek to dominate and control nature as a ruling purpose, led by the scientific knowledge construct. Other civilisations have always regarded nature as in some way sacred.' The view in this analysis is that the power that modern Western science has always sought as the defining characteristic of its predictive control, begins with the economic–military designs of Italian states and Tudor monarchs from the later fifteenth century on – with scientists like Galileo and Francis Bacon leading modern science in serving the development of scientific method and technology (missile technology, large-scale livestock farming, navigational astronomy, and so on) for state and commercial rulers. The theme of 'seizing control of living things' in which 'economics takes precedence over [disinterested] science'

expresses the interlocked system of the science–technology–capital construct which has now emerged as totalitarian.

83. The pervasive use of the pharmaeutical remedy, Prozac, is intended to prevent this pathological reiteration of thought through the action of its 'selective uptake inhibitor'. Prozac is in this way a revealing metonymy of the culture.

84. By 'life-world' I do not mean the thin referent of Husserl, Dithey, Schmidt or Habermas who all restrict its meaning to aspects of human thought. I mean all that lives in the world, which I also refer to as 'the life-ground'. Although this life-world or life-ground is 'infrastructurally homogenous' in its predictable conformity to physical and organic laws, these laws only apply to what is required for life's reproduction, not to its irreducibly unique expressions within the range of permission of these laws which, in general, become more unpredictably various in possibility the more developed the life-host's nervous system.

85. This point is to be distinguished from Descartes' famous proposition, '*Cogito ergo sum*' ('I think therefore I am'). The atomic 'I' that he posits as ultimate is assumed, not recognised as an assumption, and the material world ('extension') is segregated from thought in an ontological dualism that further posits non-human life as machines. The life-ground standpoint repudiates both of these Cartesian positions as philosophical symptoms of the mind-set of mechanistic atomism investigated here.

86. Ursula Franklin, *The Real World of Technology* (Toronto: Anansi Press, 1988), p. 16.

87. I analyse Marx's work as organised by a unitary paradigm whose independent variable is productive force development in *The Structure of Marx's World-View* (Princeton: Princeton University Press, 1978). I critically challenged this paradigm as misleadingly nomological in Chapter 5.

88. The mind-set enslavement of the academy's administrators to this global corporate model as sovereign over the university's constitutional vocation is indicated by the brutal eclectic of University of Toronto's President Emeritus, Robert Pritchard: 'We need a more market-driven, deregulated, competitive and differentiated [i.e., product-mandated] system ... production of better services to consumers. The market model give [*sic*] universities more freedom ... by allowing administrators to set fees higher and ... by more aggressively courting private [i.e., market] donors' (Congress News, *CAUT Bulletin*, June 2001, p. A50).

89. This inner logic of the military paradigm is analysed in my *Understanding War* (Toronto: Science For Peace, 1989).

90. Marx sees the connection, and writes to Engels in 1857 that the army developed the first wage system, extra-patriarchal right to moveable property, machinery on a large scale, the significance of metallic money, and the division of labour (*Karl Marx And Frederick Engels: Selected Correspondence* (Moscow: Foreign Languages Publishing House, 1953), pp. 118–19). Interestingly, Marx does not pursue this line of thought as significant in understanding the nature of the industrial model. Instead, he internalises its organising structure of thought in his conception of revolution as a military-industrial movement in nature with proletarians 'disciplined, organised and united' by industrialisation into 'revolutionary

armies'. The profound limitations of this underlying frame of mind were studied in Chapter 5.

91. Much the same meta-structure of organisation is expressed in the *mass-media sports* of the global system. Military-style command and obedience relations, life-and-death stakes attached to victory and loss, exactly ordered sequences of prescription continuously structuring all intention and action, strict division of labour and specialised functions, uniforms, insignia, rallying cries and secret formulae as communicative mediations, seizure of opponents' territories and possession with no limit of aggressive appropriation, mutual rule by the group mind as regulating individual thought and emotion, and – increasingly – final and sovereign rule by athletes' money-contracts and their transaction in the market. Professional sport in this way becomes a dramatic idealisation of the corporate system, the Rollerball image of the shellgame, the masking virility of the 'male corporate gang' analysed below.

92. Susan George discerns the pattern of effect when she writes succinctly: 'Without warning, the WTO has in this way created an "international court of justice" that is making law and establishing case law in which exisiting national laws are all "barriers" to trade, and is sweeping aside all environmental, social or public health considerations' ('Trade Before Freedom', *Le Monde Diplomatique*, November 1999, pp. 1–2). Richard Gwyn graphically describes its mode of imposition at the annual World Economic Forum in Davos, Switzerland: 'Circling the Congress Centre in Davos, there are now a series of high steel barricades. These are topped by barbed wire. At all the entrances, more than 300 police stand on guard, some carrying rifles and rubber bullets, while others are equipped with full riot gear including water cannon. In reserve behind them are 600 soldiers ... All those leaders will spend a week telling each other and the world about the importance of free markets and free trade and, just about, freedom from taxes, and their own fear of free ideas ... They can now only meet inside the equivalent of a gated community where no-one who doesn't think like them is allowed in to disturb their peace' (Richard Gwynn, 'Davos Barricades Convey Reality of Globalization', *Toronto Star*, February 2, 2001, p. A13).

93. The concept of the civil commons is developed in my *The Cancer Stage*, and in the lead article of the special issue, 'Gender, Class and the Civil Commons', *Canadian Journal of Development Studies*, Ottawa, 2002.

Part III

1. Income inequality, for example, already 'the central problem of our times' according to the UN Pearson Report in 1970, has more than doubled at the top and bottom quintile level in the heyday of the 'global market community' ('Overview', *UN Development Report*, 1999, p. 11). Income inequality, in turn, is now understood by medical researchers to have effects of significantly increased mortality and morbidity on human health known independently of other factors (e.g.,'Health Mortality: The Geography of Death', *Scientific American*, July 2000, p. 22).

2. The greater value of human life in the world of life, which does not entail its command, has been explained throughout the previous analysis, in particular in Chapters 5 and 6.

3. *A vital need is such if and only if deprivation of its object results in long-term reduction of endogenous powers of thought, felt being and/or organic function.* Thus food, shelter, clean air and water, and learning opportunity clearly qualify as vital needs, while junk-food, repetitive violence images, luxury oil-powered vehicles, and military weapons do not.

4. Constitutions more specifically refer to 'currency, coinage, and legal tender', 'banking' and 'the issue of paper money'.

5. Even the Bank of Canada Act, now levered into a servant of private money sequencing by the same financial mind-set as elsewhere, is quite clear on its constitutional function to 'regulate credit and currency in the best interests of the economic life of the nation ... and to promote the economic and financial welfare of Canada' (Bank of Canada Act, Paragraph 1). This has been understood by the financial sect whose members have occupied its Governor role over 20 years as a single-note and unconstitutional pursuit of reducing inflation for wealth-holders.

6. Benjamin Franklin reports to posterity in his *Autobiography*: 'The Colonies would have gladly borne a little tax on tea and other matters, had it not been that England took away from the Colonies their money, which created unemployment and dissatisfaction' (John McMurtry, *The Cancer Stage of Capitalism* (London: Pluto Press, 1999), p. 291).

7. Continuous monitoring and reportintg of this process of corporate-bank appropriation of government's money-and-credit powers has been provided since 1993 by *Economic Reform*, a monthly journal of the Committee on Monetary and Economic Reform, an international policy network <www.comer.org>

8. Citations from Jefferson and King have been provided in earlier text. In 1962, with the experience of private banking interests obstructing the Union behind him and his government's introduction of publicly redeemable and successful 'greenbacks' in their place, Abraham Lincoln said: 'Government possessing the power to create and issue currency and credit as money and enjoying the right to withdraw currency and credit from circulation by taxation or otherwise, need not and should not borrow capital at interest. The government should create, issue and circulate all the currency and credit needed ... The privilege of creating and issuing money is not only the supreme prerogative of the government, but is the government's greatest creative opportunity' (cited by Michael Rowbotham, *The Grip of Death* (London: Jon Carpenter Publishers, 1998), p. 220).

9. No Third World nation has yet repaid its debt to private banks, nor is likely to. William Hixson uniquely tracks the ever-growing portion of debt payments to banks as a percentage of US national income in *A Matter of Interest* (Westport CT: Praeger, 1991). William Krehm, chairman of the international policy group, Committee on Monetary and Economic Reform, has tracked the ratio of banks' cash reserve to debt income in Canada through Bank of Canada publications over a 50-year period. He reports that this ratio 'rose from 11:1 in 1946 to a peak of 405:1 in 1999', with a 300 per cent rise between 1993 and 1999 alone ('Money's Mutation in Troubled Times', *Economic Reform*, May 2001).

10. Documentation of these financial trends is provided in my *Unequal Freedoms: The Global Market As An Ethical System* (Toronto and Westport CT: Garamond and Kumarian Press, 1998), pp. 304–68 and my *The Cancer Stage*, pp. 131–275.

11. David Gracey, 'Money Illusions', *Economic Reform*, June 2001, p. 15.

12. Joseph Huber and James Robertson, 'Creating the New Money: A Monetary Reform for the Information Age', *World Affairs*, 4: 2 (2001). I am indebted to John Hermann and Robert Turnbull for this reference.

13. A valuable record of the repression of proposed alternatives to private bank control of society's credit creation is provided by Frances Hutcheson and Brian Burkitt, *The Political Economy of Social Credit and Guild Socialism* (London: Routledge, 1998).

14. As an indicator of the turning upside-down of economic doctrine on behalf of private banking interests since the prosperous postwar years, Milton Friedman argued that in the light of the part played by Wall Street in the Depression and the success of public money and credit creation systems from 1939–45, private financial institutions should be kept out of the money-creating business by a 100 per cent reserve requirement with 'the creation of money' left to the public 'monetary authorities' (Milton Friedman, 'A Monetary Framework for Economic Stability', *American Economic Review*, Vol. 38 (1948), pp. 245–64).

15. Cited by William F. Hixson, *A Matter of Interest: Re-Examining Debt, Interest and Real Economic Growth* (New York: Praeger, 1991, pp. xiii, 230). See also note 6.

16. How can banks keep their tills at adequate level when those to whom they loan claim the money they borrow at the teller's window? While this is true at one bank, it is also true at another where someone is depositing. This is the exchange of bank deposits and liabilities across the system which normally levels out the claims for cash to manageable levels, with after-hours cheque clearances and devices in place to 'top up' if short available to all banks (e.g., by purchase from the Federal Reserve).

17. Yet bankers did their best to stop the public planning of credit at low rates at the base of the Japan's ascension to the world's most effective economy. In 1950, the president of the Bank of Japan vigorously opposed investment in Japanese automobile manufacture, proclaiming that 'in the age of the international division of labour, Japan would best rely on the United States for motor vehicles' (McMurtry, *Unequal Freedoms*, p. 158). The mind-lock in the dogma of short-termism called 'comparative advantage' is here revealed in its full blinkered stupefaction.

18. See John Kenneth Galbraith's account in *Money: Whence It Came, Where It Went* (Boston: Houghton Mifflin, 1975).

19. 'Credit' is the property of the currency denominated and resides in the medium that all accept. Acceptance of a universal medium of exchange in a market depends, in turn, on the *shared confidence of all in the value store it represents*. It took centuries to move from precious-metal coinage or other direct stores of value as a medium of exchange to paper currency standing *for* this value. There is no more quintessential public institution and publicly sustained and paid-for medium of public meaning and economic value. It is a mark of the monarchial right assumed by the money-sequence faction that it has the free right not only to be parasitic on this public institution tax-free, and not only to create 95 per cent of its notes outside public accountability in the form of money-substitutes (ie., bank loans and stock purchases represented and used as legal money units), but to print its own currency directly as protected legal tender as it pleases. See, for example, J.D. Davidson and Lord Rees-Mogg, *The*

Sovereign Individual (New York: Simon and Schuster, 1997, pp. 196ff). Rees-Mogg and Davidson follow F.A. von Hayek's free-riding market absolutism in this and other matters.

20. An example clarifies the value-set's destructive entailments. Prescribing in accordance with its assumptions, the World Bank required the 'liberal reforms' of dismantling of India's Public Distribution System as a mandatory condition for receiving a loan to pay debt. This starvation condition was ignored by the ruling value-calculus, but was justified on 'economic grounds' as 'saving unproductive costs'. The World Bank ruled out *a priori*, that is, public investments in the well-being of the people, the meaning of any life economy. That the Public Distribution System was the long-evolved way for India to spend grown grain into the economy to feed hungry people who required it so as not to be malnourished and die, while at the same time reducing expenditures on expensive storage of masses of unconsumed food in a tropical climate – none of this could *compute* to the market's value-set.

21. Vandana Shiva, 'Fighting Terrorism of All Brands', *The Hindu*, September 22, 2001.

22. The quotation is from a Unilever Environment Group paper reporting to the Unilever Executive Committee on how to include sustainable development in the Unilever Corporate Purpose (Michael Gorman *et al.*, *Ethical and Environmental Challenges to Engineering*, Englewood Cliffs: NJ, 2000, p. 167).

23. David Andrews and Raymond L. Burke, 'A Crisis in Rural America', *America*, October 30, 1999. I am indebted for this citation to Wes Jackson, 'Poverty and Agricultural Policies', a paper presented to the Causes and Cures of Poverty Conference, Center for Process Studies, Claremont, California, October 2001.

24. 'Poverty and Agricultural Policies'.

25. Canada's long-serving Minister of Finance recently declared to an environmental audience that natural and human capital must be 'protected', and went on to claim that this was all part of 'a revolution in the structure of our economy in the mindset of our people' which began with his halving of the government deficit-to-GDP ratio in the 1990s. (Paul Martin, 'Protecting the Environment: A Fundamental Value', *Minister of Finance News Release*, Ottawa, May 25, 2001). The contradiction in this position is that the deficit was paid down by Martin's reduction of health, education and social assistance transfers to provinces by $24 billion in one year, and halving of the environmental budget – although these investments in human and natural capital accounted for only 6 per cent of the deficit growth by a multi-refereed study of his own Ministry. Capital accrual accounting for investment in human capital (e.g., education) and natural capital remain excluded from public accounts, while public investment in physical capital has been reportedly delayed by the Finance Ministry despite Auditor-General instructions for capital accrual accounting.

26. Ralph Nader, 'It's Time to End Corporate Welfare', *Earth Island Journal*, Spring (Southern Hemishere), 1996, p. 37. Nader's figures are from the Harvard School of Public Health.

27. Prior to January 1996, even public investments in *physical capital* such as public buildings and transportation infrastructures were written off in

one year as operating expenses. In the mid-1990s, financial planners in the Clinton administration quietly introduced capital accrual accounting for public capital – a still-hidden secret of the huge deficit reductions of this US administration, with $1.3 trillion of new assets found by the accounting switch. Even then, the US Bureau of Economic Analysis of the Commerce Department has classified expenditures on physical infra-structure as 'savings', not investment (William Krehm, 'Cash and Truth in Accounting', *Economic Reform*, July 2001, p. 4).

28. Taxation regimes can be, and are increasingly, transnational in their standards to withstand the control of servant governments by corpora-tions which demand subsidies instead of taxes as their price of domestic investment. For example, the Foreign Sales Corporations Act of the US which massively subsidises oligopolist corporations like Microsoft and Boeing at the national level has been the target of European Union complaint to the World Trade Organisation, which in August 2001 assessed damages of $45 billion per annum until the tax subsidies are dis-continued.

29. As deliberate GMO contamination of seedstock spreads (see Chapter 1), the view attributed to capital-S Science is that genetically modified organisms are perfectly safe and that only the 'misinformation' claims otherwise. Thus, the WTO enforces non-labelled GMOs on consumers across the world by trade fiats prohibiting 'discrimination' against them. From this standpoint of 'superior science', the US Environmental Protection Agency itself ruled in favour of a GMO to 'convert dead plant matter into alcohol'. The problem was that the *self-reproduction* of GMOs was not, and is not, taken into account in tests of GMOs 'substantial equivalence' and safety for use – a not unexpected failure in an economic model whose calculus is unable to tell what is alive from what is dead. Scientific tests conducted by a PhD student at University of Oregon discovered, however, that soil with the alcohol-producing GMOs killed all the plants in it. This was because the genetically engineered microbes of *Klebsiella planticola* (KP) survived and multiplied in the soil and, because it is one of the most common bacteria on the planet, its release planned by the EPA would have colonised across the world in a matter of several years and thereby converted roots across the world into alcohol. The EPA's response was to try, unsuccessfully, to block the graduation of the PhD student before it withdrew (George Lawton, 'A Voice for Eco-Agriculture', *Acres USA*, April 2001). Note that this global life-and-death set of facts, as revealing a marker of the system as one could find, is nowhere reproduced in the global corporate media.

30. 'Global Trends', *World Resources Institute*, Sustainable Development Information Service <http://www.wri.org/index.html>

31. An overview of the downstream effects on social conflict and war is provided by Michael Klare, *Resource Wars* (New York: Metropolitan Books, 2001).

32. Transnational corporate cigarette producers have responded to the half-century concealment of massive disease-and-death causation by their commodity with the forced acceptance of their advertising and sales in foreign societies by post-1995 WTO regulations, and by the assertion to governments that deaths by cigarettes *save governments money by the premature deaths they cause* (Philip Morris report to the government of the

Czech Republic on its purchase of the privatised public company, Tabac, August, 2001, cited by S. Bosely and K. Connolly, 'Smoking Can Seriously Aid Your Economy, *Guardian Weekly*, July 19–25, 2001, p. 2).

33. Cited by John Stauber and Michael Manekin, 'PR Nation', *Valley Advocate*, August 12, 2001, p. 16.

34. Herman Daly, 'Sustainable Development and OPEC', Conference on Poverty and its Solution, Claremont, California, October, 2001.

35. As I write, I receive a report from the Niger Delta Women for Justice and Environmental rights that a massive discharge from a burst rusted pipe has flooded the tropical forest villages of 150,000 people, all their water supplies, and their wetland food support system. Shell, which receives World Bank financial support for its infrastructure, has blamed villager 'sabotage' (on a pipe burst from the underside six feet below the ground which destroyed the villagers' own life-ground!). Shell has failed to provide sufficient water or medical care for the acutely ill, has pressured leaders to sign long-term agreements as an implied condition of further life means, and offered 66 US cents per person in compensation (from an *in situ* report by Dr Terisa Turner representing the NDWJE and Friends of the Earth, July 2001 (terisatu@uoguelph.ca).

36. In partial recognition, South India's former Ambassador and Permanent Representative to GATT, the forerunner of the WTO, acknowledges that rights of governments to set terms on corporate entry into their markets have been 'curtailed' by the 'proposed[WTO] agreement' (Bhagarith Lal Das, 'Why the South Should Oppose New Round in the WTO', *Third World Resurgence*, Nos 129/130, pp. 4–6).

37. United Nations Development Programme, UN Environment Programme, World Bank, and World Resources Institute, *World Resources 2000–2001: People and Ecosystems: The Fraying of Life* (Washingon DC: World Resources Institute, 2000).

38. I am indebted to Mark Anielski of the Pembina Institute, Alberta for this list.

39. In the counter-offensive of corporate globalisers, various misleading devices are used to substitute for facts here – repetitive slogans like 'global trade reduces poverty' and 'evidence' whose time-frame does not remotely justify the conclusions (e.g., improvements in majority world longevity from 1950–1970 to 2000, which depend on effects of decades prior to the first 'free trade' edicts). The proof is to follow the facts by ongoing well-being indexes to measure true economic efficiency in place of misleading public relations campaigns. For breathtaking conflict between the claims of an economy's life success and the reality of its failures, see the next section's summary of the US economic model's profile.

40. Fuller description is provided by David Ransom, *A No-Nonsense Guide To Fair Trade* (Toronto: New Internationalist Publications, 2001).

41. Ecological and environmental economics are growing industries, but every variety of them remains within a market frame of value reference and such remedies as pollution credit trading and willingness-to-pay polling. The common underlying feature of the entire field is to reproduce the very closed market value-set and calculus which assume cost and price as final value-co-ordinates, and block out life value *a priori*.

42. Paul Hellyer, Canada's youngest-ever cabinet minister, who served with distinction as a minister in the cabinets of Louis St Laurent, Lester Pearson

and Pierre Trudeau, sums up the subversion of an entire society by a relatively small gang in this way: 'In my opinion, twenty-five or thirty men and women, mostly men, have wrecked Canada in the last two decades by giving governments of the day bad advice' ('Good-bye Canada' (2001), Postscript (unpublished manuscript).

43. The armed force attack on all life-ground resistance and self-determination has, in fact, prepared the way for the unaccountable US capital and commodity imperium, but now that it is prescribed by a transnational regulatory apparatus protecting and prioritising only the private-profit rights of transnational capital-owners, convenient generals are not normally necessary as in the past. The Chilean case of an elected sovereign government that sought to restore its public ownership of the country's own principal natural resource, copper, is revealing in its pattern because its sequence, without the mass murders and tortures, has been reiterated within industrial societies themselves ever since its success there. I quote from a CIA 1970 cable sent from its headquarters to its covert operatives in Chile (from Peter Kornbluh, *The Pinochet File: A Declassified Dossier of Atrocity and Accountability* (New York: New Press, 2001), emphasis added): 'We accept axiom [of] coup ... [which requires] creation of a climate in which such a move can take place effectively. We conclude that it is our task to create a climate climaxing with a solid pretext ... moving to more vital pressure points ... Every special interest that we can contact should be financed and assisted – engage in any operation that you think will accomplish this purpose no matter how large or small ... We must create a climate in which this conclusion becomes *inevitable* ... leaving the indelible residue in the mind that an accumulation of arsenic does.' Twenty-one years later, the same US state-sponsored crimes against humanity and, under law, US war crimes, are taking place in Colombia in a 'climate created for a pretext', where mass murder is justified as 'inevitable' from a mind-set poisoned by carefully administered and cumulative propaganda – in this case to justify $1,300,000,000 of armed force attack on a sustenance-farming peasant force defending and administering their own land and taxing drug-movements for revenue. They are made the occasion of a 'drug war interdiction', when (as we have seen) the main transnational narcotic player is the US state security apparatus itself and when, at the same time, transnational corporations like Coca-Cola are 'using rightwing death squads to terrorise workers and prevent the formation of unions' and unleashing a reign of 'the systematic intimidation, kidnapping, detention and murder' of workers in Colombian plants'. The charge was laid by the United Steel Workers to a Florida court on behalf of a sister Colombian union (Peter Beaumont, 'Bush To Raise Private Army in Drugs War', *Guardian Weekly*, July 26–August 1, 2001, p. 5). Perhaps needless to say, Colombia is also a major source of oil with, for example, BP's largest single source of oil in Colombian oil-fields.

44. The first three figures are from David Korten, 'The Global Economy – Can It Be Fixed?' *Alien Invasion* (Toronto: Insomniac Press, 2001), pp. 206–16, and the *New York Times Service*, September 3, 2001. The remainder have been cited or are drawn from John McMurtry, 'A Failed Global Experiment: The Truth About the US Economic Model', *Economic Reform*, July–August, 2000, pp. 11–12 and Mel Hurtig, 'Conrad Black May Prefer the US, But Canadians Don't', *CCPA Monitor*, February 2001, p. 6.

45. This story is told succinctly by University of Ottawa economist, Michel Chossudovsky, in 'Financial Warfare', *Alien Invasion*, ibid., pp. 194–205. Principal banks involved in such financial strippings are Goldman Sachs, Morgan Stanley, Deutsche Morgan Grenfell, Lehman Brothers, Chase, Saloman Smith Barney, and Citicorp.

46. I am grateful to John Hermann, Economic Reform (Australia) for forwarding the article from which these terms are taken ('G-8 Locks World's Poor into Debt Crisis', *China Daily*, August 4, 2001).

47. Documentation of the Third World debt co-ordinates of (1)–(3) are best provided by Susan George in her *Fate Worse Than Debt* (London: Penguin Books, 1988), *Debt Boomerang: How Third World Debt Harms Us All* (London: Pluto Press, 1992), and (with G. and F. Sabelli) *Faith and Credit: The World Bank's Secular Empire* (Boulder: Westview Press, 1994).

48. 'Odious debt' arose as a legal justification for repudiating national debt when the US refused to assume the debt of Cuba when Spain ceded it at the end of the Spanish-American War. Spain alleged 'eternal principles of justice' in demanding repayment of the debt, while the US claimed it was an 'odious debt' because it was 'imposed upon the people of Cuba without their consent and by force of arms'. Legal scholars subsequently defined lawful debt as 'employed for the needs and the interests of the state' or for 'legitimate use' (Patricia Adams, *Odious Debts: Loose Lending and the Third World's Environmental Legacy*, (Toronto: Earthscan, 1991), pp. 163–70). Independent of this doctrine, international law that is binding on sovereign governments in this or other matters nowhere requires peoples to effectively forfeit their sovereignty as nations.

49. In the postwar negotiations for international currency and credit arrangements, Keynes proposed a more complicated idea of a 'Clearing Union' in which allowance for exchange-rate alterations occurred according to the size of surplus or debt balance in international trade in relation to a quota assigned in accordance with prior trade performance. The more elementary idea proposed here is simply the internationalisation, *mutatis mutandis*, of daily banking 'clearing house' arrangements that already exist at the domestic level.

50. The most compelling argument for a Tobin Tax is by Alex Michalos FRSC who patiently demolishes every counter-argument to it (*Fair Taxes* (Toronto: Science for Peace, 1998)).

51. Soros has long argued the obvious that 'commercial banks cannot afford to pay too much attention to its [currency speculation's] systemic effects' (George Soros, *The Alchemy of Finance* (New York: Simon and Schuster, 1987), pp. 46–7). In fact, they do not pay any attention to systemic effects because these do not enter into the private money-sequence value calculus they are confined within. Ten years later, Soros warned of the 'capitalist threat to the open society' ('The Capitalist Threat', *Atlantic Monthly*, 1997, pp. 45–7). That no financial reform has occurred with such warnings from the top is an indicator of the instituted mind-lock behind the global financial disorder.

52. Even those who dissent from the 'complete knowledge postulate' central to neo-classical economic choice theory continue to presuppose at a deeper level agent knowledge of the *medium of exchange itself* in their less idealised constructs (e.g., Herbert Simon's model of 'procedural rationality' (F. Hahn

and M. Hollis (eds), *Philosophy and Economic Theory* (Oxford: Oxford University Press, 1979), pp. 169ff)).

53. This general fact alone debunks the endless threats of 'Depression by protectionism' that are used as scare tactics by corporate globalisers in government and international institutions, while also refuting the pervasively rosy forecasts of 'increased prosperity by trade' which are simultaneously proclaimed by the sect.

54. Figures are provided by Dr Adhemar S. Mineiro, 'The Brazilian Economy: Recent Turbulence and Future Uncertainties', *Third World Resurgence*, Nos 129/30, pp. 36–88.

55. John Vidal, 'Brazil Sets Out on the Road to Oblivion', *Guardian Weekly*, July 19–25, 2001, p. 20.

56. Russell Mokhiber and Robert Weissman, 'Ending Wall Street's Reign', *Corporate Predators* (Boston: Common Courage Press, 1999), pp. 78–9.

57. 'Investment' is defined across these instruments in a form that can include anything whatever from which a money-profit can be made by an 'investor' – for example, 'every kind of asset and rights of any nature, tangible or intangible', including 'concessions for natural resources' and 'government procurements' (in all sectors, including educational 'courseware').

58. Global consumption of water, most by agribusiness, is doubling population growth, as over 1 billion people already lack access to fresh water. The global market solution is privatisation of water for profit, and the World Bank has adopted this policy. The for-profit corporate ownership of the world's water supplies is already worth $405 billion annually, catching up to the oil sector, and already 30 per cent past the pharmaceutical industry in market value (Sophie Tremolet, 'Going Into Battle Over Liquid Assets', *Guardian Weekly*, October 4–9, 2001). The recorded and predictable disasters of water and other means of life privatisations have been tracked through this study, but so unexposed is the unfolding life catastrophe that Project Censored 2001 selected this as its number one censored story <www.projectcensored.org>. Even the *Guardian Weekly* sustains this concealment of issue by its headline trivialisation of the control over all life all the time that private control over the world's water confers.

59. The overriding of all sovereign regulation of foreign money sequences has already been imposed on societies against the registered popular votes of all three countries involved in NAFTA – Canada, the United States and Mexico (with continual journalist murders in the latter), The NAFTA 'free trade agreement' has resulted, without any corporate press or government notice (indeed the suspension of one US government program reporting the job facts), in four consequences: universally lowered real wages, gutted social infrastructures, massively increased environmental pollution, and increasingly destabilised livelihoods of the vast majority of each society within six years. See my *Unequal Freedoms*, pp. 215–390 and David Orchard, *The Fight For Canada* (Toronto: Stoddart, 2001). The NAFTA regime is the prototype, in turn, for the WTO terms to rule all countries across the world. It is chapter by chapter repeated in the hemispheric FTAA and the World Trade Organisation's 1995 Rio Treaty and its General Agreement on Trade and Services timetabled for 2000–05. All the 'disciplines' of these corporate-rule apparatuses are incubated by trade and corporate legal bureaucrats in secret. GATS (General Agreement on

Trade in Services) is the WTO's main attack vector on public-sectors of domestic economies (for example, Article 1:3(c) and Article 6). See, for example, Richard Sanders, 'GATS? The End of Democracy?' *Australian Financial Review*, June 15, 2001, p. R6.

60. The US President has made this equation clear by famously saying: 'Every nation in every region now has a decision to make. *Either you are with us, or you are with the terrorists*' (President's Address to the Nation, September 20, 2001). Secretary of Defense, Donald Rumsfeld, has spelt it out. 'Attack on our way of life' is equated to terrorism (Donald Rumsfeld, 'A War Like No Other', Guardian Weekly, October 4–10, 2001, p. 11).

61. The Charter of Economic Rights and Freedoms of States was passed in the UN Geneva Assembly in 1974 by a vote of 120–6. It recognised 'the sovereign and inalienable right of every state to choose its economic system as well as its political, social and cultural systems in accordance with the will of its people without any outside interference.' It also recognised the right of every state 'to regulate and exercise authority over foreign investment', 'to regulate and supervise the activities of transnational corporations', to 'nationalize, expropriate or transfer ownership of foreign property ... [with] appropriate compensation', and to ensure 'appropriate measures designed to attain stable, equitable and remunerative prices for primary products' (extracted from sovereign natural resources) (Edmund Jan Osmanczyk (ed.), *The Encyclopedia of the United Nations and International Agreements* (London: Taylor and Francis, 1995). All of these 'sovereign and inalienable rights' of societies recognised by the community of nations are overridden without even a reference by every transnational trade and investment regulatory apparatus imposed since.

62. *Encyclopedia of the United Nations.*

63. By 'nuisances' I refer to externalities which are not costs under economic or legal definition or toxic pollutions, but are systematically damaging to enjoyed life capability – for example, the increasingly loud drone of corporate commodities pervading everyday life and the edgeless quiet of nature (with leisure all-terrain and aquatic machines destroying the quiet of entire ecosystems at the extreme end of these assaults on the life-ground by corporate commodities). Another example would be the increasingly pervasive corporate junk-mail and phone-calls invading the freedom of homes with no limit to non-stop nuisance to sell corporate commodities. These are the hidden life dimensions of global corporate totalitarianism.

64. I am indebted to *Independence News*, Saskatchewan, for this citation.

65. In contrast, in the US, the leader of these new social contracts, the bottom 40 per cent have negative financial wealth, and 60 per cent together own 1 per cent of US financial wealth (Statistics Canada data reported in Marc Lee, 'Are We Really All Capitalists?' *CCPA Monitor*, June 2001, p. 23).

66. For example, the American Trade Act of 1974 requires that the US Labour Advisory Council, representing all workers in the US under Congressional law, must advise the US government of any trade agreement it undertakes. The Text of NAFTA was given to the Labour Advisory Council the day before the deadline for its report (McMurtry, *Unequal Freedoms*, p. 236), while its general policy framework had been first planned by the Trilateral Commission (dominated by corporate executives and their political and ideological representatives) more than a decade before, and, as David Korten's *When Corporations Rule the World* (Westport CT: Kumarian Press,

1996), reports from the inside, honed by corporate representatives occupying government committee chairs and consultation bodies before being signed into law by corporately financed politicians. The connections reach far and wide. A decade later in Germany, where revenue from corporate taxes has fallen by over 50 per cent since 1980 while profits rose 90 per cent, transnational corporations such as Deutsche Bank, BMW and Daimler-Benz ensured that they would not rise again by threatening Finance Minister Oskar Lafontaine (soon forced out) with a loss of 14,000 German jobs to lower tax zones available under new transnational trade agreements (Noreena Hertz, 'We must Stay Silent No Longer', *Guardian Weekly*, May 10–16, 2001, p. 23). George Monbiot, *Captive State: The Corporate Takeover* (London: Macmillan, 2001), most thoroughly documents the corporate subversion of Britain's governing processes at all levels.

67. Lester Thurow, *Dangerous Currents* (New York : Random House, 1983), pp. 22–3. I have added 'or creed'.

68. The US's Council of Foreign Relations, the oldest of the three major policy planning bodies of US-led corporate world rule, along with the post-1954 Hotel Bildersberg Council and the post-1973 Trilateral Commission, have long planned for world rule. The Council of Foreign Relations, in fact, initiated a global design of rule with the Nazis. It was called 'the Grand Area', as the non-Nazi-ruled remainder of the world was called in 1940: 'to set forth the political, military, territorial and economic requirements of the United States in its potential leadership of the non-German world' (Memorandum E-A10, 19 October 1940, CFR, War-Peace Studies, Baldwin Papers, Box 117). Note that peaceful collaboration with the Nazis in world empire is implied. (I am indebted to former Deputy Prime Minister of Canada, Paul Hellyer, a leading non-quisling political figure, for this documentation from Chapter 2 of the manuscript of his book, *Good-Bye Canada*.) As reported elsewhere in this study, the major US transnational corporations also supplied *after* 1942 such military–industrial commodities for the Nazis as armoured vehicles (General Motors and Ford), concentration camp punch-cards (IBM), ovens (AT&T), and chemicals (Dupont), while the US state security apparatus subsequently deployed Nazi SS information and methods across the globe in suppression of majority world liberation movements.

69. This unaccountability is not only acknowledged, but delighted in by transnational corporate commands and their fawners. Soon-to-be-Lord Paddy Ashdown thus enthuses approvingly, 'power has migrated beyond the nation state' and so 'very radically' new thinking is required to ensure 'security' for the new power. Thus Sir Paddy accepts the chair of the new Law Enforcement and National Security Agency, with Shell Oil, British American Tobacco and Bechtel advising Interpol, the Nigerian Ministry of Justice, the UK Home Office, the US Drug Enforcement Agency and other armed-force servants to world corporate rule planning to police the globe so that 'the threat to order and stability' posed by 'social interactions based on popularisms' is silenced (Jim Carey, Globo-Cops, *Redpepper Investigations*, August 2001).

70. Cited by Jeffery Ewener, 'Management Science Ignores the Banality of Corporate Evil', *CCPA Monitor*, March 2001, p. 34.

71. See note 55, Part II and note 70, Part III.

72. Bear in mind as an exemplar of Orwellian 'consumer choice' politics here that the NAFTA and the WTO repudiate not only the labelling of genetically engineered foods that have not been tested generationally or ecologically on anything, but also prohibit real food producers from labelling their food 'non-GMO'. Libertarian academics do not blush.

73. McMurtry, *Captive State*, pp. 11–12.

74. Citations in this section are drawn from Jonathan Rowe, 'Is the Corporation Obsolete?' *Washington Monthly*, July 12, 2001. For more detailed investigation, see the investigative volume of *Atlantic Monthly* reporter, Jack Beatty, *Colossus: How the Corporation Changed America* (New York: Broadway Books, 2001).

75. At present, the US National Lawyers' Guild seeks to impeach five members of the present US Supreme Court for 'unconstitutionally assaulting civil and economic rights', including its unlawful prohibition of counting Florida state ballots in the 2000 presidential election <www.nlg.org/impeachment>.

76. This general fact is stated as a given in the middle of an article (Madeleine Bunting, 'Bosses in the Driving Seat', *Guardian Weekly*, June 21–29, 2001, p. 11) which then retracts its force by opining in the next sentence it 'is as vulnerable to spin as anything else'. 'Spin' cannot work if the failure to fulfil public conditions of incorporation is a public issue which must be settled before renewal of charter.

77. Logical analysis and resolution of this pervasive structure of falsification of communications is provided in my 'The Unspeakable: Understanding the System of Fallacy of the Mass Media', *Informal Logic*, Winter 1988. The free reign of propagandist falsehood has since increased, through such means as the unknown media-PR conglomerate, WPP, combining under one roof such world propagandist giants as Hill-Knowlton and Bursen-Marsteller (Sharon Beder and Richard Gordon, 'WPP: World Propaganda Power', *PR Watch*, Second Quarter, 2001, p. 9). The former firm constructed the video of the Kuwaiti Ambassador daughter's tearful and false report broadcast across the world's media of Iraqui soldiers killing infants in incubators just before the US and its military allies declared war on Iraq from whose effects over 500,000 have since died. See Ali and Shah, 'Iraq's Children', pp. 1837–56.

78. Media mogul Conrad Black has publicly proclaimed through his chief representative: ' If editors disagree with us, they should disagree with us when they are no longer in our employ ... I will ultimately determine what the papers say' (cited by James Winter, Black's Plans', *Globe and Mail*, March 12, 1994, p. D7).

79. Interestingly, Rupert Murdoch's Fox Television recently argued in court in defence of firing two journalists that disagreed: 'There is no law, rule or regulation against slanting the news' (Source: <www.foxBGHsuit.com>).

80. See note 40.

81. 'Is the Corporation Obsolete?'

82. These examples are reported by *Adbusters*, August 15, 2001.

83. Philip S. Golub, 'America's Imperial Longings', *Le Monde Diplomatique*, July 2001, p. 2.

84. The trope is that of Mark Morris. A valuable tracking of the non-stop habit of war crimes, crimes against humanity and continuous breaches of international as well as US law by one well-paid academic servant of the

corporate interest in US government is provided in Christopher Hitchens, 'The Case Against Henry Kissinger', Parts I and II, *Harper's Magazine*, February and March, 2001.

85. With NAFTA, for example, the US state unilaterally applies Sections 201 and 301 of the 1974 US Trade Act whenever a powerful US corporate sector complains of injury to its profits by exporters into industrial or agricultural markets – with foreign governments cap-in-hand competing against one another to secure compliance with rules the US has signed onto and applies against them.

86. The Aztec parallel occurs here again. The reason it fell to a hopelessly outmanned adversary was its dependency on a ruling mythology out of touch with what it could not compel to obey it, while its people's consumption relied on 'ecological footprints displaced to a great distance' (see, for example, P. Fernandez-Arnesto, *The Millennium* (Toronto: Doubleday, 1995)).

87. Cited in *Economic Reform*, August 2001, p. 13.

88. The trick is to report profits on the basis of 'cash accountancy' – again the reassuring term for effectively the opposite – which excludes the excess price over cash value paid for a take-over, but which is amortised as a cost which the conglomerate's long-term stockowners must pay over time. This magic of the market of countless spins ballooned Toronto Dominion Bank's profits from 5 cents a share to 84 cents, transfiguring a fall of 52 cents a share over the previous year into a gain of 27 cents (Eric Regularly, *Globe and Mail*, May 25, 2000). I am indebted to William Krehm's work for this example, as many others.

89. As well as my *The Cancer Stage*, see Rowbotham, *The Grip of Death*.

90. Shigeyuki Yoshida in personal correspondence, June 12, 2001.

91. Unregulated banking and securities transactions in external international markets have an exponential profile of growth in bank claims on assets and debtors. From their inception in the 1960s, they grew to $2.6 trillion by 1985, $5.9 trillion by 1990, and $11.1 trillion by 1999, more than doubling the entire US banking system's assets (Jane D'Arista, 'Capital Flows', *Wall Street Journal*, March 3, 2000). Bear in mind that interest-bearing debts approach and can in principle exceed the legal tender in circulation.

92. Greg Palast interview with Joseph Stiglitz, 'The Globalizer Who Came In From the Cold', *The Observer*, October 10, 2001 <www.gregplast.com>

93. See, for example, Veronika Bennholdt-Thomsen, Nicholas Faraclas, Claudia von Werlhof, *There Is An Alternative: Subsistence and Worldwide Resistance to Corporate Globalization* (London: Zed Books, 2001).

94. Peter Rosset, 'The Shift on Agrarian Reform: New Movements Show the Way', *Third World Resurgence*, Nos 129/30, pp. 43–8.

95. R. Seavoy, *Subsistence and Economic Development* (Westport CT: Praeger, 2000), p. 113.

96. Geneticist-farmer Wes Jackson has systematically proved this point on the ground at the Land Institute, Kansas, with his development of perennialised food seeds (including soy, barley, oats and sorghum) maximising life gains by endogenous ecosystem principles of inputs and food growth <http://www. land institute.org.>. For political obstruction of life-standards of food growth by national subsidy systems and transnational

trade fiat, see also James K. Boyce, 'NAFTA, the Environment and Security: The Maize Connection' and other analyses in the Committee of Women, Population and the Environment, *Political Environments*, Fall, 1997.

97. See my 'Towards the Just War' in 'Rethinking the Military Paradigm', *Inquiry*, 34, pp. 415–32.

Index